THE
BAKKE
CASE

JOEL DREYFUSS &
CHARLES LAWRENCE III

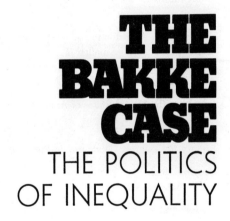

THE BAKKE CASE

THE POLITICS OF INEQUALITY

Harcourt Brace Jovanovich

New York & London

Requests for permission to make copies of any part
of the work should be mailed to:
Permissions, Harcourt Brace Jovanovich, Inc.
757 Third Avenue, New York, N.Y. 10017

Printed in the United States of America

Library of Congress Cataloging in Publication Data

Dreyfuss, Joel.
    The Bakke case.

    Bibliography: p.
    Includes index.
    1. Bakke, Allan Paul. 2. California. University.
3. Discrimination in medical education—Law and
legislation—California. 4. Medical colleges—
Admission. I. Lawrence, Charles, 1943–   joint author.
II. Title.
KF228.B34D74   344'.73'0798   78-22249
ISBN 0-15-110536-7
ISBN 0-15-616782-4 pbk.

First edition

A B C D E F G H I J

For the

HONORABLE THURGOOD MARSHALL

and for

CAROL, MAIA, AND VERONICA

ACKNOWLEDGMENTS

Our initial gratitude must go to our first teachers and supporters: our parents, Roger and Anne-Marie Dreyfuss and Charles and Margaret Lawrence; and our sisters, Jessica, Carole, Marie-Françoise, Sara, and Paula. The inspirations and ideas that shaped this book were first formed within our families.

Many friends and colleagues, particularly Derrick Bell, Ralph Smith, Eleanor Holmes Norton, Stephanie Wildman, and Stephen Arons, have been generous in sharing their ideas and reading various chapters of the book. The secretarial efforts of Jody Anderson, Angela Balestrieri, and Lani Mailes were greatly appreciated.

We are especially indebted to Dr. Daniel Collins, who encouraged us to embark on this venture, introduced us to our publisher, and provided encouragement throughout. Our editor, Peggy Brooks, played an essential role in helping us organize and clarify our final product.

Not enough has been said about the remarkable tenacity of U.S. Supreme Court justice Thurgood Marshall in retaining his vision of an integrated America long after others lost their idealism. For similar reasons, we want to acknowledge the courage of the editorial board of the *New York Times* for insisting that the public understand the complexity of the issues involved in the *Bakke* case. The editors of Pacific News Service and participants in their Cities Seminar helped place much of this material in the broader context of the nation and the world around us.

Finally, we can never adequately acknowledge the sacrifice, support, good humor, and perseverance of Veronica Pollard, Carol Munday Lawrence, and Maia Lawrence. It is their love that sustained us in this effort.

CONTENTS

THE
BAKKE
CASE

One

BITTER MEDICINE

At about four o'clock on the afternoon of Friday, August 3, 1973, Allan Paul Bakke, an engineer at NASA's Ames Research Center near Stanford University, started his car for the drive up to the University of California at Davis. The 100-mile trip would take Allan Bakke little more than two hours, but it would be a giant step toward a fate he could hardly have imagined on that sunny summer afternoon. He had applied to the medical school at Davis and had been rejected. He was applying again and would be interviewed a second time in a few weeks. But Bakke was nervous about his chances of becoming a doctor, and he was grateful that a sympathetic official at the school had agreed to meet with him informally.

One hundred miles is not a great distance at the Ames Center, where space vehicles that will travel millions of miles over several years are designed and tested. Sprawled alongside U.S. 101 on the southern peninsula of San Francisco Bay, the center is surrounded by an unsavory collection of industrial parks, drive-in movies, fast food restaurants, and flimsy residential developments that have converted the brown hilly country between the cities of San Francisco and San Jose into a classic nightmare of American urbanization. The drab green uniforms and white gloves of the U.S. Marines at the security gates help differentiate the complex from the warehouses and factories around it. The guards and the high fences hint at the difference and importance of the work inside.

A NASA spokesman calls the complex "a college campus of ideas," and there is a thin patina of the university in the formal walks, circles, and lawns that connect the jumble of brick and concrete buildings. The dominant architectural features are the giant steel and aluminum barrels suspended between the buildings. These are the wind tunnels and centrifuges where experimental aircraft and space vehicles are tested. The science fiction world is real enough with its banks of sterile control panels and flashing lights, but the more gritty side of space research is very much in evidence. There are more laborers in yellow hard hats in view than scientists in white smocks and calculators. The scale model of the space shuttle *Enterprise,* our first real spaceship, pushed over in a corner of a dimly lit hangar, wears a fine coat of grime. The coiled snake of disconnected cable, the greasy rags, and the irritating whine of high-speed drills are a reminder that the pursuit of Truth in science requires painstaking measurements, physical labor, and a tolerance of monotony rarely considered in the epics of speculative fiction.

It was in this place that Allan Bakke decided to be a physician. An engineer trained in the philosophy that all problems can be solved and all mysteries deciphered, he came into contact with the medical doctors who had to make sure the frail human cargo of the billion-dollar machines could endure the punishment of our most alien frontiers. While the practices of engineering and medicine have converged in the use of the electronics and computers that are the basic tools of our time, man—the ultimate challenge—would have been outside the conceptual universe of a mechanical engineer. One can easily understand the delight of Allan Bakke in discovering a new world to conquer. After six years at NASA, the daily routine of the engineer paled before this new mystery of flesh, blood, and emotions.

But as Bakke drove past the warehouses and drive-ins, through the eastern edge of San Francisco and its rows of pastel houses on picture-postcard hills, he knew that he was on a mission against time. He had applied to twelve medical schools over two years, and all had turned him down. Two had been honest enough to tell him why: age. He was thirty-three years old, and this single fact was a great obstacle over which he had no control. As he wound his way through the heavy Friday afternoon traffic, Allan Bakke was making a transition. Soon he would cease to be a man with a private fear of growing old and would become the symbol in a struggle that would make his name a household word and his ambition an issue that divided a nation. Despite his efforts to shun publicity, his personal goal would have repercussions he could not have foreseen as his automobile climbed through the dry brown coastal hills and plunged toward the stifling Sacramento Valley.

Four years later the issues raised at that August meeting would be the focus of an emotional debate that shattered old alliances, sparked political confrontation, and caused men of wisdom to utter the same words with totally different intent. The issue—race—was as old as the nation itself, but because of it, Allan Bakke's ambition to become a physician would concern some of the country's finest minds. Tickets for the session of the United States Supreme Court of October 12, 1977, would be as much in demand as passes to the World Series taking place between the Yankees and the Dodgers. And while six umpires would judge that confrontation of old enemies, nine men would arbitrate the dispute between Allan Bakke and the University of California.

There had been another autumn twenty-five years earlier,

when nine other important men listened to arguments about justice, law, and color, and at that time, too, the Yankees and Dodgers had met to determine the championship of the world. In 1952 the Supreme Court and the New York Yankees were all white men, and the Brooklyn Dodgers were on the leading edge of social change in America. In that year the plaintiffs argued that racial separation contradicted the ideals of democracy and should be abolished. Eventually the Court would agree and launch a profound transformation in the relationship of black and white Americans.

How far had the country come for Allan Bakke to argue that sixteen blacks, Chicanos, and Asians had violated his constitutional rights by attending the medical school at Davis? His case appeared simple enough: the medical school, in an attempt to correct the injustices of that segregated past, had set aside sixteen places in each entering class for members of minority groups. Because Allan Bakke was white, he was prevented from competing for those sixteen places. He argued that because his grades and test scores were higher than those of some of the minority students, he was better qualified to become a physician. Yet his aspirations had been dashed by his color. How ironic for the American Dilemma to come full circle in just a quarter-century. If Bakke's contention was correct, white men had lost the protection of the Constitution they had drafted in order to create a unique form of government, with all those checks and balances built in to protect them against absolute power and absolute corruption. Now Bakke took his case to the court of last appeal and pleaded for redress.

But was the issue as straightforward as many wanted to believe? Had this tall, blond, intense hero of this unusual racial epic lost his rights to a new injustice with the catchy title of "Reverse Discrimination"? What profound rearrangement of power had taken place in the space between two

World Series to provoke such a reversal of roles? To believe *Allan Bakke* v. *Regents of the University of California* that simple is to succumb to the melodrama that has been constructed of this affair, a play of shallow characters and shallow solutions. Could any fair-minded person oppose a man who wanted so much to be a physician that he volunteered to be the "pink lady" in the emergency room of a hospital after a full day at his regular job? Wasn't merit the fabric that had made America a great nation? Who would want to be treated by doctors whose abilities were so negligible that only their color made them eligible for medical school?

The issues in the *Bakke* case are hardly as straightforward as they have so often been presented, and they are hardly resolved by the decision of the Supreme Court. There are no simple solutions for complex problems, but a careful examination of the facts can reduce the melodramatic aspects of the case. There are dangers in oversimplification, and this common sin has done much to obscure the problems we have identified as racial. The instances in our history when problems of color were considered rationally have been few indeed.

At the root of this dispute is the equal protection clause of the Fourteenth Amendment, which says that no state shall "deny to any person within its jurisdiction the equal protection of the laws." The concept is engraved in the lintel over the entrance to the Supreme Court building in Washington: "Equal Justice Under Law," a simple credo that has not been enforced for most of the nation's history. The distance between laws and equality is a familiar gap in the American matrix, and much effort has been devoted to closing this gap. There was a concerted push for equality in the 1960s that evolved into the concept of real equality rather than just theoretical equality. When members of minority groups were given an advantage through preferential programs, they would be able to overcome the handicaps of history and racism.

But this generosity lasted only as long as a healthy economy promised a place at the table for everyone. The recession of the 1970s fueled intense competition for jobs, training, and education. The few who had criticized such efforts found a new and more receptive audience for their complaints. They warned of the dangers of group or "ethnic" rights in a democracy that recognized the rights of the individual and predicated advancement on merit and qualifications.

Allan Bakke's case represented a confrontation of two concepts: equality as a theoretical right and equality as a reality. The problem had appeared after Emancipation, when slaves found themselves free and penniless and, as a result, often bound to continued exploitation by their former masters. The radical demand for "forty acres and a mule" was ignored and contributed to the creation of the two racially divergent and unequal societies of the twentieth century. The parallels between Reconstruction and this era are striking. After the initial ground swell of support for black aspirations, there had been a retreat. In 1877 the Hayes-Tilden Compromise, a gesture of conciliation between North and South, removed federal troops from the South and allowed a return to white supremacy. In 1977 a southern president sat in the White House in another gesture of reunification, and once again the struggle for equality by minority groups was cast as an encroachment on the legal rights of white Americans.

Indeed, there are serious moral and philosophical issues raised by the granting of group rights. But the argument that equality cannot be legislated and will come about only in the natural course of democracy assumes that racially hostile attitudes are no longer an important element in the American equation of democracy. There is little evidence to support the contention that a profound change of attitude has taken place. A number of polls taken in 1976 showed the majority of whites to believe that blacks were at the bottom of the economic and social ladder because of a lack of effort—a variation of the "lazy and shiftless" concept. Whereas the majority of whites believed discrimination a minor issue, the perception of most blacks was the opposite. A 1978 report by the Department of Housing and Urban Development showed, in fact, that the majority of blacks continued to suffer discrimination in housing, the area whites believed to be most racially neutral.

But the inability of such reports to change white perceptions lay in the economics of the situation. As the end of the 1970s grew near, there was a painful awareness that social problems could not be solved without costs to one group or another. Already a million college graduates were unemployed or underemployed. Although the rate of joblessness among blacks was double the white rate, this provided little comfort to those whose security in society was not at all guaranteed.

Allan Bakke's case was on the cutting edge of a serious dilemma for the majority. To make a place for those underneath clamoring for a share of the rapidly dwindling privileges of affluence, some members of the majority would have to give way. To critics of affirmative action, this "reverse discrimination" was simply unjust. But to do nothing at all was to sentence entire generations of black, brown, and poor people to suffer the effects of this discrimination. The nation's highest court was expected to play Solomon in this intense melodrama. The dreams of one Allan Bakke were easier to understand than those of countless, faceless people who seemed to be asking for the unreasonable. But what the justices were being asked to do, as playwright and executioner, was to choose the victim.

There could be no resolution without injury to one side or the other. The imperative for action lay in the future shape of the nation, in the vision of a multiracial destiny that would eliminate color as a subject for debate. More than once in our history race has been a magnifying glass revealing the warts and imperfections of our most treasured myths. As one looks at Allan Bakke's case for becoming a doctor, one can also consider the irrationality of forcing 42,155 applicants to compete for 15,774 positions in medical schools. While officials admit that the majority of rejected applicants are qualified to study medicine, the United States continues to rank near the bottom among industrialized nations in the quality of health care.

It is easier for demagogues to raise cries of "merit" and "discrimination" than to consider the more serious obstacles to the education of an Allan Bakke. Few have been willing to discuss the abuse of power that had much to do with Bakke's exclusion from the medical school at Davis, California. It takes courage to admit that wealth and political power still bring advantages in our democracy. It is even more difficult to realize that we all cannot have what we want or deserve because that undermines the greatest American dream of all. Instead, we are left with the spectacle of Americans standing on both sides of the issue, crying racism while actually making a choice of victims.

The campus of the University of California at Davis would seem an unlikely setting for an important racial and legal confrontation. The university squats in the center of the valley, the broad, flat plain that slices like an incision down the middle of this rugged and mountainous state. The northern end of the valley peters out as the coastal range turns away from the Pacific and merges with the rugged Sierra Nevada, which form California's eastern Great Wall. The mountains on both sides keep out the chill coastal winds that give the coast its perpetual autumn. In winter the valley is cold, and in summer it becomes a dry, hot plain, forcibly transformed into one of the world's most productive agricultural domains by a crisscross pattern of waterways and canals.

San Francisco, that reasonable facsimile of a European city, with its cosmopolitan charm, polyglot culture, and tolerance of sexual and political aberration, is only seventy-two miles southwest of Davis, but the hills keep out more than weather. This is conservative farming country, replete with decalled pickup trucks, silos etched against an unlimited sky, and the inevitable California "Far out!" delivered to the cadence of country music. The growth of city living has encroached on the farmland around here, and the ubiquitous developments have sprouted wildly around towns like Davis. Among these boxes for living, we see the flimsiness of this new middle-class status. The builders throw up airy wooden cages, cover them with plywood and tar paper, add shingles and glass, and declare them to be homes. If this be the goal of upward mobility, then the location of this dispute is not at all difficult to understand.

On that August day in 1973, Peter Storandt, a thirty-year-old assistant to the dean of student affairs at Davis, waited inside one of the green metal prefabricated buildings that housed the medical school while permanent facilities were being completed. The medical school had begun only in 1968, and the impressive facilities on the western edge of the 4,000-acre campus were still under construction. The old green barracks at the center of the campus were relatively inconspicuous, their starkness only partially softened by the hedges around the exoskeletal structural beams.

It was six o'clock that Friday evening when Allan Bakke drove off the exit ramp from I-80 and made his way through the maze of roads and driveways that crosshatch the campus. In California the weekends begin early, and the building was deserted. The temperature had reached nearly 100 degrees, but it was dropping rapidly, and soon that part of the state would plunge into the typically cool nighttime weather that never fails to surprise tourists.

Storandt insists he never meant to provoke Bakke into suing the university. But his meeting with Bakke and their exchange of letters would make him a principal character in the melodrama. He provided a sympathetic ear, crucial information about the school's admissions procedures, and important advice on legal strategy that Bakke would follow. More than any other single event, this meeting at Davis would crystallize Bakke's resolve to sue.

Storandt, the son of an admissions officer at Cornell University, had himself toyed with the idea of becoming a physician. In one of those adolescent moments of truth that move us closer to adulthood, he decided he did not have the aggressive character and intense competitive spirit to pursue a premedical education, and he switched to English literature. He had nearly completed his course work for a doctorate at the University of Massachusetts when his wife became pregnant. Realizing that doctors of English had difficulty finding work in the late 1960s, almost by accident he found himself in admissions, first at the medical school at Wayne State University in Detroit, later at the Medical College of Pennsylvania, and then at Davis. A shy, intense man of medium height, Storandt has a clear complexion that makes him appear younger than he is and leaves his cheeks in a permanent flush. Until the *Bakke* case became a major issue, he had a reputation as a dissident in a tightly controlled administration who often took the side of students in controversial disputes. When he left Davis, students picketed in protest, not aware of the peculiar role he had played in the affair.

Storandt had always been ambiguous about the Task Force that selected minority students for the medical school. He was bothered by the fact that no whites had been selected by the Task Force, although it professed to consider all disadvantaged applicants. He felt compromised because he had to answer questions from white applicants in ways he felt were not totally honest in order to cover up the faculty's failure to develop a well-thought-out and carefully articulated rationale for the program. He saw deserving whites and blacks being excluded by both the Task Force and the regular admissions committee, and he raised the issue a number of times with administrators at the medical school.

In conversation Storandt exudes an honesty and earnestness that must have been appealing to applicants and students at the medical school. Some administrators complain that he had an inordinate desire to please and often exceeded his authority in the process. Those traits resulted in his involvement with Allan Bakke's problems. Bakke's first contact with the school was a letter he wrote in 1971 asking how his age would affect his application. Dr. Alexander Barry, an associate dean, wrote back that no fixed maximum age had been established for applicants. "However," Barry went on, "the Committee does feel that when an applicant is over thirty, his age is a serious factor which must be considered. One of the major reasons for this is that such an applicant can be expected on an actuarial basis to practice medicine for about ten years less than the applicant of average age. The Committee believes that an older applicant must be unusually highly qualified if he is to be seriously considered for one of the limited number of places in the entering class."

Despite the concern generated by this letter, Bakke applied late in 1972 and was not interviewed until the following March, after most of the places in the class had been filled. It had to be difficult for a man who had been at the top of his class at the University of Minnesota, served his country in Vietnam, and worked among the country's scientific elite to accept the form letter that rejected his application. Davis was the newest and least prestigious of the dozen medical schools Bakke had applied to. The turndown by Davis made his chances of becoming a doctor seem more remote than ever.

On May 14, 1973, Bakke wrote to Dr. George Lowrey, the dean of student affairs and the official in charge of admissions at the medical school: "Your letter denying me admission to Davis was a tremendous disappointment but I'm not yet willing to give up my commitment to becoming a physician." Bakke asked if he could be put on standby status or could audit courses until a vacancy developed. His letter went unanswered, and he wrote again on July 1, 1973. Noting the "inexorable passage of time, I feel compelled to pursue a further course of action. My commitment to becoming a physician and serving in medicine requires it."

Until now Bakke's communications with the school had concerned his age, and their tone had been respectful, even pleading. Now his anger and frustration came through clearly. Trying a new tack, he raised the issue of race for the first time: "Applicants chosen to be our doctors should be those presenting the best qualifications, both academic and personal. Most are selected according to this standard, but I am convinced that a significant fraction of every current medical class is judged by a separate criterion. I am referring to quotas, open or covert, for racial minorities. Medicine needs the ablest and most dedicated men in order to meet future health care needs. I realize that the rationale for these quotas is that they attempt to atone for past racial discrimination. But instituting a new racial bias, in favor of minorities, is not a just solution."

Bakke called quotas illegal and said he was asking friends in federal and state government about possibly challenging the school in court. "My main reason for undertaking such action," he admitted, "would be to secure admission for myself. I consider the goal worth fighting for in every legal and ethical way. Further, I believe selecting medical students on any other basis than demonstrated aptitude, ability, and motivation is wrong and should be challenged." He added that many physicians and laymen he knew opposed "reverse discrimination" and that he planned to poll the faculty of a medical school in California on the issue. After his somewhat vehement assertions, Bakke ended his letter by thanking Lowrey and adding, "I do still hope to be accepted to medical school. I won't quit trying."

Answering mail from unhappy applicants was one of the tasks assigned to Peter Storandt. Lowrey passed the letter on to him, and it was now his job to deal with Bakke, whose complaints struck a sympathetic chord in the young admissions officer. He understood Bakke's burning desire to become a physician, and while the engineer could hardly be classified as disadvantaged, neither was he a child of the privileged class.

By reading Bakke's file, Storandt quickly constructed a sketch of this troublesome applicant. Allan Bakke was born on February 4, 1940, in Minneapolis. When he was very young, his family moved to Florida, where his father was a mailman and his mother a schoolteacher. He went through the segregated public school system and Coral Gables High School. "He was one of our bright young men," recalls Harry Rath, who was principal at the time. Bakke was a star at a school with a respected academic reputation. He was a member of the National Honor Society, treasurer of his high school band, chaplain of his homeroom, and vice-president of his senior class. When he was graduated in 1958, he was a National Merit Scholarship finalist. Bakke went back to his home state and was graduated from the University of Minnesota with a degree in mechanical engineering and a 3.51 grade point average.

To defray his college costs, Bakke joined the naval ROTC, and when he was graduated in 1962, he served his four-year obligation as an officer in the Marine Corps. His tour of duty included a seven-month stint as commander of an antiaircraft unit in Vietnam. He was honorably discharged as a captain in 1967 and went to work in the space program at NASA.

Bakke's concern about lost time comes through clearly in his two applications to Davis. He starts both by referring to his age and the fact that he lost four years in military service. "Four years was a high price to pay for my undergraduate education and I would hope the admissions committee will not hold those years of service to America against me," he said in his first application. He described his good health as an argument against actuarial considerations and said he had taken courses in biology and chemistry while working full-time.

Bakke also took the Medical College Admissions Test (MCAT), an examination required by virtually every medical school in the country. He did well, scoring in the 97th percentile (top 3 percent) in scientific knowledge, 96th percentile in verbal ability, 94th percentile in mathematics, and 72d percentile in general knowledge. His scores were higher than those of the average student admitted to Davis.

But his high grades and scores did not help when he began applying to medical schools. In 1972 he applied to the University of Southern California and Northwestern and was rejected by both. Northwestern said his age was "above their stated limit." In 1973, the first year he applied to Davis, he also applied to UCLA, UC–San Francisco, Stanford, the University of Minnesota, the Mayo Medical School, Wayne State University, Georgetown, the University of Cincinnati, Bowman Gray Medical School at Wake Forest, and the University of South Dakota. He was interviewed at Stanford, Minnesota, and Mayo, an indication he was being seriously considered, but all three turned him down. This time UCSF told him age was a "negative factor."

When Bakke's first application arrived at Davis, it was one of 2,464 competing for 100 places in the class that would begin in the fall of 1973. All applications were sorted into three groups by members of the admissions committee. Line 22 of the application read: "Applicants from economically and educationally disadvantaged backgrounds are evaluated by a special subcommittee of the admissions committee. If you wish your application to be considered by this group, check this space." Applicants who had checked off "Yes" were put into a separate stack for consideration by the Task Force. The grade point averages of applicants with "No" checked off for line 22 were examined. Those with an overall GPA below 2.5 were automatically turned down. Applicants with GPAs above 2.5 were forwarded to the regular admissions committee. Bakke's file met the requirements of the third group and was moved on to further consideration. The process of selection it had undergone would become the heart of the *Bakke* case.

Bakke's mother-in-law was seriously ill with lung cancer in 1972 and required considerable attention from Bakke and his wife. As a result, his application was not completed until January 9, 1973. But his high scores, grades, and experience took him, over the next hurdle in the selection process. He was among the one out of six invited to Davis for an interview. But medical schools select their students over a period of time, and by the time Bakke was interviewed on March 21, 1973, 123 letters of acceptance had already been mailed. (Schools accept more students than they can accommodate because many choose to go elsewhere.) Only thirty-seven more letters of acceptance would go out for that fall's class. Bakke's chances for admission had already been considerably reduced by his tardiness.

However, the interview with Dr. Theodore West, a Davis faculty member, went very well. "He is a pleasant, mature person," West wrote in his interview report, "tall and strong and Teutonic in appearance (not surprising from his Minnesota background)." West called Bakke a "well-qualified candidate for admission whose main handicap is the unavoidable fact that he is now 33 years of age." West noted Bakke's service in the emergency room of a hospital near his home in Sunny-vale and his interest in applying his engineering knowledge to the problems of medicine.

"He seems completely unprepossessing," West continued. "He was not dynamic or aggressive and articulated well in all areas except his response to my request that he express for me some of his reasons for changing from engineering to medicine. During that phase his conversation was more halting, more introspective and I sensed an air of frustration and emotion which I attribute to his concern about the impact of age and the fact that this is probably about the last chance for him to apply."

The only negative comment by West was that Bakke had "apparently not looked to any extent into the problem of health care delivery." Officials at Davis were aware that problems of American medical care stemmed more from the maldistribution of physicians than from the shortages that had received so much publicity a decade or two earlier. The concept of attracting minority and rural applicants to medical schools was aimed at correcting this problem. Later another official would also complain about Bakke's lack of awareness of the nature of the delivery problem. Despite this, he went on to say that he saw Bakke as "a very desirable applicant to this medical school and I shall so recommend him." As in the case of other regular applicants, Bakke's file was then circulated among five members of the admissions committee to be rated on the basis of the test scores, grades, recommendations, and the interview with Dr. West.

At the same time the other group of applicants was going through a similar process. The Task Force, consisting primarily of minority faculty and student members, had been set up in 1969 to help bring greater diversity into the medical school.

When Allan Bakke was applying to medical school, the

atmosphere of tension and racial confrontation that marked the 1960s seemed remote. But when rioting swept through Watts, Detroit, and Newark and when the Reverend Martin Luther King, Jr., was killed in 1968, white America seemed at bay, and the need to correct the inequities of discrimination was a subject to be considered seriously. It was in this spirit that the Association of American Medical Colleges (AAMC) recommended that "medical schools must admit increased numbers of students from geographical areas, economic backgrounds and ethnic groups that are now inadequately represented." The following year an AAMC committee suggested that 12 percent of all first-year medical school classes be black by the 1975–76 academic year. This goal would not be met, but more than 100 schools responded by setting up programs similar to the one at Davis.

The Task Force at Davis was created by faculty resolution and operated in an informal manner until the dean of the school, Dr. C. John Tupper, appointed Dr. Lindy Kumagai, a Japanese-American faculty member, chairman in 1970. Kumagai had been instrumental in setting up a similar program at the University of Utah, so he seemed a logical choice. Davis was then accepting fifty medical students each year, and eight slots were allotted to the Task Force. When the class size was doubled, the number assigned to the Task Force went up to sixteen. Between 1970 and 1974 the Task Force admitted thirty-three Mexican-Americans, twenty-six blacks, and one Native American to the medical school. The fact that no whites were admitted through the program would lead to charges that it was racial and not for disadvantaged students.

But Dr. Kumagai insists he followed the recommendations of the AAMC and the faculty resolution in defining who was eligible. During the four years he was chairman, twelve Asian students were admitted through the Task Force, while forty-one other Asians came through the regular admissions process.

Kumagai says minority candidates who showed no evidence of disadvantage were referred to the regular committee but had difficulty being admitted despite excellent credentials. On the rare occasion that blacks or Chicanos were admitted by the regular committee, their records were so outstanding that it was predictable that they would not come to Davis. Task Force members say that at least three blacks were offered admission through the regular process, but only one accepted because of competition from more prestigious schools. Kumagai and others who served on the Task Force insist that they interviewed several whites during that time. Some were turned down because they made no commitment to serving in inner-city or rural areas or because their disadvantaged status was questionable. However, the statistics used in court would show only that no whites were admitted through the Task Force between 1970 and 1974.

While regular applicants with grade point averages below 2.5 were automatically turned down, this was not the case for Task Force students. Many had grades and MCAT scores somewhat lower than the regular group's. In 1973 the average GPA of Task Force students admitted was 2.88, against 3.49 for regular students. On the science section of the MCAT, Task Force students averaged a ranking in the 35th percentile, while regular students averaged in the 83d percentile. Clearly, the Task Force was giving less weight to academic credentials in selecting candidates, giving rise to charges that these students were "less qualified."

However, the *range* of scores tells more about the selection process than the *averages* used throughout the case. At least one Task Force student admitted in 1973 had a grade point average of 3.76—higher than Allan Bakke's. In addition, a considerable number of whites were admitted with grades and MCAT scores lower than Bakke's. In a number of instances white students had lower grades than did some of the students admitted through the Task Force. Because the university did not choose to make the individual scores of white students a part of the trial record but chose instead to submit only an average of their scores, these facts were never made clear.

Bakke's main problem was that he applied late in 1973, and the benchmark scores, the rating of applicants by the admissions committee, had moved upward as places became scarce to a minimum of 470 out of 500 for admission. After Bakke's application made the rounds of the committee, he had a score of 468. There were at least nineteen other applicants who scored 468 and fifteen with scores of 469. Bakke's last hope would have been the alternate or waiting list, but while some applicants with scores of 468 went on the list, Bakke was not among them. The reason he might have been excluded from the waiting list was not disclosed anywhere on the file Peter Storandt examined and would not be revealed until much later.

On July 18, 1973, Storandt sat down and carefully composed a letter to Bakke. He apologized for the delay in answering, explaining the turmoil of commencement, the start of the summer session, and changes that were taking place in the school's administration: "Your first letter involves us both in a situation as painful for us as for you. You did indeed fare well with our admissions committee and were rated in its deliberations among the top ten percent of our 2,500 applicants in the 1972–73 season.

"We can admit but one hundred students, however, and thus are faced with the distressing task of turning aside the applications of some remarkably able and well-qualified individuals, including this year, yourself," Storandt went on. "We do select a small group of alternative candidates and name individuals from that group to positions in the class made vacant by withdrawals, if any." Storandt explained that regulations did not allow part-time enrollment, as Bakke had suggested.

"Your dilemma—our dilemma, really—seems in your mind to center on your present age and the possible detrimental influence this factor may have in our consideration of your application. I can only say that older applicants have successfully entered and worked in our curriculum and that your very considerable talents can and will override any questions of age in our final determinations." Up to this point Storandt was playing the role of the concerned and sympathetic official. He encouraged Bakke to apply again through the Early Decision Plan, which would get him an interview and evaluation before October 1 and would give him time to apply elsewhere if turned down again.

Now Storandt addressed Bakke's threat to sue: "In the event that our decision is the latter [rejection] you might consider taking my other suggestion, which is then to pursue your research into admissions policies based on quota-oriented minority recruiting." Storandt said he was sending Bakke a page describing the minority admissions program at Davis. "I don't know whether you would consider our procedure to have the overtones of a quota or not, certainly its design has been to avoid such designation, but the fact remains that most applicants to such a program are members of ethnic minority groups." Storandt brought the *DeFunis* case, which challenged the use of race in admissions, to Bakke's attention and suggested two authorities on the legal aspects of minority admissions he might consult. The young admissions officer closed the letter by urging Bakke to "make a second shot at Davis."

Storandt would deny later that he was urging Bakke to sue the school, but it is difficult to interpret the letter differently. At that point Storandt felt that the Task Force was unfairly excluding whites, and in his zeal "I overstepped my bound of propriety and authority." Later he would wish he had limited his contacts with Bakke to off-the-record statements.

Finally, they were face-to-face, the man racing against time and the admissions officer who had given him new hope. They shook hands. Storandt offered Bakke a cup of coffee and tried to make small talk. Bakke brushed the chitchat aside and pressed Storandt for information about admissions procedures and the performance of minority students at the Davis Medical School. Storandt was reminded of a character out of a Bergman film, "somewhat humorless, perfectly straightforward, zealous in his approach; it was really striking; he was an extremely impressive man and I felt he deserved a straight answer." Bakke was no longer a faceless stack of forms and numbers. He was barely under six feet, taller in appearance, and his blond hair was thinning and combed across his forehead in that fruitless effort of men not yet resigned to baldness. The crew-cut youth in the picture that would be seen across America had been replaced by an older, heavier man with a determined jaw and a strong, set mouth.

Bakke did not believe the official description of the Task Force program sent to him by Storandt. As the engineer fired questions, Storandt gave him details: no whites had been accepted through the Task Force; the grades and test scores of minority applicants were lower than those of whites who applied; yes, Storandt understood the number of minority admissions was set at sixteen for each class. Bakke's resolute air and his own ambivalence made Storandt talkative. When the conversation ended, Bakke knew nearly as much as Storandt about the admissions procedures at Davis.

Yet there was one area that neither man touched. The case would go through the courts with no reference to a third method for admitting students to the medical school. Storandt had learned about it soon after he came to Davis in 1972.

From time to time the dean of the school, Dr. Tupper, would submit a name to the admissions committee for consideration. Sometimes the dean's candidate had already been rejected in the regular admissions process. But the intervention was common at many medical schools, a tradition for making sure that the children of the wealthy, the influential, and the politically powerful inherited the spoils of privilege. Although some Davis faculty members objected to the practice—especially in cases in which the candidate failed to meet the minimum standards—they thought it a privilege of the dean. The understanding was that the dean could select as many as five students in each year's class.

University officials have never satisfactorily explained their failure to mention the dean's involvement in the admissions process. They argue that it was not an issue at the time. In fact, it would not become a controversy until 1976, when a medical student wrote about the procedure and questioned the dean's right to exercise this power. A number of administrators, including Storandt, resented Tupper's interference and made strenuous objections on several occasions. But Tupper exercised much power over the waiting list, and without this quota of privilege, Allan Bakke might well have been admitted.

After his conversation with Peter Storandt, Bakke's spirits must have been lifted considerably. He had been urged to try again, and if he were turned down, he would attack what he saw to be the only obstacle between him and medical school: the special admissions program or Task Force. As he drove into the coastal fog that night, the radio droned about FBI director L. Patrick Gray's testimony before the Senate Watergate Committee and his admission that he had read Howard Hunt's files and destroyed them. President Nixon warned Congress that the impending cutoff of funds for bombing Cambodia would have "dangerous potential consequences" in Asia. The good news was that unemployment had hit a three-year low. Hardly anyone noticed that black unemployment was double the rate for whites and going up. For Allan Bakke, race was rapidly replacing age as a concern in his ambition to be a physician, and he felt a great deal less helpless than he had when he had started the drive to Davis a few hours earlier.

The following Tuesday, Bakke wrote a thank-you letter to Storandt. "Our discussion was very helpful to me in considering possible courses of action. I appreciate your professional interest in the question of moral and legal propriety of quotas and preferential admissions policies; even more impressive to me was your real concern about the effect of admissions policies on each individual applicant." Bakke reiterated that his first concern was "to be allowed to study medicine, and that challenging the concept of racial quotas is secondary. Although medical school admission is important to me personally, clarification and resolution of the quota issue is unquestionably a more significant goal because of its direct impact on all applicants." Although the personal objective remained paramount, Bakke moved for the first time into his new role as a symbol. He proposed two plans. Plan A was to apply under the Early Decision Plan at Davis and to sue Stanford and the University of California at San Francisco even if Davis admitted him. Bakke was especially interested in Stanford because it stated categorically that it had set aside twelve places in its entering class for racial minorities.

Plan B was to apply to Davis and at the same time to threaten to sue Stanford and try to force his admission "as an alternative to a legal challenge of their admitted racial quota." Bakke would sue Davis and UCSF if Stanford let him in. If also admitted to Davis, he would sue only UCSF. Bakke added that he didn't want to jeopardize his chances of being admitted at Davis under the Early Decision Plan. He wrote that he also wanted to avoid any actions Storandt might oppose "personally or professionally" because the admissions officer had been so helpful to him.

Bakke then made Storandt his mentor by asking him for suggestions or comments about the actions he proposed to take against Davis and the other schools. He also asked Storandt about the academic performance of the minority students at Davis and closed the letter by thanking Storandt again. At this point Storandt realized that Bakke was quite serious about suing. He says he went to see Dean Tupper and told him about his meeting with Bakke and the exchange of letters. Tupper took no action and told Storandt, in effect, not to worry about it.

A more prudent official might have terminated his contact with Bakke at this point. Storandt says that he was only mildly interested in Bakke and that he was just giving him the sympathy he shared with any applicant to medical school. But he sat down and wrote another letter to Bakke on August 15. "Thank you for your good letter," Storandt wrote. "It seems to me that you have carefully arranged your thinking about this matter and that the eventual result of your next actions will be of significance to many present and future medical school applicants."

Storandt went on to comment on Bakke's proposed plans to sue. He was doubtful about plan A. Could Bakke sue Stanford if he did not have a current application for admission there? Storandt preferred plan B, in which Bakke would apply at all three places and sue the schools that turned him down. He agreed with Bakke that the Stanford program seemed the most vulnerable and referred him to articles in the *Journal of Medical Education* on the performance of minority students.

"At Davis," Storandt wrote, "such students have not required 'official' tutoring, although they and many of their classmates have organized an impressive series of study sessions during the year. A few of them—perhaps ten percent—have taken longer than four years to complete the M.D. degree (but not more than one year longer)." Storandt said that about half the minority students in the third-year class had failed their National Board exams on the first try but that all had passed these tests before being graduated.

Bakke's second application was already being processed when Peter Storandt wrote his letter. It was no longer being treated as a routine application. Officials were aware of Bakke's threat to sue and had passed the word around to members of the admissions committee. There had been changes in procedure for the new application year. Davis had joined the centralized American Medical College Application System (AMCAS), which allowed applicants to fill out one form and have it distributed to all the schools where they wanted to be considered. As a result, there was a tremendous upsurge in applications to Davis, an increase of about 1,200 to 3,737 candidates for the 100 places in the class that would begin in the fall of 1974.

There was also a difference in the wording of one important question. Instead of asking about disadvantaged status, the AMCAS form made a direct reference to race. Did the applicant describe himself or herself as "White/Caucasian" or a member of some other identifiable racial group, and did he or she wish to be considered as an applicant from a minority group? Bakke checked off "White/Caucasian" and "No" once again. In his written statement he once more referred to his age and his concern about the obstacle it posed.

"The usual factors which detract from an older applicant do not apply in my case. First, my only dependent is my wife, who is well qualified to assist in earning if needed," Bakke said, stressing his recent studies as evidence of his ability to do the work in medical school. He said he was in good health and could be expected to practice as long as a younger applicant.

Bakke then decided to confront the question of why he had taken so long to decide on medicine as a career. "I was not among those blessed with a built-in motivation, such as a physician in the family, or a parent who encouraged me toward a medical career." He said that he had been considering medicine since 1963 and had made inquiries while in the Marines but that after his discharge he had gone on to finish the master's degree in engineering he had started at Minnesota. He said he thought the engineering background could be applied to medicine and emphasized that he was not changing careers for financial gain. "More than anything else in the world," Bakke stressed, "*I want to study medicine.*"

Under the new procedures at Davis, there would be two interviews instead of one, with a student and with a member of the faculty. On August 30, 1973, Bakke drove up to Davis again to see Frank Gioia, a second-year student, and Dr. Lowrey, who said later that his assignment to interview Bakke was simply the luck of the draw and not a result of his concern about the threat of legal challenge.

Gioia had heard about Bakke and was pleasantly surprised at the interview with the engineer. He found the applicant "friendly, well-tempered, conscientious and delightful to speak with." The conversation got around to minority admissions, and Gioia reported that Bakke took pains to make clear "that he was not out to sue anybody but that he simply wished to question the logic behind such policies. He simply felt that medical candidates should be selected on" the basis of qualifications. "I felt that he was at no time 'uppity' or threatening about the matter," Gioia concluded, giving Bakke a "sound recommendation" for acceptance.

Lowrey and Bakke disagreed on almost everything. "He was very unsympathetic to the concept of recruiting minority students so that they hopefully would go back to practice in the presently neglected areas of the country," Lowrey wrote in his report. "One of the main reasons for being against such programs was that this decreased his chances of getting into medical school." Lowrey found Bakke "a rather rigidly oriented young man who has the tendency to arrive at conclusions based more upon his personal impressions than upon thoughtful processes using available sources of information." He rated Bakke "acceptable but certainly not an outstanding candidate for our school."

Considering all the attention that was to focus on this case, the final process for selecting students at the Davis Medical School would never be made completely clear. None of the testimony and no interviews ever established the relationship between grades, test scores, and interviews with the benchmark ratings that actually determined acceptance or rejection. Apparently, the rating was quite arbitrary, unlike the situation in some schools, which scored each segment of the application process and produced a rating through a complicated formula. At Davis the number of people voting on applicants had been raised to six for 1974. Each scored the applicant without seeing the vote of other members of the committee.

On Bakke's second application, Storandt gave him 92 points. Gioia, who had interviewed Bakke, scored him at 94. Bakke also got a 96, a 94, and an 87. Dr. Lowrey gave him his lowest rating, 86 points. His total benchmark score was 549. He was rejected under the Early Decision Plan, and when he was reviewed the following spring, he was turned down again.

Twelve applicants with higher scores than Bakke's failed to make the alternates list for 1974, and thirty-two applicants with higher scores than 549 were not admitted at all. In the class for 1974, the overall grade point averages of whites ranged from 2.79 to a perfect 4.0. The overall GPAs of Task Force students ranged from 2.21 to 3.45. The grade point average in sciences of the top regular student was 4.0, and the science GPA of the top Task Force student was 3.89. The most profound differences between the two groups would be found in the MCAT scores and would help build the argument that the Task Force students admitted to Davis were "less qualified" than Allan Bakke.

Two

BROTHER FOX
FOR THE DEFENSE

One day Brother Fox caught Brother Goose and tied him to a tree.

"I'm going to eat you, Bro' Goose," he said, "you've been stealing my meat."

"But I don't even eat meat," Bro' Goose protested.

"Tell that to the judge and jury," said Bro' Fox.

"Who's gonna be the judge?" asked Bro' Goose.

"A fox," answered Bro' Fox.

"And who's gonna be the jury?" Bro' Goose inquired.

"They all gonna be foxes," said Bro' Fox, grinning so all his teeth showed.

"Guess my goose is cooked," said Brother Goose.

—An Afro-American folktale

The natural dramatics of a courtroom trial would have been the preferable way of resolving the issues in the *Bakke* case. The gradual exposition of fact through examination and cross-examination is a device that has attracted writers ever since the invention of the written word. For that reason plays have been written as trials and trials have served the purpose of theater. In a case that has played the national stage to such acclaim, a courtroom confrontation would have been a fitting vehicle for sorting out the complexities of law and the motivations and passions of the principal characters and for resolving it all in a firm and definitive final scene with the passage of judgment.

But this case fails to offer a neat resolution. We see no penetrating examination of nervous witnesses, no dramatic appeals to judge and jury. At least three times judgment has been rendered. But this was a battle fought with paper, delivered with little discernible drama by messengers who insisted on signatures and receipts that ended up in the record. The combatants have been not the complainants and defendants most affected by this case, but attorneys and judges.

The mass of paperwork in the *Bakke* case tends to reduce the issues to abstractions because there is little sense of the flesh and blood in legal maneuvers. But even in cases where prosecutor and defendant stand eye-to-eye in moments of high drama, these theatrically satisfying confrontations often tell us less than the processes that take place outside the public view. Decisions to include or omit, to challenge or let pass, to protest or acquiesce, are important in the overall strategy of a case.

The lack of a trial in *Bakke* remains a major criticism of the handling of the case by attorneys for the University of California. In addition, a number of important omissions and concessions by the university have muddied the defense all the way to the highest court in the land. These unspectacular events have brought into question the university's commitment to the defense of the case and cast doubt on the competence of the attorneys involved. The facts indicate that the university lawyers were hampered not so much by a lack of lawyering skills as by the competing concerns of their client and an ambivalence about the issues central to the case.

When reporters for national news organizations began calling the West Coast to find out about the attorney who would represent Allan Bakke before the United States Supreme Court, Reynold H. Colvin couldn't resist slipping into what he called his "Sam Ervin shuffle." He would tell the press he was "just an ol' country lawyer from San Francisco" and ask about the distance from the Greyhound station in the District of Columbia to the Supreme Court building. Although his law practice may not have impressed Supreme Court pundits, Colvin already had to his credit an important federal court victory in a case alleging reverse discrimination.

A jowly, jovial man of average height and stocky build who appears a decade younger than his threescore years, "Rennie" Colvin has the carefully modulated tones of the practiced public speaker. A native of San Francisco, Colvin was graduated from Lowell High School, a selective public school in the city, and got his bachelor's degree from the University of California at Berkeley in 1938. He was graduated from the university's Boalt Hall Law School before being swept into military service by World War II. After his discharge he worked as an assistant U.S. attorney until 1951, when he ventured into private practice.

An active member of San Francisco's Jewish community, Colvin served several terms as president of Temple Emanu-el, the most influential and politically powerful synagogue in the city, and he has also been president of the San Francisco chapter of the American Jewish Committee. Colvin's interest in city politics brought him indirectly to the most important case of his career. In 1964 Mayor John Shelley appointed him to the traditional "Jewish seat" on the San Francisco Board of Education, a high-visibility position that has been a traditional first step to higher political office. Despite a term as president of the school board, the gregarious attorney was unable to capitalize on his exposure because Shelley's successor, the flamboyant Joseph Alioto, declined to reappoint Colvin in 1970.

But Colvin's tenure made him a lot of friends among school officials and administrators. In 1971 Superintendent Thomas

Shaheen, facing budget cuts and declining enrollment, proposed to demote and transfer more than 200 administrators in an economy move. In order to keep the handful of minority officials who had recently joined the school system, Shaheen decided to exempt them from the effects of the reorganization. Because a strong affirmative action plan set goals for hiring and promoting minorities, the new arrangement would have virtually eliminated future advancement for white officials in the school system.

The administrators asked their friend Reynold Colvin to represent them. The "Zero Quota" case made a public figure of their attorney. After a series of confrontations with the school board, the case ended up in the federal district court. The decision in *Anderson* v. *S.F. Unified School District* did not receive a great deal of national attention. The ruling by federal judge Joseph Conti, a conservative whom San Francisco civil rights lawyers avoided when they could, concerned a specific employment situation and did not seem to have broad implications. But it was one of the few cases that had considered the issue, and it would provide important theoretical elements for subsequent attacks on preferential treatment of minorities at Davis and elsewhere.

"Preferential treatment under the guise of 'affirmative action' is the imposition of one form of racial discrimination in place of another," Conti ruled. "Any classification based on race is suspect: no authority exists which discriminates on racial or ethnic lines which is not being implemented to correct a prior discriminatory situation.

"No one race or ethnic group should ever be accorded preferential treatment over another. No one race or ethnic group should ever be granted privileges or prerogatives not given to every other race. There is no place for racial groupings in America. Only in individual accomplishment can equality be achieved," Conti concluded in reversing the school district's action.

Judge Conti's ruling turned up in the case Storandt had suggested to Allan Bakke, *DeFunis* v. *Odegaard*. Marco DeFunis, Jr., was a Phi Beta Kappa graduate of the University of Washington who sued his alma mater after he was rejected by its law school in 1971. DeFunis charged that the law school's minority admissions program had allowed less qualified applicants in ahead of him because of their race. A lower court supported DeFunis and ordered him admitted, but the Washington Supreme Court reversed the lower court and declared the university's program constitutional.

In his first letter to Bakke, Peter Storandt pointed out that DeFunis had been able to attend the University of Washington Law School while his case was in the courts. This sparked Bakke's interest, and with the thoroughness of the research scientist, he wrote to DeFunis in Seattle. By return mail he received copies of briefs and documents filed in the case. Among them was a brief by the Anti-Defamation League of B'nai B'rith on behalf of DeFunis referring to Colvin's case against the San Francisco Board of Education.

Reynold Colvin met with Allan Bakke in January of 1974 to discuss the merits of his case against the University of California. "I told Mr. Bakke he appeared to be a very sane, very intelligent, confident person and that the road of litigation was long and hard and rough." Colvin pointed out the parallels in the *DeFunis* case, which was going to the U.S. Supreme Court, and suggested that they wait to see the result.

On February 26, 1974, the High Court heard oral arguments in *DeFunis*. But the plaintiff was already completing his third year of law school. On April 23, to the bitter disappointment of both sides, the Court declared the case moot by a 5 to 4 vote. Within a couple of days, Bakke was back on the telephone with

Colvin. "Well," he said to the attorney, "what are you going to do for me now?"

There were fundamental differences between Bakke's case and that of the school administrators. The changes proposed by the superintendent had been made public; Bakke had obtained his information from conversations with Peter Storandt. While it was clear which administrators would be affected by the San Francisco plan, Bakke, as an outsider looking in, had to establish the important legal condition of standing. He had to show that he was genuinely affected by the procedures at Davis. As Colvin saw it, Bakke had to prove not only that there was a quota for minority students but that he had been injured by this quota. The crucial issue would be how close he had come to being admitted. Storandt's assurances that he had been very near admission were not enough. Bakke had to show that the Task Force students had specifically kept him out of the medical school.

While the thrust of legal action would aim at getting the special admissions program declared illegal, the real objective was to get Bakke admitted in time to join the fall class. The time element would dictate Colvin's tactics and would pay off in unexpected ways. When DeFunis sued the University of Washington, a local judge ordered him admitted, and he was able to stay in school even when the U.S. Supreme Court sidestepped the case. Colvin decided his best bet was to take the case to the superior court in Yolo County, where the medical school was located. He hoped that a state court judge at the local level, familiar with the Davis campus, would view the case in terms of real benefits and damages to Bakke. If they went to federal court in San Francisco, the judge might view the case as an abstract exercise in law and keep Bakke out until a decision was issued.

Colvin's decision to pursue Bakke's admission as a primary objective also dictated another tactic. The case would not be pursued as a class action. "While he had no constitutional right to be in medical school," said Colvin, "he did have the constitutional right not to be discriminated against. From our point of view, he was there as an individual." The emphasis on the individual, Colvin hoped, made it more likely that a judge would order Bakke admitted than if several plaintiffs were involved. This pragmatic decision would also reap benefits for Bakke. Whenever the case threatened to become too abstract, Colvin would focus attention on his client. The case would no longer involve an amorphous white person deprived for the public good. It would become a case about Allan Bakke, Vietnam veteran, aerospace engineer, and a man with a strong commitment to medicine.

On June 20, 1974, Reynold Colvin filed a complaint on behalf of Allan Bakke at the Yolo County seat in Woodland. This important first step was strangely lacking in drama. The complaint covered a modest four pages and had a fifth page asserting that Allan Bakke was telling the truth. The complaint charged that Bakke was "and is in all respects duly qualified for admission to [the Davis] Medical School and the sole reason his application was rejected was on account of his race, to-wit, Caucasian and white, and not for reasons applicable to persons of every race."

Colvin charged that "a special admissions committee composed of racial minority members evaluated applications of a special group of persons purportedly from economic and educationally disadvantaged backgrounds; that from this group, a quota of 16 percent, or 16 out of 100 first-year class members, was selected; that, in fact, all applicants admitted to said medical school as members of this group were members of racial minorities, that under this admission program racial minority and majority applicants went through separate segregated admission procedures with separate standards for admissions; that the use of such separate standards resulted in the admission of minority applicants less qualified than plaintiff and other non-minority applicants who were therefore rejected." The complaint concluded that Bakke's rights had been violated under the Fourteenth Amendment of the U.S. Constitution, the California Constitution, and the U.S. Civil Rights Act of 1964. Colvin asked that Bakke be admitted to the school while the case was being considered.

The University of California is an independent entity created by the Constitution of California. While the university depends on the state legislature for much of its funding, policy decisions are in the hands of the University Board of Regents, a body consisting of the state's top elected officials and private individuals named by the governor of California. The university is the top tier of an educational system that includes the state colleges and the community colleges, each having its own ruling body. But the university system is the most prestigious, a sprawling complex of nine campuses stretching from San Diego to Davis, an enrollment of nearly 122,000, a teaching staff of 9,400, and an annual operating budget of $1.8 billion.

On the day that Bakke's complaint was filed in Woodland, a copy was delivered to the fifth-floor offices of the university's general counsel in University Hall, Berkeley, a dull, colorless blockhouse of concrete, glass, and brick that serves as the administrative center for the entire system. All legal matters for the nine campuses are handled by the staff of eighteen attorneys under the supervision of Donald H. Reidhaar.

In many ways, Reidhaar presents a sharp contrast with his opponent in the *Bakke* case. Where Colvin is extroverted and garrulous, Reidhaar is self-effacing and closemouthed. Where Colvin is expansive and dramatic in making a point, Reidhaar has the lawyer's talent for cloaking an important point in boredom. A native of Idaho, Reidhaar is a slim, pale man, distinguished by healthy sideburns that seem out of place in his otherwise conservative demeanor. After being graduated with a degree in business from the University of Washington in 1957, Reidhaar earned his law degree at Boalt Hall and clerked for a justice on the Oregon Supreme Court. In 1961 he returned to the Bay Area and joined the prominent San Francisco law firm of Pillsbury, Madison, and Sutro. After just eleven months as an associate, Reidhaar crossed the bay to join the university counsel's office. He spent nine years as an assistant counsel, was promoted to associate, and in 1973 was rewarded with the job of general counsel. He had been in office less than a year when Bakke's complaint reached his desk.

Although the debate sparked by *DeFunis* had been raging for some time, the university had been amazingly complacent about the possible repercussions of that case. Large corporate institutions like the university retain full-time attorneys as a preventive measure against legal problems. Yet no guidelines had been issued on affirmative action, and no efforts had been made to formulate admissions guidelines for the university system. Instead, each campus and each professional school were allowed to set their own standards for admission and to draw up their own affirmative action plans. The result was a hodgepodge of approaches, some clearly more defensible than others. Reidhaar would explain that this diversity was a result of the university's policy of encouraging autonomy on the individual campuses.

The university had received complaints about affirmative action and special admissions programs from individuals and organizations such as B'nai B'rith, but Bakke's was the first definite legal action against these programs. The regents had expected that a U.S. Supreme Court decision on *DeFunis* would provide some guidance on special admissions; but less than two months had passed between the Court's rejection of *DeFunis* and the filing of Bakke's complaint, and they were no more ready in June than they had been in April.

Initial reaction to the complaint was low-keyed. Reidhaar assigned three lawyers from his staff to determine the facts of the case. They went to Davis and interviewed medical school officials involved with admissions: Dr. George Lowrey, the dean of admissions; Peter Storandt, who had corresponded with Bakke; Dr. Lindy Kumagai, who had been chairman of the Task Force; and Dr. C. John Tupper, the dean of the medical school.

Storandt remembers his own response to Bakke's complaint as a combination of concern and relief. Maybe now, he thought, his reservations about the Task Force would be resolved in court. "We believed it was going to be a strictly social issue," he recalled. "It was going to be one of those precedent-setting decisions that would help the medical school devise a better program and maintain its commitment to minority education. Maybe we were optimistic and idealistic and maybe all of these things."

But some of the people interviewed by university attorneys were not so confident about preparations to defend the program. At least one Task Force member thought the lawyers somewhat casual in their approach. "I think they tried to win the case with one hand tied behind their backs," said a faculty member. "They didn't realize they couldn't win it off the cuff." Dr. Kumagai, who had set up the guidelines for the Task Force, thought at least one of the lawyers was "overtly against affirmative action. I said to one of them, 'With friends like that, who needs enemies?' "

The facts assembled by the university attorneys would become the foundation of the case for both sides. Unfortunately, mistakes or omissions in the university's preparations would prove most harmful to the defense. There was no dispute over the fact that applications were sorted into two groups—regular and Task Force—and that members of separate subcommittees interviewed and rated applicants, then presented them to the full admissions committee for consideration.

For some reason the lawyers decided to build their defense around the testimony of Dr. Lowrey, who had never worked directly with the Task Force and was therefore not completely familiar with its operation. Two key arguments in Bakke's complaint, which would remain undisputed throughout the legal battles, might have been challenged or undermined if Task Force members had been brought into the defense of the special admissions program. Early in the case the university virtually conceded that a quota was in operation by submitting statistics showing that in each year Bakke applied, sixteen students were admitted through the Task Force. Not until later would Dr. Sarah Gray, a black faculty member, go through the records of the admissions office and find that in 1974 only fifteen students came through the Task Force. One slot was given back to the regular committee, apparently because Task Force members felt they didn't have a qualified candidate. This information would have been helpful in refuting charges that unqualified applicants were being admitted to Davis because of a rigid quota.

The most damaging evidence against the Task Force was the total absence of whites admitted as disadvantaged, although more than 200 applied. Nowhere would the university show that a number of white applicants were interviewed by the Task Force. Dr. Kumagai and Dr. Gray say none of the whites were admitted because they failed to meet the economic and social qualifications applied to minority applicants or because they indicated no plans to practice in underserved or ghetto areas. In their defense, they point out that minority candidates from middle-class backgrounds were referred to the regular committee for evaluation. Dr. Kumagai complains that the regular committee often turned down well-qualified minority applicants. "They would say he or she only has a 3.4 [GPA] instead of a 3.6," he recalled. "I would point out that they were accepting whites with 3.4 and much less." Dr. George Sutherland, who as a student at Davis studied admissions practices at the medical school, concluded that both committees failed to practice what they preached. Dr. Lowrey would admit later that good middle-class minority candidates and whites from disadvantaged backgrounds often fell in the cracks between the two committees and were turned down.

The most crucial defense omission, of course, was the dean's intervention on behalf of well-connected applicants. Long after the California Supreme Court ruling in the case, Tupper would admit to a Davis paper that he had "intervened hundreds of times" in the admissions process "on the side of fairness." One prominent instance involved Ramona Mrak, daughter-in-law of a former chancellor of the Davis campus. Another Tupper admittee was the son of B. Kent Wilson, a former president of the Yolo County Medical Society. Others included the sons of the state senator and assemblyman who headed finance committees responsible for the medical school budget. In one case, Storandt recalled, a student was not interviewed at all but simply placed on the waiting list and admitted after the admissions committee had disbanded for the summer.

At the time that university attorneys were preparing their case, most faculty members, even those opposed to the practice, believed Tupper to be within his rights. After all, most professional schools made some exceptions for wealthy and influential friends. "I don't think those places were on anybody's mind as they worked on the court case," recalled Storandt. "It never came up when we were working with the university attorneys." Considering reports that Tupper was admitting as many as five applicants each year, this was a considerable oversight. A similar practice at the university's San

Francisco medical school had been debated some years earlier and abandoned when slots traditionally controlled by the dean were used for a new affirmative action program.

Bakke's entire case rested on the premise that the "quota" of sixteen places in the first-year class at Davis left just eighty-four slots open to competition. What if he had known that he was really competing for seventy-nine places because he lacked political connections? More important, Tupper often exercised his authority by placing students on the waiting list and selecting them from that list when vacancies occurred. In each year he applied, Bakke never made the waiting list. But because the details of the admissions process remained curiously fuzzy, he would never know that social status had at least as much to do with his exclusion as race.

Thirty-three days after Bakke filed his complaint, the university made its first official response. The lawyers admitted the existence of a special program that let "officials of the Davis Medical School consider minority group status of qualified applicants as a factor in filling a limited number of spaces in each first-year class for the purpose of promoting diversity in the student body and the medical profession and expanding medical educational opportunities for persons from economically and educationally disadvantaged backgrounds."

The university argued that Allan Bakke had no standing to sue because he had fallen far short of admission and because there was nothing illegal about the special admissions program. So far the university's response followed standard procedure. But at this point the attorneys made a move that would come back to haunt them. In filing an answer to Bakke's complaint, Reidhaar filed a cross complaint explaining the stiff competition for places in the medical school and the rationale for using race as a factor.

"An actual controversy has arisen and now exists," the university lawyers said, "relating to whether the special admissions program" violated the law. They asked the superior court to determine the validity of the program "so that it may ascertain its rights and duties with respect to the evaluation of [Bakke's] application and others." With this simple statement in the cross complaint, the university had opened itself up to a new line of attack. Up to this point the legal debate centered on Allan Bakke's right to be admitted to medical school. Colvin had suggested in his complaint that the method of selecting minority students was illegal but that all he wanted the court to do was admit his client. Quite possibly, the court would touch on the legality of the program in deciding whether to admit Bakke, but state trial court judges tend to shy away from sweeping decisions. This was the reason Colvin had gone to the Yolo County court. Now the university, of its own free will, was broadening the target for Bakke.

Litigation is the sweat and blood of law, essentially an unglamorous business of nuts and bolts, technique and technicalities. One axiom of litigation is that the defense tries to narrow the grounds of a case while the plaintiff makes every effort to widen it. The university lawyers had violated this rule, and they would pay for it. Another common tactic of corporate defendants is to slow the proceedings and increase the costs to the plaintiff. Again, the university gave no sign of resorting to such practices.

Bakke was fortunate that Reidhaar and his staff were after bigger game. The general counsel would refuse to discuss his strategy on the grounds of the lawyer-client right of confidentiality, but he conceded "the great uncertainty about the validity of such programs in the wake of *DeFunis*. There certainly was an institutional interest in having their validity clarified and sustained." Like Peter Storandt, the university lawyers had decided to turn their troubled consciences over to the courts.

The next step for Bakke was to find out as much as possible about the facts of the case. Under the rules of discovery adopted by most states in recent years, one party can interview the other in a legal action to determine these facts. On July 12 Colvin filed a formal notice of his intention to take a "deposition" from Dr. Lowrey. He asked the school official to bring all records of Bakke's applications, including documents having to do with his evaluation and rejection. Colvin also wanted information about the special admissions program and any documents defining the terms *educationally disadvantaged* and *economically disadvantaged*. Understandably, most of Colvin's requests for information were vague, but there was one specific item he wanted: "documents setting forth summaries and tabulations of information relating to said special program including, without limitation, the documents prepared by the University of California, Davis School of Medicine, Office of Student Affairs, Admissions Office, entitled: 'Statistics, Admissions Office, May 20, 1974.'" This document had been prepared by the medical school at the request of the Department of Health, Education and Welfare's Office of Civil Rights in San Francisco. The reason: a complaint of reverse discrimination by Allan Bakke. Colvin knew that those statistics, marked "Confidential," would provide information essential to Bakke's case.

Dr. Lowrey was interviewed by Colvin in the presence of Reidhaar at University Hall on Tuesday, July 23. For the first time Bakke and his attorney had full access to the files and letters in Bakke's application folder and a statistical comparison of Task Force and regular students at the medical school. Colvin took Dr. Lowrey through a step-by-step explanation of the selection process at Davis: the separation of files into "disadvantaged" and regular groups; elimination of regular applicants below the 2.5 GPA limit; the interview process; and the method of grading according to benchmark scores.

Lowrey emphasized that the score was a "benchmark for selection but is not rigidly followed throughout the admission period." He explained that students were admitted in batches and that their scores were sometimes changed because of additional recommendations or material added later. He said students selected from the alternate or waiting lists were not picked strictly by scores but for "balance" or "special skills" they brought to the class.

Colvin concentrated on the statistical differences between Task Force and regular students. He pointed out that some Task Force students admitted had grades well below the 2.5 set for regular students. In one class the average science GPA of regular applicants was 3.36, but that of Task Force students was 2.42. Lowrey conceded the difference. Colvin wondered if the purpose of looking at the relative scores was to determine whether applicants could compete successfully in medical school. Lowrey said no; the process tried to judge more than just academic qualities—for example, character and motivation.

Lowrey rephrased the comment he had made in his unfavorable evaluation of Bakke: "I think we are concerned about such things as imaginativeness. We also consider the possibility of what kind of practice and where they are, at that point in their lives, thinking of practicing, recognizing these things can change." Colvin asked if benchmark scores for Task Force applicants were equivalent to those of regular applicants. Lowrey was unsure, but he conceded they might be lower than those of regular applicants, possibly as much as 30 points lower.

"Below the 468?" Colvin asked, citing Bakke's score when he was turned down the first time.

"Below the 468, right," Lowrey answered.

Colvin wanted to know if any exceptions were made to the admissions procedure described by Dr. Lowrey. Lowrey conceded there were some exceptions.

"Those exceptions were made by the committee as a whole?" Colvin asked.

"Some, yes, because of further information. A letter from a dean of the applicant's undergraduate school would come through and be very strong and this would make that original rating somewhat higher than it had been." Lowrey gave another example: when a married couple applied and one spouse had grades somewhat lower than the other's.

"Were the exceptions made by determination by yourself, Dr. Lowrey?"

"In some cases, yes."

"Some cases, I see. Was this understood by the Admissions Committee that this was the rating process: that exceptions would be made to the numerical order which was proven out by the rating?"

"Yes," said Dr. Lowrey, remembering instructions from the university's lawyers not to volunteer additional information.

This was as close as the record would get to the dean's discretionary admissions prerogative. The exceptions made by Dr. Lowrey were often made at the instructions of Dean Tupper. But Colvin dropped what might have been a revealing line of questions. The university had been very cooperative, and he had no reason to suspect that anything was being hidden. In addition, Lowrey's comments on the exceptions were not especially useful to his case. Colvin was going to argue that Bakke was better qualified than others on the basis of his benchmark scores. The concession that some students were selected without regard to their ranking on the waiting lists undermined that argument. Lowrey was painting a picture of an admissions process than was extremely subjective and arbitrary, while Colvin preferred to exploit the statistical differences between the two groups. For this reason he would never examine the grades at the upper and lower end of each group admitted, preferring instead to emphasize the averages. His interview of Lowrey would turn out to be the most critical confrontation in the case.

In every case there is a point where each side assesses its position and considers the possibility of settlement. After taking Dr. Lowrey's deposition, Colvin had to feel fairly confident. In his eyes the administrator had virtually admitted that a quota existed and that the admissions process was segregated. During the interview Reidhaar had made little effort to direct the flow of Dr. Lowrey's statements, an indication that he considered little of the information damaging to the university's case.

But time was running out for Bakke, with classes just a few weeks away, and Colvin's priority was to get his client into medical school. He met with Reidhaar to discuss the possibility of a faster and less costly resolution. "Look," he said to Reidhaar, "Allan Bakke belongs in medical school. He should have been admitted in the first place. There's a law of the universe that there is always room for one more, so why don't you find another cadaver for Mr. Bakke up there at Davis? He will go to medical school. There will be no more lawsuit, and since there are no other plaintiffs in this case, it will be over."

The proposition would have tempted the ordinary trial attorney. If the university agreed to admit Bakke, there would be a respite until another case was filed. The next plaintiff would have to go through the laborious process of preparing a case without all the information that Bakke had collected. The university would gain valuable time to prepare a defense and correct weaknesses in the Davis admissions procedure. There might even be time to issue guidelines for the entire university.

But Reidhaar rejected the offer. The "institutional interest" in a definitive resolution took precedent. In pursuing a constitutional decision, the university had discarded caution and forgotten to protect the special admissions program. In light of the growing pressures against special admissions, this concern was understandable, but what if the university lost? Little attention had been paid to the possible impact of a decision against the university. If anything, there were no indications the university attorneys ever considered that they might lose.

But where had this directive come from, to get a definitive ruling on special admissions? Reidhaar informed the regents about the case at their July meeting, but several who attended the closed-door meeting do not recall any specific instructions to the general counsel. At that point the *Bakke* case was just another lawsuit before a lower court, and few could have guessed the impact it would have in just a few months.

Reidhaar's determination to pursue a legal judgment would add to the controversy over the handling of the case. The opportunity to set legal precedents must have seduced the university's chief lawyer, but his failure to bring out the complete story of the admissions process at Davis greatly jeopardized his chances of getting a favorable ruling.

The great frustration that *Bakke* presented to minority groups was their exclusion from the preparation and defense of the case. *Brown* v. *Board of Education* and other important civil rights cases were the result of a well-prepared legal assault on segregation drawn up by black attorneys under the direction of black legal expert Charles H. Houston in the 1930s. The unraveling of the separate-but-equal doctrine had not happened suddenly with *Brown* in 1954 but had begun with a long line of victories in the courts dating back to the 1940s and all based on the master plan dictated by Houston and others. But *Bakke* was a defensive action, and minorities found themselves on the sidelines, reminded that despite the rhetoric of progress so popular in the 1970s, most American institutions remained solely in the hands of white men who made decisions that would profoundly affect their welfare.

Colvin went back to court on August 6, and armed with the new information from his interview of Lowrey, he asked the court again to admit Bakke while the issues were considered. In addition to his request for action, he filed his first detailed legal argument on behalf of Bakke. His "Memo of Points and Authorities" listed laws and court precedents in support of his arguments. Bakke had been turned down twice, Colvin argued, although his grade point average and his MCAT scores were "both high and in fact higher than those of some who were admitted." He charged that the Task Force was exclusively for the admission of "racial minority persons" despite the assertion about "disadvantage."

"The selection process for the Task Force students paralleled but never intersected that used in the selection of nonminority students so that at no time were Task Force and nonminority applicants compared." Pursuing the thrust of his complaint and his interrogation of Dr. Lowrey, Colvin argued that the two groups of students were selected by "different standards." As evidence, he listed the differences in the grades and test scores of the two groups.

Colvin then launched into a legal argument that had definite echoes of the decision in the *Anderson* case he had won in federal court. Any classification on racial grounds by a state is suspect under the equal protection clause of the Fourteenth Amendment, he said. These racial classifications had prevented Bakke from competing for all the places in the entering class of the medical school. Bakke was excluded solely because of his race from a significant number of places that were set aside and reserved for other races. Had Bakke been a member of a racial minority, Colvin contended, such exclusion would have been unconstitutional. "The intent for adopting the quota is irrelevant. Validity of state racial discrimination is measured by effect, not motive."

Following the lead of the *DeFunis* case, Colvin quoted UCLA economics professor Thomas Sowell, a black critic of affirmative action and quotas. Paraphrasing Sowell, Colvin said Task Force students were being labeled as incapable of meeting the higher standards of admission applied to non-minority candidates. Colvin concluded by noting that there was no demonstrated history of race discrimination at the University of California to justify the use of such quotas—an exception often made by the courts.

The university filed its response on September 3. Again, Reidhaar and his staff insisted that Bakke had not been rejected because of the special admissions program. Even if there had been no such program, they said, he ranked so low he would have been excluded. They also repeated their belief that the program was legal under the law. The university argued that the courts had clearly given educational institutions the right to set admission standards. "The special admissions program is designed to serve the legitimate needs of the Davis Medical School, the medical profession and society. This delicate and complex process of deciding which of the many qualified applicants best serve those needs must be left to the informed judgment of those administrative officers."

As an example, the university cited the need for family physicians over highly trained specialists. "The issue is not whether preference should be allowed; they are basic to the admissions process. The question is whether the Constitution is to deny members of minority groups from disadvantaged backgrounds the kind of preference which is routinely granted to a myriad other individuals and groups." The test of "rationality" for racial classifications, the university argued, was intended to protect minority groups from capricious acts of racial discrimination. "There is every indication that this extraordinary exception to the rational basis test is a shield protecting minorities against discrimination and not a sword preventing society from redressing the effects of historical discrimination against minorities."

Colvin was not impressed with the eloquence of the university's arguments. On September 24 he filed a response suggesting the university had admitted the existence of a racial quota. If this were true, Colvin argued, the burden of proof in the case should be shifted from his client to the university, a practice frequently used by the courts in cases involving discrimination. For the first time Colvin used the term *reverse discrimination* and argued that "qualified applicants such as plaintiff are passed over because of their race in favor of minority applicants with less potential ability."

Colvin proceeded to bolster this argument by reducing the issue to numbers. "Defense must show, statistically speaking, plaintiff would not have been admitted even if there had been no special admission program. Only in this way can defendant prove that race was not a factor in the evaluation of plaintiff's application."

Of course, the university had already admitted that race was a factor in the selection process. Colvin was making the key argument of opponents of race-conscious admissions: that race had no positive value in a selection process, that being black, Asian, or Chicano and presumably from a poor background gave an applicant no advantage over one from a middle-class background. This argument prevented race from being an experience that might make a better physician or lawyer but reduced it to the level of a somewhat superfluous characteristic such as hair or eye color.

In a deposition taken by university lawyers after his interview with Colvin, Dr. Lowrey attempted to show the positive value of the presence of minorities in the medical school class. Lowrey said that these students brought a perspective and a concern about minority communities beneficial to both students and faculty members at the medical school, that minorities were most likely to return to their communities and provide medical services as well as role models for young blacks, Asians, and Chicanos.

Nowhere would the university argue that these minority students were actually "better qualified" than Bakke and other white applicants in fulfilling these objectives. After all, the admissions committee had never made a comparison of the two groups or, as some schools had done, combined the two groups of applicants before selecting students. Bakke's attorney would emphasize the difference in tests and scores and put the university on the defensive. Much time would be devoted to explaining the history of poorer educational opportunities and financial need that forced minority applicants to work while in college—all valid enough reasons for placing less emphasis on grades.

But there was the underlying assumption that Allan Bakke had to be an unfortunate victim of temporary measures that were probably less than just. Few of the foxes in the defense could make the leap of faith to a concept that minority students with lower grades and test scores could possess human qualities growing out of their individual racial experiences that made them better qualified than some whites who wanted to be physicians.

Reidhaar defended the motives and actions of his staff and the university. He said the issues needed to be presented as "sharply and cleanly" as possible. His involvement with the case, he admitted, was a great educational experience. "A person cannot be involved with a case like this without being deeply impressed with the consequences of the legacy of discrimination against persons of color that we have in this country." The man from Grangeville, Idaho, spoke eloquently of the high qualifications and credentials of minority students admitted to the University of California through race-attentive programs. But in the end he conceded that there were no blacks or Asians and only one Chicano on his staff of eighteen attorneys. "It wouldn't be fair," he said, "to bring in someone who couldn't cut it. But we are always on the lookout for qualified applicants."

Three

MASSACRE IN
YOLO COUNTY

In late summer the coastal hills shut out the Northern Pacific breezes and turn the Sacramento Valley into a cooking pot. Along the ocean the temperatures rarely rise above the 80-degree mark, but a mass of superheated air settles over the valley, undisturbed by the moderating influence of the sea, and temperatures above the 100-degree mark are common. State Route 113 connects Woodland, the county seat of Yolo, to I-80 and Davis, eleven miles to the south. The terrain along this road gives a strong impression of the Midwest. The heat and scenery are right, the fertile fields stretching to a barely visible wall of purple and dark blue mountains in the west and as far as the eye can see at the other cardinal points. The grain elevators and the mechanized farm machines shimmer in the hot sun, vague and intriguing structures that seem concerned with far more than the production of tomatoes, sugar beets, maize, and soybeans.

The monotone of the fields is broken occasionally by the old wooden farmhouses, generous in dimensions, trimmed with Victoriana, and framed by the old shade trees planted when these houses still smelled of the sea from the long trip around the Horn. The illusion of middle America is broken by the palm trees in the yards or in gauntlets along the road, possible only in a land that doesn't know snow or ice in winter. Woodland is a modest, quiet city of 25,000, complete with its Main Street and a handful of stores touting everything from farm equipment to consumer goods. There is little of the psychedelia and poster trade that differentiates Davis from any other valley town. Agriculture dominates here, as it has for more than 100 years.

Yolo County has not always been in the mainstream of California history. The first settlers were stragglers from the mass migration across the Bering Strait, mysterious and complex people who 2,000 or 3,000 years before Columbus buried their dead stretched out in their tombs, facedown, with their heads toward the west. One of Spain's ubiquitous missionary explorers sailed up the Sacramento River in 1817 and found the Patwin Indians living modestly in a land abounding in waterfowl, salmon, deer, the now extinct tule elk and acorn.

One of the first ranchers was Francisco Guerrero y Palo-Mares, a leading citizen of San Francisco, but like most of the Spanish grantees, he was an absentee landlord. Yolo was still a backwater when the gold rush drew thousands to the Sierra Nevada, but once again the stragglers and disappointed prospectors saw the value of this flat, fertile land. "In the conflict of the races," says the official history of Yolo County, "only the fittest survive. Civilization and epidemics destroyed the California and Yolo Indians." Civilization came in the form of rough-and-ready white settlers, who made slaves of the Indians and robbed and killed each other with alarming frequency. In 1850 a sheriff in Yolo quit, complaining that "there were more cattle thieves than gold dust to pay for hunting them."

When a man known as Uncle Johnny Morris built the first log cabin in Woodland, it was a wilderness of oak trees inhabited by grizzly bears. In the 1880s Indians were still a common sight on the streets of Woodland, their women clad in many skirts, colorful bandannas, and brightly colored plaid shawls. By the end of the last century Woodland had settled into a placid agricultural life, and farmers brought their families into town in the evenings to watch the seven o'clock train come in.

A fire in 1892 destroyed most of the evidence of Woodland's colorful past, leaving only the Spanish and Indian names and a relatively poor community, where change has been slow and relatively peaceful. A new breed of educated Chicanos has refused to accept the traditional arrangements of class and color and begun a push for political power. But their efforts are hampered because the best and the brightest prefer the more exciting life of Sacramento, San Francisco, or San Jose. The older Chicanos can remember when the Chinese were not allowed to live in Yolo and when Mexican farm workers had to hitch rides to Sacramento to get their hair cut.

The county building provides a measure of how much the recent past has been rejected. Its imposing Greek columns and the sweeping staircase would fit better in a European city than in a county whose name means "the place abounding in rushes." The main courtroom on the third floor of the building is a medium-sized room, lit unsparingly by a battery of fluorescent lights that succeeds in blurring the last remaining Greek revival details of the original architect.

Court clerks and officials were excited about the case when it first appeared on the docket in 1974. They didn't think of it as an important legal landmark, just a welcome break from the normal routine of minor civil suits and domestic disputes. Still, the two sitting judges of the court were already swamped by the backlog of cases when Colvin filed his complaint on behalf of Allan Bakke. A third judge, F. Leslie Manker, sixty-seven years old and retired at the time, was called in to handle the *Bakke* case. Manker had been a prosecutor and municipal court judge in Sonoma County before being appointed to the superior court bench in 1964 by Governor Edmund ("Pat") Brown. A native of California and a Boalt Hall graduate,

Manker stepped down in 1969 but came back occasionally to help handle the overflow. Until his trip to Woodland, little of his judicial work had gained the attention of the press or the public.

With the preliminary skirmishes completed and the positions of the parties committed to paper, September 27 was set for the hearing on Colvin's motion to have Bakke admitted immediately to the Davis Medical School. With just a few days left before the start of classes, Bakke's chances of getting admitted in time seemed very slim. When time is an important factor for one party in a suit, an argument can be made for immediate relief on the grounds that irreparable injury will take place unless the court takes immediate steps.

Colvin had observed the performance of the lawyers for the university, and he understood that their primary objective was a ruling on the constitutionality of the special admissions program. "They were not taking the view of hard-nosed litigators," he said. "What it gets to is neither apathy, incompetence, nor malicious motive. They were as anxious to get the case to issue as I was, but for a different reason. I thought the best thing I could do for my client was to get to the issue as soon as possible. They saw it as a great constitutional issue."

On the day of the hearing the courtroom was nearly deserted. Bakke and Colvin sat at one table in the carpeted inner area of the courtroom, Reidhaar and members of his staff at the other. The only spectators were Bakke's wife and three-month-old daughter and Dr. Lowrey. Bakke's key pieces of evidence were Lowrey's deposition and the statistics obtained from the medical school. In its defense the university had sent a list of twenty-four questions to Bakke, asking about his background, his qualifications, and his efforts to get admitted to Davis and other medical schools. In his arguments Colvin had continued to exploit the differences between Bakke's scores and those of the Task Force students. In the deposition taken by Reidhaar, Lowrey had reemphasized the preference for attributes not measured by grades and test scores and the need for minority physicians. Lowrey continued to stick to his assertion that the Task Force was intended for disadvantaged students of all races. ". . . the special admissions committee considers the applicant's status as a member of a minority group as an element which bears on economic or educational disadvantage and indeed, almost all of those admitted through the special admissions process have been blacks, Chicanos and Asians."

This was really the essence of the case, whether race or ethnicity could be taken into consideration in selecting applicants for the medical school. In the hearing before Judge Manker the university argued that it could use race as a factor. Colvin replied that race was the main determinant of who was eligible for the Task Force and was therefore illegal. All the statements, depositions, and briefs were meant to support one side or the other of the issue. As the hearing neared an end, Colvin knew that the pressure of time was against him. Feeling he had no other choice, he told Reidhaar he was willing to let the hearing serve as the trial in the case. This meant there would be no more discussion, no further testimony, and no further discovery or gathering of evidence.

"I was somewhat surprised when Colvin made that offer," Reidhaar conceded, "because it seemed to me he had not gone as far as he might have gone in the attempt to develop evidence supportive of his claim. It seemed to me at the time the documentary record contained essentially all the evidence we had detailing and supporting the program." But considering the glaring omissions in the record, the offer was even more attractive. There would be no further investigation of admissions practices at the medical school and no contradiction or challenge of the record as it stood. Colvin had gambled on the general counsel's anxiety to get a constitutional ruling, but he had also lost any opportunity to find out about the dean's discretionary admissions. Reidhaar was so eager to agree that he forgot to make an oral argument in support of the cross complaint he had filed asking the judge to declare the program at Davis legal.

Later he would defend his decision to accept Colvin's offer as a "trial tactic," but it would add to the concern about the university's commitment to defend the program. But the second-guessing would be based on the importance the case was yet to acquire. Although the issues involved were complex, it would have taken the gift of prophecy to guess that affirmative action was about to be ambushed in the nearly empty courtroom of a small town in a relatively minor county of Northern California.

In cases involving racial preference, Judge Manker had two main categories of decisions to draw from in reaching a decision. He would be guided by the Anglo-American system of precedents, rulings by other judges and other courts that are the building blocks of important legal principles. Most of the decisions in favor of preferential treatment involved institutions in which there was clear evidence of previous discrimination: school systems that had been intentionally segregated, all-white unions and municipal departments, segregated job categories. With some reluctance the courts had ordered some form of corrective action: recruiting, hiring goals, and, in some cases, hiring quotas. The pattern was less clear in cases in which there was no documentation of earlier discrimination. Here the judges preferred to tread lightly. Without clear evidence of wrongdoing, the courts shied away from quotas and the dangers of "group rights."

There was another important legal element for Judge Manker to consider. In cases involving school desegregation, busing did not involve the exclusion of whites from schools.

Despite the protests of some white parents that their children were excluded from better schools, the judges saw no victims. At least in theory, all children were getting an integrated education. But *Bakke* picked up where *DeFunis* left off: a redistribution of opportunity. A decision to admit minorities meant the exclusion of some whites, and this posed a much more serious problem for the judges.

The Supreme Court of the State of Washington had concluded in the *DeFunis* case that there was a "compelling state interest" in making a choice by race. Lowrey's deposition had pursued this argument, saying that more minorities meant better services for the poor and benefits to both students and faculty through the presence of a minority perspective. But the university had not fleshed out these arguments with any evidence or expert testimony that might persuade a judge whose understanding of minorities was largely unknown.

The most concrete evidence available to Judge Manker was the compilation of grades and test scores. Colvin had pounded away at the differences between the average grades and the average scores of regular and Task Force students. The university had failed to point out that at least on the basis of grades, a number of the regular students ranked lower than some of the Task Force students. In the areas where the differences were most glaring, the MCAT scores, the university provided no detailed breakdown of the scores and no evidence to support the argument that these scores told little about a student's eventual ability to become a physician.

In *DeFunis*, law school applicants were given a benchmark score determined by a precise mathematical formula. The process of scoring applicants at Davis was left unclear. If the ratings were as arbitrary as the testimony implied, with little weight given to test scores and grades, there seemed little reason to segregate minority applicants. If the scoring was not so subjective, much had been omitted from the record that

Reidhaar considered complete enough for his purposes. Maybe the lawyers had planned to introduce additional evidence at a full-scale trial, but they had bargained away that opportunity by agreeing to Colvin's offer.

Bakke's hopes of quick admission faded as summer melted into fall. Classes were well under way when Manker took his first tentative steps toward a decision. On November 25 he filed a Notice of Intended Decision, a preliminary announcement that gave attorneys for both sides a chance to respond before his decision became final. In the notice Manker rejected the university's argument that Bakke had no standing to sue. Although Bakke had not proved his right to be in the medical school, the judge said, the university had admitted he was a qualified applicant, and he therefore had a definite interest in the resolution of the issues. The first round had gone to Bakke.

On the basis of figures submitted by the university, Manker said, it seemed obvious that whites were being excluded from the special admissions program. In 1973, of the 297 applicants to the Task Force, 73 were white. In 1974, of the 628 applying for minority or "disadvantaged" status, 172 were white. Since none had been accepted, the superior court judge had to conclude that the special admissions program was "in fact open to and available only to members of racial minority groups and that it excludes consideration of applicants who are members of the white race."

Manker expressed some reservation about Bakke's qualifications as a plaintiff, saying he would have preferred someone who had applied to the Task Force and been turned down. "Nevertheless," he went on, "the use of this special program did substantially reduce plaintiff's chances of successful admission to medical school for the reason that since 16 places in the class were set aside for this special program, the plaintiff was in fact competing for one place, not in a class of 100, but in a class of 84, which reduced his chances for admission by

16 per cent." Manker had decided that the sixteen places were in fact a quota.

The judge reviewed the precedents that favored the use of race, including the decision by the Washington state court in *DeFunis*. But he chose to rely on the dissenting opinions in that case in formulating his position. "Racial bigotry, prejudice and intolerance will never be ended by exalting the political rights of one group or class over that of another," Manker quoted from the dissent of Chief Justice Frank Hale on the Washington Supreme Court. "The circle of inequality cannot be broken by shifting the inequities from one man to his neighbor."

Manker now shifted to William O. Douglas's powerful dissent to the U.S. Supreme Court decision that the *DeFunis* case was moot. "What places this case in a special category is the fact that the school did not choose one set of criteria but two, and then determined which to apply to a given applicant on the basis of race." To rally additional support for his decision, Manker quoted from *Anderson* v. *S.F. Unified School District,* the case Colvin had won for the white school administrators.

"This court cannot conclude," said Manker, "that there is any compelling or even legitimate public purpose to be served by granting preference to minority students in admission to the medical school when to do so denies white persons an equal opportunity for admission." As a result, Manker concluded, the program at Davis violated the equal protection clause of the U.S. Constitution. Round two had also gone to Allan Bakke, but he had fallen short of victory.

Manker said there was not enough proof that Bakke would have been admitted if the special admissions program did not exist. In addition, "the admission of students to the medical school is so peculiarly a discretionary function of the school that the court feels it should not be interfered with absent a showing of fraud, unfairness, bad faith, arbitrariness or capriciousness, none of which has been shown." The net result was a standoff. The university's program was declared illegal, but Bakke would not be admitted. "What happened at Woodland," Colvin would say later, "was that both sides lost."

Manker's decision was still in the formative stages. He had invited the attorneys for both sides to respond, and they did, each trying to claim victory and offering to write the decision for the court. Colvin proposed a declaration that the special admissions program at the medical school was illegal and an order that Bakke's application be considered without regard to race. Reidhaar objected, noting that Colvin was now asking that the special admissions program be halted, something he had not done earlier. The university lawyer failed to mention that his cross complaint had opened up the issue. "Plaintiff's complaint sought only to compel [Bakke's] admission to Davis Medical School," Reidhaar argued. "Defendant's cross complaint sought only a declaration as to the constitutionality of its special admissions program." Now Reidhaar was arguing a technical nicety—saying that the university had asked the judge to determine if what it was doing was legal but that it never intended to stop.

Colvin was still trying to push Manker into a more active role. He pointed out that the university's cross complaint had brought up the issue of legality and that Bakke was entitled to a ruling about the special admissions program. He also told Manker that Bakke had no other recourse for getting his application considered. "Indeed, what can be more unfair than to discriminate against an applicant on the basis of race? The violation of one's constitutional right is the classic form of unfair treatment and once a constitutional violation is established, the court not only has the authority, but also the duty to intervene and grant relief."

When Manker issued his final judgment on March 7, 1975, it was apparent that Colvin's arguments had been persuasive, but the judge was still reluctant to involve himself in the admissions process at the medical school. He repeated his earlier ruling that the special admissions program was illegal, but he did not order the program halted. He did tell the university that Bakke was entitled to have his application considered without regard to race.

Now that the university had been rebuffed, it started to play the kind of game that might have been expected earlier. A few weeks afterward Reidhaar made a cavalier offer to have Bakke's application considered on the same terms as "any other application coming in at this late date." This, of course, meant that Bakke would not be admitted. This gesture could have no other effect than to make sure that Colvin joined Reidhaar in taking the case to a higher court.

Once the case left Yolo County, it would move into the special environment of appeals courts, where the legal issues would be debated in a highly abstract and unemotional atmosphere. But the facts had been established in Judge Manker's court, and his findings would have a profound impact on subsequent decisions about the right of Allan Bakke to attend medical school.

Critics would question the paucity of the record and the lack of a vigorous defense by attorneys for the university. Indeed, the defense seemed to be a litany of missed opportunities. The university's main argument against Bakke was that he was not a particularly extraordinary candidate. Yet it never made much of a case against him. On the basis of grades alone he seemed much more qualified than most applicants— black or white. But because of the peculiar blur that occurs at the most critical point in the selection process—the benchmark scores—the reasons for his low rating and his failure to make the alternate lists are never explained. Bakke's own admission that he had been turned down by twelve other medical schools was never used by the university, nor was the most obvious obstacle of all, his age.

Bakke had begun his quest for a seat at Davis with a fear that he was applying too late. But because there was so little information about the way applicants were rated, the impact of age on at least his initial rejection is not clear. At least two other schools had turned him down flatly on the basis of age. Apparently they felt secure from a suit on the basis of age discrimination.

The suspicions of minority groups would inevitably center on the racial makeup of the people defending the university. It was not difficult to conclude that a group of white male attorneys would see the *Bakke* case as a simple matter of law and an opportunity to settle once and for all a practice that was generating considerable public resistance as the mood of the nation changed and the number of opportunities declined.

The battleground had also been an important factor. Had Bakke filed a complaint in Los Angeles or San Francisco or a major eastern city, the response from minority groups might have occurred sooner and affected the process of litigation at any of its crucial points. But neither Davis nor Woodland was a flash point of racial confrontation. Both were small, basically rural communities, like much of California north of San Francisco, and racial issues there had never reached the critical status of those in large cities in the 1960s.

This, perhaps, was why Judge Manker could see no compelling state interest in having minority doctors. He had weighed the most tangible evidence before him, grades and test scores, and found the minority students less qualified than did the university. He had stayed away from the issue that subsequent decisions would also do their best to avoid: the new awareness that opportunities, like natural resources, were limited in America. To have made such an admission would run counter to the entire mythology of advancement in America and the

belief in places like Yolo County that survival was the prerogative of the fittest. As for the arguments that preference was not
unusual, they would fall by the wayside. After all, the university had failed to point out that the most ancient and honored
form of preference—wealth, power, and privilege—could still
be an obstacle when the son of a mailman and a schoolteacher
tried to become a doctor.

Four

"A VERY SAD IRONY"

Once Judge Manker's decision was made final, it was clear that the case would have to be appealed. If Bakke surrendered his struggle to get into medical school at this point, he was really giving up his dream. The university was in a worse predicament. Manker's ruling had made the program at Davis, and by implication all similar affirmative action programs in the university, illegal. Reidhaar and Colvin filed with the state's court of appeals, the next rung on the judicial ladder. But they soon decided they might as well go directly to the state's highest court for a definitive ruling on the issues.

The university's motion to the California Supreme Court made it clear that the *Bakke* case was no longer a local matter before a local judge. Reidhaar billed it as "a case of great and pressing statewide importance" and said that "a decision by this court will avoid a multiplicity of litigation." Without the court's intervention, he warned, all special admissions programs would be of "questionable legality."

The petition for transfer went to a court with an enviable reputation as one of the most active and progressive in the country. The California Supreme Court had anticipated many of the most liberal rulings of the U.S. Supreme Court in protecting the poor and extending constitutional rights. It had preceded the U.S. Supreme Court in ruling against the death penalty. When the Nixonian majority emerged on the nation's highest court and began cutting back on the rights of criminal suspects, the California court was extending those rights.

The California Supreme Court had also broken new ground by ruling that discrimination based on sex was suspect and that school financing systems that resulted in discrimination based on wealth were unconstitutional. On racial matters, it had rejected the U.S. High Court's attempt to differentiate between de jure and de facto segregation, holding that all segregation violated the rights of black children. This was a court that was viewed as a champion of the underdog and that gloried in its activist reputation.

It was not surprising that the court quickly agreed to accept the *Bakke* case. "All of the justices were concerned that this was not the ideal case upon which to decide such an important issue," recalled a court staff member, "but they also agreed that it was an issue which needed to be faced head-on." On June 26, 1975, the California Supreme Court agreed to hear the *Bakke* case, and this automatically raised it to the level of importance Reidhaar had sought. Immediately several organizations asked to file friend of the court briefs in support of one side or the other. As in the *DeFunis* case, the battle lines were quickly defined. Jewish organizations such as the Anti-Defamation League and conservative unions such as the American Federation of Teachers attacked the use of race and "quotas" on behalf of Allan Bakke. Civil rights groups such as the NAACP and associations of medical and law schools joined the university's side of the fray.

The arguments in the briefs filed by the two parties and in the oral argument of March 18, 1976, were not much different from those made in the Yolo County court. Bakke contended that the equal protection clause of the Fourteenth Amendment applied to all races and that "only in remedial situations have the courts tolerated racial discrimination." He also attacked the still-vague description of the admissions practices at the medical school in pursuit of his argument that it was up to the university to prove that he should be excluded. Because there were no clear standards by which the university judged medical school applicants, he argued, it could not objectively demonstrate that he was rejected for a reason other than race.

The university countered that there was a difference between programs instituted to assist minorities and those which discriminated against them. Reidhaar also urged the court to differentiate between programs that completely excluded whites and programs, like the university's, that attempted to include a limited number of minority students. As for Bakke's eligibility, the university renewed its arguments that Bakke was so far from acceptance that even without the special admissions program he would have been rejected.

Immediately after oral arguments, the seven members of the California Supreme Court met to discuss the merits of the *Bakke* case. It was soon clear that two members of the court would play pivotal roles in the forging of opinions on the case. Mathew Tobriner and Stanley Mosk had both been appointed to the court by Governor Edmund ("Pat") Brown, Tobriner in 1962 and Mosk in 1964. In their years on the state's highest court the two men had become close friends. They were both Jewish and longtime Californians who had acquired reputations as legal scholars and liberals, but their responses to the issues in *Bakke* could not have been more different.

Mosk remembers his family's struggle during his childhood: his father's fight for survival as a "small businessman" during the Depression, his job on Chicago's South Side for $7.50 a week during his days as a student, and his migration to Southern California in search of opportunity as a young attorney. He recalls with pride his courageous stand on civil rights as a judge in Southern California, where he outlawed restrictive racial covenants; as the state's attorney general, in which capacity he banned the segregated Professional Golfers Association from using state golf courses; and on the supreme court, where he authored many of its most liberal decisions.

But Mosk, a settled and comfortable man, is not so much at ease in discussing the *Bakke* decision, for his majority opinion has provoked strong reactions. Seated at the head of the T-shaped desk in his office, he has surrounded himself with documentation to defend his position on the case. He refers to William J. Wilson's book asserting the decline of the importance of race, and under the gold *M* on his desk he has secured a copy of Theodore Gross's *Saturday Review* article attacking open admissions at the City College of New York. He talks about quitting the Elks and the Eagles because those fraternal organizations had racially restrictive policies and adds that he also left the San Francisco Bar Association because it filed a brief supporting affirmative action in the *Bakke* case. "They're not discriminatory in their membership, but they are advocating a discriminatory position which I think is equally bad."

Mosk has been vehemently attacked by minority groups who felt forsaken by their formerly liberal ally. A conservative judge might have been viewed as the enemy, but Mosk is now seen as a traitor. Hundreds of chanting students have massed below his office window on San Francisco's Civic Center Plaza to denounce his decision, and his appearances at local campuses have been met with pickets and demonstrators. When, through bureaucratic insensitivity, Mosk was invited to give the commencement address at the Davis Law School, minority students wrote him to express their displeasure and to ask him to decline. With the same aggressive defensiveness, Mosk responded that he would not be intimidated, and he chastised the students for "their defective knowledge of the First Amendment." Yet he sees no contradiction between his insistence that they should hear his views and his own resignation from the Bar Association because he disagreed with the organization's position.

Mosk has been made tense and besieged by the outspoken opposition to his views. "I have been harassed a good deal by the Third World Coalition," he says of the protesters. "I see no difference between their position and that of George Wallace. They both want race to be a factor, and I don't."

On the other side was Mathew Tobriner, who would stand alone on the side of the university. It is clear that he has enjoyed the role of the intellectual maverick. "I was always considered the radical," he says.

Tobriner grew up in a magnificent Victorian house built by his father right after the 1906 earthquake, and he lives in that house today. "I'm not very adventurous when it comes to my own living," he explains, "but I'm more adventuresome in my theories of the law." After leaving Stanford, he went to the Harvard Law School, but he found the atmosphere isolated and repressive. "We had some wonderful teachers like Powell in constitutional law and Frankfurter, but most of the teachers were pretty orthodox."

After Harvard, Tobriner returned to San Francisco to practice labor law, and from 1928 to 1959 he represented many agricultural cooperatives and labor unions. It was during his early days as a lawyer that he met the man who would eventually appoint him to the California Supreme Court. Both he and Edmund Brown were registered Republicans, but the two young men were impressed with Franklin D. Roosevelt's New Deal. After a discussion of the merits of FDR, Tobriner talked his friend into switching to the Democratic party.

Twenty-five years later, when Brown was governor of California, he offered a vacancy on the California Court of Appeals to his old friend. Two years after his appointment to the court of appeals, Brown elevated Tobriner to the California Supreme Court.

The fact that Mosk was unhesitating and definitive in support of Bakke's position had a clear effect on the other justices. Judges are as sensitive of their image as politicians, and considering the fragile power of courts, they must often weigh public reaction to their opinions. This was, after all, a court that had great pride in its liberal reputation, and it surely was easier to believe the justices had not abandoned that image if Stanley Mosk was speaking for all of them.

While six of the justices debated the issues, one would play a minimal role. Justice Marshall McComb, eighty years old at the time, had ceased to be an active member of the court. A year after the decision in *Bakke*, the state Commission on Judicial Performance would recommend his removal for senility and incompetence. However, McComb would cast his vote with the majority that was forming around Stanley Mosk.

Although Mosk and Tobriner respected each other's independence, they both tried diligently to persuade each other. There was a steady flow of newspaper and magazine articles from the offices of one justice to the other. "I argued very loudly and long and strenuously," said Tobriner, "but as you know, I received no other vote." In a stunning 6 to 1 decision, the California Supreme Court upheld Judge Manker's ruling that the special admissions program at Davis was illegal and ordered the university to go back to the Yolo County Superior Court to determine if Bakke would have been admitted in the absence of the special admissions program.

To the educated eye, the opening sentence of a supreme court decision often tells the whole tale. In the *Bakke* case Justice Mosk stated the question before the court and answered it in the same breath: "In this case we confront a sensitive and complex issue: whether a special admission program which benefits disadvantaged minority students who apply for admission to the medical school of the University of California at Davis offends the constitutional rights of better qualified applicants denied admission because they are not identified with a minority."

The second sentence, stating the court's conclusion, had a clearly redundant ring: "We conclude that the program, as administered by the University, violates the constitutional rights of non-minority applicants because it affords preference on the basis of race to persons who, by the University's own standards, are not as qualified for the study of medicine as non-minority applicants denied admission."

The opinion was a news reporter's dream. There was no need to read beyond the first paragraph. Mosk had dealt himself four aces, and only constitutional scholars would be interested in seeing how he played the hand. But the question he had put to himself was based on the vital but unsubstantiated premise that Bakke and other rejected white applicants were "better qualified" than the sixteen minority students who had been accepted under the Task Force program. Unless the court accepted this premise as fact, Bakke had no case. He certainly could not claim he had been subjected to discriminatory treatment if the accepted minority students were better qualified. Superior qualifications had always been an acceptable reason for preferring one person over another, and if this were true, Bakke could not argue that he was denied admission *solely* because of race.

Mosk placed responsibility for this crucial finding on the "University's own standards." But what were these standards? Bakke had claimed he was better qualified on the basis of his higher undergraduate GPA and MCAT scores. Justice Mosk used these figures in his opinion to show that special admissions students were less qualified.

Applicants considered under the regular program were automatically disqualified if their undergraduate GPA was below 2.5, but minority students were admitted with GPAs as low as 2.11. (Bakke's GPA had been 3.51.) Bakke had scored above the 90th percentile in the verbal, quantitative, and science portions of the MCAT, while the average scores of the task force students were below the 50th percentile. Finally, the benchmark scores of some special admissions students were 20 to 30 points lower than Bakke's.

Despite the absence of a clear explanation of how the university determined which applicant had the best qualifications, the record indicated a strong reliance on grades and scores by the admissions committee. Dr. Lowrey's testimony that the committee looked hard at other qualities was, for Mosk, just an attempt to justify racial preference after the fact. The university had not challenged the trial court's finding that whites were barred from the special admissions program. Mosk obviously believed that the scores of the two groups were comparable and that the medical school had favored lower-scoring "less qualified" minorities over higher-scoring "better qualified" whites. But many other whites had been admitted with grades and test scores lower than Bakke's. Were they also "less qualified"?

Justice Tobriner, the lone dissenter in the court's opinion, broke with the majority at this initial stage of the analysis of the facts. ". . . the majority incorrectly asserts that the minority students accepted under the special admission program are 'less qualified'—under the medical school's own standards—than non-minority applicants rejected by the medical school. This simply is not the case. The record establishes that all the students accepted by the medical school are *fully qualified* for the study of medicine." By this assertion, Tobriner argued, the court was giving greater significance to grades and test scores "than the medical school attributes to them or than independent studies have shown they will bear."

Tobriner did not believe the court could discuss qualifications until it understood the goals of the medical school. If the school wanted to produce general practitioners as well as specialists, individuals who would practice in rural as well as urban settings, then it would have to seek a variety of skills, backgrounds, motives, and personalities for each class. In his view, the court could not speak as if there were one single, inflexible standard. The record showed that the medical school wanted an integrated student body that would lead to better services for the state's minority population. To fulfill this important goal, the school had judged the minority applicants "better qualified" than applicants like Bakke, who had been turned down.

Mosk's majority opinion moved on to a discussion of the constitutional ground rules the court would follow in considering the legality of the Task Force program. He posed two questions for the court to consider. The first was what test should be used in determining whether or not the program violated the equal protection clause, and the second was whether the program met the requirements of that test.

In considering a constitutional question, appellate courts follow the precedents established by earlier cases. When enough cases have been decided according to the same legal principle, a constitutional doctrine or rule develops. The process by which a court determines if a principle is being complied with is called a test.

"The general rule," wrote Mosk, "is that classifications made by government regulations are valid if any state of facts reasonably may be conceived in their justification. . . . This yardstick, generally called the 'rational basis' test, is employed in a variety of contexts to determine the validity of government action and its use signifies that a reviewing court will strain to find any legitimate purpose in order to uphold the propriety of the State's conduct." In this brief paragraph of legal jargon, intelligible only to the initiated, Mosk reminded his audience of lawyers how appellate courts most often looked at equal protection cases. While the terms of the equal protection clause were absolute, this did not mean that every law must apply to every person in the same way. After all, laws would serve no purpose if they could not treat people in different circumstances differently. For example, a law designed to ensure highway safety could grant a driver's license to a sighted person and refuse one to a blind man or woman. A state could provide welfare assistance to a disabled person and deny it to one who was physically able. Criminal laws treat violators and nonviolators differently, just as tax laws have different impact on rich and poor. Laws by their nature involve unequal treatment and often favor one group or individual over another.

How was this apparent paradox resolved? As two law professors had written in the *California Law Journal* forty years earlier, different treatment is not unequal treatment unless there is no good reason for the difference. In other words, a state has to show a need to make laws that treat people differently. In legal language, this is called the minimal rationality or rational basis test, and the Supreme Court of the United States told the states that different treatment had to be rationally related to some state purpose. The word *minimal* allows a state some flexibility in attempting to reach its goal. For example, a state might set the minimum drinking age at eighteen, although some people might be mature enough to drink at a younger age.

In all such cases the courts assume the wisdom of legislators and defer to them as long as the law is not clearly arbitrary or irrational. Under this practice of "minimal scrutiny," the courts do not require states to justify their motives or means.

It was clear that under this minimal scrutiny approach Allan Bakke would not have much of a chance. The state's purpose of integrating the medical school, providing better medical care in minority neighborhoods, and remedying past effects of discrimination all were legitimate societal goals. The court would not have had to "strain" to uphold the university's conduct.

But, as Mosk's opinion continued, in some cases a stricter standard of review is imposed: "Classification by race is subject to strict scrutiny, at least where the classification results in detriment to a person because of his race." Not only did the state have to show a "compelling interest," Mosk went on, but it also had to show there were no other ways to achieve this goal, and the burden of proof rested, in this case, on the university. Mosk was proposing to apply the strict scrutiny test, a different standard for looking at a state law's purposes and the means chosen to achieve them.

In this situation the court would require the state to show that the different treatment of different groups or classes of people was *both* necessary and rational. This test had been applied by the courts in situations that involved especially important or "fundamental" constitutional rights: the right to vote, to travel, to privacy, or to a fair trial. Strict scrutiny was applied in these situations because it was felt that states had to have a damned good reason to deny these important rights to an individual. The second major area where this test was applied involved laws that singled out a class of persons—blacks, aliens, or illegitimate children, for example—for less favorable treatment. The courts had recognized that in such cases the power of the majority was often used to oppress unpopular or politically powerless groups. The U.S. Supreme Court has referred to such groups as "suspect classifications."

Mosk had selected the strict scrutiny test because he believed that Bakke's exclusion from the medical school at Davis was based on the fact that he was white. The U.S. Supreme Court, he noted, had consistently held that racial classifications were suspect and should be subjected to strict scrutiny. His choice of this test was crucial to the outcome of the case.

Under the rational basis test, Bakke's lawyers would have faced the impossible task of convincing the court that the Task Force program was related to no legitimate state purpose. Under strict scrutiny the burden was now on the university to prove that there was no other way to achieve its goals.

Mosk rejected the university's contention that racial classifications were suspect only if they isolated or stigmatized a minority. He argued that racial discrimination could not be justified against one race but not another. Whites suffered a disadvantage by their exclusion from the university on racial grounds, and this discrimination could not be allowed.

Again, Mathew Tobriner chose to differ from his colleague. He noted that in previous cases the court had distinguished between invidious racial classifications and remedial classifications. Tobriner could not accept the argument that there was no difference between laws that used race to stigmatize minorities and laws intended to overcome the effects of past discrimination. Once again, the argument had reached the issue of victimization. Mosk was saying the program at Davis was illegal because it made victims of whites. Tobriner was arguing that the law attempted to halt the victimization of minorities and that it was inevitable that some whites would lose in the process.

To support his argument that there was a difference, Tobriner went to the history and purpose of the Fourteenth Amendment. The amendment had been intended to prevent states from discriminating against blacks and had gradually been extended by the U.S. Supreme Court to cover other minority groups in similar circumstances. But, Tobriner went on, nothing in the history of the Fourteenth Amendment suggested that the federal government or the states were prevented from attempting to meet the peculiar needs of minority groups.

In addition, said Tobriner, there was good reason for differentiating between invidious and benign racial classifications: "prejudice against discrete, insular minorities may be a special condition which tends to seriously curtail the political process." His argument, supported by a long list of cases, was that the strict scrutiny test was inappropriate for reviewing laws intended to benefit minorities because the majority had the protection of the normal political process and minorities did not.

"It is indeed a very sad irony," Tobriner said, that the "first admissions program aimed at promoting diversity ever to be struck down under the 14th Amendment is the program most consonant with the underlying purposes of the 14th Amendment."

Again the California court's two most liberal and intellectual judges had looked at the same set of facts and come to different conclusions. Was the strict scrutiny standard the correct one for this case? Was any governmental action that took race into account "suspect" and therefore subject to "strict scrutiny"? Or were there, as Tobriner argued, certain "benign" racial classifications that did not require the court to be suspicious? This was the crucial issue being debated. Not only would it determine the outcome of the case, but it would also affect the ways in which the modern manifestations of racial discrimination would be addressed.

The larger issue underlying the *Bakke* case was whether a school, an employer, a union, or a government agency should be allowed to notice who was black and who was white in an attempt to overcome a past that had made many of these institutions all-white. The majority opinion of the California Supreme Court was that the Constitution is color-blind and that race could never be considered.

Mosk's opinion implied that minorities were asking for more than their share of equal protection by asking for a higher degree of protection. This attitude was reminiscent of the view of a U.S. Supreme Court justice in another era. In 1883 Justice

Joseph P. Bradley struck down an act of Congress outlawing segregation in public places. Speaking of the black man who had been recently freed, Bradley said that "there must be some stage in the progress of his elevation when he takes the rank of mere citizen, and ceases to be a special favorite of the laws, and when his rights, as a citizen or man, are to be protected in the ordinary modes by which other men's rights are protected."

Tobriner's lengthy and scholarly exposition of the case law supporting the use of race as a remedial tool was virtually ignored by the majority. The dissenting opinion had pointed out that the U.S. Supreme Court had found remedial racial classifications essential in desegregation and employment cases. How else could a desegregation or hiring plan be implemented without paying attention to race? If the U.S. Supreme Court upheld such practices in overcoming past discrimination, why couldn't the medical school use them to overcome minority underrepresentation? Mosk responded to Tobriner's twenty-page analysis in several footnotes. The cases cited by Tobriner were not applicable, he said, because desegregation remedies did not "grant benefits to one race at the expense of another." Also, in all the employment cases cited "there was a finding by either a court or an administrative agency that the employer had engaged in racial discrimination in the past."

Tobriner had anticipated Mosk's first objection by pointing out that desegregation often excluded whites from the best schools in a district in order that the basic goal of integration could be achieved. Mosk's second argument assumed the absence of past discrimination in the *Bakke* case. Earlier Mosk had written that there was no evidence in the record to indicate past discrimination by the university. Neither party had argued that such discrimination had existed; therefore, the court had to presume that no past discrimination existed.

Then, in an inexplicable burst of candor, Mosk added in a footnote: "Admittedly, neither the University nor Bakke would have an interest in raising such a claim. But this fact alone would not justify us making a finding on a factual matter not presented below." This segment of the majority opinion was perhaps the best example of Mosk's ambivalence about the case. He had used the judicial fiction that an appellate judge may see only what is in the record to avoid seeing the reality of state-imposed discrimination, and in the next breath, he confessed that his blindness was artificial and self-imposed.

Just a few months earlier the California Supreme Court had found, in *Crawford* v. *L.A. Unified School District,* that the city of Los Angeles was still operating an unconstitutionally segregated school system. A few years earlier the U.S. Supreme Court had ruled in *Lau* v. *Nichols* that the San Francisco school district was violating the rights of Chinese children by failing to provide them with a bilingual education. There were numerous instances of documented discrimination against minority children in California, and this continued unequal treatment surely affected the ability of minorities to compete for admission to the university. But since none of this was in the trial record, Mosk and the other justices in the majority could choose to ignore the world around them.

Once the strict scrutiny test was adopted, Mosk went on to determine whether the university had met the heavy burden of demonstrating that the special admissions program was necessary for a compelling state interest and that its objectives could not be achieved without imposing a lesser burden on the majority. The university had made three arguments. One, integration of the school and profession would provide diversity and make both students and faculty members more sensitive to the needs of minority communities; two, an increase in minority doctors would provide needed medical services for minority communities; and three, minority doctors would have more rapport with patients of their own race and a greater interest in and sensitivity to their problems.

Considering how rarely the U.S. Supreme Court had upheld laws under the strict scrutiny test, the university's argument might seem futile, but these were the same grounds the Washington Supreme Court had used in upholding the state in *DeFunis*. Justice Mosk rejected these arguments. Quoting from Justice Douglas's dissent in *DeFunis*, he said, "The Equal Protection Clause commands the elimination of racial barriers, not their creation in order to satisfy our theory as to how society ought to be organized. The purpose of the University of Washington cannot be to produce black lawyers for blacks, Polish lawyers for Poles, Jewish lawyers for Jews, Irish lawyers for Irish. It should be to produce good lawyers for Americans. . . .'"

The sentiment was noble, but it ignored the fact that in many communities the alternative to a black doctor was none at all. It ignored the reality that in Chicano or Chinese neighborhoods the choice might be between a doctor who could communicate with his or her patients and a doctor who couldn't understand them at all. Underlying this argument were also a rejection of any societal responsibility for the nearly total absence of black and Chicano physicians and the implied assumption that paying attention to race naturally meant a lowering of quality.

Mosk was willing to assume that the other goals of the special admissions program were legitimate. But the goal of integrating the student body and improving medical care, even if legitimate, had failed the strict scrutiny test because the university had not proved to his satisfaction that they could not be achieved by other means. Mosk rejected the university's argument that the program was necessary because before the Task Force was created, only two blacks and one Mexican-American had been admitted to the medical school.

He offered three "less restrictive" alternatives for achieving the university's aims. He suggested the university increase minority enrollment by instituting aggressive programs to identify, recruit, and provide remedial schooling for disadvantaged students of all races. He suggested the university expand its enrollment. And finally, he recommended the introduction of more flexible admissions standards that relied less heavily on quantitative factors such as test scores and grade point averages.

If the majority opinion seemed somewhat less than compelling in its consistency and logic up to this point, it had now crossed the threshold into the disingenuous. Recruitment and remedial programs aimed only at minorities would involve the same race consciousness Mosk considered unconstitutional. Furthermore, while racial minorities are disproportionately disadvantaged, when one looks at the absolute numbers there are more disadvantaged whites than blacks. Racially neutral recruiting might bring about a needed change in the economic structure of the profession but drastically reduce the number of minority students in the process.

As for increasing medical school enrollment, Mosk must have thought he was offering a hypothetical solution. But the increase had already taken place. Between 1968 and 1976 medical school enrollment had nearly doubled, with first-year medical school registration up from 9,479 to 15,351 during that period. The new opportunities had been swallowed up in the surge of competition for places in medical school. Tobriner had dismissed his friend's suggestions caustically. "It is a cruel hoax to deny minorities participation in the medical profession on the basis of such clearly fanciful speculation," he said.

But Mosk's third alternative did offer a ray of hope for continued minority presence in the medical school. The use of flexible standards was surely the best of his suggestions. But this was precisely what the medical school had tried to do in its somewhat clumsy fashion. Mosk would not accept Tobriner's assertion that his opinion compelled the university to use only "the highest objective academic credentials" as the criteria for admission. Yet he had used these same academic credentials to determine that Allan Bakke was more qualified than the minority students.

Mosk offered similar alternatives for meeting the need for more doctors to serve the minority community. He suggested that applicants be selected by evidence of demonstrated concern for minorities and by declarations of intent to practice in such communities. How ironic that this "alternative" standard sounded precisely like the method the Task Force said it had used in selecting applicants. Two former Task Force chairmen, Dr. Kumagai and Dr. Gray, insisted they had interviewed a number of whites and minority students and rejected them because of a lack of demonstrated commitment to minority communities. But of course, neither Gray nor Kumagai had been given the opportunity to present this evidence to the trial court. On the basis of the evidence in the record, Mosk could only conclude that whites were excluded from the program. Once again the formality of court proceedings had done little to uncover the reality of what had actually taken place.

"Few legal issues in recent years have troubled and divided legal commentators as much as that we decide today," wrote Justice Mosk. He was convinced that his position was correct, and he would not apologize for it; but he felt a need to share the difficulties he had experienced in reaching his decision. Mosk outlined the major arguments made by proponents of special admissions. Preferential treatment is essential in order to give minorities the opportunity to enjoy the benefits that would have been theirs but for more than a century of exploitation and discrimination. Although racially discriminatory laws have been removed by the courts and the Congress, minorities still are faced with severe handicaps. To achieve the American goal of equal opportunity for all races, more is required than the mere removal of the shackles of past formal restrictions.

These were strong arguments, but Mosk had not referred to them because he considered them credible. His purpose was to contrast them with other "more forceful policy reasons against preferential admissions based on race." "The divisive effect of such preferences needs no explication," declared Mosk, "and raises serious doubt whether the advantages obtained by the few preferred are worth the inevitable costs to racial harmony." Once again he was not seeing the victims created by the status quo. Two decades earlier, judges in the South had argued that school desegregation would upset the harmony between the races. Now Mosk was speaking as if racial divisions had been eliminated in our society and we were in danger of creating new ones. As long as our society favored its white members, resentment came from minorities. If steps were taken to adjust these preferences, it was inevitable that some whites, finding themselves in a less advantageous position, would react disharmoniously. By leaving things as they were, Mosk was only making sure that the resentment would stay on the minority side of the racial line, as witness the angry pickets he resented.

Mosk argued that an overemphasis on race would be counterproductive. Once again Justice Mosk had identified the crime, but he had blamed the wrong culprit. It is not because of preferential treatment that the mention of Arthur Ashe, Thurgood Marshall, Edward Brooke, or Stevie Wonder brings race to mind. Mosk was rejecting racism as an entity that lingered despite the best intentions of judges and politicians.

Mosk listed several additional drawbacks. There would be pragmatic problems in deciding which groups should be preferred and in identifying who belonged to those groups. Once a preference was established it would be difficult to get rid of it. "Human nature suggests a preferred minority will be no more willing than others to relinquish an advantage once it is bestowed," Mosk warned.

A number of critics had raised the problem of identification after small numbers of white males attempted to list themselves as "Cherokee Indian" or "Spanish-surnamed" in an effort to reap the benefits of affirmative action. But were the pragmatic problems of correctly identifying these individuals more difficult than spotting welfare cheats or tax swindlers? Few whites were willing to accept full-time minority status despite their complaints that minorities were being given unfair advantage. The prediction that preferred minorities would want to retain their advantages was no doubt an accurate assessment of human nature. But advantages bestowed by the majority on a minority can easily be taken away. The specter of a permanent black ruling class was reminiscent of the nightmares of Klansmen, not the basis for a reasoned judicial decision.

"Perhaps most important," said Mosk, summing up, "the principle that the Constitution sanctions racial discrimination against a race—any race—is a dangerous concept fraught with potential for misuse in situations which involve far less laudatory objectives than are manifest in the present case." Had the university asked the court to sanction "racial discrimination," or was it asking, as Justice Tobriner had argued, only for the sanction of the use of race to correct the effects of prior discrimination? If such classifications were misused, the court could easily enough identify and outlaw such practices.

In closing, Mosk, who suspected that his son had once been subjected to an anti-Semitic quota at an Ivy League college, spoke of the evil he feared most: the "revival of quotas." "No college admissions policy in history has been so thoroughly discredited in contemporary times as the use of racial percentages," he said, now convinced that his decision was both legally and morally correct. "Originated as a means of exclusion of racial and religious minorities from higher education, a quota becomes no less offensive when it seeks to exclude a racial majority. No form of discrimination should be opposed more vigorously than the quota system."

Mosk argued that to decide in the university's favor would be to "sacrifice principle for the sake of dubious expediency" and would represent a retreat from recent court decisions removing legal barriers to racial equality. The Davis special admissions program was unconstitutional "because it violate[d] the rights guaranteed to the majority by the equal protection clause of the 14th Amendment and of the United States Constitution."

Justice Tobriner did not choose to respond to Mosk's argument that the burdens of special admissions outweighed the benefits except to say that such considerations were out of place. Mosk and his colleagues in the majority were perfectly free to agree with those persons who felt it was preferable to avoid any use of racial classifications as a matter of policy. But they were wrong to equate their own personal views of appropriate policy with what the Constitution required.

Once again Tobriner's conclusions differed sharply from those of his colleague and friend. Mosk perceived a society that had nearly won the battle for equality and was on the brink of retreat at the expense of whites. Tobriner saw a world where whites were still dominant and discrimination against minorities was still the rule. Where Mosk feared "principle sacrificed for the sake of dubious expediency," Tobriner saw a clumsy but necessary step in the right direction. "Two centuries of slavery and racial discrimination have left our nation an awful legacy, a largely separated society in which wealth, educational resources, employment opportunities—indeed all of society's benefits—remain largely the preserve of the white-Anglo majority. Until recently, most attempts to overcome the effects of this heritage of discrimination have proven unavailing. In the past decade, however, the implementation of numerous 'affirmative action' programs, much like the program challenged in this case, have resulted in at least some degree of integration in many of our institutions." Citing a series of decisions by the court of which he and Mosk were members, Tobriner summed up: "It is anomalous that the 14th Amendment that served as the basis for the requirement that elementary and secondary schools be *compelled* to integrate should now be turned around to *forbid* graduate schools from voluntarily seeking that very objective."

In the end, it was clear that what had most influenced these two men in reaching their conclusions was their vision of the world around them. Justice Mosk and those who agreed with him saw the movement toward equality progressing without need of special protection and intervention on behalf of groups and individuals whose status at the lower end of the social scale was the result of centuries of unequal and often brutal treatment. In fact, they believed fervently that racial prejudice had ceased to be a major factor in determining opportunity. Such a theory was attractive to a majority that had lost faith in the ability of the nation to provide for all its citizens. Philosophies that proposed to limit expectations among those on the bottom were comforting to the segment of the population that already had its share or could reasonably expect to acquire it. The flaw in such theories and in legal opinions that gave support to such attitudes was the lack of an alternative. Mosk's opinion was an elegant exercise in legal theory, but his attempt to present solutions failed because it ended up preserving the arrangements that had failed to work for so many for so long.

From the same bench, Justice Tobriner had a startlingly different view. He saw a country that had taken small, tentative steps toward the ideals it had ignored for so long but was now backing off because it had lost the courage to pursue its objectives. Those who chose the most comfortable solution, he was warning, would reap the harvest of their shortsightedness.

The California Supreme Court's surprising decision was

announced on September 16, 1976. Within hours, Reidhaar held a news conference to predict the regents would appeal the case to the U.S. Supreme Court. But many of the organizations that had been united in their opposition to *Bakke* and to the court's decision were not in agreement about what the next step should be. On the basis of the record and the university's defense, many believed there was little chance of obtaining a favorable ruling before a body with a decidedly less liberal reputation than the California court. Ralph Smith, a law professor at the University of Pennsylvania and adviser to the National Conference of Black Lawyers, declared, "We are trying to tell the university, 'You do not have a good case. You did not do all that could have been done in this case. Let's not compound the error.'" The NAACP Legal Defense Fund, the Mexican-American Legal Defense Fund, and several other organizations joined in opposing an appeal. In their view, the decision affected public institutions in the state but left considerable leeway for private institutions in California and for affirmative action throughout the country.

However, Nathaniel Colley, the general counsel of the NAACP's Western Region, took the view that the damage had been done. Because of the California Supreme Court's prestige, he predicted, many courts in other states would use Mosk's opinion as a precedent in similar cases. Without an appeal, affirmative action would not recover from this crippling blow. In addition, Colley argued, the issue was not strictly a matter of liberal or conservative ideologies. He believed there was a good chance of winning at the U.S. Supreme Court. While Colley's position was not popular among the minority organizations, it had some influence on the university. One of his closest friends was William Coblentz, an influential San Francisco attorney and former Yale classmate, who was chairman of the Board of Regents. The regents met in Los Angeles a week after the state supreme court decision. In a closed-door meeting, they decided to petition the state court for a rehearing and, failing that, to go ahead with the appeal to the U.S. Supreme Court.

Once again the university's attorneys made a move that fueled the controversy surrounding the defense. In declaring the special admissions program at Davis illegal, the California Supreme Court had ordered the case sent back to Yolo to determine if Bakke should be admitted. But in the petition for rehearing, Reidhaar said the university had already produced all the available evidence on the admissions process and, therefore, could not prove that Bakke would have been rejected if there were no special admissions program.

"Mr. Bakke was a highly qualified applicant and came extremely close to admission in 1973 even with the special admission program being in operation," said the university. "It cannot be clearly demonstrated that the special admission program did not operate to deny Mr. Bakke admission in that year."

The turnaround in the university's position was peculiar. Two years earlier Reidhaar had argued that Bakke had done "fairly well" in the admissions process. In his deposition Dr. Lowrey had gone to great pains to enumerate the number of rejected applicants with higher scores than Bakke's who had not been accepted by the medical school. Lowrey's arguments, used again and again in university briefs, stated that when Bakke applied in 1973, most of the places in the class were already filled. Of the 160 letters of acceptance sent out to fill the 100 places, only 37 remained to be sent when Bakke's application was completed. According to Lowrey, there were at least nineteen applicants with Bakke's identical score of 468 and fifteen others with scores of 469. Throughout, the university had insisted that the statistics simply did not warrant Bakke's contention that he was discriminated against.

In an effort to explain this reversal to the California Supreme

Court, Reidhaar admitted that the university had "a strong interest in obtaining review by the U.S. Supreme Court" to determine whether the special admissions program at the Davis Medical School and other similar programs were unconstitutional. "It is far more important for the University to obtain the most authoritative decision possible of the legality of its admission process than to argue over whether Mr. Bakke would or would not have been admitted in the absence of the special admission program," he wrote.

Later Reidhaar would give two reasons for the shift. One, he admitted that the university could simply not meet the burden of proof asked by the court. "It simply could not be demonstrated with any assurance that he would or would not have been admitted in the absence of the Task Force program," he said. The second reason, of course, was the desire for quick resolution that had always affected the defensive strategy of the university.

But these explanations did not quell the skepticism. At no time in two years had the university ever indicated that there was any doubt about Bakke's lack of standing. Lowrey had specifically pointed out that he would have been excluded even without the special admissions program. As for the desire for a definitive ruling, the state supreme court had split the case into two parts, and it seemed that the university could have pursued the issue of affirmative action while Bakke's application was reconsidered.

But to determine Bakke's right to attend Davis, the entire admissions process would have to be examined again, and this time it was likely that the Yolo County court would have wanted much more information about the methods used at Davis. While the university argued it had provided all the information available, this was simply not true. In *DeFunis* the university had been required to submit a complete list of students, their grades, test scores, and benchmark ratings. The

Davis Medical School had provided only a range of grades and an average of student test scores. At no time did it ever provide the benchmark ratings that were so crucial to the admissions process.

While the case was making its way through the courts, an important political event occurred on the Davis campus. During the 1975–76 school year, George Sutherland, a student at the Davis Medical School, investigated the admissions practices at the school and raised questions about Dean Tupper's special authority to admit students. When faculty members discovered that Tupper's authority to overrule the admissions committee was not clear, a running battle erupted over the practice. The flames were fueled by the disclosure that one white student whose grade point average was 2.19, well below the 2.5 cutoff for regular admissions, had been admitted by Tupper. The controversy was picked up by the local Davis newspaper and by the *Los Angeles Times* in the summer of 1976.

For the first time the dean's admissions procedure was in the minds of faculty members and administrators at the medical school. A review of the admissions process would inevitably disclose the gaps in the university's defense of the case. Sutherland, who was still a student at Davis at the time, believes the decision not to review Bakke's application was strictly political. "They sacrificed the minority admissions program rather than the dean," he says. "They made the choice."

On October 28, 1976, the state court denied the university's request for a rehearing of the issues, despite a new study showing that the number of minorities admitted to the university would decline sharply without race-sensitive admissions procedures. On October 28, 1976, the California Supreme Court issued its final decision: "On appeal the University has conceded it cannot meet the burden of proving that the special admission program did not result in Bakke's exclusion. Therefore, he is entitled to an order that he be admitted to the

University." The Yolo County Superior Court was directed to "enter judgment ordering Bakke to be admitted."

Reidhaar went back to the California Supreme Court on November 15 and obtained a thirty-day stay of the ruling so that the university could decide whether to appeal. The state court agreed to delay enforcement of its decision indefinitely if the United States Supreme Court agreed to hear the case. Four days later the regents met again in a private session and voted 11 to 1 to appeal to the nation's highest court despite pressure from minority and civil rights groups to abandon the pursuit of a final decision.

The university counsel remained optimistic about the chances of getting the California decision overturned. "There is a very genuine prospect we can win the case," he argued. "It is not a foregone conclusion we will lose it." By the time the regents gave him the go-ahead, Reidhaar had already hired two specialists to help prepare the university's case: constitutional scholar Paul Mishkin and former U.S. Supreme Court clerk Jack Owens.

The university filed its first brief with the U.S. Supreme Court on December 14, 1976, pleading that the urgency of the problem and the fundamental questions raised by the California Supreme Court's decision made a decision at the highest level an essential one. At the same time a number of the organizations that had opposed the university's plan to appeal the decision filed briefs asking the U.S. Supreme Court to deny the writ of certiorari. Most of the critics argued that the case lacked the kind of record necessary for resolution of such an important issue and that the university had failed to make a vigorous defense. Despite these charges, it was clear that the nation's highest court had finally decided to take on a controversy that gave no sign of disappearing. On February 22, 1977, the U.S. Supreme Court agreed to hear *Regents of the University of California* v. *Allan Bakke*.

Five

THE CONTINUING
SIGNIFICANCE OF RACE

Ultimately, all the arguments about strict scrutiny and state interest and equality lead back to race. Why *is* race such a dangerous and troublesome issue in the *Bakke* case? A common argument made in discussions of the case takes this tack: "Bakke should be judged as an individual when the medical school decides whether to take him or not. He should not be denied admission just because he is a member of a particular group." The legal version of this argument was made by the American Jewish Committee's brief: "It is well settled that the right to equal protection granted by the 14th Amendment is an individual and personal one, not a group right. . . . If an individual is denied admission to a state institution even though he is better qualified than others who have been accepted, and if the denial is due to the fact that he is not a member of a particular racial or ethnic group, his personal and individual right to be free from discrimination has been infringed."

There is a strong respect for the individual in many of our traditions. America is a nation whose founders came to a wilderness to escape the poverty, classism, and religious intolerance of Europe. The Declaration of Independence and the Constitution document the ideal of the equality of individuals and the concern for protecting the rights of the individual against government. In a frontier land with infinite resources to be shared, the only limits on an individual's opportunities and development were his own.

But through a remarkable self-serving schizophrenia, American whites were able to define nonwhites as subhuman and exclude them from this value system that held the individual in such high regard. Despite the contradictions, the ideal of the individual grew and flourished with America. And although this ideal has never overcome the restrictions of race, class, and religion, Americans have continued to view their society as an open one, where a poor boy can become a millionaire and a woodcutter can one day sit in the White House. All this, of course, runs in the face of evidence that a poor man's son is as likely to be as poor as his father and probably more so now than 100 years ago. Still, we continue to believe that success in this society comes by virtue of hard work and superior ability.

In an amicus brief for the Anti-Defamation League in the *DeFunis* case, the late Alexander Bickel argued that special admissions programs subverted the ideal of individualism. Bickel, an eloquent opponent of race-conscious programs, wrote: "In a society in which men and women expect to succeed by hard work and to better themselves by making themselves better, it is no trivial moral wrong to proceed systematically to defeat this expectation." But is Bickel's concern about the subversion of individualism warranted in this case? When it is suggested that Bakke has not been treated as an individual, there is a danger that oversimplification has led us to a righteous but erroneous conclusion.

There are many situations in which individuals are identified and treated differently because of membership in a group we find perfectly acceptable. If Allan Bakke had not been graduated from college, we would not be outraged if he were denied admission to medical school. If he had never taken a chemistry course or had been turned down at Davis because he planned to practice plastic surgery in Hollywood, the case would have never reached the California or U.S. Supreme Courts. Two medical schools had no qualms about telling Allan Bakke he was too old. Yet each of these reasons for denying a student is based on a generalization about members of a group. Any admissions procedure relies on standards or generalizations about groups which may not be true for every individual in that group.

When the regular admissions committee at Davis set a cut-off point of 2.5 for GPAs, applicants who fell below that figure were automatically rejected and never interviewed. An applicant whose average was one-tenth of a point below the cutoff might well have demonstrated qualities of dedication, motivation, and sensitivity in an interview which would have made that person a better candidate for medical school than an applicant whose grade point average was above the cutoff. But inclusion with the group below the 2.5 minimum prevents the individual from being considered on individual merits. Few would argue that such an arbitrary grouping deprives that person of a constitutional right.

However, identification by racial group is seen as very different because we are told that Bakke can't do anything about his race and because skin color has nothing to do with his ability to be a good doctor. It is true that individuals do not control their color and their sex. But we also have little control of our intelligence, mechanical aptitude, athletic ability, or place of birth. Our inability to change these personal attributes does not make them an improper basis for awarding scholarships or diversifying a student body.

Race seems a more bothersome immutable personal trait than intelligence or athletic ability, not because it is harder to change but because we like to think of race as irrelevant. Those who oppose minority admissions programs say they take a superficial characteristic like race and turn it into something important. Professor Philip Kurland of the University of Chicago Law School made this argument when he condemned any use of race as a criterion for admission in a brief on Bakke's behalf for the Anti-Defamation League. "A racial quota cannot be benign," he wrote, echoing Justice Mosk, "it must always be malignant because it defies the constitutional pronouncement of equal protection of the law; malignant because it reduces individuals to a single attribute, *skin color,* and this is the very antithesis of equal opportunity."

Kurland's argument is seductive because it is familiar. How often have we heard people say, "I don't care if he's black or blue or green and from Mars as long as he's competent." The relevance of race to qualifications is often compared to the relevance of hair color or skin color. The consistent substitution of *skin color* for *race* in this debate makes it clear how misunderstood the issue is in this society and why we need to remain conscious of race until its meaning is changed.

One of the most persuasive arguments for the use of race in admission and employment has been made by Richard Wasserstrom in a UCLA *Law Review* article entitled "Racism, Sexism and Preferential Treatment: An Approach to the Topics." Wasserstrom, who teaches law and philosophy at UCLA, had witnessed the debate within his own faculty over the propriety of race-conscious admissions and hiring. He had heard his colleagues profess the irrelevance of race, arguing that they didn't care whether their students and colleagues were green and from a red planet. "It is truly possible to imagine a culture in which race would be an unimportant insignificant characteristic of individuals," he wrote. "In such a culture race would be largely if not exclusively a matter of superficial physiology; a matter, we might say, simply of the way one looked."

But that imagined culture is not this culture, said Wasserstrom, pointing to the phenomenon of "passing" as evidence of that fact. "Passing" is the practice among some blacks of identifying themselves as "white" because they look white. Many black Americans recall stories of family members who used their light skins temporarily to get access to jobs reserved for whites or permanently to gain the benefits afforded the white race in our society. This phenomenon has been packaged for popular consumption in Sinclair Lewis's novel *Kingsblood Royal* and in films such as *Imitation of Life* and *I Passed for White.*

In Wasserstrom's imaginary culture, in which race is just a matter of the way one looks, the concept of "passing" would make no sense. The phenomenon can be understood in our own culture because race is much more than physical appearance. The fact that a person may look white and still be defined and treated as black makes it obvious that race is not the same thing as skin color and that although skin color may be irrelevant, race is not.

In America to be nonwhite—and especially to be black—is to be treated as a member of a group that is viewed by the dominant group as different and—in too many instances—as inferior. Despite the gains made by a segment of the black population in recent years, membership in this minority is membership in a disliked and oppressed group.

Wasserstrom examined the apparently trivial practice of segregated bathrooms that was so common some years ago: "The point of maintaining racially segregated bathrooms was not in any simple or direct sense to keep both whites and blacks from using each other's bathrooms; it was to make sure that blacks would not contaminate bathrooms used by whites. The practice also taught both whites and blacks that certain kinds of contacts were forbidden because whites would be degraded by contact with blacks.

". . . The ideology was [not only] that blacks were . . . less than fully developed humans, but that they were also dirty and impure. This ideology was intimately related to a set of institutional arrangements and power relationships in which whites were politically, economically and socially dominant. The ideology supported the institutional arrangements and the institutional arrangements reinforced the ideology."

The primary evil of racial classifications in cases cited by supporters of Bakke as evidence that race should be suspect involved the designation of black persons as degraded, dirty, less than fully developed persons who were unfit for full membership in the political, social, and moral community. Many of the opponents of race consciousness cite court decisions in miscegenation cases to support their arguments, but these laws did not operate equally against blacks and whites any more than laws that segregated trolley cars and toilets. Their purpose was not to keep blacks and whites from marrying each other but to label blacks as unfit to marry whites. The argument that Bakke was being subjected to practices that had been outlawed some years earlier obviously was not true because he was not being stigmatized or marked as inferior.

The "race is irrelevant" argument confuses another important point. Those who argue that race is a superficial characteristic that should not be considered inevitably fall back on the argument that grades and test scores are the only proper criteria for evaluating applicants. By claiming that individuals applying for professional schools and employment should be judged only according to this specific "merit" system, they ignore the entire scope of crucial human factors that also measure an individual's qualifications.

Although skin color may be a legitimate factor in choosing Richard Burton to play Richard III or James Earl Jones for Othello, it is clearly not a legitimate factor in choosing who should attend medical school. But by equating race with skin color, the critics imply that the experience of being black or a member of another minority group has no value. There are few who would dare tell survivors of the Nazi Holocaust that their experiences have given them no special insight, no special compassion, and no special qualification.

Once we begin to understand that the significance of race is not color but experience, then it is no longer an irrelevant or superficial characteristic. After all, an individual's experience has traditionally been considered an important criterion in determining qualifications for employment or school admission. While this racial experience may not automatically qualify an individual as a member of a group, neither does the requirement that this individual complete a number of courses in biology, physics, and organic chemistry.

The goal of the University of California of integrating the medical school and the medical profession did not come out of an aesthetic preference for a variety of skin color in its classrooms and hospital wards. The purpose was to bring a wider variety of backgrounds and experiences to the school and profession. Bringing in these experiences would help eliminate the causes and effects of past and present discrimination.

Individuals who had experienced racial discrimination shared a common qualification that would help achieve the university's goal. Persons who had not been subjected to racial oppression lacked that experience and were likely to be less qualified for pursuing that goal. Once race was viewed as an important criterion, like successful completion of a college degree or a number of science prerequisites, then it could become an appropriate and constitutional criterion.

Another reason for so much reservation about government's paying attention to race is that racial classifications have historically been used as a tool of oppression. By certifying racial classifications in the law, racial groups without power have been defined as inferior and denied equal access to the benefits of society. In this way a permanent underclass, defined by race, is created, and the racial group in power is assured of permanent and superior status. Official race consciousness reminds us of Nazi Germany, South Africa, and our own history of slavery segregation and legalized apartheid.

The Fourteenth Amendment was adopted for the specific purpose of putting an end to distinctions based on race. The Thirteenth Amendment had abolished slavery, but the former slaveholder refused to surrender. He enacted the Black Codes in the years after the Civil War to maintain the arrangements that had existed before Emancipation. These codes severely restricted the movement of freedmen under vagrancy and apprenticeship laws. In some states blacks were forbidden to practice any occupations but farming and menial service; a special license was required to do other work. In other states blacks could be punished for "insulting gestures," "seditious speech," or walking off the job.

This new form of slavery led the Congress, under the guidance of Charles Sumner and Thaddeus Stevens, to enact the Freedmen's Bureau Bill and the first Civil Rights Act. Both these bills were passed under the mandate given to the Congress by the Thirteenth Amendment to enforce the right of freedom. These laws were drafted to protect the "civil rights" and "immunities" of freedom, making clear that Congress believed there could be no liberty without equality. Blacks were given the right to make and enforce contracts; to buy, sell, and own real and personal property; to sue and be parties to legal action; and to have "full and equal protection of all laws."

But congressional conservatives argued that these laws were illegal because the Thirteenth Amendment required not the equal treatment of blacks and whites but only the end of the legal relationship that had existed between the master and his African slave. Stevens and his fellow Radical Reconstructionists saw the necessity of placing the new rights of the freedmen beyond the reach of future congressional majorities and conservative courts which might interpret the Thirteenth Amendment more narrowly. The Fourteenth Amendment was the answer, spelling out the rights of black Americans in explicit and sweeping language.

Much of the debate about the *Bakke* case in the legal community has focused on the purpose of the Fourteenth Amendment. The Supreme Court often attempts to assess the intent of the framers of the Constitution in order to determine the scope and meaning of particular provisions of that vaguely worded document. In the landmark desegregation case of *Brown* v. *Board of Education,* the Court had asked for additional briefs and a second oral argument on the issue of whether the framers of the amendment intended to abolish segregation. Supporters of minority admissions have argued that the history of the amendment proves beyond doubt that its purpose was to secure full citizenship for the newly freed slaves and that remedial policies designed to upgrade the status of blacks by providing special services and programs were not only permissible but specifically contemplated by the congressmen who drafted the Fourteenth Amendment.

Legal scholars who oppose minority admissions argue that the framers intended to abolish *all* distinctions based on race. They argue that the evil or mischief that the Fourteenth Amendment was intended to abolish was not just the particular oppression of slaves by whites but all oppression based on race and other arbitrary characteristics.

The first position was extensively documented in an amicus brief filed with the U.S. Supreme Court by the NAACP Legal Defense Fund, Inc. The Fund chose to focus on the history of the adoption of the amendment, partly because this had not been explored by other briefs and partly because the Fund had a good head start on collecting the evidence. When the *Brown* case had been argued in 1952 and 1953, Thurgood

Marshall, then the Fund's chief attorney, had organized a massive effort to answer questions put by the U.S. Supreme Court on the intentions of the framers of the Fourteenth Amendment.

The Fund's brief argued that while the amendment's history is often unclear, it is neither ambiguous nor inconclusive on the issues presented by the *Bakke* case.

". . . the precise question at issue in this case—the permissibility of providing educational benefits to blacks but not whites—was heatedly debated and self-consciously resolved by the same Congress which approved the 14th Amendment," the Fund argued. The Congress that fashioned the amendment believed that race-conscious remedial programs were not only permissible but necessary. The brief examines the legislative history of eight different social welfare laws adopted during that time. Each of these laws expressly delineated the racial groups entitled to benefit from its programs, and each of these race-specific measures was adopted over strong and vocal objections by a minority of Congress and President Andrew Johnson, who opposed special assistance to a single racial group as "class-conscious legislation discriminating against whites."

The most far-reaching of these programs, the 1866 Freedmen's Bureau Act, was enacted less than a month after Congress approved the Fourteenth Amendment. The bureau not only was authorized to provide land, buildings, and funds for "the education of the freed people" but could also provide such aid to refugees and other whites. The act also conveyed some disputed lands to "heads of families of the African races." A report from the commissioner of the Freedmen's Bureau provided a long list of programs intended to benefit only the freed slaves. Both the 1865 and 1866 Freedmen's Bureau bills were opposed on the grounds that they applied only to blacks. The arguments sound uncannily familiar to those we have heard in recent debates over the *Bakke* case. Most opponents of the bills complained that they made a distinction between the two races. Some congressmen contended that the bills would result in two separate governments, "one government for one race and another for another." These measures were adopted despite this opposition, and the Fund argued that the Congress that passed the Fourteenth Amendment deliberately enacted race-conscious remedies.

But opponents of race-conscious admissions have not been persuaded by the Legal Defense Fund's exhaustive account of the history of these amendments. The courts, they say, should not make their decisions according to what some men in the Thirty-ninth Congress thought necessary and proper in 1866. The only history that is binding on the courts is legal precedent. They argue that the Constitution is not a static document and that its purposes and principles must be adaptable to new conditions beyond the specific evils that gave them birth.

"There is no evidence that the equal protection clause can still be interpreted to protect only blacks," argued the brief of the Anti-Defamation League, "for such a construction has the Orwellian flavor of requiring that blacks be treated as equals to members of all other races, but no persons of another race would be constitutionally entitled to equality with blacks. Surely it is too late in the day for such an interpretation of the equal protection clause." Bakke's supporters saw race consciousness as the more general evil to which the Fourteenth Amendment must be directed. They turned to the language of the U.S. Supreme Court's own decisions to support their arguments that the amendment required the Constitution to be "color-blind."

"While the principal purpose of the 14th Amendment was to protect persons of color, the broad language used was deemed sufficient to protect all persons, white or black, against discriminatory legislation by the state," the brief went on to say. "The Equal Protection Clause, like the Civil Rights Act from which it derives, in the words of Senator Trumbull, 'applies to white men as well as black men.'"

There is no argument about the fact that the equal protection clause protects all persons regardless of race. The real issue is whether race consciousness, in every instance, denies whites equal protection. Certainly, the equal protection clause protects whites, as it does everyone, from arbitrary and irrational treatment by government. It protects them from being treated differently for no good reason. The question before the Court, however, was not whether whites received the benefits of the equal protection clause but whether, in applying the clause, the Court has any reason to suspect foul play on the part of government, whether there is any need to apply the strict-scrutiny test.

All the cases cited in the Anti-Defamation League brief to support the proposition that the amendment applied to "white men as well as black men" involved groups that had traditionally been subjected to discrimination for no other reason than oppression. *Yick Wo* v. *Hopkins* and *Oyama* v. *California* found the use of race unconstitutional because Asians (in California), like blacks (in the South), had historically been the objects of discrimination and oppression. Likewise, *Graham* v. *Richardson, Sugarman* v. *Dougal,* and *In re Griffiths* found discrimination against aliens unconstitutional because they were a traditionally disfavored and relatively powerless group. Discrimination against illegitimate children was struck down in *Levy* v. *Louisiana* and *Gomez* v. *Perez* for the same reason. The laws in these cases received more careful attention, not because the plaintiffs were white, as the authors of the Anti-Defamation brief would have us believe, but because they were members of disadvantaged minority groups. In addition, the government could offer no good reason for the discrepancy in treatment that was not related to hostilities toward those groups.

In *Yick Wo*, for example, the city of San Francisco had systematically denied licenses to Chinese laundries that were built of wood. Wood laundries owned by whites were granted licenses. The rationale was safety, but the white-owned laundries were clearly no safer. The obvious purpose was to put the Chinese out of business.

Other cases used to argue that race consciousness is always unconstitutional include *Memorial Hospital* v. *Maricopa County* and *Shapiro* v. *Thompson,* but these cases involved residency requirements, and the Supreme Court applied strict scrutiny because the issues involved the important right to travel.

Similar arguments were made in a brief to the U.S. Supreme Court from the American Jewish Committee, the American Jewish Congress, and several white ethnic organizations. The brief argued that the Supreme Court has held that application of the Fourteenth Amendment "has not been restricted to those forms of racial discrimination that are regarded as 'invidious' because they stigmatize and denote the inferiority of a minority group. Racial classifications which oppress members of the minority and majority racial groups with equal force have been found constitutionally defective without reference to the issue of stigma." The cases cited—*McLaughlin* v. *Florida* and *Loving* v. *Virginia*—were cases in which the Court ruled antimiscegenation laws unconstitutional. Once again we are back to the distortions of the original intent of such laws as pointed out by Wasserstrom. The oppression suffered by whites under such laws was clearly less than that suffered by blacks. To argue that the laws involved in these cases did not "stigmatize and denote the inferiority of a minority group" is simply dishonest.

Other popular references in this line of argument are *Shelley* v. *Kraemer* and *Buchanan* v. *Warley,* which involved racially restrictive housing. Again the argument is that such laws hurt both whites and blacks equally. But the purpose of housing segregation, like other forms of racial separation, is to demean and stigmatize the excluded group, and that group suffers in a wholly different way from those who are doing the excluding.

Bakke's supporters have argued that it is judicial precedent, not congressional history, which should control the issues in this case. If there was a strong precedent to support their position, it was not found in the cases they have relied upon.

Once again we come face-to-face with the differing perceptions of the issues and problems involved in the *Bakke* case. The argument that no special consideration need be given to race or racial groups is based on the view that these groups no longer need the special protection of the Fourteenth Amendment. One line of argument in this debate suggests that race is no longer an issue in the success or degree of opportunity available to Americans.

In its annual report, "The State of Black America 1978," the National Urban League presents a very different picture. The League points to the growing divergence of perceptions of discrimination between whites and blacks. Most whites have come to believe that bigotry is no longer an important factor in the progress of minorities in this country. But, as the report points out, there are twice as many blacks out of work in 1978 as there were ten years earlier. The number of unemployed black men tripled between 1967 and 1977, and the unemployment rate among black teenagers increased from 26.5 to 38.6 percent in that decade. "There are just as many poor black families today as there were ten years ago, although the number of poor white families has dropped over that period. . . .

Black families are still four times more likely to be poor than white families."

The report concedes that much progress has been made, especially among black middle-class families, who have narrowed the gap with the rest of the middle class. "Still, the harsh truth remains . . . that the majority of blacks have not seen their status materially improved over the past decade, and that for many, their lives are still lived out in despair and deprivation."

Six

THE BEST DOCTORS

When a great deal is at stake in a struggle of ideas and principles, words become weapons, loaded with connotations designed to trigger an emotional response that will benefit a specific point of view. Many words have achieved this status in the *Bakke* case but probably none more than *qualifications*. Allan Bakke launched his campaign for admission to Davis on the grounds that minority students selected by the medical school did not have the "best qualifications, both academic and personal." In writing the majority opinion of the California Supreme Court, Stanley Mosk cast the issue as a choice between "better qualified whites" and "less qualified minorities." The University of California insisted that all its students were "fully qualified," but opponents of special admissions saw the difference between the grades and test scores of the two groups as evidence that standards were being perilously lowered. One formerly liberal magazine concluded that affirmative action succeeded only in replacing "mediocre whites with mediocre blacks."

These comments seem gentle when compared to statements in a brief filed with the U.S. Supreme Court by a group of prominent scholars and academicians who supported Allan Bakke: ". . . it is a distinct disservice to these young people to admit them to schools where they cannot succeed, and where their poor performance confirms rather than dispels the false stereotypes about minority abilities." Of course, it takes an admirable manipulation of the facts to reach a position that strengthens a stereotype of minority students under the guise of protecting them from humiliation.

The brief by the Committee on Academic Nondiscrimination and Integrity and the Mid-America Legal Foundation is one of the most fascinating documents submitted to the Supreme Court. Important figures such as Bruno Bettelheim, Sidney Hook, Daniel Boorstin, and Nathan Glazer have endorsed a document that concludes that a choice has to be made between excellence and race-conscious admissions practices. Bakke's situation is compared to that of blacks before the passage of the Fourteenth Amendment, and the authors assert that Bakke "is far better qualified than most if not all of the preferentially admitted minority applicants."

What is worth remembering is that the distinguished members of this committee are surely aware that their position is not supported by the facts, which clearly show that the great majority of special admissions students complete their studies successfully. In some cases, despite their lower grades and test scores, special admissions students have surpassed the achievements of their white classmates. According to the Association of American Medical Colleges, "for the 1970 and 1971 entering classes, the retention rates for blacks were 95 and 91 percent respectively, as compared to 98 and 97 percent for white students."

Obviously, some affirmative action students have not done as well as students selected by traditional methods. But special admissions is relatively new, and school officials have had to work on a trial-and-error basis. In nearly every year since these programs were instituted, the retention and achievement rates of special admissions students have improved. According to the American Medical Association, 11 percent of blacks and 9 percent of Mexican-Americans admitted to medical schools in 1976 had to repeat their first year, against 1.2 percent of whites. The critics use these figures to attack special admissions, but proponents point out that these programs involve a calculated risk that is paid off when nine out of ten blacks and Chicanos are promoted with their classmates. In addition, the higher repeat rate is a sign that schools are not promoting students until they successfully complete the requirements.

But in making a choice between a class that is one-tenth empty or nine-tenths full, the critics have persisted in their attacks on minority students, their abilities and credentials. To some, the ease with which these attacks have been embraced tells much about a new form of racial McCarthyism which deliberately ignores and distorts the truth. But then, the perception of minorities as less competent and less qualified than the majority whites is hardly a new concept in America.

One reason, of course, was the image of the Task Force students created by the vague use of terms such as *less qualified* during the litigation of the case. If the Task Force students existed at all, they were an amorphous, undeserving, and unqualified group hardly likely to find understanding in the new, less compassionate racial atmosphere of the 1970s. It was easier for most of the public to sympathize with Allan Bakke—blond, blue-eyed, hard-working, individual—the victim of a misdirected sense of social obligation. Considering the vague and ambiguous quality of most of the issues in the case, the numbers had a comforting solidity. Bakke's 3.51 GPA was higher than the 3.49 and 3.29 average of regular students admitted to Davis in 1973 and 1974. The averages for Task Force students in those years were 2.88 and 2.62. Some had GPAs as low as 2.11 in 1973, and 2.21 in 1974, well below the school's cutoff point of 2.5. On the MCAT, Bakke scored in the 90th percentiles in the verbal, quantitative, and scientific categories, higher than most of the regular students and far higher than the Task Force students.

Of course, as we pointed out earlier, some of the Task Force students had higher grades than some of the whites admitted (and higher than Bakke and other whites rejected). A number of regular students also had grades and test scores lower than those of Allan Bakke. The most consistent area of difference was in the MCAT scores. In this area, however, there is an impressive body of research to show that these scores, while useful in predicting student performance in the first two years of medical school, have little value in assessing talent in the clinical aspects of medicine (the last two years of school) or performance as medical professionals. To improve the situation, medical schools asked the AAMC, which administers the test, to "explore the development of additional instruments to measure personal qualities deemed necessary for the practice of medicine."

It would seem that personal qualities had much to do with the selection of Task Force students and regular students with lower scores and grades. Such exceptions reflect the growing recognition of the limits of numbers in the admissions process throughout the country. The AAMC reports that nearly a third of white applicants to medical school in 1976 had undergraduate GPAs of 3.30 or better and MCAT science scores above 600 (on a 205–795 scale). "Yet," says the association, "31 percent of these applicants were not accepted to any medical school, while 882 white applicants whose grades and MCAT science scores were *both* lower than these levels were accepted. Therefore it is clear that admissions committees have looked beyond grades and test scores in selecting students to be admitted."

But arguments persist that separate standards of selection were unfair to white applicants because minorities with lower "qualifications" were picked. If human qualities, character, and motivation are as important as officials say, then the method of selection is unfair for different reasons. If as much emphasis were placed on commitment as on academic qualifications, medical schools would choose white students who are more humane and more compassionate individuals and provide better doctors for everybody.

When Allan Bakke was turned down by the University of California at Davis in 1973, sixteen minority students were chosen who, in his estimation, did not deserve places in the medical school. Once these students were admitted, the only special treatment they received was a three-week tutorial before the start of classes. The special program was designed to familiarize them with study and examination procedures in medical school and to help them identify their areas of weakness. After completing the program, they were plunged into the same highly competitive and intense atmosphere that their other classmates had faced from the first day of school. Four years later, thirteen of the original sixteen were graduated from Davis, and their accomplishments do much to undermine the stereotypes promoted by groups like the Committee on Academic Nondiscrimination and Integrity. No figures are available for the success rate of regular admissions students at Davis, but the national rate is close to 99 percent.

Orel Knight would probably have enjoyed a discussion of "qualifications" and "standards" with Bruno Bettelheim and Sidney Hook. Knight was completing his first year at Davis when Allan Bakke sued the university for letting in "less qualified" minorities. When Knight was graduated in 1977, he had won the medical school's most coveted prize: the senior class award for the qualities most likely to produce an outstanding physician. The vote by the Class of 1977 paid tribute to Knight's outstanding academic and clinical record by designating him the best doctor in the class.

Like some of the most ardent opponents of special admissions, Knight was a poor immigrant who made good in America. He was born on October 18, 1944, in Georgetown, Guyana, a former British colony on the northern rim of South America. Knight's father supported his wife and six children by working as an accountant. Like many of his fellow countrymen, Orel dreamed of emigrating to a country where he would have greater opportunities. After being graduated from high school, he went to work and began saving his money. After four years he had enough for his passage, tuition, and, he hoped, a year of living expenses in the United States.

In 1966 Knight settled in the predominantly Hispanic community of East Los Angeles, where he rented a room for $25 a month and stretched his meager savings by riding a bicycle to classes at East Los Angeles College. "I was living on close to $7.50 a week," he recalled. "I was riding a bicycle when they weren't 'in' yet. I looked funny, an adult, riding down Brooklyn Avenue." Knight's wry sense of humor comes through easily in conversation. He is an impressive six-footer, a *café au lait* Clark Gable with a square jaw, prominent cheekbones, a thin mustache, and a wave of black hair. "It was a cultural shock, coming from a poor, underdeveloped country to the richest nation in the world. East L.A. was a sort of buffer. My main goal was to do as well as I could in school."

In his first year in America, his social life was "next to nil," but his concentration on studies paid off. He had close to a straight A average in junior college and won a scholarship to the University of Southern California. He retains fond memories of his early days in East Los Angeles: "The people were my own kind." After taking a class in biological sciences, Knight decided to study medicine. "I realized if I wanted to become a doctor, the time shouldn't matter."

But after a year of full-time study, his funds were running low. He had found a job at Blue Cross of Southern California, where he worked as a claims examiner while carrying a full load of courses at USC. "It was fortunate the job was related to the medical field," he said. "You learn a lot of [medical] terms. I also learned there are ways a physician can bill to get more money for his patients."

The years at USC did not have the warmth and comfort of his days in East Los Angeles. He was in a highly competitive environment, where premedical students sometimes sabotaged each other's laboratory experiments in the furious struggle for places in medical school. "I was the only black premed in 1968, and in the entire time I was there, I took one science class with another black. There was only one professor whom I thought might have been prejudiced. Once he mentioned William Shockley [the Nobel Prize–winning physicist who is an advocate of white genetic superiority] in a class on genetics. I never really felt comfortable in his class. But there were a lot of professors who were quite anxious to help."

In 1971 Knight sent out his first applications to medical schools, but he found that few slots were available for foreign students. By the time he was graduated in 1972, he had obtained permanent resident status—the first step toward U.S. citizenship—and he was admitted to Davis through the Task Force. Knight says he enjoyed his years in medical school. He says he worked hard and feels he was rewarded for his efforts. In his first medical school exam he had the highest score. "I remember the chairman of the Task Force coming to congratulate me, as if to say, 'I told them so.'" Knight feels he had advantages in getting through medical school because he was older than most of his classmates and because his background in Guyana had spared him the history of racial discrimination experienced by most black Americans. "In Guyana there were six races and we united against the common enemy: the British."

Knight strongly supports programs like the Task Force. "While I was at Davis, only one black came through the regular admissions, but there were [Task Force] students in my classes whose grades were just as good as the whites'. If you're trying to pick people with 3.9s, you don't need interviews. You can use a computer." He says grades are misleading because they don't take other circumstances into account. He says he didn't do as well at USC as he did in junior college because he had to work. In his last year at Davis, Knight scored "honors" (on a fail/pass/honors grading system) in all but one of his courses. "People get the impression minority students barely get through medical school and that minority physicians can only deal with minorities. I didn't need the Task Force to get my commitment. I want to treat minorities, but it's my own choice. I feel somebody has to take care of my own."

After leaving Davis, Knight got his first choice for his internship, the nationally recognized obstetrics and gynecology program at the USC–Los Angeles County Medical Center. He plans to practice in an area of Northern California with a large minority population, possibly Oakland or Sacramento.

Patrick Chavis and his wife, Toni Johnson-Chavis, were also among the sixteen Task Force students admitted in 1973. Pat Chavis decided to become a doctor when he was still a junior high student in Watts. He was one of five children in a poor family, and he stuck by his ambition despite an uncle's warning that he would be a financial burden on his mother. He earned a bachelor's degree in human biology at Albion College in Michigan, and a GPA of close to 3.5 helped him get into Davis. According to members of the medical school faculty, Chavis did well academically and even earned a master's degree in public health at UCLA "on the side" while completing his last year of medical school.

Like Orel Knight, Chavis's high ranking in medical school helped him get his first choice, the OB-GYN program at L.A. County. In the spring of 1978 he took a National Board exam in his specialty and had the highest score among the interns at L.A. County. "All the efforts people have made over the years to advance the cause of minorities are going down the drain with Bakke," Chavis said. "It's more than just a color issue. We're talking about affirmative action, about trying to make things better and giving people who are poor and oppressed a chance for a better life."

Toni Johnson-Chavis is an even more ardent advocate of special admissions. Her father worked on the Santa Fe Railroad for twenty-seven years. She was the oldest of five children reared in the poor black enclave of Compton, just outside Los Angeles. "Ever since I can remember, all my life, I wanted to be a doctor," she said. "My father was an extremely intelligent man, but he had to do demeaning jobs because he came from a poor family and never got a chance for a good education. Through his children, my father felt he had his chance to do something."

At Compton High School her education included hand-me-down books from Beverly Hills High School and science classes in poorly equipped laboratories. "I had to do double time to keep up when I went to Stanford [on a scholarship], not knowing even how to use a slide rule, not having basic chemistry, competing with people from top prep schools in the nation. In addition to the educational disadvantages that poor students face when they get to college, I lived with white people burning crosses on my dormitory lawn and putting swastikas on my dormitory door. Nobody did anything special for me. I finished in three years to get the hell out of that kind of environment." After being graduated from Stanford in 1972, she completed a master's degree in public health at UCLA before going to Davis.

"There's a whole public misconception about the Task Force program. The thinking is that somehow the people who came in through the program are different from the rest of the class. They can't understand why we weren't admitted through regular admissions. That's why I'm angry. The people who came through special admissions programs were as qualified or more qualified because, believe me, I feel more qualified than the average person who came in. I have done more. There have been no favors, no corner cutting. They've only addressed themselves to the fact that there are not enough black physicians and we must make some kind of goal and commitment to get more people in."

She and three other Task Force students set up a weight reduction clinic in Del Paso Heights, a poor area of Sacramento, and found that more poor whites than blacks came to the clinic. But she says she was never able to recruit her white classmates to help. "One of the students told me straight. He told me he wanted a nice Wilshire Boulevard practice and didn't want to be bothered with poor people, white or black.

"Twenty percent of the white students who came into the class at Davis had grade point averages less than Bakke's. The dean was able to let people in for straight political reasons. There are three applicants for every spot in medical school. There are just not enough medical school spots, and unfortunately someone gets the shaft. It's unfair to everyone. People have never complained about nepotism being a way of getting into medical school or about having a lot of money giving you an advantage. But now that they're considering affirmative action programs, it's a big deal. People can't tolerate the idea that you're going to let that spot be filled by a black person and a poor black person at that. The people who were let in for special reasons were rich white people who had poorer grades than Bakke. Why not complain about these people? Why single out the sixteen in the Task Force?"

The treatment of Task Force students by the news media is one reason Vivian Legette refused to be interviewed until after she was graduated from Davis. She had seen reporters storm the campus after the California Supreme Court decision, stick microphones in the path of minority students, and ask how it felt to be "less qualified." According to Allan Bakke's logic, Vivian Legette was one of the students who deprived him of a place the second time he applied to the medical school in 1974.

Vivian's grandparents were farmers in the hamlet of Hemingway, South Carolina. Her parents owned a "fish joint" until her mother refused to say "sir" to a local sheriff in 1951. The Legettes were advised that their lives would be safer in Charleston, and their father joined the Air Force to support his family. Military assignments took the Legettes all over the country and to the Far East, but whenever possible Vivian and her two brothers spent the summers with relatives in Hemingway, picking cotton and tying tobacco. Her father stayed in California after retiring from the Air Force and bought a modest house in a black area of Sacramento.

Vivian had considered becoming a lawyer or a writer; but circumstances made her go to business school, and she found a job as a secretary for Planned Parenthood in Sacramento. Her efficiency and initiative prompted some of the doctors she met through her work to encourage her to go back to school. She took some courses at Sacramento State before transferring to the University of California in San Diego. She did so well academically that she was able to apply to medical schools as a junior. She was accepted at Howard, Northwestern, and UC–San Francisco, but she chose Davis to be near her parents.

"I was really afraid. I didn't have the background of students with master's degrees, Ph.D.'s or even B.A.'s," she said of her early days in medical school. She believes there was a great deal of hostility because of racist and sexist attitudes among the faculty. "During the basic science years we only had to contend with attitudes because the tests were objective. How much help you received from faculty depended on how they felt about the Task Force. I sought very little help." On one occasion she went to a professor to discuss some material she was having trouble with. He was condescending, unfriendly, and dismissed her after five minutes. A white classmate who went to the same instructor was given ninety minutes. She shared her notes on the subject with Vivian.

After two years in the basic science curriculum, students at Davis move into the clinical courses more closely related to medical practice. Here, said Legette, attitudes were more difficult to judge because ratings and grades were extremely subjective. She believed that in many instances minority students were given lower scores than they deserved. "It depended not only on scores and exams but on impressions." When she became interested in surgery as a specialty, she discovered a great deal of resistance to women in this traditionally male preserve. During a fourth-year clerkship at a hospital in the Midwest, a staff physician started his evaluation of her work by describing her "sweet and charming disposition." In another instance a surgical resident kept "forgetting" to call her when important cases came to the hospital. "They barely tolerate women in surgery," she concluded. Despite the obstacles, Legette's work impressed the hospital staff so much that they offered her a residency in surgery at the hospital. Eventually she hopes to become an ear, nose, and throat specialist on the South Side of Chicago. Despite her successes, her memories of Davis remain bittersweet. "I wish I could have had more than I got. If I could do it over again, I would go to another school that had more experience with minorities and women."

•

Understandably, Task Force students who did well at Davis spend little time dwelling on the kind of atmosphere they encountered at Davis. The sudden plunge into the intense academic grind of the first two years is intimidating enough for all students. Those Task Force students who had early academic successes found the burden of their roles as minority group representatives easier to bear. But many of the others had to contend with negative attitudes as well as the pressures of the curriculum. As could be expected, faculty opinions on special admissions reflected the entire spectrum of public opinion. Small segments of the faculty were strongly for or against affirmative action. The great majority fell into the middle and shifted with the prevailing winds. Many former and present Task Force students say the polarization increased once the *Bakke* case became a national issue.

In 1975 one medical school faculty member circulated a memo suggesting that Task Force students had lowered the standards of the medical school. "By introduction of Task Force students into the student body," he wrote, "we have invalidated this mechanism of determination of quality. It is my contention that the presence of Task Force students has resulted in a decrease of the mean and an increase in the standard deviation [a statistical measure] of virtually all of our examinations." The memo concluded by suggesting that the introduction of twenty first graders into the class would have had the same impact as the sixteen Task Force students. The medical school administration did a statistical study that refuted the memo's suggestions, but many Task Force students say the incident reinforced their feeling that they were simply not wanted at the medical school.

While admissions officials may have put less emphasis on grades, these remained the main determinants of excellence in the minds of most faculty and students. Arthur Chen, an Asian student admitted through the regular committee with a 3.0 GPA and average MCAT scores, remembered fearing conversations with his classmates. "I was always feeling my statistics were nothing to brag about. I was happy they didn't ask me what my GPA was because they'd make the judgment that 'you probably got in through the Task Force' or 'Oh. I have a friend with a 3.5, and *he* didn't get in.' I can admit I was influenced by that, and I tended to stifle talk about it." Ironically, when Chen was graduated, he was chosen by his classmates to deliver the valedictory speech at commencement exercises.

Some students felt a stricter standard was in effect for Task Force students because of faculty doubts about their ability. They believed that passing marks in courses were often set arbitrarily to eliminate Task Force students at the bottom of classes and that makeup exams were often given to whites but denied to blacks and Chicanos. There are many stories of racist and sexist remarks made by professors not accustomed to dealing with women and minorities. In one course on human reproduction, the instructor said he would concentrate only on male orgasm and leave female orgasm for the course on psychiatry. When half the class was absent from a seminar during the spring, the instructor asked, "Where are the Task Force students? That's why they don't do well here." Such remarks prompted one class to file a petition in protest.

Donald Parks, a student admitted through the Task Force in 1974 and dropped in 1976, said these incidents underlined the hostility of faculty members who had not been educated to understand the process used in picking students in nontraditional fashion. Since he was dismissed for academic reasons, Parks has waged a private war for readmission to Davis. A native of New York City, Parks was the first member of his family to go to college. He majored in education at New York University and went into the Air Force in 1965 to serve an

ROTC obligation. He worked in race relations and counseling in the Far East and became interested in medicine after working for a base psychiatrist.

Parks admits his grades were "average" and his MCAT scores mediocre, but he believes he was accepted at Davis because interviewers took into consideration his eight-year absence from school as well as his background in the military. But soon after the start of classes in 1974, Parks developed eye trouble. He says the eye problems and the side effects of steroids used in treating him contributed to his failing a course in his second year. He was put on probation and asked to repeat the entire year. When his eye problems started again, he was refused a chance to drop a course and reduce his load. He failed the course and was dismissed. His appeals were turned down, and he has been trying ever since to get readmitted.

Parks, who gets a captain's disability retirement pay from the Air Force, has compiled a foot-thick file of memos, transcripts, and letters to document his charges of discrimination and arbitrary treatment by the medical school. Even officials who are skeptical about Parks's claims admit that he has forced the medical school to reform many of its disciplinary and review procedures, which were often vague and arbitrary. After seeing the carefully cross-indexed file, some people half-jokingly suggest that Parks switch to law. But he is determined to get reinstated. "What I want to do," he says, "is get my record straight. I don't have a choice. If I don't get back in here, I can't get into an accredited medical school anywhere. What I'm trying to do is set a model, not just for minority students, but for all students to know their rights. I want to feel that I'm accomplishing something." Charges brought up by Don Parks and other students are difficult to prove. But they do expose the vulnerability of students who are admitted to medical schools with academic deficiencies and who get little help in correcting those shortcomings. In an atmosphere where there is serious doubt about their talents and abilities, the fact that most Task Force students are able to do well, and that some do outstanding work, must serve as testimony to their drive and determination. As for those who fail, one has to conclude that they were simply too far behind, that they had too many deficiencies and difficulties to overcome, and that, in their own way, they will continue to be victims.

If there is one area that both critics and proponents of affirmative action can agree about, it is the fact that students admitted through such programs often suffer from stigmatization. But while all may agree about the effect of such programs, the solutions offered are much different. For critics of special admissions, the final authority on the subject is Thomas Sowell, an economist at UCLA, who, they are careful to point out, is black:

"What the arguments and campaigns for quotas are really saying, loud and clear, is that black people just don't have it, and that they will have to be given something in order to have something. The devastating impact of this message on black people—particularly young black people—will outweigh any extra few jobs that may result from this strategy. Those black people who are already competent, and who could be instrumental in producing more competence among the rising generation, will be completely undermined, as black becomes synonymous—in the minds of black and white alike—with incompetence, and black achievement becomes synonymous with charity payoffs."

One flaw in the "Sowell Defense" is the assumption that special admissions (here called quotas) must always be associated with inferiority. If the majority perceives members of minority groups as less competent because of affirmative action, isn't there a choice other than ending all such programs? A more fruitful solution might be to educate the public about the false logic of such associations. The same might be said of charges that affirmative action polarizes ethnic and racial groups. This suggests that racial harmony is the responsibility of the victim of racial harmony—the excluded minorities. This logic is not much different from that which blamed racial unrest in the 1960s on outside agitators. The truth is that the impact of minorities on the competitive pool has been minor. The makeup of professional and graduate schools has been drastically changed by the presence of women, and they are the real competition for white males. The percentage of women in medical schools has risen sharply from 5.7 in 1959 to 22.4 in 1977. The total enrollment of minorities in U.S. medical schools was 8.2 percent in 1977, and because of the limited pool of minority applicants with training in sciences, the number is expected to decline in the next few years.

What the critics of special admissions try to do is to substitute one myth for another. Viewing blacks as incompetent, which Professor Sowell fears, did not begin with affirmative action and would not end if minorities were excluded. Caught between the rock and the hard place, minority groups have no choice but to continue to push for a fair share of opportunities and hope that at some point they will be accepted on their own merits. The crucial fact remains that special admissions is not as revolutionary as some would like to believe. Consider this report from the admissions committee to the Faculty of Arts and Science at Harvard University, a recognized bastion of the meritocracy:

"Faced with the dilemma of choosing among a large number of qualified candidates, the Committee on Admissions could use the single criterion of scholarly excellence and attempt to determine who among the candidates were likely to perform best academically. But for the past 30 years the Committee on Admissions has never adopted this approach. The belief has been that if scholarly excellence were the sole or even predominant criterion, Harvard College would lose a great deal of its vitality and intellectual excellence and that the quality of the educational experience offered to all students would suffer. Consequently, after selecting those students whose intellectual potential will seem extraordinary to the faculty—perhaps 150 or so out of an entering class of 1100—the committee seeks . . . variety in making its choices."

What is remarkable is that this report was written in 1960, long before the advent of affirmative action. It makes clear that in their zeal to discredit programs that would bring members of minority groups into the mainstream, the critics create precedents that never existed. The ancient meritocratic process that is being so valiantly defended simply never existed. Of course, many of the ardent foes of special admissions were themselves victims of quotas and admissions policies that didn't see members of certain ethnic groups as adding "vitality" to the Harvard experience. But it surely is a commendable sign of progress that the definition of diversity has been expanding to encompass all groups and segments of society. Once again, because of the large pool, many qualified individuals will be excluded, as they were in the past for an infinite variety of reasons over which they had no control. The apparent "fairness" of this approach would lead Justice Powell to laud the "Harvard Plan" when he grappled with a decision in *Bakke*. From the minority point of view, the injustice of quotas is not difficult to understand, but their benefits are also obvious. To a group that was subjected to a quota of zero, a quota of 10 percent was a distinct advantage of opportunity, helping form a core of highly educated individuals over several decades. Had racial minorities been recipients of this essentially perverse paternalism, the makeup of our society in the last quarter of this century would be fundamentally different from what it has turned out to be.

•

The crush of competition for places in professional and graduate schools today obscures the historical fact that just twenty years ago the opportunities for whites were much greater than they are today. Until 1961 the Boalt Hall Law School automatically admitted any college graduate with a B average. The LSAT was required only for those with less than a B who could not talk an admissions official into admitting them without it. And in those days a score of 500 was enough for admission. According to a brief filed by the deans of several law schools, in 1960, 708 persons applied to Boalt and 517 were admitted. In the fall of that year, 268 or 53 percent of those admitted enrolled in the first-year class.

The postwar boom of babies impacted on admissions in the 1960s, and applications rose sharply. In 1966, 1,500 applied for 278 places at Boalt Hall. In 1972, 5,000 applied and 271 were enrolled—5 percent of all the applicants. The LSAT was now required of all applicants, and the median scores were 638 in 1967 and 712 in 1976. The grade point average of entering law students in 1976 was 3.66. "It is quite clear," said the law school deans, "that the level of record achievement required to gain admission to Boalt Hall is far in excess of the level which would be required if the sole criterion were a record sufficient to justify a confident prediction that the applicant could successfully complete the program and become a competent member of the bar."

The history of medical school during the last two decades is similar. In the early 1960s some schools complained they could not fill all their available places. The Medical College Aptitude Test was introduced in the 1950s to help reduce the attrition rate "by providing a standardized measurement of knowledge and ability in order to predict success in the basic science curriculum, which usually comprises the first two years of medical school." The high attrition rate of the time was the result of a basically "open admissions" policy at many medical schools. The mean MCAT science score of accepted students was 516 in 1957 and 615 in 1975. The quantitative score on the test went from 517 to 620 in that period. "Because of the larger pool of academically qualified students," said the AAMC, "medical schools have raised their admissions standards well beyond the minimum level necessary to ensure completion of the course of study leading to the M.D. degree."

In these cases the pressure of competition has raised the level of academic qualifications far beyond what is needed to succeed. The medical schools point out that minority applicants are scoring at the level of whites who were admitted to medical schools twenty years ago. "The qualified minority applicant, who is perhaps just catching up to the level of educational ability and achievement attained by the qualified white applicant of twenty years ago, cannot compete with the even more highly academically qualified white applicant of today," the AAMC concludes. The additional irony may be that some of those who complain loudly about lowered standards are complaining about students who match and even surpass the "qualifications" they used to get into professional schools just a generation ago.

Still, the argument about the "better qualified" would be valid if a connection could be made between the MCAT scores and the quality of physicians produced. If a science score of 700 meant a better doctor than one of 500, it would be immoral to choose a student with the lower score. But extensive studies over the last two decades simply do not support such conclusions. In 1972 Ralph Friedan and several other medical investigators reported: "Several investigators have observed that the criteria for selecting medical applicants correlate poorly with the student's performance in medical school and not at all with their performance as physicians. In particular, investigators have not been able to predict physician performance by college grade point average, a criterion greatly emphasized by medical school admissions committees. Similarly, the grade point average obtained as a medical student, considered an important factor in acceptance in internship-residency programs, has been found to have a zero correlation with a physician's clinical performance."

Robert Montoya, a California health official, cites a 1975 study of twenty-three minority students admitted in 1970 and 1971 to the medical school at the University of California in San Diego. "Under traditional admissions criteria," said Montoya, "only one of these 23 would have been accepted; 22 out of 23 would have been rejected." On the first part of the National Board Examination, which physicians must pass to be able to practice medicine, 17 of these students passed on the first try, and all the rest eventually completed the test successfully. "In terms of clinical performance, the minority students have been performing at an average level. All 23 passed pediatrics and surgery clerkships on their first attempt, but two had to repeat the medicine clerkship. A randomly selected group of 21 of their traditionally selected cohorts showed one had to repeat the medicine clerkship and one had to repeat the surgery clerkship." The average GPA of the minority students in the study was 2.93 overall and 2.84 in science. Their average MCAT scores were in the 45th percentile in science and in the 37th percentile in the quantitative segment.

What these studies confirm is what the medical school administrators have been saying: minority students do less well on standardized tests, but this does not imply they are any less able. In fact, a 1967 study of 180 physicians working in Public Health Service hospitals (most of them white, we can safely assume) showed a *negative* correlation between their MCAT scores and rating of their work by supervisors. "If an admissions committee were to follow literally the implications of studies relating MCAT scores to physician performance," facetiously suggests a brief in support of special admissions, filed in the *Bakke* case by an organization of black law students, "it should prefer candidates with lower scores."

There is a clear link between race and rating in the MCAT test. Even within the same income range, minorities do worse on the test than white applicants. Since performance cannot be related to MCAT scores or ethnic identification, it becomes clear that, in a purely objective sense, the MCAT discriminates racially. David White, an authority on testing at the University of California at Berkeley, has pointed out similar problems with the LSAT. His solution: "If admissions had been determined on undergraduate grades without the LSAT, there would be more minority students in law school than there are with the LSAT and special admissions." White found that 10 percent of black applicants to law school had an academic average over 3.2, while only 3 percent had an LSAT over 600 and only 1 percent had both. But the grades and test scores of white applicants were more evenly matched. "This is the most dramatic, persuasive evidence ever of the independent racial bias of the LSAT," White concluded.

If the evidence is so overwhelming about the irrelevance and racial bias of standardized tests, why do officials continue to use them? Primarily because they are a convenient tool for paring down an overwhelming number of applicants. A semblance of fairness is created by having every applicant take the same examination, although the test itself has virtually no value in predicting what contribution the student will make to the profession he or she is about to enter. Also, the basic reforms in medical education, begun in the early part of the century after Abraham Flexner's seminal report on the state of medicine in America, have escalated to a point where most schools in the United States train scientific researchers rather than physicians. Demands for better primary care are not being met because doctors are taught to depend on a high level of technology that ties them to major urban research centers.

Dr. George Silver, professor of public health at the Yale University School of Medicine, who takes the position that *all* current admissions methods are unfair, suggests an admissions policy that admits all applicants. Silver believes the costs could be met by shifting funds away from biomedical research to the preparation of physicians. The essential research could be done at a few key institutions, and attrition would eliminate the unqualified from medical programs. But Silver admits that the medical establishment is not likely to adopt his proposals, which point out that faculty-heavy medical schools in the United States drive up the costs of training doctors far beyond those of other industrialized countries.

But as long as major reforms are resisted by the majority, special admissions and other similar programs are the only alternatives to total exclusion from professions that have profound impact on the economic, professional, and social well-being of all citizens. In an atmosphere of growing conservatism and self-interest, opportunistic scholars and intellectuals, who have access to all the research on testing and achievement, can callously assert that attempts to select minorities more fairly are a form of discrimination.

The practice of using numbers to exclude racial groups is not at all new. In his book *The Legacy of Malthus: The Social Costs of the New Scientific Racism,* Allen Chase traces the development of intelligence tests and their enthusiastic use by the eugenics movement in the early part of the twentieth century. The eugenicists, who had in their ranks some of the world's most prominent scientists, believed in the superiority of Northern Europeans over all other racial groups. They believed in limiting the propagation of "undesirable" genes by limiting immigration and forced sterilization.

Racial and anti-Semitic prejudices predated the eugenics movement, but testing seemed to provide an "objective" tool for confirming these prejudices. One of the many ironies of the battles around the *Bakke* case is the willingness of ethnic groups that were once the victims of testing procedures to line up in support of examinations that work to exclude certain minorities. The language of the early intelligence testers reflected the ancient historical prejudices against those who were not white, Anglo-Saxon, and Protestant.

In 1912 psychologist Henry Herbert Goddard used a version of the intelligence test invented by Frenchman Alfred Binet to "prove" the inferiority of immigrant Jews, Italians, Hungarians, Poles, Russians, and others. Lewis M. Terman of Stanford University developed the Revised Stanford-Binet IQ test and concluded: "Common observation would itself suggest that the social class to which the family belongs depends less on chance than on the parents' native [hereditary] qualities of intellect and character." After testing Indian, Chicano, and black children in the Southwest and California, Terman and his associates concluded from their IQ tests: "Their dullness seems to be racial, or at least inherent in the family stocks from which they come. . . . They cannot master abstractions, but they can often be made efficient workers, able to look out for themselves."

Their theories would be amusing except for the fact that these scientists exerted considerable influence on government and social policy. The restrictive immigration laws passed by Congress in 1924 followed almost exactly the ranking of ethnic European groups devised by the eugenicists. Northern Europeans were the most desirable immigrants; Jews and Eastern Europeans were the least welcome. One impact of these tests, said Chase, was the exclusion from sanctuary in the United States of millions who would become victims of the Nazi Holocaust. Not surprisingly, the theories of the eugenicists had great influence on the development of Nazi racial theories.

The influence of IQ and World War I intelligence tests declined sharply in the 1930s, when more thorough analyses of their findings pointed out the discrepancies of education and environment that provided racial differentials in the scores. But the use of the tests had a resurgence in the 1950s after the U.S. Supreme Court ordered an end to school segregation. Politicians and educators in the South used IQ scores and studies that deliberately distorted the findings of prominent researchers to meet their political needs. But the eugenicists had a second rebirth in 1969, when Arthur Jensen's landmark article on race and IQ was published in the *Harvard Education Review*. "Is there a danger that current welfare policies," Jensen wrote, "unaided by eugenic foresight, could lead to the genetic enslavement of a substantial segment of our population?"

Jensen was clearly aware of the political repercussions of his research. "Since much of the current thinking behind civil rights, fair employment, and equality of educational opportunity appeals to the fact that there is a disproportionate representation of different racial groups in the various levels of the educational, occupational and socioeconomic hierarchy, we are forced to examine all the possible reasons for this inequality among racial groups in the attainments and rewards generally valued by all groups within our society."

After reviewing the literature, Jensen suggested that black and white children had different learning abilities and that black children could not easily grasp abstractions. He concluded that compensatory education programs had failed because they tried to achieve too much. He suggested they concentrate on the basic skills minority children would find most useful in their eventual low status as adults. *Newsweek's* summary of his ideas reflected the prevalent interpretation by mass media. "Since intelligence is fixed at birth anyway, he claims, it is senseless to waste vast sums of money and resources on such remedial programs as Head Start, which assumes that a child's intellect is malleable and can be improved."

Jensen's ideas were immediately challenged by an influential segment of experts in the fields of genetics and intelligence research, and even those who praised his methods disagreed strongly with his conclusions. In a subsequent issue of the *Review,* Martin Deutsch, who had co-authored a book with Jensen in 1968, took issue with his associate: ". . . I believe the impact of Jensen's article was destructive; that it had negative implication for the struggle against racism and for the improvement of the educational system," said Deutsch. "The conclusions he draws are, I believe, unwarranted by the existing data, and reflect a consistent bias toward a racist hypothesis."

Deutsch's understandable concern about the political implications was reflected in the attention given to Jensen's ideas by the press. A nation torn by the war in Southeast Asia and racial confrontation had its purse strained by military expenditures and the vestiges of the Great Society programs. A rationale for eliminating compensatory programs was extremely attractive. Jensen's theories were extended by Richard Herrnstein, Edward Banfield, and others into programs for political action that found acceptability in political and journalistic circles.

Historians of science have noted the common practice among promoters of racial superiority of distorting the facts and ignoring the research that contradicts their findings. Recently, much of the work of Dr. Cyril Burt on intelligence has been discredited because of evidence that he made up many of his figures. Burt's work was an important source for Jensen's research, as he conceded in his *Harvard Education Review* article: "Probably the most distinguished exponent of the application of these methods to the study of intelligence is Sir Cyril Burt, whose major writings on the subject are a 'must' for students of individual differences." But when other researchers went back to Burt's original data and found serious discrepancies, Jensen was forced to retreat from his reliance on the work of the man he admired so much.

The new scientific racism comes full circle when one finds that some of its most ardent advocates hail from racial and ethnic groups that were targets of the early eugenicists. William Green, an early president of the American Federation of Labor, argued that "our republican institutions are the outgrowth of ten centuries of the same people in England and America. They can only be preserved if the country contains at all times a great preponderance of those of British descent." The concept of preservation against an onslaught of outsiders can still be found in the positions of many opponents of special admissions. The concept of pure racial stock has now been converted into the preservation of "high standards" in the meritocratic argument. This argument dwells on the dangers to the institutions of democracy of programs of affirmative action and race consciousness. Yet, since these fragile institutions survived the inequities of slavery and racial segregation, why must they collapse under efforts to achieve an end that even the critics admit to be admirable?

The most disturbing aspect of the opposition is that it offers no real alternatives to special admissions programs. Numerical apportionment is attacked as a dangerous quota. Race sensitivity is described as "reverse discrimination," and the rejection of rigid numerical standards is seen as a serious assault on standards. The best alternatives that can be offered are increased recruiting and special tutoring. But the deans of medical and law schools have made it clear: without special programs, most professional and graduate schools would once again become virtually lily-white. And most of these officials, who surely have to be concerned about the reputations of their institutions, insist that the quality of education and training provided has not been harmed by the presence of minority students.

Considering the body of independent evidence to support these arguments, one has next to consider the motivation of the critics. What they end up saying to minority groups is that they need to wait longer for equality—not the equality of paper and law, but the real equality that reflects the random distribution of skills and talents through all ethnic and racial groups, Jensen notwithstanding. In the end, the issue becomes one of the preparedness of the majority to accept minorities in unaccustomed roles as lawyers and doctors, supervisors and university intellectuals. In the effort to measure black progress in recent years, little attention has been paid to white progress toward acceptance of a racially diverse society.

Black Americans especially find bitter humor in the new concern that special admissions casts doubt on the talents and abilities of members of minority groups. Somewhere in the folklore of every black family is the story of the relative or ancestor who suffered under the burden of this doubt. There are enough stories about black doctors who couldn't practice at local hospitals because the American Medical Association excluded them, about black Ph.D.'s who spent their lives working in the Post Office, about black college graduates who were messengers and stock clerks on Wall Street. Yet distinguished scholars feel comfortable enough in rewriting history to argue that the treatment of blacks earlier in American history was equivalent to the treatment of Jews and ethnic whites. To refuse to differentiate between partial and total exclusion becomes the highest form of demagoguery.

The basic assumption adopted by the opponents of corrective programs is that American society has suddenly become generous and open in a free market of talent and initiative.

Even the most ardent advocates of the free enterprise economy would be embarrassed to suggest that such a state of openness exists. Somehow the creeping economic socialism about which Milton Friedman complains has not yet corrupted the intellectual meritocracy. The doors are allegedly open to all, and the complaints of minority groups that they are not getting their fair share are interpreted as evidence of their unwillingness and inability to compete.

In 1976, 42,155 applicants competed for 15,774 positions in medical schools. Of these applicants, 33,762 were white and 9,393 were from minority groups. In that year 8.3 percent of those accepted, or about 1,300 of the students accepted, were from minorities. If these 1,300 were excluded, 25,000 applicants would still be left out of medical school, many of them highly qualified applicants.

In arguments about qualifications race serves as a mechanism for avoiding an analysis of the broader issues. If minority demands, and confrontations like the *Bakke* case, serve to expose broad injustices, those with the least to gain from such disclosures are those who already benefit from privilege and whose chances for access are highest. One lesson of the civil rights movement was that many of the victories won by blacks benefited not only other minority groups but many whites. The doubling of class sizes in medical schools under pressure for minority access is one example of unexpected benefits to the majority.

In truth affirmative action, special admissions, and other such devices are imperfect remedies. Many of the basic problems of American society have been exposed by racial confrontation because the discomfort of confronting color leads to an examination of other factors that are not at all racial. There was little dialogue about the exclusion of disadvantaged whites from professional schools until the *Bakke* case. But if a solution is limited to a racial basis, one basic inequity is resolved at the expense of another. This would not be the first time that race has been used to preserve privilege. Racial issues are easier to confront than broad philosophical problems about the inequality of classes in America.

Opponents of broad political and social reform can retreat into the glass house of their own standards without having to listen to dissidents who insist on bringing up issues of race, color, and opportunity. If there ever is a confrontation in America over these issues, as there was in the 1960s, it will probably not have the cloaking in morality that existed in the last decade. At this point the shaping of moral indignation is too firmly in the hands of those who reap the benefits of this alleged meritocracy. That is one reason that recent efforts by black leaders to appeal to moral and ethical obligations have failed. These leaders have been wedded to the traditions of Martin Luther King, Jr., and others who forged the civil rights movement. But this emphasis on morality ignores a definite shift in the movement's strategy that was cut off by Dr. King's death. In 1968 he was attempting to form a coalition along class lines that would counter the impact of the growing conservative movement that was to put Nixon in office.

It is becoming increasingly clear as the nation approaches a new decade that there is little hope of creating a movement along racial lines. Advocates of equality have the unenviable task of broadening their struggle so the majority will understand that the underdogs are not only black and brown but often white as well. The main obstacle to such a political movement is a lack of access to the information industry. Given a choice between "better" and "less" qualified individuals, the public has little doubt about who should be picked. The function of minority groups has always been to serve as point men in ferreting out the contradictions of American democracy. They begin by noticing the color-coded aspects of privilege, and they end up raising questions about fundamental issues of rights and the distribution of benefits. It becomes extremely difficult to convince minorities that the present order of things is the just result of the Medical College Aptitude Test or God's will.

Seven

A CHANGE OF MOOD

On a Sunday afternoon a small group of young and success-ful black professionals sat around the remains of a sumptuous dinner and engaged in a ritual that had accompanied many of the Sunday dinners of their parents and grandparents before them. After covering the latest developments in foreign policy, presidential politics, and the arts, the conversation drifted into what used to be called "the state of the race." Under the in-fluence of several bottles of fine California wine and the hyp-notic flicker of the fireplace, they shared their views of the one issue that separated them from other groups of young American professionals.

One of the diners was excited about a new venture in tele-vision. He had planned meticulously, brought in the best minds to help him develop his project, and had obtained the funding for an ambitious program aimed at teenagers. In retracing his steps, he described in a matter-of-fact tone his struggle against an indifference caused partly by the bureaucratic inertia that can be found in any institution and partly by the fact that he, like everyone else in the room, was black. He was not com-plaining about the racism he had encountered, for he would have been surprised if it had been absent. After a decade in white organizations he had simply learned to isolate and outflank that peculiar irrationality in the thinking of his white colleagues.

The reporter nodded in sympathy and launched into a convoluted and hilarious story about a confrontation with an editor who could not understand why a magazine article derogated the abllities and the competence of blacks. The journalist had lost the argument, but he hoped that the fuss he raised would raise the consciousness of the editor. He had learned along the line that his influence on the prestigious publication he worked for was only incremental.

The others around the table agreed and recalled their own experiences. In each case there was that instant of conflict which revealed a chasm between their own perception of the world and that of the people they worked with. None of them would have been classified as militants in the 1960s, and they all had impressive credentials to verify their ability to compete successfully in the mainstream of society. Yet they had no doubt that the color of their skin still set them apart and to some degree increased the odds against achieving their goals.

Just as their individual accomplishments would be used as evidence of black progress in the years since the civil rights era, their collective view of the world would just as vehemently be denied by the majority of Americans. For the irony of the time is that the views of blacks and whites about the nature of racism in American society are now probably more in conflict than they have been since the Supreme Court ruled that separate was not necessarily equal. When Stanford University professor Seymour Martin Lipset analyzed polls of racial attitudes recently, he concluded that "most whites do not believe discrimination is the principal cause of black inequality." But the majority of blacks, on the other hand, even those who are relatively affluent, continue to believe that their opportunities are still circumscribed by hostile racial attitudes. This difference of opinion is important in assessing the meaning and impact of the *Bakke* case.

On the tenth anniversary of the assassination of Martin Luther King, Jr., there was the predictable flurry of reports on black progress in America. The neat pile of statistics documented the gains made by the middle class and warned about the continued existence of an "underclass" that had not benefited from the victories of the civil rights movement. But these reports told more about the changes in race relations in the country through their style than through their content. After decades of moral indignation, fear, protest, and hostility, the dialog on race had been reduced to dry economic terms that could be charted on graph paper.

Clearly, race no longer had the fire or importance it demanded in the last decade. A 1978 Gallup poll found that whites ranked "the problems of black Americans" last on a list of thirty-one concerns. The issue may not have gone completely away, but it could not hold the national attention in the same manner as demonstrations, protests, and riots. Even *Bakke,* with all the hoopla about its landmark status, failed to provoke much of a debate on race relations. Most of the discussions centered on the legal and ethical issues raised by affirmative action and peripherally on the relative economic status of the races.

But there were other indications that white attitudes had not changed so fundamentally as to warrant this kind of complacency. The case itself could not have reached such prominence without a national sentiment for reassessing the obligations of the majority toward minority groups. And for the first time in history most whites were willing to believe that equality had been achieved and that programs to improve the status of minorities were giving these groups an unfair—and possibly an unnecessary—advantage. This was clearly the appeal of a term like *reverse discrimination.*

This shift in attitude was not isolated from other political and economic issues that had developed in the aftermath of the economic recession and the end of the Vietnam War. The resurgence of political conservatism could be attributed to the profound disappointment of the middle class in government and the growing sense of economic insecurity. Inflation and "making ends meet" were the major concerns of Americans, and the fear of economic competition from minorities had always intensified racial antagonism.

The difference in the 1970s was that this antagonism was not as simple as it had been in the past. A much more complicated set of ideas and assumptions had replaced the old arguments for racial superiority. As late as 1970 a Louis Harris survey showed that 76 percent of whites believed that blacks experienced discrimination in trying to achieve full equality. The majority of whites also believed that there was discrimination in housing, employment, and education. But in 1977 another Harris poll showed the extent of the change in attitude. Only one out of three whites believed that discrimination existed, and even fewer thought racism to be a factor in housing, education, and employment. At the same time 55 percent of whites believed blacks were pushing "too fast" for equality.

Since the majority of whites had concluded that race was no longer an important issue, they could turn their attention to other problems without feeling guilty. If blacks were at the bottom, most of them believed, it was because of their own shortcomings. Since minorities were dependent on the goodwill of the majority, this new attitude could have a strong impact on their struggle for parity.

This change of mind was a result of many factors. For one, the world of most whites was no longer racially exclusive. They might still live in segregated neighborhoods, but minorities appeared in most of the other areas of their lives. Blacks were more prominent than ever on television, in entertainment, and on the playing field. Whites had to work with blacks, ride public transportation with them, and generally adjust to a multiethnic world. The fact that change had taken place was easier to assess than the degree of change. The layman's gut reaction was reinforced by an intellectual and political campaign that touted black progress. Nixon adviser Daniel P. Moynihan's infamous "benign neglect" memo suggested that enough progress had been made to warrant a pause in government efforts on behalf of minorities. As early as 1965 Moynihan suggested that 50 percent of black families were in the middle class. *Commentary* made the same argument in 1973 with an additional suggestion that black leaders were covering up these gains for their own political ends. A few months later *Time* devoted a cover to the black middle class, and CBS News did a one-hour special on four black "middle-class" families, including one with an income of $8,000 a year. Although the figures and charges were disputed by other experts, the image of middle-class advancement dominated the 1970s.

The statistics on black progress were impressive. Between 1966 and 1976 the proportion of black families with incomes of $15,000 or more increased from 19 to 30 percent. Black families with incomes of $25,000 or more went from 3 to 8 percent. There were more white families, 53 and 19 percent respectively, in these categories, but the rate of change among blacks was faster. During that decade black college enrollment increased from 4.6 to 10.7 percent of the total, although the majority of blacks were enrolled in two-year and vocational schools.

But there were other numbers that did not bode well. Between 1967 and 1977 black unemployment doubled from 638,000 to 1.5 million. The black unemployment rate went from 7.4 to 13.2 percent, and black teenage unemployment soared from 26.5 to 38.5 percent. As one economist put it, the financial profile of the black community was being transformed from a pyramid to an hourglass. While the number of affluent blacks was increasing, the number of poor families was also growing. One sign of the impact of the poor was that despite the gains of the middle class, the median income for blacks in 1977 was 59 percent of white income—just one point higher than it was in 1966. The Kerner Commission's warning that America was moving toward two separate and unequal societies was being reflected in the black population. And beyond the numbers was the toll of human waste: the infant mortality rate matched only by Third World countries; the third and fourth generations of families on welfare; homicide as the greatest cause of death among young black men. The negative statistics were all higher than they had been during the era of urban violence.

The new class division among blacks was a reflection of what economists were calling the dual labor market. Young, educated blacks were reaping the benefits of affirmative action and moving into the middle-class income group while the poor were entering a job market of dead-end jobs which often did not pay enough to support the worker. Reflecting the values of the larger society, many of the poor were refusing to enter this lower track with no promise of advancement and dropping out of the labor market.

A University of Michigan study of 5,000 families showed that in 1967, after working six years, blacks between twenty and twenty-nine earned $2.40 an hour while whites were paid $3.30. Over the next eight years, the study found, the disparity in income grew from three-fourths to two-thirds. University of Chicago sociologist William J. Wilson suggests that middle-class blacks were able to move into white-collar and management positions because that sector of the economy was expanding during the past decade. But the economic recession of the mid-1970s slowed growth in this area and was reflected in the intense competition for places in professional schools. Already more than 1 million college graduates were classified as un-employed or underemployed, and the U.S. Census Bureau warned about intense competition over the next few decades as the baby boom of the 1940s played out its actuarial course.

The financial stresses on the middle class, caught between inflation and their own rising expectations, were reflected by the passage of California's Proposition 13, which attempted to limit government spending to relieve the tax burden of prop-erty owners. But this act, apparently lacking in strong political ideology, had strong class and race implications. Some 72 per-cent of those who voted for the proposition said they hoped the cuts would be made in welfare costs. No wonder that many minorities were skeptical about arguments that race was no longer a factor in the social equation. For many, *Bakke* was nothing less than a reaction to competition from minorities at the middle-class level.

Other studies of the labor market showed that blacks made the greatest gains in areas where there was not much competi-tion from whites. In fact, when the recession drove large num-bers of white women into the employment area, the number of blacks in the service workers' category declined significantly. As Wharton School economist Bernard Anderson described it, blacks were still in the caboose of the train that was the econ-omy, and they stayed at the rear whether the train speeded up or slowed down.

Despite this evidence, the concept of a racially neutral so-ciety was too attractive to give up easily. When the Depart-ment of Housing and Urban Development did a study of hous-ing discrimination in 1978, it found that only a fraction of blacks received equal treatment. The study said that blacks had a 62 percent chance of being discriminated against in buying a house and a 75 percent chance in trying to rent. "Even I am surprised at the figures," said HUD assistant secretary Donna E. Shalala. "We made every effort to be on the conservative side. We're talking about turning away people, the most overt form." Recent surveys of white attitudes showed most of them believed that housing was one area where blacks were least likely to encounter racism.

To many observers of the civil rights movement, the shift of national attitudes was signaled by the election of Richard Milhous Nixon in 1968. Urban violence was very much in the minds of most Americans, and the new administration moved quickly to establish some distance between the White House and the black masses whose militancy was so disturbing. The antipoverty and legal assistance programs which were seen as centers of provocation were quickly dismantled. The Republicans shifted government activities on behalf of equality to the middle class under the guise of "Black Capitalism." Not only was this kind of activity appealing to a conservative electorate, but the images it projected were much less threatening. Commerce secretary Maurice Stans made cameo appearances in black communities in striped pants and homburg to shake hands with black bank presidents and company executives.

Nixon's master stroke was his transformation of the civil rights movement from a moral to a political issue. Blacks were simply another special interest group deserving of no more—and often much less—attention than other competing interests. This practice of reducing all issues to their basic political essence would ultimately reach its fatal conclusion in Watergate, but that was still some years away. There was a war in Southeast Asia, and the young whites who had waged a holy crusade in Selma, Oxford, and Tupelo were redirecting their efforts on Saigon, Washington, and the Pentagon.

In the eyes of many whites the essential issues of race had been resolved by passage of the Civil Rights and Voting Rights acts. In addition, the demands made by blacks demanded more than the benevolent acquiescence of liberalism. The coalitions that had lobbied for equality in the 1960s were breaking down, and the black movement was becoming more isolated.

Thomas Blair observes that the militant organizations which evolved out of the Student Nonviolent Coordinating Committee and CORE "introduced new imperatives into the process of race relations and turned black protest organizations toward a concern with economic and social problems of the masses." In the summer of 1966, Stokely Carmichael's outline for Black Power called for the formation of political organizations outside the traditional political parties to speak and act for blacks. The most effective instrument for change was not moral judgment, he said, but the exercise of power. What drew national attention was Carmichael's rejection of the philosophy of nonviolence, the need for strong black organizations before the formation of coalitions with whites, and his suggestion that whites go work within their own communities on racial issues. "Black Power is not black supremacy," said Floyd McKissick, "it is a unified black voice reflecting racial pride in the tradition of our heterogeneous nation."

But the positive aspects of the Black Power message never reached the white majority. "The thrust of Black Power into national politics sounded the death knell of the civil rights alliance," says Blair in *Retreat to the Ghetto*. "It brought the black masses into what Frederick Douglass called the 'awful roar of the struggle.'" The mild-mannered civil rights leader was displaced in the public mind by the fiery young men calling for the overthrow of the system. The new generation of activists melded easily into the stereotype of the dangerous black male that still lurked in the psyches of white America.

There is a tendency now to forget how much fear was a catalyst in race relations. In major cities whites barricaded themselves in their homes or fled to the suburbs on the weekend following the death of King. Many of the reforms made in the wake of King's death were prompted as much by the aura of martyrdom as by the concern that militancy would gain credibility among blacks. In 1968 J. Edgar Hoover declared the Black Panther party the "number one threat to national security" and launched a plan to destroy it that would be the envy of any totalitarian government. But what was taking place was a division along class lines that had been dramatized by King's failure to extend his campaign in northern cities. The movement that had shifted from protest to politics was now making another crucial shift to economics and to much more fundamental questions about American society.

The Black Political Convention in Gary, Indiana, in 1972 was a momentous event in the evolution of black political thought. Throughout the country, grass-roots organizations brought into the political debate blacks who had never before participated; they voted on the issues and elected delegates to the convention. But it soon became clear that the growing class divisions within the black community had also spread to the political ideologies. Middle-class delegates wanted to strengthen their hand for the Democratic National Convention in Miami. Blacks from inner-city organizations and rural areas were committed to a black nationalist perspective and wanted to create an independent entity with no commitment to either party. There were several thousand delegates to the convention and as many observers and curiosity seekers. Every major news organization as well as many smaller journals and black newspapers staffed the convention.

Only a masterful diplomatic effort by the convention organizers prevented a full-scale debacle, but in one last defiant slap at the elected officials the nationalist groups forced through a resolution condemning Israel's policies in the Middle East. Most of the elected officials, dependent on Jewish support, retreated from the organization, and without the administrative superstructure they could have provided, the convention lost

an opportunity to develop a cohesive black political organization.

The right to vote was one of the great victories of the civil
rights era, but the impact of the black electorate remains
marginal because of inconsistent turnouts and the lack of unified views on many issues. Blacks have been elected in unpre-
cedented numbers at the local, county, and municipal levels,
but black elected officials consist of just one-half of 1 percent
of the nation's total.

At the national level, blacks have depended on coalition
politics to strengthen their impact. The sixteen black House
members are loosely organized into the Congressional Black
Caucus and through political pressure have been able to acquire key positions on committees and subcommittees. But
their most effective tool has been their ability to persuade
white members with large black constituencies to support legislation that serves black interests. This strategy was used to
win home rule for the District of Columbia and to extend the
life of the Office of Equal Opportunity. "As individuals," says
Howard University political scientist Marguerite Barnett,
"most CBC members are 'good liberals'; as a collectivity, they
hold the possibility of joint effective action for the beleaguered
black community."

But because most members have different aims and different
constituencies, they are more a symbol of black political aspirations than a real force in the Congress. The often tense relationship between President Carter and black leaders during
the early days of his presidency reflected doubts about the real
political clout of blacks at the polls. Until blacks demonstrate
the same ability as other ethnic groups to switch their loyalties
according to the issues and to deliver more than an average
election turnout, they will not have much of an impact on the
political process.

The political clout of blacks was diminished to a large degree by the breakup of traditional alliances. Many important pieces of civil rights legislation were supported by a triumvirate of blacks, labor, and Jews. But once the civil rights struggle turned to economic issues, this alliance was seriously weakened. The kind of economic reordering demanded by affirmative action, quotas, and efforts to overturn seniority systems put blacks and labor at odds. When the *Bakke* case went to the Supreme Court, neither the AFL-CIO nor the once-powerful Leadership Conference on Civil Rights filed a brief because of strong internal disagreements about a position.

Perhaps the most widely publicized split involved the long and honorable alliance between blacks and American Jews. In *Bakke* most of the major Jewish organizations filed briefs on behalf of Allan Bakke. Some commentators suggested that the black-Jewish conflict was unimportant in the larger context of the black-white struggle, but the civil rights movement had grown up depending on Jewish support, and the withdrawal of that support was extremely harmful. American Jews, with their disproportionate impact on national sentiment, intellectual debate, and journalism, had been a valuable ally.

Many northern liberals had doubts from early on about the tactics of the civil rights movement, and *Commentary*, the influential publication of the American Jewish Committee, reflected these concerns early. An early supporter of the civil rights movement, the magazine's shift to the right preceded a similar shift of the national sentiment. Many of the positions its editors and authors now hold can be safely considered to be in the mainstream of current thought.

In 1961 Tom Brooks wrote a prophetic article entitled "Negro Militants, Jewish Liberals and the Unions," which examined the conflict that erupted when black unionist A. Philip Randolph attempted to organize a Negro American Labor Council along the lines of the powerful Jewish Labor Council.

"One wonders if the growing antagonism between Jewish and Negro labor camps is a precursor of strained relations between the larger Jewish and Negro defense agencies," Brooks asked, "and ultimately between the two minority communities in general."

In March 1964 *Commentary* sponsored a round-table discussion on "Liberalism and the New Negro," featuring James Baldwin, Nathan Glazer, Sidney Hook, and Gunnar Myrdal. Editor Norman Podhoretz defined traditional liberalism as "society being made up not of competing economic classes and ethnic groups but rather of competing individuals who confront a neutral body of law and a neutral institutional complex." Podhoretz called "radical" the thought that "the Negro community *as a whole* has been crippled by 300 years of slavery and persecution and that the simple removal of legal and other barriers to the advancement of individual Negroes can therefore only result in what is derisively called 'tokenism.' "

Hook, who would later come to embrace Podhoretz's concerns about the inviolability of the individual, said he saw "no conflict with the traditional principles of liberalism, as I understand them, in the idea of *temporary* crash programs to improve the position of the Negro community." He compared this kind of effort to aid for earthquake victims but warned that he was opposed to any lowering of standards. Later on he would equate crash programs with lower standards in becoming a prominent neoconservative.

Glazer, who was still a liberal, admitted that "formal equality simply hasn't worked to produce actual equality, or rather, it has been working too slowly." To counter inequalities that had existed in the past, Glazer cited the use of such mechanisms as the ethnically balanced political ticket, a sensitivity to ethnicity which he would later renounce. Hook pressed for continuing efforts by arguing, "There's a difference between collective guilt and collective responsibility in the present for such responsibility can ultimately be brought home to each individual's door."

Professor Hook's casual statement during the discussion that there were few racial problems on university faculties drew a perceptive letter from a reader who wondered if "there would still be no problem if those same academic communities were suddenly to acquire a proper proportion of Negroes . . . enough indeed to threaten faculty jobs." At that point the concept of whites competing with blacks was just beginning to trouble the white liberals who had supported equality as an ideal.

In December 1964 Glazer wrote that the demands of black organizations for "preferential union membership" and "preferential hiring" simply could not serve as a basis for a common effort by blacks and Jews. Minority pressures for busing and school integration, he warned, would cause conflict. "The insistence on the primacy of integration over all other educational objectives breeds antagonism among former Negro allies." The black push for inclusion, Glazer concluded, was "a serious threat to the ability of other groups to maintain their communities."

The first serious conflict between blacks and their allies had been defined. As long as whites had been able to direct the thrust of the struggle for liberation, it had posed no threat to their self-interest. But blacks were beginning to see that laws were not enough to bring about equality. Bayard Rustin noted this shift in February 1965: "At issue, after all, is not civil rights, strictly speaking, but social and economic conditions." The liberal admonitions "of moderation are, for all practical purposes, admonitions to the Negro to adjust to the status quo and are therefore immoral."

But the concept of morality had died with Martin Luther King, Jr.'s, disastrous Chicago campaign. His inability to affect complex social, economic, and political issues in the urban ghettos gave credence to the nationalist militants and hastened the retreat of liberals from the battle. *Commentary* carried a running debate over the value and danger of Black Power. When Moynihan analyzed the 1966 elections, he concluded that "the electorate is fed up to the teeth with demonstrations and riots and perhaps more particularly with the assertion of the right to resist open threats of violence." A year later Moynihan would admit the failure of Congress to enact real economic reforms, but in 1968 he observed that "plain physical fear of the Negro is now a political fact of American life and not a happy one for liberals."

Moynihan's assessment of the national mood was reflected by the changing character of the magazine. After the confrontations over community control of education in New York, many Jews concluded that blacks were anti-Semitic and began to reconsider their involvement in civil rights. Earl Rabb's "The Black Revolution and the Jewish Question" reemphasized the Jewish commitment to a pluralistic society (which black nationalism seemed to threaten) and concluded that the key question had to be: "Is it good for Jews?" Over the next few years *Commentary* and its editors would usually conclude that it wasn't. The magazine published attacks on government intervention in social problems, affirmative action, and school integration. Arthur Jensen and other advocates of black genetic deficiency were given space to defend their right to express their views. Understandably, after the Jewish experience with Nazism, the magazine was somewhat uncomfortable about giving outright support to genetic theories. A few years later the magazine would not be so anxious to support the First Amendment rights of American Nazis.

The initial retreat from the alliance with blacks was primarily emotional, over charges of black anti-Semitism which had been greatly exaggerated. But the efforts to shift the civil rights struggle to economic issues were a much more real threat. Jews were an ethnic group that continued to live in proximity to blacks in large cities. Demands for quotas and affirmative action threatened Jewish jobs that were most directly accessible to black pressure: civil service, education, city government. The pressure for community control posed a direct threat to the base of Jewish political power in the cities. Many blacks saw this movement as the inevitable result of expectations raised by the newly acquired freedoms, but they had underestimated Jewish insecurity.

The love-hate relationship between blacks and Jews grew out of a combination of admiration and envy. The influence of Jews on American institutions and their representation in the most desirable professions was viewed as a guide for the development of black communities and political organizations. But the pressure of black competition was aimed at the very group blacks most admired. There were serious discussions in *Commentary* and other publications about possible linkups between black militants and the white Anglo-Saxon establishment. The concept of the meritocracy was refurbished for use in cases like *Bakke.*

But the Jewish establishment found unexpected support in its uneasy battle against minority demands. Many Gentiles were also threatened by pressures for massive structural readjustments and economic redistribution. The neoconservative line honed in *Commentary* and *Social Policy* was well received in *Harper's, The Atlantic,* and the newsweeklies. The reservations about minority demands no longer had to be the Jewish position. The Jewish establishment's concern about the image of Jews as radicals, Communists, and civil rights advocates as a possible trigger to anti-Semitism could be alleviated. Milton Friedman, Glazer, and Podhoretz could help Jews merge with the mainstream while they still preserved the group's interest. After all, their work was full of reaffirmations of American institutions and American ideals. The neoconservatives could wrap their views in the flag and reject demands for equality on patriotic grounds.

The New Racism was not a resurrection of the old ideas of racial superiority but a much more sophisticated attack on the abilities and motivations of minority groups. By rewriting the history of white ethnics in America, the neoconservatives could resolve the ticklish problem of societal obligation (or guilt). Glazer's *Affirmative Discrimination* outlined the argument for the washing of hands by white ethnics: "These groups were not particularly involved in the enslavement of the Negro or the creation of the Jim Crow pattern in the South, the conquest of part of Mexico, or the near extermination of the American Indian. They came to a country which provided them with [fewer] benefits than it now provides the protected groups. There is little reason for them to feel they should bear the burden of the redress of a past in which they had no or little part, or to assist those who presently receive more assistance than they did. We are indeed a nation of minorities; to enshrine some minorities as deserving of special benefits means not to defend minority rights against a discriminating majority but to favor some of these minorities over others."

This version of history, reprinted in the B'nai B'rith brief in support of Bakke, ignores the active role of ethnic whites in excluding blacks from the city political patronage machines they developed at the turn of the century, in excluding blacks from the labor movement from its inception to World War II, all acts that can be linked directly to the high unemployment figures and the relatively low economic and political status of blacks and other minorities today. These "favored minorities" need assistance today because they were denied the basic human rights of political power and full-time employment that gave other ethnic groups their first step into the economic mainstream.

But if guilt could be eliminated, the subordinate role of minorities still had to be explained. The new eugenicists stepped in with refurbished versions of nineteenth-century Social Darwinism to explain the oppression of blacks in terms of the "culture of poverty" and the genetic deficiencies promoted by Jensen, Shockley, and others. "The lower class individual lives in the slum and sees no reason to complain," wrote Edward C. Banfield, an adviser to Nixon and Rockefeller. "He does not care how dirty and dilapidated his housing is either inside or out, nor does he mind the inadequacy of such public facilities as schools, parks, libraries: indeed where such things exist, he destroys them by acts of vandalism if he can. Features that make the slum repellent to others actually please him." Banfield's *The Unheavenly City* became a popular college textbook in the 1970s by reviving ideas of motivation among the poor that had been abandoned thirty or forty years earlier.

But while these theories were enough to hold back the hordes in the inner city, ways had to be found to justify the retreat on affirmative action, which involved middle-class jobs. New code words came into use: *qualifications, competence, reverse discrimination, inarticulate.* All these fed into the new consensus that minority groups were making unreasonable demands. The initial rush into affirmative action had brought hundreds, even thousands, of minorities into jobs that put them into direct contact and competition with whites. Inevitably, some did not do well. Others could not cope with the pressures or lacked the proper preparation. The people doing the hiring meant well, but they often lacked experience to select members of these minority groups. Still, failures were used to justify the claims of lowered standards and unqualification.

But if minorities were not moved by such rationalizations, it was because an entire generation had gone to school and worked with whites. There no longer was any mystique about white superiority. Minorities saw whites who were competent and others who were not. They saw those who succeeded and those who failed, and many began to suspect that a double standard was in operation.

Dr. Price Cobbs, a San Francisco psychiatrist and management consultant for large corporations, has studied the dynamics of racial interaction at the middle-class level. "I don't have any question," says Cobbs, "that racism is alive and well." The coauthor of *Black Rage*, a 1960s best-seller on race relations, Cobbs says the subtlety of the New Racism makes it no less real. "A primary manifestation of this is the perception that white middle and top managers have about blacks. We are dealing with a range of preconscious assumptions about the relative competence of blacks, about the intelligence of blacks. You run into good, well-motivated people who think they are fair, who feel they have turned around attitudes and beliefs of ten to fifteen years ago but who continue to view blacks in a deficit model: 'less than,' 'not as good as,' 'if we could only do so-and-so to bring them up to speed.'

"If you look back," Cobbs goes on, "much of what passed for benign race relations was some kind of social comfort on the part of whites who were dealing with blacks. There are many whites who can be comfortable socially but who don't have any idea of the depth and degree of their remaining negative assumptions about people who are different."

Many of these preconscious assumptions can be found in the reporting on the *Bakke* case. *Less qualified minorities* is a term that was not supported by any evidence in the *Bakke* case, but the term followed the case from its early days to the morning of the Supreme Court's decision. These same assumptions make Allan Bakke a sympathetic victim but fail to see the minorities who are victims on a much greater scale and in far greater numbers.

The greatest danger that the New Racism poses to minority efforts at equality is its assumption that racism no longer exists, that whites have finally overcome several hundred years of cultural reinforcement, and that they can make objective judgments about the ability and performance of minority-group individuals. Neither history nor experience gives minorities reason to believe that is so. It is extremely difficult to develop mutual trust in a relationship where power is shared so unequally.

The racism that has been a virulent and violent force through most of our history has been changed greatly in the last two or three decades. Just the fact that open racism is no longer socially acceptable is one measure of the tremendous progress that has been made. But there is a danger as well in assuming that it is not there at all. What is less tangible is no less real.

The neoconservative catechism preaches assimilation of those who have gained entry into the middle class and isolation and punishment of those who have been unfortunate enough to become victims of society. Putting aside considerations of race, one has to wonder if such a dispassionate vision can appeal to the majority of Americans. Even the most ardent liberals would admit that there were failures and excesses in the Great Society experiment of the last decade, but rather than reject wholesale the concept of a helping hand, isn't there a way to build on this experience for a better future?

The desire of Americans for simple solutions to complicated problems has made them susceptible to demagoguery. The experience of minorities has always been dichotomous and has often been a catalyst for appealing to the better instincts of the majority. For a group of young blacks discussing the state of the race on a Sunday afternoon, there is no contradiction between their individual successes and their concern about the fate of those who have not been fortunate.

The duality of the minority experience in America helps them understand why a struggle for equality can often appear to be a threat to individual liberties. This experience helps explain why laws intended to protect minorities from oppression can be turned against them in convoluted debates over legal technicalities.

But there are people who understand that the *Bakke* case does not exist in a vacuum, that it is not isolated from the shifting political and economic winds of its time. But because the idea of justice has long been debated by men, they will not let this complicated process be reduced into a kind of athletic competition where the bottom line is the question of whether Allan Bakke wins or loses.

Eight

THE SOLICITOR'S
BRIEF

The Carter administration had been in office only a month when the U.S. Supreme Court agreed to hear the *Bakke* case. The various groups that claimed responsibility for Jimmy Carter's victory looked to his political appointments for evidence of his gratitude, and they were difficult to keep happy. Blacks complained about tokenism. Women were upset about the paucity of top-level appointments. Hispanics and labor expressed concern about the direction of selections. It was just about what could be expected in a new Democratic administration.

Carter's nomination of his good friend Griffin Bell to be attorney general of the United States provoked bitter complaints from some liberal and black groups, and they remained unhappy after his confirmation. Bell's selection of two blacks for top posts in the Justice Department was clearly intended to appease the critics. Wade McCree, a judge on the Sixth Circuit Court of Appeals, was named solicitor general. Drew Days, an attorney with the NAACP Legal Defense Fund, was appointed assistant attorney general for civil rights. Both men had impeccable establishment credentials and strong ties in the black political community, and their selection was universally hailed. But the case of the white aerospace engineer would become a controversial issue in their lives and demonstrate that the divisions over the *Bakke* case were not strictly along racial lines.

On the day the Supreme Court agreed to hear the case, attorneys for the University of California were in Washington soliciting the support of McCree and Days. Under federal law, the attorney general or the solicitor general can file a brief or appear before the Supreme Court in almost any case in which the government feels it has an interest. By tradition, parties in a suit are allowed to seek support from the government, which can often influence the decision of the Court. But the meeting was not very productive. University constitutional expert Paul Mishkin and Harvard Law professor Archibald Cox, who had been chosen to argue the case before the Court, urged the government to support their side of the case. They told the two Justice Department officials that the case was going to be a constitutional landmark which would have direct impact on the many federal programs that used affirmative action. But McCree and Days would make no firm commitment. They pointed to the weaknesses in the case record and gave Mishkin and Cox the impression they were not anxious to become involved.

Soon afterward Days, as the government's chief civil attorney, asked the major federal agencies whether the government should intervene as a friend of the court in *Bakke*. Often the Court will ask the government to participate in a case that has obvious federal interest. But the Supreme Court had not asked the government's input in *DeFunis*, nor, for reasons known only to the nine justices, had this invitation been extended in *Bakke*.

Over the next few months all the major federal agencies and departments informed Days that they would support intervention. In June, Days and McCree met with representatives of the various agencies to work out a basic position for the solicitor general's brief. The discussion was in general terms, but it was understood that the government would come out against fixed quotas but in favor of affirmative action.

At this point the process seemed to be moving along smoothly. The importance of the *Bakke* case was clear to both sides, and all the parties concerned were busy preparing and filing the 160 amicus briefs that presented their views. When a group of black attorneys made an informal inquiry through a White House aide, Griffin Bell said he would go along with whatever Days and McCree decided. The cause of affirmative action seemed to be in safe hands.

The first disturbance to the somewhat somnolent atmosphere around the government's brief took place on June 5, 1977, when HEW secretary Joseph Califano delivered the commencement address at the City College of New York. Califano called for a renewed commitment to an equal educational opportunity for all Americans. "We cannot rest as a society—and we will not rest as a government—until full minority participation in American education is a fact rather than a dream," Califano told his audience, which included a *New York Times* reporter. "And if we are serious about doing that, we must have a way of measuring our progress.

"I know the dangers and potential for injustice that are inherent in any system of arbitrary, long-term quotas. For in our efforts to eliminate differences and inequalities, quotas may actually aggravate them. Arbitrary quotas will not be a part of our enforcement programs; we want to rely on the good faith and special effort of all who join us in the final march against discrimination. But we will also rely—because we must rely—on numerical goals as a benchmark of progress."

The headline on the next day's *Times* read: "Califano Asks 'Goals' Not 'Quotas.'" Many Jewish organizations, which were already uneasy about the new administration, were outraged by the speech and demanded a retraction. One group took a full-page advertisement in the *Times* calling for Califano's resignation. The president was in trouble with an important group of supporters. He extracted a retreat from Califano and issued a somewhat ambiguous statement condemning rigid quotas but affirming his commitment to equal opportunity.

Maybe because it was summer in Washington or maybe because no direct link had been made between the president's position and the government's brief in the *Bakke* case, the tempest died down almost as rapidly as it had erupted. One additional factor was also the fact that the two top officials in the government's brief were black.

Both Days and McCree could have been called representatives of the talented tenth by W. E. B. Du Bois. Despite their differences in age, they were examples of the best of the black "old guard," men who had achieved success long before affirmative action came to be the vogue. McCree was a native of Iowa who had attended the exclusive Boston Latin School, Fisk University, and Harvard Law School, where former Transportation secretary William Coleman had been a classmate. McCree had been an elected judge in Michigan, and he had earned a reputation on the court of appeals for his finely crafted opinions.

Days, a decade younger than McCree, was the first black assistant attorney general to head any division of the Justice Department in its 187-year history. Born in Tampa, Florida, and reared in suburban New Rochelle, New York, Days had his share of memories of blatant discrimination. But he had clearly overcome the obstacles. In the 1960s he was one of five blacks in his Yale Law School class. His involvement with the Yale Russian Chorus led him to meet his wife, Ann Ramsey Langdon, a direct descendant of Sarah Ball, a cousin of George Washington's. In addition to working for the Legal Defense Fund, Days had spent two years teaching at the Temple University Law School.

The first draft of the government's brief was written by Days and two attorneys on his staff. The draft went to McCree, who gave it to an assistant to revise. Beyond that, responsibility for the contents become vague. Until it went to the government printer, the different versions would appear to be the work of many hands. Sections were pasted up, cut, crossed out, and corrected by hand.

Toward the end of August the White House gave the first signs of concern about the brief. There were some casual inquiries, but the message from McCree's office made it clear that it thought it none of the White House's business. Traditionally, the attorney general was considered the top political job in the Justice Department. The solicitor general had a more scholarly and abstract image, and McCree clearly wanted to keep that aura of independence. When a newspaper story appeared suggesting that the government would support the university, the White House renewed its efforts to determine the contents of the brief. White House aides extracted a concession from McCree's assistants that the president had the right to have his views expressed in the government's brief, but they were told to route their suggestions through Bell.

Finally, a draft was delivered to President Carter by the attorney general on September 1. Carter turned it over to the chief of his domestic policy staff, Stuart Eizenstat. The brief was obviously in preparation, Eizenstat noted from the corrections, additions, and revisions. He criticized its style, organization, and tone. But the content was even more important, and Eizenstat considered that a political disaster. The brief supported the admission of Bakke, declared the admissions program at Davis unconstitutional, and gave tentative support to the use of race in admissions.

In a long memo to the president, Eizenstat warned that the brief would be regarded as the administration's definitive statement on affirmative action. He said the language of the brief would harm the government's affirmative action programs and added that the trial record was too thin to warrant support for Bakke's admission. The memo was passed to Bell, who once again had it transmitted to the solicitor general.

By this time the rumors about the Justice Department's position had alarmed civil rights advocates enough that the Congressional Black Caucus arranged for University of Pennsylvania professor Ralph Smith and several other attorneys to discuss the case with them. Many had been involved in Capitol Hill politics and had paid little attention to the controversy surrounding *Bakke*. The lawyers warned them that it was important that the Justice Department take a strong position on the issues or affirmative action would be jeopardized. The caucus was scheduled to meet with President Carter on September 7, and before that meeting they discussed their concern about *Bakke* with Vice-President Mondale. Mondale said he had not read the brief, but he arranged a meeting with Bell and other Justice Department officials for that afternoon. But the meeting was not very productive. The legislators knew very little about the facts of the case, and they did not know what was in the government's brief. In the words of one participant, "McCree just whipped them."

By now the controversy had spilled into the public arena. The *New York Times* published a story on September 8 declaring "Justice Dept. Brief Opposes Race Quotas at Coast University." At a second meeting between the caucus and the Justice Department officials the next day, it became clear that there were profound disagreements between the politicians' concern about political repercussions and McCree's intellectual approach to the law.

The politicians and their lawyers decided that political action was the next step, and they made plans to stop the brief at the White House. They found an unexpected ally. There was an anonymous telephone call to one of the concerned officials. If he went outside, he would meet a taxicab with a copy of the brief on the backseat. Finally, the civil rights forces had a copy of the government's brief. They saw immediately that their concerns had been well founded.

The brief was not a political document at all. It was written in a scholarly, neutral tone reminiscent of a law review discussion. In discussing "minority-sensitive" programs, the brief said: "We conclude that the case for such programs, although not one-sided, is compelling. We discuss all the arguments not because we doubt the constitutionality of such programs but because they are serious arguments and not all arguments advanced in support of such programs are persuasive."

In different type the argument continued: "It is better, we conclude, to face the difficulties and to identify the arguments on which we do not rely here."

The brief criticized programs like the one at Davis, which only compared minority applicants to one another. This would result in the selection of "those minority applicants who have suffered the least from discrimination. The pertinent comparison should be between the most highly qualified whites and the most highly qualified blacks, Chicanos and Asian-Americans." The concern about quality could be attributed to McCree and Days, two men who had met the best standards of excellence and who clearly resented any implication that minorities could not compete with whites, but the ponderous style did not seem to be the work of McCree, with his reputation as a legal stylist.

The problems with the argument were clear. Opponents of affirmative action had used the most strident and extreme arguments to support Allan Bakke. The proponents of affirmative action could not afford the tentative and hesitant tone of the brief as the government's position on the issues. Through the weekend a group of black attorneys shut themselves up in a hotel room with "fried chicken and Chivas Regal" and prepared an analysis and critique for a third meeting with McCree and Days the following Monday. The lawyers tried to get in touch with McCree, but they were told he had gone to Detroit. They reached through the small network of black professionals and had contacts in Detroit corner McCree.

They expressed their concern about the offending passages in the brief. How could they know? he asked; they hadn't read the brief. They quoted some of the most disturbing passages. The solicitor general was furious about the breach of confidentiality. But copies of the draft were already circulating among members of the president's Cabinet, which would also meet on the following Monday. Califano was outraged and ordered an assistant to prepare an alternative brief. Eizenstat and other White House officials were dissatisfied with this latest version and expressed their displeasure to Justice Department officials. Caucus members approached HUD secretary Patricia Harris and UN ambassador Andrew Young about the problem. That Saturday, September 10, McCree, under heavy political pressure, called his office from Detroit and dictated four points that would become the core of government's brief. The ambiguous and tentative language of the earlier drafts was replaced with a call for strong support of affirmative action that allowed the use of race, opposed rigid racial quotas, declared there was an inadequate finding of facts, and urged the case be sent back to California. The new brief also made it clear that the government's interest was primarily in affirmative action—not in Allan Bakke.

On Monday the political assault on the Justice Department's brief was two-pronged. At the Cabinet meeting Califano, Harris, and Young made a spirited defense of affirmative action and deplored the strong position against quotas. The meeting between the caucus members, their legal advisers, and the Justice Department officials was better orchestrated. Representative Parren Mitchell of Maryland, the Democratic chairman of the caucus, made some brief opening remarks and gave the floor to Representative Louis Stokes, who talked about the need for partnership between the legislative and executive branches of government. James Nabrit, Jr., an attorney with the NAACP Legal Defense Fund, traced the historical basis of the Fourteenth Amendment in protecting the rights of blacks. University of Pennsylvania Law School dean Louis Pollak talked about the role of the solicitor general as the attorney representing the interests of all the people. McCree's predecessor, Robert Bork, a conservative Yale law professor, had argued forcefully for the consideration of race in drawing legislative district lines to strengthen the vote of minorities. Pollak quoted Bork's argument that to be colorblind was to be blind to reality. Smith pointed to the shortcomings of the court record and argued against support for Bakke.

The second hour of the meeting was given over to questions, and again, there seemed to be a curious gap between McCree's assertion about the brief and what it actually contained. On one occasion Days seemed surprised when one of the attorneys read from the document. The confusion remained, but it seemed clear that the political pressures would have an impact. After the meeting the caucus warned that President Carter would "discredit his presidency in the eyes of history" if he endorsed the existing version of the brief. "The brief's legal positions pronounce a death sentence for programs which use race or ethnicity to achieve integration or equality," the caucus said in a position paper issued after the meeting with McCree and Days.

After this latest salvo of criticism, McCree and Days took personal charge of the final drafting of the government's position and took a line much closer to what the caucus and the Cabinet members had advocated. The brief supported the use of race for affirmative action and urged the Supreme Court to send the case back to California to determine if Bakke's rights had been violated. The influence that the black and liberal forces were able to exert on the White House was testimony to the structural changes that had taken place within the country's political system. Minority groups had complained that they had no input into the defense of the case, but they had been able to change the direction of government in the preparation of its position on the issue.

But the sequence of events also reflected on the peculiar situation of blacks who find themselves in positions of power. At one point in the discussions, McCree rejected the suggestion that he should be true to "the black community." "I have to be true to myself," he asserted. His concerns probably did reflect the fears among some blacks that affirmative action programs would be used to cheapen the achievements of minorities. In addition, what was the obligation of a member of a minority group to his or her community and what was his obligation to his own deep-seated convictions? The problem for the solicitor general was that his position was much more political than he wanted it to be. Maybe there would be a time when men and women like McCree could carry out the duties of their office without giving consideration to race and ethnic origin. But as with the argument about color blindness, it would be some time still before that ideal could be translated into a reality.

Nine

A DISCUSSION
AMONG GENTLEMEN

The intensity of the game the night before had been excep-
tional, a classic confrontation of athletes at the peak of ability.
The arguments over contracts, free agents, and salaries were
set aside for a moment, and it was just baseball again, that
synthesis of body and mind that raises sport to the level of art.
At the White House, General Olusegun Obasanjo, the Nigerian
head of state, warned President Carter that armed conflict was
inevitable in southern Africa and would result in black rule.
His statements were a reminder that the balance of power in
the world had shifted to a point where black Africa could
chart its own course with destiny and simply inform the
world's most powerful nation out of simple courtesy.

Against the background of conflicts in sports and world
politics, the nine justices of the United States Supreme Court
prepared to hear the case of *Regents of the University of California* v. *Allan Bakke*. At Yankee Stadium, Paul Blair's sharp
single in the twelfth inning gave the home team a 4–3 victory
over the Los Angeles Dodgers in the hundredth World Series
game played in the House That Ruth Built. No one had kept
count, but confrontations over race were as common to the
Supreme Court as extra-inning victories in the South Bronx.
The dilemma of discrimination in a democracy had been discussed often in this imposing building with the words *Equal*

Justice Under Law carved over the entrance. Once more the application of this slogan would play to a full house on a bright, sunny day full of the golds and reds that mark the end of the baseball season.

Certain news items on that October 12, 1977, made the day more familiar than might be expected. In New York two white policemen were accused of killing a black postal worker, resulting in a meeting between the police commissioner and a group of angry black citizens, led by a Baptist minister from Brooklyn. The *Washington Post,* basking in the afterglow of Watergate, devoted considerable space to a sociological study of pimps—complete with a vocabulary list that was closer to Iceberg Slim than Pulitzer Prize–quality journalism. It all made a tableau of autumnal *déjà vu,* American style: diplomacy, racial conflict, and now a debate on inequality with a peculiar O. Henry twist. The complainant this time was white, the defendants were white, and the most affected parties, the blacks and browns who still sought to have the generous motto of equality apply to them, sat on the sidelines like spectators along the first-base line.

Few bothered to discuss baseball as the long line of people wound its way toward the building that had prompted Charles Evans Hughes to proclaim, "The Republic endures and this is the symbol of its faith," when the cornerstone was laid in 1932. In hope of seeing the process of democracy unfold, the most determined had camped at four o'clock the day before in the shadow of this Greek temple to American law. Such all-night vigils were not uncommon outside baseball stadiums at World Series time, but here they served as testimony to the intensity of this confrontation. Across the street from the court, several hundred demonstrators raised placards and banners they hoped would influence the events taking place inside.

Court officials could not accommodate the crush of spectators, so they finally decided to rotate groups through the courtroom, limiting their participation in history to three-minute intervals. Most would have to wait for eyewitness reports and news stories from the media representatives who had competed fiercely for the 100 ringside seats. For once, representatives of print and electronic media would operate under the same handicaps because the Court allowed no intrusion of modern technology. All the reporters would have to depend on pad and pen to record the event. Even as the crowds waited, Court employees placed ten-inch white quill pens on writing pads at the counsel tables in the courtroom. All these gestures were in keeping with the image of tradition promoted by the sixteen Corinthian columns of the Court's facade, the black robes of the justices, and the red velvet curtains around the courtroom's perimeter. The mystique of tradition and formality gave the Court its power, and this power was guarded jealously.

The guards began admitting spectators at about nine-thirty, guiding them through the metal detectors that were one concession to the political realities of the time. Members of the press were shuffled off to the packed narrow alcove on the left side of the courtroom, where their view of the events would be partially obscured by the red curtains and the proliferation of Greek columns. Admission to the press area and the main courtroom were, in fact, reasons for triumph, for access to tickets had been at least as difficult as to seats for the World Series.

This was a select audience of government officials, attorneys, and interested parties. The men wore the vested suits of dark blue and gray that were the uniform of the legal profession, and they greeted each other with the enthusiasm of old classmates at the Harvard-Yale game. In fact, most of them were graduates of the best law schools: Harvard, Yale, Stanford, Columbia. This was the eastern legal establishment, divided now by this troublesome issue but still united by their common experiences in education and society. The scarcity of women was testimony to the years when they were exceptions in this professional elite of law. There were a number of blacks, but few if one considered the special interest this case had for them. In 1952, when the Court had heard *Brown,* almost half the audience was black. The lack of a strong black presence here illustrated the peculiar sideline role that minority groups had played in this case and the divergence of the propaganda of equality from the reality of justice that was at the heart of this case.

Those blacks who had gained admission to this session had survived the rigorous process of selection by the establishment. They held many "firsts" at important schools and prestigious law firms, the peculiar honorific measure that had somewhere distorted advancements in the attitudes of whites into a measure of progress for blacks. The men and women who were now members of this club had struggled for their equality before the advent of affirmative action, quotas, and special programs, and while they were at ease with their white colleagues, their presence here was an indication that they had not abandoned their struggle for equality.

Despite the tensions surrounding this case, the mood of the courtroom was clearly festive as the crowd filed in. This was a social event divorced from the real-life passions that enveloped the case. Like opening night at the theater, the show was not limited to the stage. The attorneys—Archibald Cox and Donald Reidhaar for the university, Wade McCree for the United States government, Colvin and Robert Links for Bakke —took their places at the long tables below the elevated mahogany bench. Out of sight of the audience, the justices performed one final ritual, the round of handshakes, each justice with every other, a reminder of common purpose despite serious differences.

The sharp rap of the gavel brought an end to the rumble

of conversation, and the audience stood in the traditional display of respect for authority. The justices took their seats according to the custom of seniority: Chief Justice Warren Burger at the center, the most senior members of the Court at his immediate right and left, the newest justices, William Rehnquist and John Paul Stevens, at the far ends of the bench. Burger read the docket number of the first case on the day's calendar and nodded toward the university counsel's table. "Mr. Cox, you may proceed whenever you're ready."

Cox, a tall, thin, and scholarly man who had been chosen to argue for the university, rose to address the court. He was no stranger to the nine men seated in a half circle before him. Like three of the justices, he was a Harvard man. He had argued many cases before this Court, first as solicitor general during the Kennedy administration and later as the first Watergate special prosecutor. He had been fired after five months by President Nixon in the infamous "Saturday Night Massacre" which ended with the resignations of Attorney General Elliot Richardson and Deputy Attorney General William Ruckelshaus. Cox had gone back to Harvard to be Williston Professor of Law. He was more peer than supplicant, and the justices understood this. He was formal enough to buoy the traditions of the Court, yet familiar enough to participate in a discussion among gentlemen.

There had been much speculation in California about who would argue for the university before the Supreme Court. No one doubted the university would follow the common practice in such cases and hire an outside counsel. The regents were concerned about the charges of collusion and incompetence generated by the early handling of the case. To rehabilitate its image, the university needed an attorney whose integrity and reputation were at least as impressive as his ability and credentials.

Paul Mishkin, a respected constitutional scholar on the Berkeley campus, was given primary responsibility for preparing the university's brief, but his reputation was limited to scholarly circles. Nathaniel Colley, a Yale graduate who was probably the most successful and prominent black attorney in California, was recommended by minority organizations, along with William Coleman, the secretary of transportation in the Ford administration, whose academic and professional credentials few white attorneys could match. But neither Colley nor Coleman was approached. The regents wanted to make it clear that their lawyer represented the university and higher education and not the interests of minority groups. By this curious turn of logic, Cox became the obvious choice.

Cox made the traditional opening statement: "Mr. Chief Justice, and may it please the Court." He spoke deliberately and conversationally. He might have been conducting a seminar at the Harvard Law School, picking his words carefully but with the full assurance of a man among his peers. That unspoken kinship would assert itself throughout the day.

This case, here on certiorari from the Supreme Court of California, presents a single vital question: whether a State university, which is forced by limited resources to select a relatively small number of students from a much larger number of well-qualified applicants, is free, voluntarily, to take into account the fact that a qualified applicant is black, Chicano, Asian or Native American in order to increase the number of qualified members of those minority groups trained for the educated professions and participating in them, professions from which minorities were long excluded because of generations of pervasive racial discrimination.

Cox's opening had been carefully drafted, with each word selected for a purpose. He had condensed the vital elements of the case he was about to make into one forceful sentence. He told the Court that the California Supreme Court had answered the wrong question. This was not a matter of whether the university could prefer less qualified minorities over better qualified whites, but a question of whether the university could consider race as a factor in selecting from a large pool of qualified applicants. He reminded the Court that the university's choice in allocating these resources was a *voluntary* decision by a responsible (white) policy-making body. It was a choice no different from many other choices made at functioning academic institutions. The Court had to choose whether the states would remain "free" to make such choices. And finally, he pointed out that the decision to consider race was made not in order to discriminate against whites but to remedy the effects of "generations of pervasive discrimination against minorities."

Cox's argument was aimed at the conservative wing of the Court. Justices Rehnquist, Burger, Harry Blackmun, and Lewis Powell, all Nixon appointees, were often joined by Potter Stewart and Byron White in a majority that took a jaundiced view of Supreme Court intervention in state efforts to resolve social problems. This Burger Court had begun to reverse a trend toward government by judiciary that had been the hallmark of the Court under Earl Warren but that this group viewed as constitutionally suspect.

The Court's record on racial issues was mixed. Many of its decisions involving minority plaintiffs had actually aimed at limiting federal protection of individual rights. In *International Brotherhood of Teamsters* v. *U.S.*, a case with profound implications that received little media attention, the Supreme Court had refused to overturn union seniority systems that continued favored privilege for whites despite evidence of past discrimination against blacks. What it had done was doom an entire generation of black workers to permanent inequality. Yet, in a case involving voting rights in New York, the Court had allowed the creation of a predominantly black election district despite white protests that their political power was being diluted.

Cox outlined the "three facts or realities" dominating the situation at the Davis Medical School which he felt the Court had to consider:

The first is that the number of qualified applicants for the nation's professional schools is vastly greater than the number of places available. This is a fact and an inescapable fact. In 1975–76, for example, there were roughly 30,000 qualified applicants for admission to medical school, a much greater number of actual applicants, and there were only about 14,000 places. At Davis, there were 25 applicants for every seat in 1973; in 1974, the ratio had risen to 37 to 1. So the problem is one of selection among qualified applicants, not of ability to gain from a professional education.

The second fact, on which there is no need for me to elaborate, but it is a fact, for generations racial discrimination in the United States, much of it stimulated by unconstitutional State action, isolated certain minorities, condemned them to inferior education, and shut them out of the most important and satisfying aspects of American life, including higher education and the professions.

And then there is one third fact. There is no racially blind method of selection which will enroll today more than a trickle of minority students in the nation's colleges and professions. These are the realities which the University of California at Davis faced in 1968, and which, I say, I think the Court must face when it comes to its decision.

It was a succinct and forceful opening. Cox's pace quickened somewhat, and he began to outline the history of the Task Force program at Davis. He was interrupted by Justice White, who asked if there was something in the record to indicate *who* proposed or adopted the Task Force program.

cox: It's indicated that it was adopted by the faculty of the school or was voted by the faculty. That appears in Dr. Lowrey's testimony. And it also appears——

WHITE: Of course he [Dr. Lowrey] wasn't there then, was he?

COX: No, I guess he must have learned when he came somewhat later. There is nothing more than his testimony gained on—I may say I have seen minutes that——

WHITE: Is there anything on the record indicating the approval of the Regents [of the Task Force program] other than the fact that they are defendants in the suit?

COX: No, because the Regents had delegated to each faculty of the school the responsibility for admissions.

WHITE: Thank you.

Cox seemed to be floundering. He was arguing from a trial court record not of his own making, and although he had studied it well, he could not correct its deficiencies. His answers appeared evasive and detracted from the impact of his opening statement. He tried to regain his ground by adding his personal endorsement of the decision by the regents to delegate admission standards to each college.

"So that this was left to the different colleges, and very wisely I think because autonomous institutions, each trying to solve this problem in their own way, may give all of us the benefit of the experience of trial and error, creativity. That's the virtue of not constitutionalizing problems of this kind."

Cox was relying on his own personal status to lend weight to his argument. He was also reinforcing his theme of judicial restraint and nonintervention. At this point Cox unexpectedly opened the Pandora's box of the quota issue: "I want to emphasize that the designation of 16 places was not a quota, at least as I would use that word. Certainly it was not a quota in the older sense of an arbitrary limit put on the number of members of a nonpopular group who would be admitted to an institution which was looking down its nose at them."

The fact that a certain number of places was set aside for minority students was the most vulnerable aspect of the program Cox had been hired to defend. The California Supreme Court had flatly rejected the practice of setting aside sixteen places. The quota issue had, more than anything else in the *Bakke* case, aroused the passion of traditionally liberal Jewish and labor organizations in supporting Bakke's position. Much of the discussion of the case in the media had focused on quotas. Apparently, Cox had decided to take the issue head-on. The Court would raise it sooner or later, and by starting the discussion himself, he could choose his ground in making a defense. The justices were not about to let him off easily.

STEWART: It did put a limit on the number of white people, didn't it?

COX: I think that it limited the number of non-minority, and therefore, essentially white[s], yes. But there are two things to be said about that. One is that this was not pointing the finger at a group which had been marked as inferior in any sense and it was undifferentiated. It operated against a wide variety of people. So I think it was not stigmatizing in the sense of the old quota against Jews was stigmatizing, in any way.

STEWART: But it did put a limit on their number in each class?

COX: I'm sorry?

STEWART: But it did put a limit on the number of non-minority people in each class?

COX: It did put a limit, no question about that, and I don't mean to infer that. And I will direct myself to it a little later, if I may.

STEVENS: Do you agree, then, that there was a quota of 84?

COX: Well, I would deny that it was a quota. We agree that there were 16 places set aside for qualified disadvantaged minority students. Now, if that number—if setting aside a number, if the amount of resources——

STEVENS: No, the question is not whether the 16 is a quota. The question is whether the 84 is a quota. And what is your answer to that?

COX: I would say that neither is properly defined as a quota.

STEVENS: And then, why not?

COX: Because, in the first place—because of my understanding of the meaning of "quota." And I think the decisive things are the facts. And the operative facts are: this is not something imposed from outside, as the quotas are in employment, or the targets are in employment sometimes, today. It was not a limit on the number of minority students. Other minority students were in fact accepted through the regular admissions program. It was not a guarantee of a minimum number of minority students, because all of them had to be—and the testimony is that all of them were—fully qualified . . .

It did say that if there are 16 qualified minority students, and they were also disadvantaged, then 16 places shall be filled by them and only 84 places will be available to others.

POWELL: Mr. Cox, the facts are not in dispute. Does it really matter what we call this program?

COX: No. I quite agree with you, Mr. Justice. I was trying to emphasize that the facts here have none of the aspects . . . that lead us to think of "quota" as a bad word. What we call this doesn't matter, and if we call it a quota, knowing the facts and deciding according to the operative facts and [we are] not influenced by the semantics, it couldn't matter less.

In asking the Court to look beyond the connotations of the word, Cox was saying the system did not stigmatize whites.

But again the facts he and Justice Powell wanted so much to agree on did not exist. The number sixteen had become established in the case as the goal or quota or whatever for the Task Force, and the university was stuck with it. But a later search had shown that only fifteen minority students had been admitted in 1974. One place had been given back to the regular admissions committee, apparently because the Task Force felt the sixteenth minority candidate was not strong enough. But because this fact was not in the trial record, it could not rescue Cox in his effort to convince the justices that the process was not unconstitutional. He tried to clarify his point by using an analogy.

COX: Justice Stevens, let us suppose that . . . the school was much concerned by the lack of qualified general practitioners in Northern California, as indeed it was, . . . and it told the admissions committee: "Get people who come from rural communities, if they are qualified, and who express the intention of going back there." And the Dean of Admissions might well say: "Well, how much importance do you give this?" And the members of the faculty might say, by vote or otherwise, "We think it's terribly important. As long as they are qualified, try and get ten in that group." I don't think I would say that it was a quota of 90 students for others. And I think this, while it involves race, of course, that's why we're here, or color, really it is essentially the same thing. The decision of the University was that there are social purposes, or purposes aimed in the end at eliminating racial injustice in this country and in bringing equality of opportunity, there will be purposes served by including minority students.

BLACKMUN: Is it the same as an athletic scholarship?

COX: Well, I——

BLACKMUN: So many places reserved for athletic scholarships.

Cox hesitated. The analogy was correct, but there was the unflattering comparison of minority students with athletes whose intellectual abilities were questionable.

COX: In the sense—I don't like to liken it to that in terms of its importance, but I think there are a number of places that may be set aside for an institution's different aims, and the aim of some institutions does seem to be to have athletic prowess. So that in that sense this is a choice made to promote the schools, the faculty's choice of educational and professional objectives.

With a sarcastic note in his voice, Blackmun asked Cox if it were not true that athletic prowess was the aim of most institutions.

COX: Well, I come from Harvard, sir.

A ripple of laughter swept through the courtroom.

COX: I don't know whether it's our aim, but we don't do very well.
BLACKMUN: But I can remember a time when—Mr. Cox. I can remember a time when you did . . .
COX: Yes. Yes. You're quite right.

This time the laughter in the courtroom was unrestrained as the audience shared the joke between two Harvard men. The tension had been unbearable as Cox negotiated the thicket of the quota issue without too much success, in the eyes of most observers. But the banter broke the suspense while restoring the special kinship of those on the bench and the attorney for the university in this lament for Harvard football and their common interest in preserving the quality of higher education.

One exception to the laughter was Justice Thurgood Marshall. The black justice found it difficult to share in the levity of the moment when so much was at stake. As chief counsel of the NAACP Marshall had acquired a reputation for a good sense of humor he used well to get out of difficult situations. But now, as a Supreme Court justice, he needed to laugh only when he thought something was funny. A veteran of ten years on the Court, he was junior only to Brennan, Stewart, and White. At age sixty-nine, the toll of his thirty years as chief counsel of the NAACP was visible in his pale complexion and his puffy, jowly features. He must have thought of the day twenty-five years earlier, when he still cut a matinee idol figure, when he stood on the other side of this high bench, arguing a case that was the culmination of the most extensive master plan for litigation ever devised.

In the days that had begun with his case against the law school of the University of Maryland in his hometown, Baltimore, Marshall was a driven man: traveling long, hard miles on dirt roads in South Carolina, Mississippi, and Texas; holding strategy sessions in the back rooms of bars over fried fish and chicken; sleeping in beds too short for his six-foot-three frame. Marshall had performed a mammoth task of picking cases carefully, making the best possible record, finding expert witnesses, and taking the cases up to the Supreme Court. The task had required an incredible commitment of mind and soul against overwhelming odds.

Marshall understood that the long struggle to end the caste system of legal segregation was just a beginning in the effort to give blacks equal access to the benefits of society. But despite *Brown,* he had seen segregation in the North increase rather than decrease. He had seen the exodus of whites from the cities to the suburbs. And he had been on the Court when it overturned a Detroit desegregation order that would have bused blacks into predominantly white suburbs. Marshall did not need evidence in the record to verify past discrimination against minorities. He had lived with it for seventy years, and he could see how far the nation had to go to achieve what most of his people still dreamed about.

He remained silent through the arguments of Cox and Wade McCree, the solicitor general. He might have argued the case differently, with more emphasis on the historical and moral justifications for such programs and less on the importance of university autonomy. But he was no longer the field general of his memories, and this was not his battle to fight. His turn would come later.

Justice Rehnquist wanted to know whether Cox felt the program would still be constitutional if Davis had decided "that instead of setting aside 16 seats for minority doctors, they would set aside 50 seats until the balance was redressed and the minority population of doctors equaled that of the population as a whole." The question was a trap that Cox knew he needed to avoid. If he conceded fifty was wrong, what was right with forty, thirty, or sixteen? He also understood what troubled the Court's youngest member. If the Court allowed the university to set sixteen seats aside, what was to prevent fifty seats from being set aside, a figure most people would consider unacceptable?

Had Cox been discussing the case over a drink at the Harvard Club he might have told Rehnquist that he knew damn well that such a possibility was out of the question. But here Cox clearly floundered. He first tried to frame a constitutional principle:

COX: . . . So long as the numbers are chosen . . . and they are shown to be reasonably adaptable to the social goal . . . then there is no reason to condemn a program because a particular number is chosen.

I would say that as the number goes up, the danger of invidiousness or the danger that this is being done not for social purposes but to favor one group . . . is great.

Cox had finally hemmed and hawed his way to a firmer footing. The civil rights lawyers in the audience sighed. That was the best argument. It was simply a matter of the majority's being reasonable; after all, they were in control of the process.

Justice Powell wanted to pursue the numbers a bit longer:

POWELL: Mr. Cox, along this same line of discussion, would you relate the number in any way to population, and if so, the population of the state, the city or to what standard?

COX: Well, the number 16 here is not in any way linked to the population in California.

POWELL: It's 23 per cent, I think, for minorities.

On the surface, Powell's question was a simple request for information, but Cox recognized an issue raised in many of the amicus briefs on behalf of Bakke and took it on.

COX: Well, this was 16 . . . I'll be quite frank to say that I think one of the things which causes all of us concern about these programs is the danger that they will give rise to some notion of group entitlement to numbers regardless either of the ability of the individual . . . or of their potential contribution to society.

This conversation of gentlemen was in full bloom now. The "causes all of us concern" could not have been uttered by Nat Colley or William Coleman, no matter how suave and patrician they were. No black man could have been secure enough in the "us" to get away with that. Cox took the opportunity to talk about qualifications, another of the emotionally charged words associated with the case.

COX: The other thing I was going to say . . . is that while it is true that Mr. Bakke and some others, under conventional standards for admission, would be ranked above the minority applicant, I want to emphasize that, . . .

there's nothing that shows that after the first two years at medical school the grade point averages will make the minority students poorer medical students, and still less to show that it makes them poorer doctors or poorer citizens or poorer people.

Justice Brennan picked up the pursuit of facts. He wanted to know if the record indicated how race was taken into account in the benchmark ratings of applicants. The vaguest area of the record was under scrutiny again. Cox could speculate that race had or had not been considered, but he didn't know. Brennan wanted to know if the benchmark scores of regular and Task Force students was comparable, but there was no way to tell. During his deposition, Dr. Lowrey had suggested that benchmark scores for the Task Force might be 30 points lower, but there had never been a comparison.

cox: There wasn't any occasion to put them on the same scale. Because if you were qualified, minority and disadvantaged, then you were eligible for one of the 16 places and there was no occasion for you to be compared with anyone in the general pool.

The California Supreme Court had based its decision on the premise that "by the university's own standards Bakke was better qualified" than Task Force students. But Cox was saying that minority applicants were judged on an entirely different set of standards and that relative qualification was not anywhere in the record despite the most common characterization of the case.

Cox's time was running out. The justices asked him about alternatives. He said that minorities were but a small segment of the disadvantaged and that only by taking race into consideration could the numbers be improved. Warren Burger wanted to know about Orientals:

BURGER: Is there . . . a specific finding in this record that Orientals, as one identifiable group, have been disadvantaged?

COX: Well, I think the decisions of this Court show better than anything else that they have been the victims of de jure discrimination over the years.

The truth was that once again the record was lacking. Cox could cite several cases involving discrimination against Asians, and the Court switched to another line of questions. They would take the issue up with McCree. What about Title VI of the Civil Rights Act of 1964, they asked Cox; could they use that to make their finding and avoid a constitutional decision?

Title VI, which forbids discrimination "on the ground of race, color, or national origin," was viewed by legal scholars as an escape valve for the Court. By ruling on the basis of a statute, the Court could avoid the thundering implications of a judgment rooted in the Constitution. But asking the university to choose its battlefield put Cox in a difficult position. If he agreed that Title VI applied, the Court might avoid the issues the university wanted them to confront.

After a few hesitant thrusts at the issue, Cox suggested he be allowed to answer in written form. A week later the Court would ask for supplemental briefs and cause a rash of speculation about its decision.

Cox asked if he could save his last few minutes for rebuttal. Burger said he had little time left, but since the Court had asked an inordinate number of questions, each side would get an additional five minutes. Cox thanked the chief justice and sat down.

The only friend of the court ordinarily allowed to make an oral argument before the Supreme Court is the government of the United States. This concession is made in recognition of the fact that some cases have an impact far beyond the interests of the parties to the dispute. Often the government's presentation is only a formality, but in a case like *Bakke,* the decision could affect millions of citizens and many important federal programs. Despite Reynold Colvin's argument that this was a simple case of one man trying to get into medical school, this disagreement involved major national policy issues.

On this day the citizens of the United States were represented by Solicitor General Wade McCree, Jr., only the second black man to hold this post; Thurgood Marshall had been the first. If McCree had not been speaking for the government, he would have been in the audience. Except for the medium brown complexion and the black, wavy crop of hair, he would have blended in easily with the high-priced attorneys in the audience.

But McCree's reputation had been seriously undermined by the controversy surrounding the Justice Department brief. He had struggled with conflicting roles as representatives of the United States and as President Carter's spokesman in the Supreme Court. He would also be the only black person to address the Court on the issue. His color made him a spokesman for blacks and other minority groups whether he liked it or not. How many bright young black men had been reminded that at a crucial moment the entire race would be accountable for their actions? Few blacks could escape this demand for racial responsibility.

McCree spoke from a prepared text, deliberately, with just a touch of the resonance found among preachers and orators. By education, achievement, and position he was formally a member of this small circle of gentlemen. But his understanding of the workings of American society and the role he was to play on this day precluded any resemblance to the informality of Cox.

MC CREE: The interest of the United States as amicus curiae stems from the fact that the Congress and the Executive branch have adopted many minority-sensitive programs that take race or minority status into account in order to achieve the goal of equal opportunity.

The final version of the government's brief had substantially supported the university's position. The government supported the use of racial classifications only to correct past discrimination. But instead of asking the Supreme Court to overrule the California decision, the government wanted it sent back for more facts.

McCree's oral argument followed the central theme of the Justice Department brief but emphasized the pervasive nature of discrimination in American life that made remedial programs necessary. He traced the history of racism through the Constitution and pointed to the crowded federal dockets as evidence of continued resistance.

MC CREE: Indeed, many children born in 1954, when *Brown* was decided, are today, 23 years later, the very persons knocking on the doors of professional schools, seeking admission, about the country. They are persons who, in many instances, have been denied fulfillment of the promise of that decision because of resistance to this court's decision that was such a landmark when it was handed down.

McCree's presentation was not the most dynamic the justices had heard, but it served to remind the Court that the country was still involved in a struggle for equality and that many victims of that struggle existed outside the sheltered atmosphere of the Court and the intellectual debate now taking place. There was one of those strange juxtapositions of history and irony here. McCree quoted a phrase he had heard at the meeting with the Congressional Black Caucus, a phrase originated by his predecessor, Robert Bork.

MC CREE: To be blind to race today is to be blind to reality.

While the solicitor general urged the Court to send the case back for evidence of prior and continuing discrimination, it was clear he did not agree with the California Supreme Court's position that such evidence should be limited to acts at the Davis Medical School. McCree reminded the Court of its decisions in cases involving school discrimination in Los Angeles, Pasadena, and San Francisco. He pointed out census data indicating that as many as 40 percent of black students in California had spent some of their school years in states that had practiced legal segregation.

Chief Justice Burger wanted to know if McCree would include evidence of conduct outside California.

MC CREE: I would include conduct throughout the nation, because we are a nation without barriers to travel, and indeed California seems to have been—seems to be currently —one of the principal recipients of the flow of population from other parts of the country. And many of them bring with them the handicaps imposed upon them by conditions to which they were subjected before they went west. We suggest that it is not enough, really, to look at the visible wounds imposed by unconstitutional discrimination based upon race or ethnic status, because the very identification of race or ethnic status in America today is, itself, a handicap. And it is something that the California University at Davis Medical School could and should properly consider in affording a remedy to correct the denial of racial justice in this nation. We submit that the Fourteenth

Amendment, instead of outlawing this, indeed should welcome it as part of its intent and purpose.

After all his expressed doubts about race-conscious programs, McCree was now making an argument some justices might have considered extremely radical. If the Davis Medical School could take into account discrimination in other states, the effects of slavery, the Black Codes, and poll taxes, was there any need to send the case back for a new trial? The solicitor general's position went unchallenged, maybe because the Court was being deferential. More likely, it found McCree's statements too radical to consider seriously.

The justices picked up on the Asian issue again. If Asian-Americans were well represented in the professions, was there any point to including them in the Task Force? The government brief had suggested they shouldn't have been and wanted the case sent back to determine the reasons.

STEVENS: Supposing the evidence shows that the reason they were included was because they had in the past been the victims of discrimination. What inference should we draw from that kind of conclusion? Would that mean the program is good or bad? Is that a sufficient justification?

McCree rambled in his response. He said the government's position was not intended to suggest that Asian-Americans should be excluded but only that the continuing impact of discrimination against the group could not be learned from the record. What Stevens seemed to be asking was whether the real intent of such programs was integration rather than the correction of past discrimination. Furthermore, many other ethnic groups not considered minorities had filed briefs arguing they, too, had been subjected to discrimination.

Again, because of the paucity of the record, the Court could not know that the Task Force considered only Asians who were disadvantaged and sent applicants whom they considered middle-class to the regular admissions committee. After some commiseration over the record, McCree found the right answer. "Asian-Americans" was such a broad category that he could not determine if discrimination had impacted equally on the diverse groups within this category. McCree closed with a brief rhetorical plea.

MC CREE: I would like to conclude that this is not the kind of case that should be decided just by extrapolating from other precedents; that we are here asking the Court to give us the full dimensions of the Fourteenth Amendment that was intended to afford equal protection. And we suggest that the Fourteenth Amendment should not only require equality of treatment, but should also permit persons who were held back to be brought up to the starting line, where the opportunity for equality will be meaningful.

McCree had turned in a commendable perfomance. He had said little that would be critical to the Court's decision, but he had managed to speak for both the president and his people without doing grave injury to either.

Of the three lawyers to address the Supreme Court that day, Reynold Colvin was the least at home. He had never been before the High Court and he had been admitted to practice before this august body only the January before. He had not been to Harvard, as had three of the justices, Cox, and McCree. He had not been to Yale, as had Stewart and White. And unlike Rehnquist, he had not gone to Stanford, the western outpost of the elite circuit. He was the son of California, that distant place of rootless people, of tinsel and tourists, of strange politics and cultures that ran against, or sometimes ahead of, the mainstream. He was not a judge or a professor but a trial lawyer, a tradesman, like the majority of lawyers whom the chief justice found little reason to respect. His speech, his carriage, and his style marked him a commoner among the gentlemen assembled at court. Colvin was obviously aware of his status as an interloper. But far from being ashamed of his position, he reveled in it.

"I would be a fool to pretend I'm a great constitutional lawyer or a social philosopher. But the facts of this particular case are very, very strong facts, and as long as I remember my place, somehow I'll get through." He had made this statement to an interviewer before he went to Washington, and it ended up being his game plan. And why shouldn't it? So far the "country lawyer from San Francisco" had beaten some very sophisticated opponents.

COLVIN: It seems to me that the first thing I ought to say to this honorable court is that I am Allan Bakke's lawyer and Allan Bakke is my client. And I do not say that in any formal or perfunctory way. I say that because this is a lawsuit. It was a lawsuit brought by Allan Bakke up at Woodland in Yolo County, California, in which Allan Bakke, from the very beginning of this lawsuit in the first paper we ever filed, stated the case. And he stated the case in terms of his individual right.

Colvin was a storyteller and this talent was useful in addressing juries. After the presentations by Cox and McCree, it jarred with the atmosphere of the Court. But Colvin had a specific reason for choosing the homespun approach. By retelling Bakke's struggle for admission, he would make the justices see the individual behind all the legal arguments. He would remind them that there was a real plaintiff who only wanted to have his rights protected from the arbitrary power of government. He had used the same approach in his brief, in which twenty-two pages were devoted to the facts of the case.

COLVIN: The name of the game is not to represent Allan Bakke as a representative of a class. We are not representing Allan Bakke as a representative of some organization. This is not an exercise in a law review argument or a bar examination question. This is a question of getting Mr. Bakke into medical school—and that's the name of the game.

Now Colvin sounded more like Robert Blake selling STP than Sam Ervin pushing American Express. His reduction of the issues to the basic level made the Court impatient. When he began a description of his efforts to move the case forward, he was interrupted by Justice Rehnquist.

REHNQUIST: But no one is charging you with *laches* [neglect of duty].

Again there was laughter in the courtroom. But unlike the joke shared with Cox, Colvin had been made the brunt of the Court's humor.

POWELL: We are here—at least I am here—primarily to hear a constitutional argument. You have devoted twenty minutes to laboring the facts, if I may say so. I would like help, I really would, on the constitutional issues. Would you address that?

Colvin's tactic of focusing attention on the facts alone seemed as unlikely to succeed as Cox's attempts to ignore the facts and get an opinion on the abstract issues. Colvin cited the laws he believed had been violated in depriving Bakke "the right to admission" at Davis.

STEWART: You spoke, Mr. Colvin, of the right to admission. You don't seriously submit that he had a right to be admitted?

COLVIN: That is not Allan Bakke's position. Allan Bakke's position is that he has a right, and that right is not to be discriminated against by reason of his race. And that's what brings Allan Bakke to this court. We have the deepest difficulty in dealing with this problem of quota, and many, many questions arise. For example, there is a question of numbers. What is the appropriate quota? What is the appropriate quota for a medical school? Sixteen, eight, 32, 64, 100? On what basis is that quota determined? And there is a problem, a very serious problem of judicial determination. Does the Court leave open to the school the right to choose any number it wants in order to satisfy that quota? Would the Court be satisfied to allow an institution such as the University of California to adopt a quota of 100 per cent and thus deprive all persons who are not within selected minority groups?

Colvin had chosen an absolute position on racial classifications. The California Supreme Court had said they were unconstitutional. This position was attractive to Bakke's attorney because he did not have to worry about conceding a point to a crafty justice only to discover he had conceded too much. But the absolute position had little support in the law. Even the California court had said only that racial classifications were wrong because less restrictive alternatives had not been tried. Such a rigid position could not be attractive to the U.S. Supreme Court, always willing to postpone taking a position on a constitutional issue. Why should it declare all race classifications illegal when it didn't have to in this case? Justice White attempted to push Colvin toward a compromise position.

WHITE: Part of your submission is: Even if these are compelling interests, even if there is no alternative, the use of the race classification is unconstitutional?

COLVIN: We believe it is unconstitutional. We do.

BURGER: Because it is limited rigidly to 16?

COLVIN: No. Not because it is limited to 16, but because the concept of race itself as a classification becomes in our history and in our understanding an unjust and improper basis on which to judge people. We do not believe that intelligence, that achievement, that ability are measured by skin pigmentation or by the last surname of an individual, whether or not it sounds Spanish.

Colvin's absolute opposition to the use of race roused Justice Marshall, and he entered the fray with a vengeance.

MARSHALL: Your client did compete for the 84 seats, didn't he?

COLVIN: Yes, he did.

MARSHALL: And he lost?

COLVIN: Yes, he did.

MARSHALL: Now, would your argument be the same if one, instead of 16 seats, were left open?

COLVIN: Most respectfully, the argument does not turn on the numbers.

MARSHALL: My question is: Would you make the same argument?

COLVIN: Yes.

MARSHALL: If it was one?

COLVIN: If it was one and if there was an agreement, as there is in this case, that he was kept out by his race. Whether it is one, one hundred, two——

MARSHALL: I said that the regulation said that one seat would be left open for an underprivileged minority person.

COLVIN: Yes. We don't think we would ever get to that point——

MARSHALL: So numbers are just unimportant?

COLVIN: Numbers are unimportant. It is the principle of keeping a man out because of his race that is important.

MARSHALL: You are arguing about keeping somebody out and the other side is arguing about getting somebody in?

COLVIN: That's right.

MARSHALL: So it depends on which way you look at it, doesn't it?

COLVIN: It depends on which way you look at the problem.

MARSHALL: It does?

COLVIN: If I may finish. The problem——

MARSHALL: You are talking about your client's rights. Don't these underprivileged people have some rights?

COLVIN: They certainly have the right to compete——

MARSHALL: To eat cake.

The black justice's remark was a visceral reaction to Colvin's magnanimous offer to allow disadvantaged minorities the "right to compete." The reaction went to the heart of the "color-blind" argument. Colvin was offering blacks who had not yet eaten the bread of equal educational opportunities promised by the *Brown* decision the right to eat cake by competing with whites who had all the advantages. Once again it was a choice of victims.

Justice Powell offered Colvin another compromise position. What if race was just one of many factors used to select students and if Bakke had been turned down under this system, which differed from the two-track process at Davis?

COLVIN: Our argument would be the same, to the extent that race itself was the crucial matter in the admissions situation.

POWELL: Well, my hypothetical listed race as one of eight or ten factors or elements the committee might fairly weigh in the interest of diversity of a student body, for example. Would that be constitutional, in your opinion?

COLVIN: In our opinion . . . race itself is an improper ground for selection or rejection for the medical school.

If, as Reynold Colvin had claimed throughout the case, his only goal was to get his client admitted, why had he refused the very argument most favorable to his cause? If the justices had given any hint of their leanings during this grueling session, it was their search for a decision on narrow grounds. If they could avoid a ruling on race classification, they might find the program at Davis illegal anyway because of the two-track admissions process. Colvin had missed the cues and plowed ahead with his absolutist argument.

The rebuttal by Cox was brief.

cox: There is no per se rule of color blindness incorporated in the Equal Protection clause . . . the educational, professional and social purposes accomplished by race conscious admissions programs are compelling objectives, or to put it practically, they are sufficient justification for those losses, those problems that are created by the use of race . . . there is no other way of accomplishing those purposes.

Once more Cox attacked the California decision. As for Colvin's position, Cox used it to counter McCree's argument for sending the case back. Colvin was either right or wrong under the law, he was saying, and no further facts were needed to make a decision.

Cox's closing remarks returned to his theme of judicial restraint. Interference by the courts would dampen creativity and take away the independence of the universities. Cox did not mention race in his last sentences. This case involved much larger issues: the creative allocation of scarce resources and the privilege of allowing state legislatures and faculties to be free to handle the sensitive area of admissions. They could be trusted because after all, their interests were not so different from the Court's. Weren't they all gentlemen?

The session ended abruptly with Justice Burger's formal closing: "Thank you, gentlemen; the case is submitted." The time was 11:58 A.M. The nine justices rose and quickly left the courtroom.

Once again the tone of the gathering reverted to the festive and social atmosphere of the morning. Reporters surrounded Cox, who had been joined by his wife, and queried him about the fine points in his argument. The press also had questions for Colvin, but they were brief and more critical. The consensus was that Bakke's attorney had not done well. Many felt that some of the justices had been clearly sympathetic to his arguments but that he had missed the cues they offered. His abrasive tone, his insistence on the facts, and his reluctance to stray into the abstractions of the law, they felt, were not only crucial errors but additional proof that the "country lawyer from San Francisco" was ignorant of the rules of gentlemanly play. The dean of an Ivy League law school joked with his friends that the event had not been a fair fight. Maybe, he said, Bakke could appeal the ruling for lack of effective counsel.

The distinguished audience filed slowly out of the courtroom: James M. Nabrit, who had argued important civil rights cases at the side of Thurgood Marshall; his son, who now worked for the NAACP Legal Defense Fund; the widow of Chief Justice Earl Warren; Eleanor Holmes Norton, a Yale Law School graduate and chair of the Equal Employment Opportunities Commission; all those who had been fortunate enough to wangle admission to this important event. They lingered in the halls of the Court, on the steps outside, in restaurants on Capitol Hill, for one moment oblivious of the politicians, whose normal standing in the Washington spotlight had been displaced by an argument over the meaning of justice.

But in the press room reporters debated the possible results of the two-hour hearing, sifting their recollections of the event much as the Greeks had read the entrails of freshly killed animals. The reporters from major publications had pooled to pay the expenses of an unofficial reporter and they chafed at the wait for a transcript. Within hours they would sit down at desks all over Washington and attempt to make sense of an event that had not yet ended.

It is easier to review plays once the curtain has come down, or to analyze baseball games because there are winners and losers. But in this case the transcript would be a box score without a final tally. The desire of the media for firm and final resolution left little tolerance for confrontations the final outcome of which was many months away.

Ten

A GENTLEMANLY

SOLUTION

More than eight months would pass between that brisk October day when Cox, Colvin, and McCree appealed to the best judgment of the nine justices and the public announcement of the Supreme Court's decision in *Regents of the University of California* v. *Bakke*. The East Coast had survived one of the worst winters in recent memory, and the successes of the New York Yankees in the autumn before had long been forgotten. The excitement of baseball fever had drifted up the coast to Boston and the Red Sox, and most of the Yankee headlines concerned the varied personality clashes of Reggie Jackson and Billy Martin.

The public had been anticipating the *Bakke* decision since early in the year, but Court experts had predicted accurately that the opinion would not come until late in the term, as was common practice in difficult cases. Sharp divisions on the Court and the tenacious commitment of individual justices to their own positions meant that the weekly judicial conferences would not be tranquil. If there was substantial agreement on the Court, there would be an effort to persuade the dissenters to join the majority. In a case where public sentiment was so sharply divided, a unanimous Court would have a moderating influence. Chief Justice Warren had spent the better part of the 1953–54 term prodding a sharply divided Court into a unified decision outlawing segregation. Warren had avoided an early vote on the case and brought it up for discussion over coffee and lunch as well as in conference. But Chief Justice Burger lacked his predecessor's skills as a statesman, and it was not apparent that either side had even a solid majority. If the Court were evenly divided, then the two sides would struggle for the vote of the uncommitted members. It would take time to find a compromise solution on which five justices could agree and to write an opinion they all could endorse. Late in the spring a Washington newspaper reported that Justice Blackmun was overheard telling a friend, "We all wish this *Bakke* case would go away." There was also some speculation that the justices would delay their release of the decision until the last possible moment in order to avoid the brunt of the inevitable political repercussions. Student groups had organized "Anti-Bakke" demonstrations all over the country, including a march by some 10,000 people past the Supreme Court building. "The Court is going to wait until school is out," predicted a student leader, "and then run for the hills."

The U.S. Supreme Court gives no advance notice of its decisions. It may well be the last institution in Washington where a secret remains secret. But as the end of the Court's term grew near, the rumors of an impending decision in *Bakke* spread like the choicest bits of Capitol Hill gossip. Weekly, from about the middle of April, the Washington grapevine reported from "sources close to the Court" that *this* would be the week. The experts purporting to have discovered the content of the decision were not quite so numerous but just as unreliable. There was a rumor that the justices had voted 9 to 0 in favor of Bakke, a report made even less plausible by the identification of Justice Marshall as the source of this information. Another story reported that the Court would duck the issue by asking the parties to reargue a particular aspect of the case in the fall. The Court had done this in *Brown* when they were still badly split at the end of the 1953 term. But in light of the sharp criticism of the Court's avoidance of *DeFunis*, this solution seemed unlikely. Still, as the Court entered the last month of the term, the reports persisted that the split was 4 to 4 with each faction courting the vote of a usually conservative justice.

On a hot muggy Wednesday, June 29, the Court was ready to announce what one reporter, sounding suspiciously like a boxing promoter, called "one of the most anxiously awaited legal decisions of the century." The Court was approaching the end of its term and was handing down several decisions each week, but the public was interested only in *Bakke*. Reporters and camera crews had been camped out at the Court since the beginning of May, and they had grown weary of the long vigil. The first hint of the long-awaited decision was the arrival of Mrs. William Brennan and Mrs. Thurgood Marshall at a side entrance to the building. When other family members and Court employees began to drift into the courtroom, there was no doubt that the time of decision had finally arrived.

At 10:01 A.M. the nine justices pushed the velvet curtains aside and took their seats on the dais. The U.S. Supreme Court is one of the last American appellate courts to announce its decisions orally, and the presentation can range from a brief summary to a verbatim rendition of the entire opinion. After quickly disposing of two minor decisions, Chief Justice Burger announced that Justice Powell would deliver the judgment of the Court in Number 76-811.

Powell, a soft-spoken Virginia aristocrat, addressed his listeners in a conversational tone. "I will now try to explain how we divided on this issue," he began with a smile. "It may not be self-evident." There was a ripple of nervous, polite laughter. Powell noted that "perhaps no case in memory has received so much attention and scholarly commentary . . . and advice." Then, acknowledging the difficulties the Court had faced in its deliberations, he said, "As we speak today, with a notable lack of unanimity, it may be evident we needed all this advice." It was apparent that those who had predicted a closely divided Court and a Delphic decision had been proved right.

Powell was the first of five justices who read excerpts from their separate opinions from the bench. The entire process took just over an hour. The full text of the opinion, which was not made public until the justices had completed their oral pronouncements, ran in excess of 40,000 words. Six separate opinions had been filed, and no single opinion commanded the majority of the votes on the Court. Powell explained how he and his fellow justices had sifted through the competing claims and gave the results of the final vote.

The arithmetic on the final scorecard was not hard to follow. Four justices (Stevens, Burger, Stewart, and Rehnquist) had voted to order Allan Bakke admitted to the medical school at Davis. They concluded that the Task Force program had treated him unlawfully under Title VI of the Civil Rights Act of 1964. They had refused to consider the constitutional question but believed the California Supreme Court decision should be affirmed. Another four (Brennan, White, Marshall, and Blackmun) had voted to uphold the Davis admissions program. They had found that it violated neither the 1964 Civil Rights Act nor the Fourteenth Amendment of the Constitution. They felt the California decision should be reversed. Justice Powell had broken the deadlock. He voted with the first four on the issue of Bakke's admission and with the second four on the constitutionality of race-conscious affirmative action. The portion of Stanley Mosk's decision ordering Bakke admitted had been upheld 5 to 4. But the part of that decision which said that race was an unconstitutional factor in admissions had been reversed. Still, the score was the only obvious aspect of the decision. As Powell, Stevens, Brennan, Blackmun, and Marshall took turns reading portions of their opinions, it was clear that the Court had left many important questions unanswered.

Lewis F. Powell, Jr., had come to the Supreme Court in 1971. A skilled and successful corporate lawyer, he had been appointed by Richard Nixon to fill the seat vacated by the late Hugo Black. Black, an Alabamian, had proved one of the Court's strongest advocates of civil rights despite a youthful flirtation with the Ku Klux Klan. Powell, a Harvard Law School graduate, millionaire, and former president of the Richmond School Board and the American Bar Association, came to the Court with a reputation as an intelligent and thoughtful southern moderate. In six years on the Court, his frequent association with the other three Nixon appointees, Burger, Blackmun, and Rehnquist, had earned him a conservative label. But Powell had also, on occasion, displayed a sensitivity and realism about racial issues that his northern brethren did not share. In a separate opinion in the Supreme Court's first northern desegregation case, Powell had pointed out that segregation had the same harmful effect on black children whether it was practiced in the North or the South. The majority of the Court seemed to miss this obvious point in differentiating between de jure and de facto segregation.

Powell's opinion straddled the two camps in the Court. He agreed with four of his colleagues that Bakke had been wronged by the Davis Medical School. But he agreed with the other four that it was legitimate to use race as a factor in selecting applicants. Powell's penchant for compromise would make his opinion the "judgment of the Court" despite the fact that no other justice chose to sign his opinion. If anything had been settled by this massive outlay of words and positions, it would be found among the carefully chosen words of Lewis Powell. Though Powell's opinion had its poetic moments, it was characteristically the work of a legal craftsman rather than a stylist. The first twelve pages were directed to a careful recitation of the facts. He then disposed of the procedural claim by the university that Bakke did not have the right to bring suit under Title VI of the Civil Rights Act. The question had not been raised until the parties reached the Supreme Court, he said, so it was unnecessary to consider it. He would assume for purposes of this case that Bakke had a right to sue under the statute.

Powell turned to the question of whether the university's admissions program violated Title VI. He noted that the language in the statute that outlawed "discrimination" in federally funded programs, such as the phrase *equal protection of the laws,* was susceptible to varying interpretations. It was not by chance that the language of Title VI and that of the equal protection clause were equally cryptic, he argued. Congressmen supporting Title VI had "repeatedly declared that the bill enacted constitutional principles," and when opponents criticized their failure to define the term *discrimination* more precisely, they had answered that the definition would be made clear by reference to the Constitution.

It was clear, he said, that the legislators were responding to the real and pressing problem of guaranteeing minority citizens equal treatment. The pronouncements of "color blindness" referred to by Justice Stevens in his dissenting argument had "occurred in the midst of extended remarks dealing with the evils of segregation in federally funded programs." "In view of the clear legislative intent," Powell concluded, "Title VI must be held to proscribe only those racial classifications that would violate the Equal Protection Clause or the Fifth Amendment."

By finding Title VI in agreement with the equal protection clause, Powell avoided further discussion of the statute. If the Davis admissions program violated the equal protection clause, it also violated Title VI. If it was constitutional, it also satisfied Title VI.

Powell moved on to the meat of his opinion. Had the Davis program violated Bakke's right under the equal protection clause? Had Justice Mosk and the majority of the California Supreme Court been correct in concluding that the clause prohibited any consideration of an individual's race in admissions programs? Powell followed the traditional approach in his analysis of the constitutional question. He began by dismissing the debate over whether the medical school had established a "goal" or a "quota." "This semantic distinction is beside the point: the special admissions program is undeniably a classification based on race and ethnic background." Powell had made the same point during the oral argument when, after a long series of questions by Justice Stevens about the meaning of "quota," he had interjected, "Does it really matter what we call this program?"

Having established that a racial classification was involved, Powell approached the question on which California justices Mosk and Tobriner had differed, the question that legal scholars had been debating since *DeFunis*. Were all racial classifications suspect and therefore subject to the Court's highest level of scrutiny? Powell's answer was yes. "Racial and ethnic distinctions of *any sort* are suspect," he said. The fact that Bakke was not a member of a "discrete insular minority" was of no consequence. Borrowing from the reasoning of Justice Mosk and former U.S. Supreme Court justice Douglas, he argued that the United States had become "a nation of minorities." Powell rejected Tobriner's notion that racial classifications that operated against the white majority might be benign. "The concepts of majority and minority necessarily reflect temporary arrangements and political judgments," he said. "There is no principled basis for deciding which groups would merit heightened judicial solicitude and which would not." American blacks would surely question Powell's use of the word *temporary* to refer to the 300-year arrangement that continued to keep them at the bottom of the ladder. They might well argue that their struggle against discrimination had differed in both quality and quantity from that of white "minorities."

Powell went on to apply the strict scrutiny test to the case. Since the test required the state to show a purpose or interest that was both substantial and necessary, he listed the goals that the special admissions program was designed to serve. They were (1) increasing the number of traditionally disfavored minorities in medical schools and the medical profession; (2) countering the effects of societal discrimination; (3) increasing the number of physicians who will practice in communities currently underserved; and (4) obtaining the educational benefits that flow from an ethnically diverse student body.

Powell rejected the first goal as "facially invalid." "Preferring members of any one group for no reason other than race or ethnic origin is discrimination for its own sake." To the argument that the program was necessary for improving health care in underserved communities, he echoed Justice Mosk's argument that there was "no evidence in the record indicating that petitioner's special admissions program is either needed or geared to promote that goal." Even at this stage the skimpy trial court record had come back to haunt the university lawyers.

Powell's approach to the remaining goals of the university was less direct. Here he would exercise his skills as a statesman and respond to political pressures by attempting to give something to both sides. "The state certainly has a legitimate and substantial interest in ameliorating or eliminating, where feasible, the disabling effects of identified discrimination," he said, addressing the university's argument that it wanted to counter the effects of societal discrimination. Earlier Powell had made clear that he thought the use of racial classifications appropriate in school desegregation cases. But in these cases, he noted, the classifications involved were "designed as remedies for the vindication of constitutional entitlement" and "the scope of the remedies was not permitted to exceed the extent of the violation." In other words, the school cases used race to remedy the effects of discrimination found by a court. In employment cases, Powell went on, the courts had fashioned racial preferences as "remedies for constitutional or statutory violations resulting in identified, race-based injuries. . . . Such preferences have also been upheld where a legislative or administrative body charged with the responsibility made determinations of past discrimination by the industries affected and fashioned remedies deemed appropriate to rectify the discrimination."

Powell had referred to these cases to support his argument that the university's more amorphous goal of remedying "societal discrimination" was insufficient. But he had also made an important concession to the forces supporting affirmative action. If a state legislature or federal agency wanted to use race as a criterion, it had to show past discrimination that made a race-conscious remedy necessary. Powell the statesman was aware of the two-edged effect of his argument.

But the university's fourth goal would allow Powell to uphold the concept of affirmative action and still order Bakke admitted. Using a somewhat novel approach, he argued that the pursuit of a diverse student body was essential to the university's exercise of academic freedom: the right to select its own student body. Although academic freedom was not a specifically enumerated constitutional right, it had long been viewed as a special concern of the First Amendment. Because the university's purpose of achieving diversity involved the exercise of a constitutional right, it was sufficiently compelling to meet the first requirement of the strict scrutiny test.

But the second part of the test had not been met, according

to Powell. "Petitioner's argument that this is the only effective means of serving the interest of diversity is seriously flawed. The diversity that furthers a compelling state interest encompasses a far broader array of qualifications and characteristics of which racial or ethnic origin is but a single though important element," Powell went on. "The experience of other university admissions programs, which take race into account in achieving the educational diversity valued by the First Amendment, demonstrates that the assignment of a fixed number of places to a minority group is not a necessary means toward that end."

Powell then referred to the Harvard College admissions procedure as an example of an acceptable program. "In such an admissions program, race or ethnic background may be deemed a 'plus' in a particular applicant's file, yet it does not insulate the individual from comparison with all other candidates for available seats."

The special admissions program at Davis had failed the strict scrutiny test because a set number of places had been set aside, and Powell found this not "necessary." Justice Brennan would find the necessity to which Powell referred more political than constitutional. The chief advantage of the Harvard program seemed to be that it did not make its system public. In dissent Brennan wrote, "It may be that the Harvard Plan is more acceptable to the public than is the Davis 'quota.' If it is, any state, including California, is free to adopt it in preference to a less acceptable alternative. . . . But there is no [constitutional] basis for preferring a particular preference program simply because in achieving the same goals that the Davis medical school is pursuing, it proceeds in a manner that is not immediately apparent to the public."

The gentleman from Virginia had written the ultimate political opinion. He had neutralized the anti-affirmative-action forces by admitting Bakke and holding that quotas were illegal.

And he had given his friends in the academic establishment what Mr. Cox had asked for: the freedom to continue to run their business the way they pleased. It was not clear that he had given minorities anything, but he had not shut the door on them entirely. It would be possible for them to claim victory and difficult for them to say they had been ignored.

Justice John Paul Stevens had authored the opinion for the bloc of four justices who had voted to order Bakke admitted because the Davis Medical School had violated Title VI of the 1964 Civil Rights Act. Stevens, the Court's most junior member, had been appointed by Gerald Ford in 1975 to replace an ailing Justice Douglas. A moderate Republican, Stevens had a reputation as a scholar at the University of Chicago and an able circuit court judge. He had not yet established a reputation on the highest court, but in his first years he had evidenced a strong, hard-eyed independence that led him to write more than his share of separate concurrences and dissents. There was some surprise that Stevens should align himself with the conservative wing of the Court, but the *Bakke* case had made for strange bedfellows. Stevens's eagerness to decide the case on the narrowest of grounds was not uncharacteristic, and it was certainly plausible that each of the justices who had joined his opinion had done so for very different reasons.

"It is always important at the outset to focus precisely on the controversy before the Court," began Justice Stevens. "This is not a class action. The controversy is between two specific litigants." Stevens was echoing the theme that Reynold Colvin had so often repeated to the Court. The critics in the eastern establishment had panned his performance at oral argument, but the "country lawyer" had made his point well. Colvin had focused on Bakke as an individual to stress the real human injury to his client. Justice Stevens's purpose was to frame the narrowest possible question for the Court's consideration. If it was possible for the Court to decide this case without saying anything about the broader constitutional and societal issues that had so sharply divided the nation, it should do so.

With this goal in mind Stevens pointed out that the trial court had ordered the university to consider only Bakke's application without regard to his race and that the order did not include any broad prohibition against the use of race in the admissions process. "There is no outstanding injunction forbidding any consideration of racial criteria in processing applications." Said Justice Stevens, "It is therefore perfectly clear that the question whether race can *ever* be used as a factor in admissions is not an issue in this case, and that discussion of that issue is inappropriate."

In his eagerness to avoid the more far-reaching and politically volatile constitutional issue, Stevens had ignored the language in the California Supreme Court's decision which stated in no uncertain terms that *"no applicant* may be rejected because of his race," an omission that Justice Powell was quick to call to his attention.

Stevens continued. "Both petitioner and respondent have asked us to determine the legality of the university's special admissions program by reference to the Constitution. Our settled practice, however, it to avoid the decision of a Constitutional issue if a case can be fairly decided on a statutory ground."

The statutory ground that provided Stevens with a way out of the constitutional issue was the Civil Rights Act of 1964. Colvin had made it part of his original complaint and then forgotten about it until Justice Brennan had brought it up during oral argument.

Section 601 of the 1964 act provides: "No person in the United States shall, on the ground of race, color, or national origin, be excluded from participation in, be denied the benefits of, or subjected to discrimination under any program or activity receiving federal financial assistance."

Stevens's position was that, as an admitted recipient of federal funds, the university was in clear violation of the statute. The university had excluded Bakke from participation in the Task Force program because of his race, an action expressly prohibited by the plain language of the statute. There could be no other result, argued Stevens, unless the statute's language misstated the central intent of Congress. Stevens was convinced that it did not. "It seems clear that the proponents of Title VI assumed that the Constitution itself required a color-blind standard on the part of government," he argued, quoting sections of the *Congressional Record* for support. Stevens had adopted the "color-blind" argument advanced by Bakke's supporters but he had carefully avoided giving it constitutional status by attributing this interpretation of the Constitution to the Congress rather than to the Court. "Congress' expression of its policy to end racial discrimination may independently proscribe conduct that the Constitution does not. However, we need not decide the congruence—or lack of congruence—of the controlling statute and the Constitution since the meaning of Title VI's ban on exclusion is crystal clear: Race cannot be the basis of excluding anyone from participation in a federally funded program."

By confining their decision to the statute, Stevens, Burger, Stewart, and Rehnquist had managed to say nothing about where they stood on the issue of whether race-conscious affirmative action violated the equal protection clause of the Fourteenth Amendment. Their insistence that Title VI required a color-blind administration of federally assisted programs may have been one indication of how they would have stood on the Fourteenth Amendment, but Stevens had gone to some length to make clear the fact that they were not expressing their own views on whether the Constitution required the same thing as the statute, and this may well have been an indication that even this group of four had joined together only after mutual compromise—that perhaps the only thing that all four agreed on was the propriety of not divulging their views on the ultimate question.

Because Justice Powell chose to say what he thought about the meaning of the equal protection clause the four justices who signed the Stevens opinion would neither agree nor disagree with anything he had said except that Bakke should be admitted. "Accordingly, I concur in the Court's judgment insofar as it affirms the judgment of the Supreme Court of California," wrote Stevens at the close of his brief and rather cryptic opinion, "to the extent that it purports to do anything else, I respectfully dissent."

There was some speculation that the opinion authored by William J. Brennan had once been a draft of the majority opinion of the Court. In several places Brennan had used the active tense usually reserved for a justice who speaks for five or more justices rather than the subjunctive normally used in concurrence and dissent. Justice Stevens had openly chided him for presuming to explain the "central meaning of today's opinion." "It is hardly necessary to state that only a majority can speak for the Court or determine what is the 'central meaning' of any judgment of the Court," wrote Stevens in his opening footnote.

Had Brennan found himself speaking for more than four justices in this crucial case on race he is likely to have been at least as much surprised as pleased. The most senior justice on the Court, he had come to the high bench in 1956 and was one of only four justices remaining from the activist Warren Court. But two of those four, Stewart and White, were often found in the chief justice's camp, and increasingly Brennan found himself dissenting in important civil rights cases with only Marshall for company.

"Our Nation was founded on the principle that 'all men are created equal' yet candor requires acknowledgment that the framers of our Constitution, to forge the thirteen colonies into one Nation, openly compromised this principle of equality with its antithesis: slavery. The consequences of this compromise are well known and have aptly been called our 'American Dilemma.'" Brennan had begun the body of his opinion by calling to mind the initial hypocrisy in America's commitment to the equality of all men. It was an appropriate introduction. For the central theme of this opinion would be that law must be more than empty words. It must ensure the actuality of equal opportunity in a society where all were not yet equal. "We cannot . . . let color blindness become a myopia which masks the reality that many 'created equal' have been treated within our lifetimes as inferior both by the law and their fellow citizens," Brennan wrote at the close of a brief history of the Fourteenth Amendment.

Having established his theme in the clear rhetorical tones of an orator, Brennan would support it with an exhaustive marshaling of legislative history and case law that ran in excess of fifty pages. His first task was to give the lie to his brothers on the Court who had argued that Title VI standing by itself barred all race-conscious efforts to extend the benefits of federally funded programs to minorities. He agreed with Powell that Title VI prohibited only those uses of racial criteria that would violate the Fourteenth Amendment. "The history of Title VI," argued Brennan, "reveals one fixed purpose: to give the executive branch of government clear authority to terminate federal funding of private programs that use race as a means of disadvantaging minorities in a manner that would be prohibited by the Constitution if engaged in by government." He followed with seven pages of references to the legislative history to support his position that Title VI was intended to help eliminate privately initiated segregation and that race-conscious affirmative action had been anticipated as a means of carrying out that purpose.

Brennan further buttressed his position on the intent of Congress by referring to the regulations that had been devised to administer the statute. In several cases the Court had recognized that such regulations were a reliable indication of congressional intent, and the Court had found regulations construing a statute particularly deserving of attention when Congress had subsequently considered the regulations and left them unaltered. Brennan cited four different HEW regulations adopted to ensure the enforcement of Title VI. Where there was evidence of past discrimination these regulations not only were permitted but required race-conscious affirmative action. Even in the absence of prior discrimination, the regulation clearly allowed the consideration of race. In adopting subsequent legislation, Brennan noted, Congress had discussed these regulations and allowed them to stand.

Congress had also made clear that it did not intend Title VI to bar consideration of race in its passage of the recent Public Works Act. That legislation explicitly required that no grants be made for any local public works project unless the applicant gives satisfactory assurance that at least 10 percent of the amount of the grant will go to minority businesses. Congress was fully aware that Title VI would apply to these federal grants. "The enactment of the 10% 'set aside' for minority enterprises reflects a congressional judgment that remedial use of race is permissible under Title VI," concluded Brennan.

Finally, Brennan pointed to the Court's own prior decisions, noting that it had interpreted Title VI to require recipients of federal funds to depart from a policy of color blindness in a case in which the San Francisco schools were ordered to provide bilingual education for Chinese children. The Court had also, Brennan said, declined to adopt a "color-blind" interpretation of the voting rights and employment discrimination statutes by upholding Court-ordered racial preferences for minorities as a remedy for Title VII violations and by permitting states voluntarily to take race into account in establishing voting districts that would fairly represent the voting strength of minority groups.

Now Brennan turned to the equal protection argument. "The position summed up by the shorthand phrase 'our constitution is color-blind' has never been adopted by this Court as the proper meaning of the Equal Protection Clause," he began. "Indeed, we have expressly rejected this proposition on a number of occasions." With a brief flurry of case citations Brennan quickly disposed of Colvin's argument that racial classifications are per se invalid under the Fourteenth Amendment.

Then, adding a new twist to traditional equal protection analysis, he rejected both Bakke's claim that racial classifications always require strict scrutiny and the university's argument that the minimal scrutiny or rational basis test should apply when the purpose of such a classification is benign. Because the Court was faced with a problem it had never before confronted, the old definitions and tests were in many respects inapplicable.

The Court's prior cases made it clear that statutes that restricted "fundamental rights" or contained "suspect classifications" must be subjected to strict scrutiny; but no fundamental right was involved here, and whites as a class had none of the "traditional indicia of suspectness." As a group, whites had not been subjected to a history of purposeful unequal treatment, nor were they in a position of political powerlessness that required the Court to protect them from the majoritarian process. Finally, this was not a case in which racial considerations should be prohibited because they were irrelevant. But Brennan was equally uncomfortable with allowing a racial classification to be shielded against any real judicial scrutiny by the rational basis test.

The test that Brennan proposed lay somewhere in between the "we'll look with our eyes closed" approach of the rational basis test and the "hanging judge" approach of the strict scrutiny test. It was a test the Court had used in cases involving sex discrimination and statutes that discriminated against illegitimate children. In those cases the Court had held that the classification involved "must serve important governmental objectives and must be substantially related to the achievement of those objectives." Elaborating on this test in order to account for the "significant risk that racial classifications established for ostensibly benign purposes can be misused," Brennan proposed that to justify a benign racial classification, "an important articulated purpose for its use must be shown." Then he added that "any statute must be stricken that stigmatizes any group or that singles out those least well represented in the political process to bear the brunt of a benign program." This last requirement was designed to quell the fears that discrete white minority groups might be singled out for less favorable treatment.

Having stated his new test, Brennan spent the next ten pages of his opinion in another exhaustive chronicling of the law in support of his position that the Davis Medical School's stated purpose of remedying the effects of past societal discrimination was sufficiently important to justify the use of a race-conscious admissions program. One passage in this generally compelling analysis is worth special note because it places Bakke's claim in a perspective that has been lost amid the cries of "reverse discrimination." Brennan wrote, "If it was reasonable to conclude—as we hold it was—that the failure of minorities to qualify for admission at Davis under regular procedures was due principally to the effects of past discrimination, then there is a reasonable likelihood that, but for pervasive racial discrimination, respondent would have failed to qualify for admission even in the absence of Davis' special admissions program."

Brennan closed, first, by echoing Justice Tobriner's sentiments that the alternatives to considering race proposed by the majority of the California Supreme Court were fraudulent, and second, by exposing Justice Powell's baseless distinction between Davis's "quota" and what would surely become known as "the Harvard Plan":

"Davis' special admissions program cannot be said to violate the Constitution simply because it has set aside a predetermined number of places for minority applicants rather than using minority status as a positive factor to be considered in evaluating the applications of minority applicants. For purposes of constitutional adjudication, there is no difference between the two approaches. In any admissions program which accords special consideration to disadvantaged racial minorities, a determination of the degree of preference to be given is unavoidable, and any given preference that results in the exclusion of a white candidate is no more or less constitutionally acceptable than a program such as that at Davis."

That an opinion as strong as Brennan's should be joined by White and Blackmun as well as Marshall was perhaps the most encouraging note of the decision for minorities. Blackmun had been the biggest surprise for those who did not look past his rather consistent alliance with Burger on most issues. But for those who had followed the case closely, the Minnesota Republican's vote had come as less of a shock. While Blackmun was considered a "conservative" and a "strict constructionist," his record in the area of race and civil rights had been moderate. He had written for the majority in decisions that had given more protection to aliens and joined Brennan and Marshall in dissenting from the Court's decision in a California case which upheld a state constitutional amendment that had the effect of keeping blacks and poor people out of the suburbs.

It was Blackmun who had asked Cox whether racial preferences were not similar to athletic scholarships, and during oral argument in the *DeFunis* case he had asked a similar question, inquiring whether it would not be appropriate for a professional school to give preference to an applicant from an underserved geographic location. Blackmun's ten years as general counsel to the Mayo Clinic, located in his hometown of Rochester, Minnesota, had no doubt made him more aware of the peculiar problems connected with medical school admissions than were many of his brothers in the Court.

In a separate opinion Blackmun added some observations to the joint opinion written by Brennan. Repeating the theme he had pressed in oral argument, he said, "It is somewhat ironic to have us so deeply disturbed over a program where race is an element of consciousness, and yet to be aware of the fact, as we are, that institutions of higher learning . . . have given conceded preferences up to a point to those possessed of athletic skills, to children of alumni, to the affluent who may bestow their largesse on the institution, and to those having connections with celebrities, the famous, and the powerful."

And then, in an eloquent closing, he rephrased the words of Bork and McCree. "I suspect that it would be impossible to arrange an affirmative action program in a racially neutral way and have it successful. . . . In order to get beyond racism, we must first take account of race. There is no other way. And in order to treat some persons equally, we must treat them differently. We cannot—we dare not—let the Equal Protection Clause perpetrate racial supremacy."

There could be little doubt that Thurgood Marshall's presence at the secret deliberations of the Court had a profound effect on those deliberations and on the final decision. It is difficult to ignore the reality of race in America with a black man looking you in the eye. And Justice Marshall would not have been shy about verbally reminding his colleagues of that reality if for some his presence were not enough. His "to eat cake" exchange with Colvin at oral argument was evidence of the fact that age and position had not blinded Marshall to the plight of his people.

He had not been able to argue this case in Court, as he had in *Brown,* but as their peer his influence on the justices could be even greater. Behind the closed doors of the Supreme Court conference room and in private chats with his colleagues he was not limited by the same restrictions of time, form, and deference.

There were limits to what Marshall could do, for this was a different Court and a different issue from *Brown.* But his presence surely had far greater impact than his single vote. His hand was clearly evident in the joint opinion authored by Brennan. And no member of the Court dared offer the empty alternatives proffered by Mosk and the California Supreme Court. In his own separate opinion, Marshall articulated the thoughts of millions of black Americans. Unlike the other members of the Court, Marshall could not differentiate between the laws of the country and the treatment of blacks under those laws. "Three hundred and fifty years ago, the Negro was dragged to this country in chains to be sold into slavery," Marshall began. "Uprooted from his homeland and thrust into bondage for forced labor, the slave was deprived of all legal rights." Marshall was establishing the unique status of blacks in America, an experience that had been deliberately blurred by opponents of affirmative action and by members of the Court who argued that blacks were just one more ethnic group.

He reminded the Court of its own responsibility in relegating blacks to inferior status. "The position of the Negro slave as mere property was confirmed by this Court in *Dred Scott* v. *Sandford,* holding that the Missouri Compromise—which prohibited slavery in the portion of the Louisiana Purchase territory north of the Missouri—was unconstitutional because it deprived slaveowners of their property without due process." He noted that the Court had concluded that blacks were not intended to be regarded as citizens but were "regarded as beings of an inferior order . . . altogether unfit to associate with the white race, either in social or political relations: and so far inferior that they had no rights which the white man was bound to respect."

Marshall then traced the repeated failure of the Supreme Court to protect the rights of blacks after Emancipation, noting that even *Brown,* the case to which he had devoted most of his legal career, "did not automatically end segregation" or "move Negroes from a position of legal inferiority to one of equality."

"The position of the Negro today in America is the tragic but inevitable consequence of centuries of unequal treatment," he continued. "Measured by any benchmark of comfort or achievement, meaningful equality remains a distant dream for the Negro." Marshall's value to the Court once again was to touch on the reality of the black existence in America, a reality often lost in the efforts of the other justices to find a politically acceptable solution. "It is unnecessary in twentieth century America to have individual Negroes demonstrate that they have been victims of racial discrimination," wrote the Supreme Court justice whose color might still disqualify him from membership in some of Washington's most exclusive private clubs. "The racism of our society has been so pervasive that none, regardless of wealth or position, has managed to escape its impact.

"It is more than a little ironic," Marshall concluded, "that after several hundred years of class-based discrimination against Negroes, the Court is unwilling to hold that a class-based remedy for that discrimination is permissible."

Even as the justices attempted to explain the convolutions of their opinions, the major news organizations rushed to inform the world. In the early minutes the desire to score a "beat" outweighed the prudence required by such a complicated decision. The Associated Press scored a six-minute "beat" over UPI with a flat declaration that Allan Bakke had won his case. The wire service would spend the rest of the morning attempting to explain its initial bulletin.

It was just a few minutes after seven on the West Coast when the *CBS Morning News* was interrupted so correspondent Terry Drinkwater could inform early-morning viewers about the decision. Allan Bakke had won, Drinkwater told his audience, and the Supreme Court had outlawed racial quotas. "Some of these quotas are called affirmative action," he rambled with uncharacteristic partisanship. "But the important thing is—Allan Bakke won." On the other side of Los Angeles, the struggling *Herald-Examiner*'s morning edition would scream, "Bakke Wins." If the initial reports were something less than objective, it was a reflection of the perception in some quarters that the rights of white men were under siege. In the Washington bureau of the *New York Times*, an editor glanced at the wire stories about the decision and declared, "Well, that's one for our side."

As the news organizations scrambled to formulate more accurate assessments of the decision, various interests rushed to claim victory. A flock of reporters had been camped on the street outside the home of the most important figure in the case since the night before. But Allan Bakke remained true to his decision to avoid public comment about the case. He dashed out of his home with a newspaper over his face, slid behind the wheel of his Volkswagen Rabbit with only a mumbled acknowledgment that he had heard the Court's decision, and drove to work at NASA. He would leave it to his attorneys to declare that he was pleased with the outcome and that he intended to attend medical school in the fall.

Across the bay in Berkeley, University of California president David Saxon addressed a packed news conference. "I consider it a victory for the University of California," he declared. "The overall bulk of our admissions programs appear to be entirely lawful." Some days later university lawyers would issue guidelines to all branches of the institution about revisions in their affirmative action programs.

In Washington, Attorney General Griffin Bell said he and President Carter regarded the decision as a "great gain for affirmative action." Bell told White House reporters, "That is what we thought the law was."

In New York, Benjamin Hooks, the executive director of the NAACP, called the decision "a clear-cut victory for voluntary affirmative action." Hooks said he was disappointed that Bakke had won, but he added that he saw a strong ray of hope in the Court's decision. Urban League head Vernon Jordan also looked for the silver lining: "The most important thing is that a majority of the Supreme Court backed the use of race as a permissible factor in affirmative action programs."

But not all minority spokesmen viewed the decision with such immediate optimism. Operation PUSH president Jesse Jackson viewed the decision as part of a national move "to the right" and suggested that minorities might organize boycotts or sit-ins to emphasize their concerns. His reservations were echoed by Representative Parren Mitchell, chairman of the Congressional Black Caucus, who said the group's members were not pleased but did not view the outcome as "the death knell for affirmative action."

The greatest outrage at the decision was expressed by the groups that had organized to campaign against the case. The National Committee to Overturn the Bakke Decision and the Anti-Bakke Decision Coalition overcame their internal political differences to denounce jointly the Court's finding as "a bad decision with potentially devastating impact on race relations in this country." Within hours chapters of the organizations staged protests in a number of major cities.

Even the Jewish organizations, which had opposed any use of racial consideration, could find comfort in the decision. Arnold Forster, general counsel of the Anti-Defamation League of B'nai B'rith, said his organization was "comforted that, once and for all, the United States Supreme Court has held that racial quotas are flatly illegal."

The central message to the public seemed to be that everybody had won. Many commentators referred to the "Solomonic decision" of the Court and declared that the justices had given "half a loaf" to each side. The liberal position was that this decision was the best one possible because quotas were clearly indefensible and because the tenuous support for affirmative action was the most that could be hoped for. But many of the black spokesmen would begin to develop reservations as they analyzed the decision more carefully. They realized that the decision made affirmative action permissible and not mandatory. The white majority which Justice Powell suggested did not exist would be allowed to continue to provide minorities with access to the mainstream as long as it desired. But what the minorities recognized was that the *Bakke* case reflected a growing sense among the more fortunate that the poor had been given enough. In the words of pollster Mervin Field, "It has become much more acceptable to be less generous."

Because of the narrow scope of the decision, it was not immediately apparent what its effect would be in the important area of employment. But even if the Court upheld laws mandating affirmative action in employment, minorities had to worry about a possible translation of the national mood into congressional action. Already, conservative members of Congress had introduced legislation to undercut the government's ability to enforce affirmative action requirements.

None of America's traditional victims would be winners in the *Bakke* case. The Court had by the slimmest of margins held affirmative action programs permissible under certain circumstances, but there was no guarantee that white Americans would choose to continue these programs, which had only just begun to bring equal opportunity to racial minorities. Allan Bakke had been admitted to medical school, but while he had become a symbol for America's "forgotten" white men, Bakke, with his $28,000 NASA salary and engineer's degree, was hardly representative of the poor and working-class whites who the polls showed identified with him so strongly. And few of them would gain by his "victory."

The real winners had been the country's economically and educationally privileged. Mr. Cox had asked that the Court not interfere with the university's right to choose its students as it saw fit. Not only had his request been granted, but his own school, Harvard, the pinnacle of the academic elite, had been pointed to as the example of the way things should be done.

Shortly after the Court's decision, Derrick Bell, the Harvard Law School's first black professor and the author of a text on racism in American law, noted that once again the legitimate frustrations and angers of the majority of white Americans had been displaced onto blacks. At most schools minority admissions programs provided token access by minorities to an admissions process heavily weighted toward the upper classes. Poorer whites, Bell pointed out, considering their virtual exclusion from elite educational institutions, had every reason to complain, but the concern and hostility of whites focused not on the general admissions process and the most favored status it provided for well-to-do applicants but on the minuscule number of seats set aside for minorities.

"Opposition to racial quotas has been the slogan," said Bell, "but retention of superior societal status based on race has been the goal. Otherwise, why challenge a minority admissions procedure accounting for ten percent of the seats when class-based standards equally exclusionary for all but a few account for 90 percent of the seats?"

The Court had failed to address itself to the issues at the core of the national debate provoked by Bakke. By their silence, the justices who took the Stevens position alleging a violation of Title VI had sidestepped the serious questions raised about the meaning of race and the scope of racial problems still existing in the United States. And because of Justice Powell's concern about responding to the most immediate political pressures, he too had written an opinion that had avoided any clear position on the nature of the Constitution's commitment to resolving the American Dilemma of race and equality. Only the four justices who had joined the Brennan opinion had seen fit to confront the reality that a history of American racism had left the country divided by race and opportunity. The question of the meaning of the equal protection clause could not be answered without a decision on what equality meant. Did the Constitution require a maintenance of the existing inequities of opportunity, or did it require a fundamental readjustment of those opportunities?

Ultimately the greatest impact of the Court's decision would be outside the bounds of the laws it had handed down. Americans had looked to this respected and still-hallowed institution for guidance on a difficult and troubling issue. The justices had been aware of the most melodramatic aspects of the case and had done their best to sidestep the most obvious pitfalls by refusing to entangle themselves in semantic problems such as "goals," "quotas," and "qualifications." After all, one reason the Court had maintained its aura in a time of growing mistrust of government was its very cautious approach to jurisprudence. Even the favorite term of the meritocrats and journalists, *reverse discrimination*, was referred to only once in the massive opinions, and Justice Powell took care to wrap it in quotation marks.

It is not a little ironic that the script for this legal melodrama was little more than a reasonable facsimile of what had really transpired at Davis. Much of the Court's decision had turned on crucial "facts" that had become a part of the record through the stipulations and omissions of the university. Powell had held that the Task Force program constituted an unconstitutional quota because the record showed that whites were not allowed to compete for seats in the special admissions program while minorities were considered for every seat in the class. But a full examination of the admissions process as it actually operated raises considerable doubt whether either of these "facts" was true.

The final decision to order Bakke's admission was compelled because the university had conceded its inability to prove that Bakke would not have been admitted if the special admissions program did not exist. This concession had clearly been influenced as much by the university's anxiety to get to the Supreme Court and avoid a close examination of its admissions practices as by its belief that it could not meet the burden of proof.

Despite the fact that Justice Powell's opinion represented the views of only one member of the Court, schools throughout the country looked to his words for guidance in revamping their minority admissions programs. They argued that it was all they had to go on and that since Powell had taken such pains to chart a "middle course," it made perfect sense for them to follow his lead. But the lack of a clear majority position also provided a perfect excuse for institutions that wanted to rid themselves of minority admissions. They could argue that because of the murky nature of the Supreme Court's decision, they had to choose a conservative interpretation to avoid further legal challenges.

At some schools special committees for minority applicants were eliminated. On other campuses the definition of *disadvantaged* was broadened to include whites. Others tried to balance traditional admissions criteria with new ones that took race and economic background into consideration.

The new admissions procedure at Davis, introduced in the fall of 1978, sought that elusive "middle course." Under a computer-graded point system, applicants had to score at least 15 out of a possible 30 points to make the first cut. Points were awarded primarily on the basis of grades and test scores. Minority applicants automatically received an additional 5 points. Students who claimed to be disadvantaged also received 5 points and were asked to submit a brief written description of the nature of their disadvantage.

The 2,000 applicants to survive the first cut then were considered by a series of subcommittees. The first committee examined the credentials of applicants. A second group interviewed applicants, and a third subcommittee made the final decision on admission or rejection. Interestingly, the new plan took away the medical school dean's power to admit students at his own discretion.

But the decision ordering Bakke admitted legitimized the concept of a majority discriminating against itself, and there was a danger that zealots opposed to this practice would harm genuine efforts toward equality. If there was a serious omission by the Court, it was the failure to address the national mood which lurked around the edges of the stage on which the Bakke affair was played. The justices, no matter what their political or legal positions on the issues, surely could have addressed this important element in the melodrama and declared the continuing commitment of America to a real and tangible equality for all its citizens. By their failure to chastise the hecklers in the audience, they had given opponents of affirmative action the courage to continue their campaign.

Minority groups had sought some guarantee from the Court that the process of amelioration begun in the last decade would continue. But this was not a Supreme Court that wanted the role of protector which the Warren Court had accepted courageously. The frail majorities in this decision said simply that efforts to bring minorities closer to equality were allowable under the laws of the land. This caution, too, was in keeping with the traditions of this Court in avoiding a leadership role in the formulation of a national consensus. The broader issues of class and privilege sidestepped this time would undoubtedly come back to the Court in future cases.

For the time being, medical schools would continue to favor the children of the wealthy and exclude thousands of well-qualified applicants of all races. Just a few months before the decision, the *New York Times* had reported on a growing pattern of abuses of the admissions process by wealthy parents attempting to avoid the stiff competition for places. A study by Grace Ziem at Harvard University of the composition of medical students at U.S. universities shows that the percentage of students below the national median income has remained at 12 since 1920. It would probably have been unreasonable to assume that the Court would address the most serious problems of the medical profession which are rooted at least as much in class issues as in the racial history of this country. The exorbitant costs of medical care would not at all be affected, nor the basic nature of that care. The decision would have little impact on the infant mortality rate in the black and Hispanic ghettos of the country and would not visibly alter the racial makeup of the medical profession. While the chances for whites of being admitted into their desired professions had not been changed much by the *Bakke* decision, the ruling would clearly have a negative impact on the opportunities for minorities. The Supreme Court had attempted to find a neutral ground for a political decision, but because there could be no "benign" solution, the justices had not strayed from the traditions of America in their choice of victims.

Eleven

AFTER BAKKE: QUOTAS
AND A WHITE CLUB
BY THE BAY

Reporters have grown fond of referring to the *Bakke* case as "perhaps the most important Supreme Court decision since *Brown* v. *Board of Education*." In the 1954 *Brown* decision, the Court declared segregated school systems unconstitutional because they deprived black schoolchildren of the opportunity for an equal education. The decision itself was a narrow one; it did not outlaw all segregation but applied only to segregated schools. Only school systems where segregation was sanctioned by law were compelled to desegregate, and that was to be accomplished with "all deliberate speed." The narrow score and cautious tenor of the decision were dictated by the Court's sensitivity to the southern temperament and by Chief Justice Earl Warren's desire to achieve a unanimous ruling on the controversial case. The decision to treat the South gently meant that segregated school systems remained virtually intact for ten years following the decision.

But the importance of the *Brown* decision cannot be measured simply by its scope or the success of its implementation. Despite the Court's effort to limit the language of *Brown*, it became clear that the decision had, in effect, declared illegal all forms of state-sanctioned segregation. The Court went on to rely on *Brown* to declare unconstitutional segregated municipal buses, public parks and beaches, public golf courses, and other government-owned services and facilities.

Even more important was the fact that *Brown* spawned the mass movement for racial equality by declaring that the Constitution was squarely on the side of the struggle for equality and human rights. Equality was not just a gift to be bestowed by whites, but a birthright. Less than a year after the decision, Rosa Parks, a forty-three-year-old seamstress in Montgomery, Alabama, refused to give up her seat to a white man and sparked a yearlong boycott of public transportation led by Martin Luther King, Jr. The success of Montgomery led to other boycotts throughout the South. In 1960 college students launched the second stage of the movement with sit-ins at segregated lunch counters in North Carolina. The all-out campaign for civil rights had begun.

But while the Supreme Court had outlawed segregation in publicly owned facilities, lunch counters, hotels, barbershops, movies, and restaurants were privately owned and protected from court action by a constitutional rule called the state action doctrine. In 1883, in the Civil Rights Cases, the Supreme Court had struck down a provision of the federal Civil Rights Law of 1875 which had outlawed racial discrimination in inns, public conveyances, theaters, and other places of public amusement. The Court had said the Fourteenth Amendment applied only when the *state* deprived an individual of equal protection and said the law did not apply to wrongs that blacks might suffer at the hands of private individuals.

This decision was an invitation to discrimination by making it clear that government would do nothing to interfere with the discriminatory practices of individuals. The courts were also inactive in protecting the right of blacks to vote. The civil remedies for discriminatory administration of election laws depended on private litigation and even when a complainant could be found, the problems of collecting evidence or securing a favorable verdict in southern communities were insurmountable. But in 1963 the campaign of nonviolent confrontation with southern segregation reached its peak. National television audiences saw "Bull" Connor's troops use dogs, hoses, and cattle prods against children. When three little black girls were killed by a bomb in a Birmingham church, President Kennedy could no longer remain silent. His televised speech to the country challenged America to make freedom a reality for blacks as well as whites. "We are confronted primarily with a moral issue," he declared. "It is as old as the Scriptures and is as clear as the Constitution. If an American, because his skin is dark, cannot eat lunch in a restaurant open to the public; if he cannot send his children to the best public schools available; if he cannot vote for the public officials who represent him; if, in short, he cannot enjoy the full and free life which all of us want, then who among us would be content to have the color of his skin changed and stand in his place?"

A week after this extraordinary speech, Kennedy sent to Congress a comprehensive Civil Rights Bill. But it would take his assassination in Dallas, the killing of a white woman, Viola Liuzzo, in Alabama, massive marches in Washington and Selma, and the arm-twisting tactics of a southern president to enact the Civil Rights Act of 1964. The act outlawed discrimination in public accommodations, federally assisted programs, education, and employment. The relatively weak voting rights provisions were substantially strengthened by the Voting Rights Act in 1965. The mood of the country—despite some strong resistance—was one that supported equality for blacks, and Congress reflected that mood with a willingness to support Johnson's Great Society legislation.

Southerners quickly challenged the new legislation in the courts. The Supreme Court, however, supported the national mood in two public accommodations cases, avoiding the state action doctrine and declaring that racial discrimination in public places affected interstate commerce. In the two cases, *Heart of Atlanta Motel* v. *United States* and *Katzenbach* v. *McClung,* the Supreme Court made it clear that it was reversing its long-standing acquiescence in discrimination.

The High Court went on to affirm the Voting Rights Act in *South Carolina* v. *Katzenbach* and declared that "the time for deliberate speed has run out on school desegregation. The Court struck down freedom-of-choice plans and placed the burden on school boards "to come forward with a plan that promises realistically to work now."

Because the initial confrontations following the *Brown* decision had centered on desegregation and the vote, the employment provisions of the 1964 Civil Rights Act, Title VII, had received little attention. But it soon became clear that Title VII was the most radical provision of the 1964 law, for it contained the only hope of eradicating the economic caste system which placed blacks on the lowest rung of the employment ladder.

Title VII prohibited an employer from hiring, firing, promoting, or in any other way discriminating against an employee on the basis of race, color, religion, sex, or national origin. It also prohibited any segregation or classification of employees or applicants that would deprive the individual of employment opportunities or in any other way affect his or her status adversely. The act, originally applied to private employers, was amended to cover government employers in 1972 and also affected labor unions, employment agencies, and job-training programs.

It was not until 1971 that the Supreme Court addressed the legality of Title VII. *Griggs* v. *Duke Power Company* involved a class action suit brought by blacks working at the Dean River power-generating facilities operated by Duke in

Draper, North Carolina. Before Title VII became effective, the company had openly discriminated in hiring and assigned all blacks to the labor department, where the highest-paying jobs paid less than the lowest salaries in the other four departments.

In 1965 the power company had discontinued the overt policy of restricting blacks but, for the first time, made graduation from high school and satisfactory performance on two professionally prepared aptitude tests a condition for employment in the more desirable departments. White employees who had been hired prior to the adoption of the new requirements were allowed to continue working in the higher-paying departments and were promoted whether or not they had been graduated from high school and without having to take the new tests.

According to the 1960 census, only 12 percent of black males in North Carolina had graduated from high school, compared to 34 percent of white males. It was not surprising that 58 percent of the whites and only 6 percent of blacks who took the test passed. A crucial factor in the case was that neither of the aptitude tests measured the ability to learn or perform the jobs the company had to offer.

The federal district court that considered the case found that Title VII had not been violated and said that the law was not intended to be retroactive or to apply to discrimination in the past or to the impact of past discrimination on the racial composition of the company's work force, and the court of appeals agreed.

But the U.S. Supreme Court reversed the lower court's decision. The Court said the intent of Congress in enacting Title VII was clear: "It was to achieve equality of employment opportunity and remove barriers that have operated in the past to favor an identifiable group of white employees over other employees." Under the act, said Chief Justice

Warren Burger, writing for a unanimous Court, "practices, procedures or tests neutral on their face, and even neutral in terms of intent, cannot be maintained if they operate to 'freeze' the status quo of prior discriminatory employment practices.

"Congress has now provided that tests or other criteria for employment or promotion may not provide equality of opportunity only in the sense of the fabled offer of milk to the stork and the fox. On the contrary, Congress has now required that the posture and condition of the job seeker be taken into account. It has—to resort again to the fable—provided that the vessel in which the milk is proffered be one all seekers can use. The act proscribed not only overt discrimination but also practices that are fair in form but discriminatory in operation. The touchstone is business necessity. If an employment practice which operates to exclude Negroes cannot be shown to be related to job performance, the practice is prohibited," the Court asserted. "Good intent or absence of discriminatory intent does not redeem employment procedures or testing mechanisms that operate as headwinds for minority groups and are unrelated to measuring job capability."

Although the Court was technically just interpreting the provisions of the statute, its reasoning recognized a reality that had never before been articulated in its decisions. After 200 years of oppression, the Court said, equality could not be achieved by simply removing the mechanisms of political domination. It was fraudulent to speak of "neutral requirements" or a "fair contest" when a contestant had suffered the consequences of this oppression. The *Griggs* opinion also recognized that any requirement of intent would destroy any chances of achieving equal opportunity. Intent would be almost impossible to prove, especially since employers knew that racial discrimination was illegal. The new business necessity test assumed that any requirement that excluded blacks for reasons not related to the job had a discriminatory intent. In addition, intent was really irrelevant since the purpose of the law was not to punish evil employers but to ensure the removal of the barriers to equal employment.

The decision of the Supreme Court to look at results makes the *Griggs* case its most radical and far-reaching decision on the issue of race. The Court recognized that a conversion to a nonracist society required the removal of barriers much more complex and subtle than laws. Once it was demonstrated that the employer was using a test or requirement that had the effect of excluding minorities or maintaining the status quo, the burden was on the employer to prove there was a business reason for this practice. If *Brown* established racial equality in principle, *Griggs* required it in fact.

San Francisco is an unlikely setting for racial conflict. There is little evidence here, even in the poorest neighborhoods, of the bombed-out blocks of the South Bronx or the rows of deserted houses in Philadelphia or Detroit. The neighborhoods are culturally distinct: the Mission, with its Latin flavor and "English spoken here" signs; the Fillmore, still predominantly black but turning over to gay and white; North Beach, where the Chinese are replacing the Italians. But racial tensions are remarkably low. Whites, blacks, browns, and yellows move easily within integrated neighborhoods and interracial couples rarely attract attention. There is little evidence now of the attitude of twenty-five years ago when Nob Hill's famous Mark Hopkins Hotel had to clear its dining room of all white patrons before seating the family of one of the city's most prominent black doctors. San Franciscans today would find it difficult to believe that Willie Mays had so much trouble finding a house when the Giants abandoned New York in 1958.

Poverty is also well disguised in San Francisco. Tourists gape out of bubble-topped charter buses and never see a slum. The only obvious poverty is the self-imposed version among the remnants of the Haight-Ashbury counterculture.

But there is one section of San Francisco that has neither the look nor the feel of the rest of the city. Bayview-Hunters Point is on the southeastern tip of the city, isolated from more affluent and picturesque areas by the barrier of Highway 101. Chinatown may be the only ghetto that is a tourist attraction, but few casual visitors ever see the city's only nonintegrated black enclave. The best parts of Hunters Point look like neighborhoods in a slightly seedy southern town, but the barracks-like projects, built for the influx of blacks who worked in the shipyards during World War II, make it clear that this is what the social planners call the inner city. And it was here that another kind of racial conflict would bring up the question of "quotas," in a different context from the *Bakke* case.

For years the San Francisco Fire Department had operated as an exclusive white club. In 1967 the department had just one black member. Most of the fire fighters were Irish Catholic, and they ran the department like a family business, passing the jobs from father to son and from uncle to nephew. At one time in the city's history this might have been a reflection of the ethnic makeup of San Francisco. But according to the 1970 census, 43 percent of the city's population consisted of minority groups (15 percent black, 23 percent Asians, and 5 percent others). The city's high schools were more than 60 percent nonwhite. In the summer of 1969 a newspaper article had disclosed that there were only four black firemen in San Francisco. City fire fighters were well paid, and the twenty-four-hour shift system meant they worked only a three-day week, which gave them time to moonlight in second jobs. To the residents of Hunters Point, these jobs seemed very desirable, and they wanted to get more blacks in.

Another community concern was safety. After the riots of 1966, white firemen had declared that they were afraid to venture into Hunters Point and other black areas of the city. The residents were angered and naturally concerned that a result of the segregated fire department would be unanswered alarms and a loss of lives and property in their communities.

It took some time to collect the data, to find complainants, and to prepare the case, but in August 1970 the NAACP Legal Defense Fund and the California Rural Legal Assistance program joined the Neighborhood Legal Assistance in a suit against the San Francisco Civil Service Commission on behalf of the Western Addition Community Organization, the NAACP, and the Mexican-American Political Association. The complaint said the organizations represented "all Negro and Mexican-American San Francisco area adults fully qualified to be firemen" and "all Negro and Mexican-American San Francisco adults desirous of having their homes protected by an integrated department." The suit charged that the written examination used to select firemen violated the plaintiffs' rights to due process and equal protection of the laws.

WACO v. *Alioto* was an example of the kind of lawsuit that would become commonplace in the 1970s, attacking patterns and practices that had long been taken for granted and demanding a redistribution of opportunity and a more equal share of the nation's jobs. The cases aroused opposition among whites, like Bakke, for whom affirmative action programs amounted to reverse discrimination.

Although the U.S. Supreme Court's decision in *Regents* v. *Bakke* related to race-conscious admissions programs in the country's graduate schools and colleges, several of the justices had drawn analogies to employment cases. The Court had already agreed to hear several important job discrimination cases in the 1978–79 term, and the *Bakke* decision would ultimately have its greatest impact on the nation's working men and women.

Any measure of black opinion reports that employment is the primary concern. For the past twenty-five years, black unemployment has stayed nearly double the white rate, no matter what the economic situation. In 1966 the median non-white income was equal to the median white income in 1947. A 1967 study of poverty among nonwhites found that even when one discounted such variables as differences in education, "the sheer fact of being black explained 38 percent of the difference between the incidence of poverty for whites and Negroes." But while the pattern of economic exclusion was clear, the first stages of the struggle for equality did little to address these issues.

The Supreme Court's reasoning in *Griggs* was the basis of WACO's suit against San Francisco's all-white fire department. At the crux of the case was the city civil service examination results, used to fill vacancies in the department. Although applicants were also required to take an athletic ability test and a medical examination, the results merely determined minimal requirements. The sole factor in determining an applicant's position on the hiring list was his score on the written test.

The minority applicants complained that the written test was discriminatory because it was unrelated to the job of fire fighting and served as a barrier to minorities in competing for positions in the fire department. The exam's emphasis was on math, verbal ability, and reading comprehension. While 47 percent of the 150 questions tested these skills, 16 percent related to the general knowledge of mechanics and the physical properties of various materials, 11 percent to basic chemistry and physics, and 13 percent to responses in situations with which a fireman might be confronted. An item on one exam depicted a famous painting and asked the applicant to identify the artist. Perhaps a fire fighter might have to choose one day between saving a Van Gogh or a Cézanne, but the question seemed somewhat removed from "business necessity."

The job required physical ability and the capacity to perform under stress, the suit argued, but not mathematical, verbal, and reading skills. The emphasis of the examination and its weight in the selection process seemed misplaced. In fact, a report from the National Board of Underwriters had recommended that a written examination should constitute no more than 30 percent of the factors in selecting firemen. But San Francisco's fire department had chosen to ignore this recommendation.

The negative impact of the test on minority applicants was illustrated by the result of examinations given in December 1968. Just 101 of the 1,883 applicants allowed to take the test after meeting the physical, medical, and character investigations were black. Of the 662 who passed the test, 12 were black. Of the 350 who qualified for the hiring list, just 3 were black, and they ranked 239th, 304th, and 308th. Since 160 men would be hired from the list, none of the blacks would qualify for the fire department. On the basis of the *Griggs* decision, the department had to show that the test was related to the actual task of fire fighters, or it was illegal under Title VII.

On July 23, 1970, the lawyers at Public Advocates, the public interest firm now representing the minority organizations, filed a motion in the federal district court in San Francisco to stop the city's Civil Service Commission from using the results of the 1968 test and from using its format in future examinations.

The judge hearing the case was William Sweigert, a seventy-year-old Republican who had been appointed to the federal bench by President Eisenhower in 1959. A product of San Francisco's parochial school system, he had many old friends in the largely Irish-Catholic fire department hierarchy, and he was reluctant to find them directly at fault. Throughout the litigation, Sweigert would give the city every benefit of doubt, ruling against the defense only when the evidence was uncontradicted and when the law clearly allowed no other result.

Sweigert's initial response to the suit was to delay the administration of the written examination and request the city to devise a new, fairer test. But in the three years and numerous court hearings that followed, the Civil Service Commission seemed content to do little more than procrastinate and make excuses. Two new tests were proposed, but each test proved almost as discriminatory as, and no more job-related than, its predecessor. Sweigert considered the imposition of a quota an "extensive type of relief" and felt it "should be avoided, even if legal, unless necessary as a last resort."

By November of 1973 Sweigert's patience was at an end. There was still no valid written exam, and the more than 200 vacancies in the fire department were endangering the safety of the city's inhabitants. He went back to the most recently administered test and found a pool of 314 white and 118 minority applicants who had passed all segments of the test. He ordered the Civil Service Commission to create a dual list and to fill the vacancies by picking alternately from the list of white applicants and the list of minority applicants until the pool of minorities was exhausted. The quota order was temporary and could be altered or ended at Sweigert's discretion.

The ruling was received with a mixture of shock and resentment in the firehouses of San Francisco. The firemen's union had intervened in the suit and opposed any change of the old system. Although the case had been based on the *Griggs* theory of unlawful impact, it soon became clear that racial bias in San Francisco's fire department was not at all theoretical.

On January 21, 1974, the first class of recruits entered the Fire College. Forty-eight men had been selected—twenty-four whites and twenty-four minorities. Nine of the minority recruits were black, two were Asian, one was an East Indian, and twelve had Spanish surnames. Before 1957 new recruits had been immediately assigned to fire stations, where they received their training on an individual basis. The Fire College made that training more formal and socialized the recruit for his professional family. Because men's lives depended on skills and cooperative efforts, the Fire College placed great emphasis on building camaraderie and commitment to the team. The best and most respected veterans were assigned to teach at the college. The training was vigorous, but there was little formal testing. Instructors stayed after class to give recruits who needed help additional pointers, and the recruits were allowed to work with the equipment until they had mastered the necessary skills. In the entire history of the Fire College no man had ever been terminated because of substandard performance. One man had been dismissed for being drunk on the job.

But in the forty-eighth Fire College class the emphasis was not on training but on testing. Recruits were graded on attitude as well as on written and practical skills. Tests were given each Friday, and during the first six weeks of the eight-week course more than twenty-five different tests were administered. Tests were scored in an apparently arbitrary manner, and the passing score fluctuated from week to week. There were no provisions for retesting or makeups. Instructors refused to stay after class to give the recruits additional help.

Little of the family spirit remained, and the minority recruits felt they were being made to pay for the court order. Black candidates who were told by instructors immediately after a practical test that their performance was outstanding discovered later that they had been given failing grades. Others who took tests as part of a team that included white recruits were the only members of their team to receive low scores. Despite these pressures, after three weeks nearly all the recruits had passing grades.

On February 18, the fifth week of classes, a new grading system was introduced. The new deficiency point system meant that failure in one practical test could mean failure for the entire week. Within a few days eleven recruits were called to individual conferences and warned that their performance was substandard. They were told that they were in danger of termination and that they had two weeks to improve their records. Nine of the eleven were minorities, and none had received any prior indication that their performances had any serious deficiencies.

On March 1 three black recruits, Carl English, George Drake, and Jimmy Oates, received letters warning them that termination was imminent. Four days later they were called in and given letters of dismissal.

Ironically, two of the three blacks who had become scapegoats would have made it into the Fire College without the help of Judge Sweigert. Drake, a twenty-year-old Vietnam veteran and the winner of eight combat decorations, had scored 998.50 of the possible 1,000 on the 1971 test, which ranked him twenty-second on the master civil service list. English, an outstanding high school athlete who had completed a year at the University of California at Berkeley, was twenty-third on the original list.

A fourth recruit also dismissed had not been warned as the others had been. Dennis O'Leary had all the traditional San Francisco Fire Department credentials. His father and his uncle were firemen. After being graduated from high school, he had completed two years of junior college and received a degree in fire sciences. He told the court later, "I believe my termination was part of an active cover-up by the Department designed to obscure its efforts to remove black candidates from the Fire College." The fact that he had not received a warning letter seemed to support his suspicion that integration of the dismissals was an afterthought. He believed that he had been chosen because he had been friendly with some of the black recruits.

The recruits contacted Public Advocates, the public interest law firm that had taken over the original suit. The firm immediately filed a motion to reinstate the four recruits. The affidavits of the dismissed recruits were accompanied by a petition signed by 250 firemen who believed the terminations had been "arbitrary and unfair." Seventy-seven firemen agreed to assist in any additional instruction the four might need. The story of the dismissals had spread through the grapevine, and a large number of the club members were unwilling to go along. A similar petition signed by the forty-three remaining recruits was also attached to the motion. Two respected battalion chiefs were leading the campaign for decency. Robert and John Sherratt had witnessed the arbitrary and abusive treatment of the new recruits and refused to go along at great personal risk. But the leaders of the department stood firm and denied any wrongdoing. It would take four weeks of trial before the city agreed to a settlement, which reinstated the four plaintiffs in the next available Fire College class.

What this incident illustrates is both the power and the limitation of the law. In a city with the liberal reputation of San Francisco, the resistance to racial change was as real in the 1970s as it had been in the South a decade earlier. The law had bypassed the barriers to opportunity for minority groups, but it could not protect them from a will to resist. Critics of quotas might point to this resistance as an unavoidable result of groups pitted against each other by court decisions. But would there have been justice in allowing the selection process to continue unchanged because of fears that racial antagonisms would be exacerbated? The *Griggs* decision was an admission that racial attitudes were often subtle and extremely difficult to assess. Examining the impact of an apparently neutral selection process on minority groups revealed discrimination. Opponents of numerical goals avoid the reality of white resistance to the invasion of their exclusive little club. Sometimes the very real concern about social discomfort obscures the equally real right of economic opportunity, and in the more sophisticated language of our time, we tend to forget that resistance to change is not limited to one specific ethnic or economic group.

Judge Sweigert was not the only one to order employers to hire a specific percentage of minorities to correct the effects of discriminatory tests or former job requirements. Between 1971 and 1975 federal courts in virtually every circuit issued and sustained similar quota orders. Police and fire departments were ordered to hire according to numerical ratios in Minneapolis, Boston, Bridgeport, Los Angeles, Baltimore, Philadelphia, Montgomery, and San Francisco. When past discriminatory practices could be proved, unions were also subjected to numerical quotas. In the private sector, racial quotas were imposed on United States Steel, Goodyear Tire and Rubber, Detroit Edison, and other large corporations.

When it became clear that federal judges were willing to require that employers do something about desegregating their work force, many employers entered into consent decrees or voluntary affirmative action programs, either out of a new sense of social responsibility or concern about the costs of defending their actions in court. The battleground for equality was clearly economic, and state and federal agencies had become active advocates for minorities.

Executive Order 11246 gave the Labor Department the

power to require every federal contractor to have an affirmative action program. The Supreme Court upheld this order issued by President Johnson in a case attacking the Philadelphia Plan, which required goals for hiring minorities by contractors involved in federally assisted construction projects. In 1977 Congress would pass the Public Works Employment Act in an attempt to stimulate the economy and fight unemployment. The act required that all contractors receiving funds under the law set aside at least 10 percent of all construction funds for "minority business enterprises" when such businesses were available to do the work. This little-noticed provision would provoke a series of court battles over the concept of the economic quota.

But the enthusiasm for economic redistribution which had evolved out of the civil rights era began to wane in 1971, when the worldwide economic recession began to have an impact on the American economy. The continued expansion of the middle-class sector was no longer assured, and inevitably white males who were competing with women and minorities would soon be rushing into court with their own complaints. Like Bakke, they argued that employment programs which reserved a certain number of slots for minorities and women discriminated against them. Jobs and promotions should go to the best qualified and the most senior, they argued. They favored civil service examinations, like the one used to select firemen for San Francisco, which had been introduced by reformers to remove political favoritism and make sure jobs were awarded on merit alone.

Reynold Colvin's suit on behalf of the San Francisco school administrators had been one of the first of these "reverse discrimination" attacks on affirmative action in employment. The famous baby boom of the post–World War II period had made education a growth industry in the 1950s and 1960s, but the demographic changes in the 1970s forced a rapid contraction. School districts closed schools and laid off teachers. There was no longer a job in education for anyone who wanted one. The competition between blacks and whites was soon translated into a growing flood of challenges to affirmative action.

Brian Weber, a white laboratory technician at a Kaiser Aluminum plant in Gramercy, Louisiana, succeeded Bakke as the central character in the continuing racial melodrama plaguing the Supreme Court. His case, *Weber* v. *Kaiser Aluminum and Chemical Corporation,* was considered by the Court during its 1978–79 session. While he had not captured the public's attention as easily as Allan Bakke, his legal efforts promised to have a much broader impact on affirmative action.

Weber had applied for an on-the-job training program that would qualify him for a position with higher pay and better job security. But Kaiser had signed an agreement with the United Steel Workers Union to set up a program that would bring more minority workers into skilled positions. The minority population in the area around the Louisiana plant was about 43 percent, but until the affirmative action plan was implemented, only 5 of the approximately 290 skilled craftsmen at the plant were black. Under the agreement, one minority worker was to be picked for every white chosen until the percentage of minorities in skilled jobs was roughly equal to their representation in the population. Candidates for the program were picked from separate seniority lists for whites and minorities. When Weber applied for the general repairman program, three blacks and two whites were selected. He was not one of them.

Weber sued, charging that the labor agreement violated Title VII's prohibition of discrimination based on race. The federal district court and the Fifth Circuit Court of Appeals ruled in Weber's favor. The appeals court said there was insufficient evidence to show that Kaiser had engaged in past discrimination and that in the absence of such discrimination the quota system imposed by the company and the union violated Title VII.

American Telephone and Telegraph's affirmative action program was not exactly voluntary, but the company soon found itself a defendant in a reverse discrimination suit. In what had been described as the largest civil rights settlement ever, AT&T agreed in 1973 to a consent decree designed to end job bias against women, blacks, and other racial minorities. After months of negotiation, the Justice Department, the Equal Employment Opportunity Commission, and the Department of Labor filed a suit charging AT&T with discrimination against women and minorities in its 700,000-member work force. The same day a federal judge approved a consent decree the government had negotiated before filing the suit.

The agreement required AT&T to establish goals and time-tables for preferential hiring and for promoting and transferring minority and women employees. Three unions representing company employees refused to accept the agreement and sued both AT&T and the government. In *Communications Workers of America* v. *EEOC* they argued that the program undercut seniority rights won in collective bargaining and violated the due process and equal protection clauses of the Fourteenth Amendment. In May 1977 the Third Circuit Court of Appeals upheld federal district judge Leon Higginbotham's ruling in favor of the consent decree. The circuit court ruled that "the use of employment goals and quotas admittedly involves tensions" with the Fourteenth Amendment but that the plan was "permissible because it seems reasonably calculated to counteract the detrimental effects of a particular identifiable pattern of discrimination." The U.S. Supreme Court would let the decision stand by refusing to review the lower court's ruling.

In *Kreps* v. *Associated Contractors of California* a group of contractors challenged the 10 percent "set-aside" provision of the 1977 Public Works Employment Act on the grounds that it violated Title VI of the Civil Rights Act of 1964, which bars discrimination in federally funded programs and the due process clause of the Fourteenth Amendment. A federal judge agreed, but the Supreme Court ducked the issue by sending the case back to determine whether it was moot because the money allocated to the act had already been spent.

In a case similar to the San Francisco suit against the fire department, a federal judge in Los Angeles found that city's fire department screening tests did not meet the *Griggs* standard of business necessity and set a quota of 20 percent for blacks and 20 percent for Mexican-Americans for new employees. The case, *County of Los Angeles* v. *Davis*, was taken to the U.S. Supreme Court.

Cramer v. *Virginia Commonwealth University* brought the issues raised by Bakke back to the academic setting and raised the additional issue of reverse discrimination by sex. James Cramer, a thirty-two-year-old sociologist who had taught at Virginia Commonwealth for a year, claimed he was denied tenure because the university chose to hire a "less qualified" woman under a voluntary affirmative action plan.

The common thread in all these cases is the argument by white males that they are being treated unfairly and that through no fault of their own they are being moved from the front to the back of the line. Their argument is that affirmative action changes the rules of the game and replaces mechanisms designed to assure fair competition. They are being made victims simply because they are white and male.

What these statements ignore is precisely what the Supreme Court recognized in *Griggs*—that the old rules of the game were not fair and that the merit system was limited to white males. Before 1954 the right of white men to superior and preferential treatment in the job market was never seriously questioned. When Congress and the courts made white male supremacy illegal in employment, both the formal and the informal systems of selection remained intact. There were the "old boy" systems of filling vacancies by word of mouth, the preferences for sons and nephews of employees, the stereotypes held by personnel directors about the kinds of people best suited for certain positions, the assumptions that certain ethnic groups had a natural monopoly in other positions, and the seniority systems that perpetuated the effects of past discrimination. During a period when federal agencies and the courts were willing to confront these much more complex obstacles to equality, they imposed goals and quotas with the objective of achieving results.

The "reverse discrimination" argument argues against any large-scale societal readjustments. It assumes that the pre-affirmative-action procedures were fairer than ones that take into account the dynamics and legacies of a racially conscious society. Both *Griggs* and Title VII address systemic and institutional policies that serve to exclude by race or sex. If an employer has used such devices or has discriminated against minorities in the past, the courts have allowed numerical readjustments.

Those who advocate a return to a nominally neutral system disclaim any societal responsibility for the position of minority groups, but they also want to reap the benefits of the acts in which they claim to have played no role. "Why should I be laid off when I've put in fifteen years at the plant when this black guy has only been here four?" says the white worker in defense of his seniority rights. But if the plant would not hire blacks ten or fifteen years ago, the black worker will never reap the equality of security granted his white counterpart. He will be laid off in recessions and be barred from promotion because of discriminatory acts ten or twenty years old. He continues to pay for the sins of those who would not hire him because of color.

When the U.S. Supreme Court agreed to hear the *Bakke* case, it had already made two substantial retreats from the spirit and principle of the *Griggs* case. *Washington* v. *Davis*, a 1976 decision, was almost identical to the San Francisco Fire Department case. Black applicants to the District of Columbia police force claimed that the written test used to help select recruits denied them equal protection by excluding a disproportionate number of blacks. The test failed blacks at four times the rate of whites and had no relationship to job performance, the plaintiffs argued. They made no claim of discriminatory intent or purpose. Then the police force in the nation's capital had been active and rather successful in attracting blacks. Using *Griggs* as a standard, a federal court of appeals agreed with the black applicants, saying that intent was irrelevant and that the discriminatory impact of the test was sufficient proof of a constitutional violation.

But the U.S. Supreme Court disagreed. When the applicants filed their suit, they were not yet protected by the amendments that extended Title VII to public employees. Their case was based on the Fifth and Fourteenth Amendments, and the question was whether the Court would extend the *Griggs* standard to the Constitution. Justice White, writing for a five-man majority, said the court of appeals was in error in applying *Griggs:* "We have never held that the constitutional standard for adjudicating claims of invidious racial discrimination is identical to standards applicable under Title VII and we decline to do so today. . . .

"The central purpose of the Equal Protection Clause of the

14th Amendment is the prevention of official conduct on the basis of race. . . . But our cases have not embraced the proposition that a law or other official act, without regard to whether it reflects a racially discriminatory purpose, is unconstitutional *solely* because it has a racially disproportionate impact."

In other words, the Court was requiring individuals or groups seeking constitutional protection from racial discrimination to prove intent or purpose. Where the Constitution was involved, the Court would ignore what it seemed to see so clearly in *Griggs*. Where tests and zoning ordinances had replaced "whites only" signs, the intention of institutions and individuals would be nearly impossible to prove. This apparent backward step was important because Title VII covered a limited area of conduct.

A year later the Court decided the case of *International Brotherhood of Teamsters* v. *United States*. This case involved a suit brought by the Civil Rights Division of the Justice Department against a large national trucking company and the union that represented most of its employees. The suit said the company had discriminated against minorities by hiring them only as servicemen or local drivers while reserving higher-paying long-distance jobs for whites. The suit charged that the seniority system in the collective bargaining agreements between the company and the union perpetuated or "locked in" the effects of past discrimination, because if a city driver wanted to transfer to the higher-paying positions, he had to forfeit all his seniority rights and start at the bottom. The government proved at the trial that the company had engaged in a pattern of discrimination against minorities in violation of Title VII. The vital question before the Court was whether, given proof of past discrimination, a seniority system that perpetuated past discrimination was unlawful.

The Supreme Court upheld the seniority system by making a distinction between seniority lost as a result of "post-Act discrimination" and seniority lost because of discrimination before the law was passed. The courts could make up for discrimination since 1964, but there would be no relief for "pre-Act discrimination." What happened was that the labor establishment, a powerful element in the civil rights struggle during the 1960s, had managed to insert a clause in the law immunizing seniority systems despite their discriminatory impact.

The Court rejected the government's argument that the clause was illegal by saying that such a finding "would place an affirmative obligation on the parties to the seniority agreement to subordinate [their] rights in favor of the claims of pre-Act discriminatees without seniority." After reviewing the legislative history, the justices concluded that "Congress did not intend to make it illegal for employees with vested seniority rights to continue to exercise those rights, even at the expense of pre-Act discriminatees." In the *Teamsters* case, the Court had attributed the choice of victims to Congress, and that choice was clear.

The Supreme Court had not been required to confront the issue of employment discrimination in the *Bakke* case, which centered on graduate school admissions. But the implications of *Bakke* for working men and women was clear enough. If affirmative action programs were outlawed, what was to prevent a return to the ancient practices that had always denied minorities access to the marketplace? The consensus for affirmative action was clearly a thing of the past in the face of tremendous economic problems and the intense competition for desirable positions.

Because the Court did not have the power to create full employment, it would have to decide whether the competition would be governed by the old rules that placed whites at the front of the lines or by the new laws that attempted to break the well-entrenched patterns of discrimination. Because, just like the men at the bottom of the San Francisco Fire Department hiring list, not all the people at the end of the line would get jobs, there could not be a neutral position that would harm no one. Someone had to be at the end of the line, and the Supreme Court was being asked to choose.

The Court would not make this choice in one crucial landmark decision. The *Bakke* case had proved that the Court was of many minds and that it would move cautiously on this very sensitive issue. In the cases challenging affirmative action in employment that were scheduled to come before the court in the 1978–79 term the Court was likely to base its decisions on the narrowest of grounds. It was also likely to attempt to avoid responsibility for the choice by throwing the issue back into the political arena as it had done in *Bakke*. But even if the Court upheld laws mandating affirmative action in employment, minorities had to worry about a possible translation of the national mood into congressional action. Already conservative members of Congress had introduced legislation to undercut the government's ability to enforce affirmative action requirements.

In California, the trend-setting state where it had all begun, the voters had overwhelmingly passed Proposition 13, a measure designed to limit property taxes and government spending, which would have a devastating effect on local governments' social welfare and affirmative action programs. Allan Bakke had left NASA and his suburban San Francisco home to enroll in his first year of medical studies amid the broad stretches of farmland at Davis. There were now 65 minority firemen among the 1,501 in San Francisco's previously all-white club. In the best tradition of the department several of them had found outside jobs to occupy their off days and supplement their income. Like all firemen, they tried to repress the constant fear that the next time they entered a burning building might be their last. They also tried not to think about Proposition 13 and the *Bakke* case. They had been given a piece of the American pie, but their position was a precarious one. Any combination of job layoffs or "reverse discrimination" suits might put their jobs in jeopardy.

Twelve

A CHOICE OF

VICTIMS

On Monday, September 25, 1978, Allan Paul Bakke joined 100 other first-year students to form the medical school Class of 1982 of the University of California at Davis. If Bakke's efforts over a five-year period had simply been one man's struggle to bring his dreams to reality, then the first day of classes would have provided a fit and anticlimactic end to the story. But the presence of reporters, cameras, and chanting pickets on the Davis campus thwarted any ideas Bakke might have had of ending his role as a symbol.

The story could not really end because some very serious issues remained. The U.S. Supreme Court had set down some rules that applied to only a very small segment of a very broad problem. The broader conflicts exposed by Bakke's determination to attend medical school had not yet been resolved. He had achieved a personal victory and given comfort to many who had serious questions about some of the methods used in the quest for equality in America. But there were also some who believed that Allan Bakke had helped curtail the aspirations of many others.

If there was a lesson in this case, it was that all the dreams of young Americans could not be fulfilled. The medical school process was a microcosm of a competitive process that was spreading to many areas of American life. According to the

U.S. Census Bureau, there would be more than 60 million Americans between the ages of twenty-five and forty-four by 1990. The competitive crush for places in professional schools would soon be extended into an intense and emotional struggle for scarce opportunities in other fields. The old myths about individual ambition and individual choice would now clash with the needs of society and the political realities of a very crowded future.

The *Bakke* case should have forced a sober examination of some very complex issues. How were we to choose the best doctors? How were we to choose from many well-qualified applicants for a few openings in many fields? What did tests really tell us, and what were their limits and values? What did "merit" really mean? Had we really achieved the equality that was so valued in America? But for the most part, the debate had not been enlightening. Too often it had got sidetracked into semantic cul-de-sacs such as "better qualified" and "less qualified." The issue of race dominated the debate around *Bakke*, and as often happened in American history, it helped obscure some fundamental economic problems.

At least the case had shown how artificial was the racial peace of the 1970s. There was plenty of evidence that the most cruel aspects of legal racism had been eliminated. Fundamental changes had taken place in the relationship between white and nonwhite Americans, and considerable progress had been made in employment, income, and social interaction. Because of such visible gains, many Americans found it difficult to accept the fact that so much more remained to be done.

The emotional rhetoric generated by the case pointed to a fundamental change in the country's perception of race relations. The problem posed was no longer a matter of granting rights to everyone but of allocating a limited number of opportunities. If there were no racial minorities, coming to grips with this fundamental challenge to our American myths would have been difficult enough. Now racial minorities were adding to the difficulties by demanding their fair share of these opportunities. If everyone who wanted to—and who had the ability—could not become a doctor or a lawyer or president, who would be chosen, and who would make that choice? It was easier to fall back on the ancient assumptions that those demanding their share who were not white were making unreasonable demands.

The country had clearly shifted away from the economic and political generosity that made the civil rights movement so successful in the 1960s. The Tax Revolt, highlighted by passage of California's Proposition 13, was an obvious sign of rebellion in the middle classes against the cost of government. Because this movement lacked ideology, minority groups feared it could be turned against them. Blacks and Hispanics had come to depend on government for employment and legal protection, and they worried that programs designed to help them particularly might be made scapegoats for fiscal problems for which they were not responsible.

A fundamental difference between blacks and whites lay in their different concepts of the role that government should play in their lives. The expression of middle-class sentiment in Proposition 13 had its applications in *Bakke* as well. At its core was a racial difference in perceptions of America. Most whites believed that our major racial problems had been solved, but most blacks did not. Justice Marshall, in arguing that the melting pot had not worked for blacks, reflected that minority perception. Without a national consensus to provide energy and momentum, the movement toward equality was stalled. Opponents of race-sensitive measures saw the country as a collection of competing ethnic groups whose only rights were individual and whose achievements were simply the result of merit. Such a vision of America was comforting to those in the best position to reap the benefits of privilege.

Racial minorities would find it difficult, in light of their own experiences, to accept such a picture of America. As long as opportunities were color-coded, there was a contradiction between the comfortable mythology of the meritocracy and the realities of American life. The sharp racial differences in life expectancy, medical care, income, job categories, education, and political power all were a part of that reality. Those who argued for improved educational opportunities rather than more drastic adjustments were ignoring disparities that went beyond differences in schooling. How would they explain that white high school dropouts had lower unemployment rates than black youths with some college education or that the economic gap between blacks and whites was widening despite growing numbers of blacks in higher education? The experience of professional schools and corporations had shown that *qualifications* was not such an easy term to define. A very real resistance to affirmative action came from a justifiable fear of competition. Just as whites wanted to narrow the competitive field as much as possible, minorities saw they needed government intervention to get a fair share.

"Victory for a White" said the subhead on the *New York Times* story about the Supreme Court's decision in the *Bakke* case. The year before, *Newsweek* had portrayed a black and a white in a tug-of-war over a diploma in its cover story on reverse discrimination. The presentation of whites as victims of affirmative action was the key to the controversy around the *Bakke* case, and considering the relative positions of whites and nonwhites in America in the 1970s, it was a gross distortion of reality. But the struggle for power had always been at the root of racial conflict in the country, and white resistance to civil rights had always been fed by a fear of losing control. Lost in the debate over preferential admissions was the fact that medical schools were more than 90 percent white, that 95 percent of law students were white, and that in virtually every desirable job category, minorities came nowhere near having representation approaching their numbers in the population. After two decades of civil rights activism and ten years of feminism, being born white and male continued to be the best guarantee of success in America.

Historical and economic circumstances at the turn of the last century had enabled white ethnic groups to gain control of a number of powerful institutions—labor unions, political patronage systems, the film and information industries. These institutions had served as a base of power for the Irish, Italians, and Jews in their negotiations with the majority. In many instances the same institutions had opposed minority efforts to enter the political and economic mainstream. Blacks had been able to use a fortuitous combination of political and economic developments to apply *moral* pressure in the 1960s to make some gains. Attempts to disclaim any responsibility for past events were an effort to distort history and deny moral obligation for the majority to do something about the present.

Political and psychological resistance to the claims of minorities is an old tradition in America. As each new wave of immigrants arrived—and blacks took on the status of immigrants in 1954, when the U.S. Supreme Court granted them the rights guaranteed to the newcomers from Europe over the centuries—there was always a great deal of concern among the entrenched groups about the impact of those "fresh off the boat." At the turn of the last century white Anglo-Saxons worried that the character of the country would be altered by the influx of Jews and Eastern Europeans. The arguments made seventy-five years ago about preserving standards and "quality" are quite similar to those made today.

The American melting pot had actually been a divided plate, with each distinct group claiming its share by wielding its particular political and economic weapon. What the black and Hispanic newcomers now feared was that the plate would no longer expand to accommodate them. Economists were talking about a dual economy, with most minorities concentrated in the dead-end, low-paying jobs on the lower rung. For them affirmative action was a gateway into the more desirable track, and ruling in *Bakke*, the Supreme Court was defining not only their legal rights but their economic future.

The case had exposed the fragility of political alliances that had supported the cause of minorities in the past. Jews and blacks, old allies in the romantic days of the civil rights movement, had parted company over affirmative action. The labor movement had been so divided on the issue that the AFL-CIO had failed to file a brief in the case. After the Supreme Court's decision there were efforts by both sides to patch up the old wounds. But *Bakke* had provoked a great deal of bitterness, and many of the fundamental issues had not been resolved. Jews saw themselves as a beleaguered minority, one step away from an anti-Semitic backlash. But to blacks, Jews had achieved an enviable amount of power and the ability to manipulate public opinion in their own interest. The fundamental economic problems remained and the differences would not be resolved easily.

There was some discussion of new alliances between blacks and Hispanics, between the poor of different races, and between urban residents of various classes. But the old mistrusts continued to outweigh the new political necessities. The greatest obstacle of all, the absence of a political movement or figure that could provide common ground for unifying these divergent racial and ethnic groups, remained a major factor. In *Bakke* no major political figure had stepped forward to attempt a reconciliation of the opposing sides. The Carter administration had sought a political solution that pleased no one—and that did little to enlighten Americans about the real issue at stake.

The Supreme Court had disappointed the public by its failure to take a definitive stand on the issues, but the multiplicity of opinions was just a reflection of the complexities of the problem. Vietnam had taught America about the infinite shades of right and wrong in foreign policy. *Bakke* might extend this hard-earned wisdom into domestic policies and race relations. Efforts to define minority progress strictly with statistics avoided less tangible but equally important aspects of equality. In fewer than twenty-five years, blacks and other minorities had made great strides in overcoming hundreds of years of psychological damage caused by political oppression and white cultural supremacy. True equality would come only when people not only felt equal but also believed they were playing a role in determining the destiny of the country.

Finding a solution for the problems posed by the *Bakke* case would require a great deal of wisdom and an even greater degree of trust by both sides. The unequal nature of power in America would make this task extremely difficult. How would minorities be persuaded that institutions would do what was right without the pressure of law and government? Could they believe that the white majority had become "color-blind" in just two decades? Could whites be made to understand the real nature of economic struggles taking place and that minorities did not want lowered standards?

As long as race remains an issue in America, we will be unable to address the country's major structural deficiencies. In *Bakke* the issue of color had enabled many Americans to avoid the issues of class and privilege that contradict our most enduring myths. But as the nation matures and the conflicts deepen, we will have no choice but to confront the injustices that contradict these democratic ideals. No society can make winners of all its people. There are those who will not succeed in a system because of the flaws of that society or their own shortcomings. There are still some elements of American society who are anxious to assume—unobtrusively—that color is a justification for failure. It is perilous for any society to become comfortable with injustice. As America enters its third century, we see disturbing signs of complacency and intolerance. It is at our own peril that we become comfortable with our choice of victims.

SELECTED BIBLIOGRAPHY

Bell, Derrick. *Race, Racism and American Law*. Boston: Little, Brown & Co., 1973.

Blum, Jeffrey M. *Pseudoscience and Mental Ability*. New York and London: Monthly Review Press, 1978.

Carnegie Council on Policy Studies in Higher Education. *Selective Admissions in Higher Education*. San Francisco, Washington, D.C., London: Jossey-Bass Publishers, 1977.

Chase, Allan. *The Legacy of Malthus: The Social Costs of the New Scientific Racism*. New York: Knopf, 1977.

Ginger, Ann Fagan, ed. *DeFunis v. Odegaard and the University of Washington*. Dobbs Ferry, N.Y.: Oceana Publications, 1974.

Glazer, Nathan. *Affirmative Discrimination: Ethnic Inequality and Public Policy*. New York: Basic Books, 1975.

Jones, F. C. *The Changing Mood in America: Eroding Commitment?* Washington, D.C.: Howard University Press, 1977.

Kluger, Richard. *Simple Justice*. New York: Knopf, 1976.

National Urban League. "The State of Black America 1978." New York, 1978.

INDEX

MONEY
MADNE$$

MONEY
MADNE$$

The Psychology of
Saving, Spending,
Loving, and
Hating Money

HERB GOLDBERG and
ROBERT T. LEWIS

WILLIAM MORROW AND COMPANY, INC.
NEW YORK   1978

Library of Congress Cataloging in Publication Data

Goldberg, Herb (date)
   Money madne$$.

   Includes bibliographical references and index.
   1. Money—Psychological aspects. 2. Wealth—Psychological aspects. I. Lewis, Robert T., joint author. II. Title: Money madness.
HG221.G59   1978   332.4'.01'9   77-25444
ISBN 0-688-03296-6

BOOK DESIGN AND BINDING   CARL WEISS

Printed in the United States of America.

First Edition

1   2   3   4   5   6   7   8   9   10

PREFACE

WE LIVE IN AN AGE OF INCREASING SELF-AWARENESS, A TIME when many are striving for honesty in emotions, desiring personal growth, and seeking to realize the maximum of human potential. People today are more willing than ever to get in touch with and express their anger, to experience their sexuality guiltlessly, and to assert themselves in positive, self-caring ways. Yet many of these same emotionally emancipated people are stuck in self-defeating money traps. They engage in hidden money manipulations and are preoccupied with secret money obsessions that motivate much of their behavior. The way they deal with money seems incongruous with their otherwise liberated, humanistic life-style. For example, a man whose parents were both well-known psychiatrists relates that when he was a child, his parents talked freely in front of him about sex and aggression but went into the bedroom and closed the door when they discussed money.

Unraveling the psychological threads that entangle most of us in one form or another of money madness is the aim of this book. More than anything, we feel that it is time to examine the psychology of money behavior and to explore the self-destructive patterns, magical notions, and unrealistic fantasies that surround and generate people's money attitudes. To the extent that people can disentangle themselves from their irrational involvement with money and deal with it appropriately, they will be able to experience life in a more satisfying and spontaneous manner. As a contribution toward that goal, we undertook the writing of this book.

HERB GOLDBERG
ROBERT T. LEWIS

Los Angeles, California
February 1, 1978

CONTENTS

MONEY
MADNE$$

INTRODUCTION–MONEY
MADNESS

If "It's a mad world. Mad as Bedlam," as Charles Dickens wrote, at least part of that madness has to do with money.

There is probably nothing that someone won't do for money. The German lyric poet Heinrich Heine claimed, "Money is the god of our time." And the dramatist Sophocles observed, "For money you would sell your soul." Even George Bernard Shaw called it the "most important thing in the world." [1]

Money destroys friendships, marriages, and family unity. Money, which in itself has essentially no value, exerts more power over human lives than any other single commodity. It brings out the best and the worst in people. An elderly woman is mugged and beaten by two youths for less than a dollar, while across town a couple on unemployment take in a runaway teenager and feed him because he has even less than they do.

A priest in St. Louis turned out counterfeit money on a press he installed in his rectory.[2]

A firm in California converts new Cadillacs into pickup trucks for customers who are willing to pay $18,000 to $24,000 for a truck in which they will never haul anything.

At least a dozen Michigan store owners cashed bogus checks of over a hundred dollars each, which were made out to I. M. Slick and signed U. R. Stuck.[3]

A few years ago, the Boy Scouts of America, an organization which has practically become synonymous with honesty, found that some of its staff were padding their membership rolls with nonexistent boys in order to receive more federal funds.[4]

The strange and illogical things that people do with and for money fill the newspapers and bring a smile to the lips of millions of readers, whose own money behavior is almost as strange. In the United States, for example, it is estimated that there are approximately eight million compulsive gamblers, men and women whose primary purpose in life is to bet money. To them, gambling is more important than their families or their careers. They will often steal money or cause their children to go hungry in order to get money to make another bet. One compulsive gambler confessed in a meeting of Gamblers Anonymous that, although he had no regular employment or income, he had lost as much as thirty thousand dollars in a single week. He had been in jail on more than one occasion for swindling in order to get enough money to pay his losses at the track. Yet he was unable to control his compulsion or learn from his mistakes.

On the other side are the millions of compulsive savers, who are compelled to save money with the same vengeance that compulsive gamblers are driven to bet it. In the same class are the millions of compulsive bargain hunters, who drive miles out of their way to save two cents on a gallon of gasoline, or who buy potato peelers by the dozen because they are on sale at half price, or who haunt swap meets and garage sales buying anything that is cheap even though they have no use for it. Today, Overspenders Anonymous has been added to Gamblers Anonymous in an attempt to help people break their compulsive money habits.

Billions of dollars change hands every year because dishonest salesmen appeal to the greed and gullibility of millions of people who eagerly hand over their money in the hope of "turning an easy buck."

Approximately ninety percent of all crime is committed for money. Robbery, forgery, embezzlement, and kidnapping are money motivated. Even murder is sometimes done for a price. Organized crime is one of the largest industries in the United States, netting billions of dollars a year. Free-lance crime adds billions more. Americans are probably as moral as anyone, yet few would dispute the adage that "Everyone has his price." Morality is frequently bought off with money.

Money is a necessary commodity for survival in the modern world. Its uses are many and its role in business and society is well established. But it seems to bring out the irrational in people. It taps the deepest layers of the personality and triggers emotions such as greed and envy, love and security. The desire to obtain enough money to achieve one's desired standard of living is in the realm of realistic behavior. The desire to accumulate extreme wealth is irrational. Beyond a certain point, added wealth cannot increase the opulence of one's style of living or increase one's happiness. Yet the dream of having millions is common to most Americans.

Howard Hughes made more than a billion dollars in his lifetime and J. Paul Getty made several billion. This was much more than either could possibly spend. If one spent a thousand dollars an hour, twenty-four hours a day, three hundred and sixty-five days a year, it would take over a hundred years to get rid of a billion dollars. What is the drive that made them continue to pursue money when they already had more than they could ever count, let alone spend? Surely not happiness, since both of them apparently became more and more unhappy as their wealth increased.

In his earlier years, Howard Hughes was considered a typical rich playboy, with a passion for parties and beautiful women. As he grew older and shrewder and turned his inheritance into a vast fortune, he underwent a transformation. He became more aloof and suspicious, and it would seem that his wealth created an ever-increasing barrier between himself and other people. In his last years he lived in seclusion and for years very few people knew whether he was dead or alive. In spite of his wealth and influence, he turned more and more inward, becoming a recluse whose life was devoted to avoiding germs and people.

To most people, perhaps, the lure of money seems to be a natural phenomenon. "Everyone wants money" is a common belief. The rumor of a new gold rush will cause people to scurry to the far corners of the earth and endure untold hardships. Most would agree the sacrifice is worth it. They have become so indoctrinated with the idea that having money is important, that they no longer question why. They are unaware that perhaps what they are truly seeking is an increase in self-respect, or security, or freedom, or love, or power. While they may not be aware of what it is they truly want from life, they feel sure that money will provide it for them.

1

ASSORTED MONEY GAMES, GAMBITS, PLOYS, AND PASTIMES

AT 6:55 ON A MONDAY MORNING, RICHARD BENNETT ARRIVED at the breakfast table.* "Marsha," he said curtly, "with the price of bacon what it is, don't you think two slices apiece would be enough? And fresh orange juice this time of year? That must cost a small fortune!"

While sipping his juice, he turned to the financial page of the morning paper. "Hmmm," he observed half aloud, "the price of gold went up fifty cents an ounce."

"Speaking of gold," his wife interrupted, "I saw this lovely gold bracelet yesterday at Bronson's. It has a wide band with—"

"Marsha, if there is one thing in this world you don't need, it's another gold bracelet!"

"I know, darling, but it would really be perfect with my new black dress."

"My God! Not another dress?"

"But Richard, I only bought it because I thought you would

_____

* In all of the case histories cited, with the exception of historical figures, the authors have used fictitious names and described traits not identifiable to any particular person or persons.

like me to wear something special when we go out with Jim and Lisa Saturday night."

"I forgot we were going out with them Saturday night! Why can't we ever just stay home and watch television like other people? What is it this time, and how much is it going to cost me?"

"You remember, darling," Marsha answered, trying not to sound annoyed. "We're going out to dinner and then to the opening of that new play we talked about. It won't be all that expensive, and it will be a lot of fun. Actually, we haven't been out in ages."

"Not expensive? Everything you do is expensive! You act as if I'm the U.S. Treasury."

"You're just not any fun anymore, Richard!" she said, on the verge of crying. "I don't know what's happening with you. All you ever do is complain about money!"

"And all you ever do is spend it!" he shouted.

The dialogue at the Bennett's breakfast table had been going on, with only minor variations, for almost twenty-five years. No matter how trivial or how extravagant a purchase his wife made, Richard automatically reacted in anger. It was as if every dollar she spent was robbing him of some inner sense of well-being and security. Ironically, before they were married, he was attracted to Marsha largely because of her easy, carefree attitude toward life. As was not the case with him, money seemed to be unimportant to her except as a means of enjoyment. Soon after they were married, however, her casual disregard for money became an irritation rather than a fascination. As his earnings continued to increase, so did his annoyance.

On the other hand, Marsha initially had been attracted to Richard because he appeared so responsible and his financial stability was a welcome balance to her own impulsive and irresponsible handling of money. Later, she began to see him as "tight" rather than conservative. She resented his inability to loosen up and enjoy what money could buy. To her it seemed he was interested only in hoarding it in the bank and that he measured everything in terms of its cost.

To Richard, money in the bank meant security, while spending it unnecessarily made him feel anxious and vulnerable. Marsha liked to spend money because it made her feel fulfilled and free, as though she were sharing her abundance with the world. While Richard and Marsha fought about money almost continuously, neither really understood how the other felt about it.

As Richard arrived at work and pulled into the company parking lot at exactly 7:25 A.M., he waved to the night security man, who was driving out. "I just don't understand people like that," Richard muttered to himself. "How can he drive a new Lincoln on the salary I pay him? And with a wife and two children! Such irresponsibility!"

At the same time, the night security man was thinking, "I just don't understand people like that. With all his money and driving a cheap compact car! How tight can you get? No wonder he's rich!"

Later that morning, Richard made a point of taking his office manager, Harvey Willenski, aside for a chat during the coffee break.

"Harvey," he said, "if you have a minute, why don't you bring your coffee into my office? I'd like to talk to you."

"Of course, Mr. Bennett. I'll be right in."

"Please call me Richard. You don't have to be formal with me," he replied in a warm tone of voice as he closed the office door behind them. "I've been meaning to tell you what a really fine job you've been doing, Harvey. It's awfully hard to get good workers these days, as you well know. And with business as rough as it's been, it's nice to know that some departments are running efficiently. Please tell the new typist that I haven't forgotten about her and that we'll get her a new electric typewriter as soon as possible. But I'm afraid we'll have to get along with the old copying machine for a little longer. You know we lost that Takayama order we thought we had in the bag, and things will be a little tight around here for a while. But if we all work together, I'm sure we'll make it and not have to let anyone go."

"I didn't know things were that bad," replied Harvey in a concerned tone. "That's strange," he thought to himself. "I'm sure the latest audit showed a big jump in profits."

"It's just temporary, I'm sure," Richard continued. "If we all pitch in and cut the fat, it will turn out okay. Thanks, Harvey. It's always good to talk to you."

As the owner of a small manufacturing plant, Richard Bennett tried to maintain an informal, friendly relationship with his employees. Although it didn't really come naturally, he had worked at being the warm and friendly employer for so many years that it was almost automatic. In a management training workshop years ago, he had been taught that many employees would rather have a friendly relationship with the boss than a raise in salary. That appealed to him. He also learned from observation that contented employees had fewer absences and turned out more work.

While Richard's behavior was partly contrived and his motivation at least partly conscious, Harvey, like many employees, was lured into a pseudo-friendship for primarily unconscious reasons. His need for recognition and the ego satisfaction he received from being made to feel on an equal plane with his employer was apparently sufficient to compensate for working for less money. The trade-off was friendship instead of money. Harvey would feel disloyal in asking a "friend" for a raise. Also, when the boss "confides" in him about the financial difficulties of the business, it makes asking for a raise even more difficult. In the end, Harvey is likely to wind up sharing the boss's problems rather than the boss's money.

Just before lunch, Richard's twenty-two-year-old daughter, Honey, stopped by his office to see him. He immediately became defensive when he saw that particular look in her eye which meant she wanted something from him.

"Hi, Daddy!" she greeted him warmly. "I know you're super busy and I hate to bother you like this, but I do need your advice."

She then proceeded to tell him the following:

1. The service manager at the auto agency warned her that her car was unsafe to drive and that she might have an accident if she continued to drive it.

2. The price of a new car was prohibitive, and she couldn't afford one on her salary.

3. She wouldn't really feel right about asking him to buy her a new one, although she knew he would because he was so "generous."

4. The service manager conceded that a new transmission and relining the brakes would keep her old car going for another year or so.

5. The service department happened to have a special on transmissions for the next two days and she could save twenty percent, but she didn't have enough money to pay for the repairs.

6. What did he think?

By the time she had finished, Richard was so relieved that she was not asking him to buy her a new car, that he readily agreed to pay for having her old one fixed.

Honey knew that she had a special relationship with her father and that he had trouble denying her anything. Unlike her mother, she never saw him as tight, at least not with her. In addition, she learned early in life that it made him feel important to be consulted on financial matters and he was less reluctant to spend money if he felt it was his decision. She also knew that he had trouble passing up a bargain. Therefore, any request for money would be most likely to succeed if it incorporated all of these elements. For her part, it was less a conscious manipulation than a habitual way of relating to him. As for Richard, no matter how often he resolved to resist giving in to her bid for money, he usually wound up agreeing with her "good judgment" and paying the bill. Despite the intensity of his anxiety about spending money, his need for his daughter's approval and admiration was stronger.

After she left her father's office, Honey met Daryl, her current boy friend, for lunch. Since she had invited him, she intended to pay. All through lunch, however, she was uncomfortable since she didn't know how he would react and she hadn't been able to discuss it with him ahead of time. Talking about money seemed like such a tacky thing to do. They had gone together only a short time and she didn't know him very well. He had paid for the other dates, and she was somewhat concerned about it. Although it was comfortable for her to slip into a dependent role with men as she did with her father, she was also trying to become more liberated and autonomous and to see male-female relationships as equal.

When lunch was finished, the waitress placed the check in front of Daryl, but Honey quickly reached over and took it. A surprised look came over Daryl's face and he started to protest, but she laughed a little uneasily and said, "No, I really want to. I invited you and I'd feel better if I paid."

No more was said, but all afternoon Honey was concerned about whether Daryl was offended and whether this would mess up their relationship. Would it threaten his masculinity? Or was he happy? Maybe he'd respect her more. She was equally confused about how *she* really felt about paying her share of the expenses on dates. Partly she resented being dependent on a man, but partly she liked it. Did she really feel guilty when a date paid all the expenses? Did she feel more independent when she paid half? She couldn't decide.

When Daryl left Honey that afternoon he was asking himself similar questions. "On what I make as a graduate assistant at the university, it's kind of nice to have someone share expenses on a date, but I don't feel quite right about it. I really like Honey even though I have a hard time figuring her out. But then I never did understand women very well.

"Which reminds me, today is Mom's birthday. I know she said, 'Don't buy me a present. There's nothing I want and I wish you wouldn't spend your money. Just come over for dinner. That's enough for me.' But does no mean no or does no mean yes? With my mother I'm never sure. If I buy her a present, will she be mad because she told me not to, or if I don't will she be mad because that means I don't love her?"

Daryl's mother had him in what is known as a "double-bind." It is a situation in which he cannot possibly win because there is no correct answer. He can wind up feeling guilty no matter which way he goes. She can portray herself as a victim of his inconsiderate behavior or accuse him of being wasteful and extravagant.

In thinking about his mother, Daryl knew she had always played the role of a martyr when it came to money. He remembered how she had been with his father. A few years before he died, his dad had seen a set of expensive golf clubs he really wanted to buy, but felt he shouldn't. For weeks he would go and look at them whenever he got a chance, but could never bring himself to spend the money. Finally his wife said to him, "Go ahead and buy the clubs. You know you really want them. Besides, playing golf is good for your health. You need more exercise. And the next time your boss asks you to play, you'll have a set of clubs you can be proud of. Besides, by next year they will cost more. You can save money by buying them now."

Having persuaded her husband to buy the golf clubs, she never missed an opportunity to mention the new dress, the new stove, the new vacuum cleaner, the new watch, and numerous other things she had denied herself because he had spent so much money on the golf clubs.

During the lunch hour, Harvey Willenski, Richard Bennett's office manager, went home to get the mail before his wife returned from her dental appointment. He had just finished scrutinizing the telephone bill when his wife drove up. "If you will notice," he greeted her, waving the bill in his hand, "I had the phone company send an itemized statement this time, and I see that you called your mother three times last month. Don't you think that's a little wasteful?"

Caught off guard, his wife became defensive and started to justify her actions, but soon regained her composure and went on the offensive. "Look who's talking! Those three phone calls were only about $2.50. When we drove out to see *your* mother last Sunday, we spent $7.50 on gasoline alone, not counting the wear and tear on the car."

Harvey and Miriam Willenski were both products of depression families. They grew up with the idea that bad times were always imminent and that frugality was the greatest possible virtue. Each received considerable approval in his and her respective families for having learned that lesson well. They were first attracted to each other because of their similar philosophy about money. At times, however, they found themselves competing with each other and checking up on each other's handling of money.

Most of their arguments and disagreements centered around some minor "extravagance" such as leaving a hall light burning all night. Being confronted with some example of wastefulness was akin to an attack on each other's character. For both, that was their most vulnerable area. If, for example, Harvey felt that Miriam was not responsive sexually, he was not likely to accuse her of being cold, but would go out of his way to find where she overpaid for a bar of soap or forgot to get a parking ticket validated. To accuse her of being frigid would be far less shattering than to accuse her of being wasteful.

Most of the time Harvey and Miriam were in agreement about money matters. They both scrimped on clothes, rarely entertained, and almost never spent money for luxuries or recreation. But when one or the other felt threatened, or frustrated, or angry with the other, he or she would compete to see who was the superior person or who was "right." That meant, who was the most miserly.

After Harvey went back to work, Miriam stopped by to visit her next-door neighbor, Carmen Herrera. Carmen and her husband, Al, had recently moved into the neighborhood, and Miriam had taken it upon herself to make them feel welcome. When Miriam complimented her on her coffee, Carmen beamed. "The new coffee maker we bought does make a difference. It's certainly worth the extra money it cost."

"Carmen," Miriam chided in a maternal tone, "I hope you

didn't go to Blumfield's and pay full price again. I can show you where you can buy things like that at a discount."

"I know, but I don't like to bother you. You've already done so much for us. And it's kind of fun to go to Blumfield's. They have so many pretty things! I love to go and browse, and the salespeople are so friendly."

While she couldn't admit it to Miriam, and she was only partially aware of the reasons herself, Carmen preferred to patronize Blumfield's rather than some large, overcrowded discount store, even though it cost her more money to do so. For her it was a symbol of having arrived. When Al was promoted to foreman, it seemed for the first time that their dream of moving into a house of their own would become a reality. When it finally happened, she felt a little like Cinderella and she wanted to hold onto that euphoric feeling as long as possible. They had traded exclusively in discount stores for years and she felt it would be a step backward to go there now. Besides, she and Al felt a little insecure in moving into a higher income neighborhood. They were aware that some of their new neighbors looked down on them and, by trading at the most expensive store in the area, they were trying to prove that they could well afford their new environment.

Shortly after lunch, Marsha Bennett drove over to her friend Elizabeth Levin's house, where her bridge club was having its weekly meeting. She was not looking forward to it. Since Elizabeth's husband, Ron, had joined an influential law firm and become a highly paid corporate attorney, Marsha felt less comfortable around her. Until a few years ago, Marsha had had more money to spend than Elizabeth, and now that the situation was reversed, Marsha had the feeling that Elizabeth was flaunting her new status.

Even though Ron gave her a generous amount of money for her personal use, Elizabeth, as she had done since they were first married, took ten percent of the total of all the household money and put it in a personal bank account, which not even Ron knew she had. Despite an air of snobbishness, which seemed to be more pronounced as their income grew, Elizabeth had always felt insecure with other people and in her marriage. She secretly believed that someday Ron would leave her, so she put away a nest egg as a protection for when that time would come. In addition, she pushed for a bigger house in a more expensive neighborhood, and spent money to gain the "respect" from others that she felt she could never warrant on her own merits.

Ron, on the other hand, was not so much concerned about status or impressing others. Rather, he was an ambitious, driving person whose life was dedicated to providing his family with the kind of life he had never had himself. He had come from a deprived family background where everyone had to struggle for a bare existence and where there were no luxuries. What he remembered from his childhood was hunger, and anger, and a resolve that when he grew up and had a family of his own, things would be different.

True to his vow, Ron was able to provide his children with fine clothes, good schools, nourishing food, and a comfortable home. In addition, there were music lessons, expensive vacations, elaborate parties, an abundance of toys, and much, much more. It made him feel proud to know that he could satisfy his children's every desire and protect them from the harsh life that he had experienced. The vicarious satisfaction he obtained by doing this for his children had been his greatest reward.

At times, however, Ron found himself becoming angry when the children seemed to take their affluence for granted and were either unappreciative, demanding, or complaining about things they didn't have. And there was the time when he exploded in rage and smashed an expensive new toy to pieces because his son ignored it in favor of a tin pan and a spoon from the cupboard.

When he stops to think about it, now that the children are grown, Ron feels confused about life and a little bitter. "After all I've done for them, the only time they ever seem to come around is when they want money!" Since he feels that what he gave his children as a result of his affluence was a sign of his love for them, it is difficult for him to see why they don't respond warmly and affectionately toward him in return.

Ron tolerates Elizabeth's preoccupation with social status and spending money to impress her friends because it gives her something to occupy her time so she will be less demanding of him. He believes, however, that she, too, is interested in him only for the money he provides and that if he went broke, he would probably lose her. Feeling unloved by his wife and children, he has spent more and more time working the past few years, which, in turn, has made him even more money. He feels useful and appreciated at work, but emotionally drained at home. "I give and I give," he complains, "but no matter how much I give, it's never enough!"

The couple that Elizabeth Levin envies most is Cliff and Rosemary Donaldson. They are the center of their social circle and everything revolves around them. They throw the most expensive parties and make the biggest splash. While the Levins and many of their neighbors started with virtually nothing and have made money, the Donaldsons have always had it—not only their parents, but their grandparents. As far back as anyone can remember, the Donaldsons and money have been synonymous.

Cliff and Rosemary belong to two country clubs and have season tickets to the horse races and the light opera series. No one can remember when they last turned down a social invitation, and they have the clothes and equipment to participate in any of the chic sporting events. Every two years they go to Europe to buy the hottest, newest, and most expensive sports car. Friends consider them the most fun-loving, relaxed couple in town.

Cliff works at the bank once owned by his family, but he doesn't really have much responsibility there. One of the conditions his father made when he sold the bank was that Cliff would have a position as vice-president for life. Except for that foresight, the Donaldsons would be forced to drastically change their life-style. They have no assets except a small equity in their heavily mortgaged house. They live to the full extent of their income and not infrequently run out of money before the end of the month. If Cliff died tomorrow, Rosemary would be left with two teenage children, a large number of debts, and no provision for contingencies like the children's education.

Although envied by Elizabeth and other friends, the Donaldsons are actually less well off financially than any of them. Yet they continue to spend money with no concern about tomorrow. They are like fun-loving teenagers who omnipotently think that no matter what they do, they will somehow survive. Life is to be enjoyed, and money will always magically be there when it is needed.

Although they are seemingly affectionate and accepting of their children, they have abandoned some of their parental responsibility by not providing for the children's education or their future, an oversight that suggests some underlying denial of their parental role and the responsibilities inherent in that role.

The recreation center where Dick Levin, Ron and Elizabeth's twenty-two-year-old son, works is in a racially integrated, lower-middle-class neighborhood. As a reward for winning their respective tournaments, Dick decided to take the boys' and girls' junior and senior Ping-Pong champions to a special restaurant for lunch. The children were quiet and respectful and noticeably uncomfortable. They picked at their food and when Dick tried to put them at ease by engaging in light conversation, they would politely reply, "Yes, sir," or "No, sir," but little else. After lunch was over, he heard one of the girls say, "It was all right, but with all his money I thought he would take us to some really neat place like McDonald's."

Because he didn't feel very comfortable with these children, Dick had tried to impress them with money and buy their respect. He was now beginning to see what he had done and was disgusted with himself.

When he returned to the center, Dick had an appointment with Jeff Washington's parents. Jeff was the best guard on the center's basketball team but hadn't shown up for practice for over a week. Dick was concerned. When he called Jeff's parents, they agreed to meet with him.

"Mr. Levin," Jeff's father began, "We want you to know how

much we appreciate what the center has done for Jeff. He never got into drugs or trouble with the police and never gave us any worry. We're thankful for that. But he's sixteen now and it's time for him to get a job and make some money."

"Does that mean he won't be able to play on the basketball team this year? We were counting on him, you know. He's the best player we have."

"Play is for kids, Mr. Levin. Jeff is grown up and grown-ups should work. I got him a job with a plumbing company where he can learn a trade."

"But what about college?" Dick inquired. "He's such a bright boy and he had his heart set on going to college. With his grades and his basketball ability, I know he can get a scholarship."

"There's no point in him going to school all his life. What's he going to be if he goes to college, a schoolteacher? Plumbers make more money than schoolteachers."

"Think of the long run, Mr. Washington. Surely you want Jeff to be happy. The money can't be that important right now."

"That's easy for you to say, Mr. Levin. You've always had money. We haven't. What do you know about money and happiness? I don't know that much about happiness 'cause I haven't had that easy a life, but I do know something about money. And I know that without it there isn't much happiness."

When the Washingtons had gone, Dick felt frustrated and depressed. He tried to understand their position, but he was angry when he thought about what they were doing to Jeff. He also felt that he had let Jeff down since he hadn't been able to come up with any effective counter to Mr. Washington's position. He had never known parents who didn't push their kids to go to college, let alone block it. He spent a long time trying to figure out the Washingtons. What were they really saying? What was the underlying motive for their behavior toward Jeff? He wasn't sure. At last, he decided to do what he usually did when he had similar problems trying to understand people. He would talk with his older brother, Andy.

By the time Dick arrived at Andy's office, however, he found that his brother had left work early. Andy's girl friend, Janice, had been in a bad mood when he left for work that morning and, even though it was unlike her, she stayed in bed all day instead of going to work. Andy decided to go home and see if he could cheer her up.

"Hi, Babe!" he greeted her, "I bought a bottle of Chablis. I thought it might improve your disposition. As Lord Byron used to say, 'Let us have wine and women, mirth and laughter. Sermons and hangovers we'll save for the day after,' or something like that."

"You're a nut, Andy," she laughed, "and I love you. I'm sorry about this morning, but I'm still mad about yesterday! When we had Dave and Susan over we had T-bones. When they had us back yesterday, what did we get? Hamburger! That's twice they've pulled that. And for her birthday, I bought her some really expensive French perfume. What did she give me? Cheap costume jewelry! I know it sounds petty, but I've had it with them! I'm tired of always getting taken! And I'm especially tired of hearing how much money they are saving and investing. It makes me feel mercenary when I act like this and I hate it. It's not really the money, it's just . . . oh, let's forget it."

After Janice had calmed down, Andy skimmed through the evening paper while she poured the wine. "Well, here's another congressman who got caught with his hand in the cookie jar," he remarked disgustedly. "I'll bet there isn't an honest politician in Washington. This whole country is run by a bunch of crooks! I guess that's what it takes to make it in politics!"

A few minutes later, however, Andy was gleefully telling Janice how he planned to pad his expense account and manipulate it in such a way that he could not only get more money than he was entitled to from his employer but also not declare it as income for tax purposes. Nor was he aware of the incongruity of his own behavior and his expressed disgust for the dishonesty of others. When Janice made a teasing reference, he got defensive. "That's different! You have to survive somehow the way taxes are! And the company doesn't feel it. Besides, everyone does it. It's one of the fringe benefits."

At 7:15 that evening, Richard Bennett sat across from his wife at the dinner table and stared glumly at his salad.

"Avocados again?" he snapped.

"I thought you liked avocados!" Marsha replied.

"I do, but at the prices they charge for them, they're a little hard to swallow."

"They were on sale, dear."

"Hmmmph!"

"How was your day, Richard? Did anything interesting happen?" she inquired.

"No, not really."

"Did Honey stop by? She said she might."

"Yes."

"What did she want?"

"Nothing special," he answered reluctantly, not wanting to admit that he had given her money to fix her car. "How much did you lose at the bridge game?"

"I didn't! I won three dollars."

"What did you spend it on? I'm sure you couldn't come home with three dollars more in your purse than you had when you left!"

"Oh, Richard . . ."

2

THE LAST TABOO

TODAY MONEY IS A FAVORITE TOPIC OF CONVERSATION IN MANY settings. The financial page of the daily newspaper is read about as avidly as the sports page or the comics. There has probably never been a cocktail party at which the subject of taxes, the cost of living, or the price of real estate has not been discussed. In gossip circles, who did what with whom is rivaled only by who paid how much for what.

Money is on the minds of most people every day. It is impossible to hide from it for long. Regardless of how one feels about the subject of money, it is certainly here to stay. In fact, with many people it has become an obsession. No matter how they try to deny the hold it has on them, their preoccupation with it is such that they think of practically nothing else.

Bruce and Nancy Clarke had planned their housewarming party for weeks. In a way, years had gone into the preparation. They had worked and saved and denied themselves many luxuries in order to someday purchase the house of their dreams. Now they finally had it and they wanted to share the joy with their friends.

They were excited and feeling happy as they welcomed their guests and proudly displayed their new home. The guests, in turn, recognized the warmth and charm the house exuded, and were lavish in their praise of Nancy's taste in furnishings and Bruce's landscaping efforts. Waiters moved about offering champagne and hors d'oeuvres. Laughter and pleasant conversation all but drowned out the music in the background. Everyone seemed to be having a good time.

And then it happened!

One of the guests, in a voice loud enough to be heard above the rest, remarked to Bruce, "This is a great place you have here. How much did you pay for it?"

There was an embarrassed silence. People standing nearby looked at each other self-consciously. Nancy pretended she hadn't heard the remark. Bruce avoided a direct answer, mumbled something about "a good buy," and started another conversation.

One might ask, of course, why a guest would display such poor manners as to ask the owner what he had paid for his house. Certainly everyone should know that that sort of thing is just not done.

The more interesting question from a psychological point of view, however, is why is such a straightforward question considered shocking? Why is there so much secretiveness attached to the subject of money? Why, especially, is it acceptable to talk freely about money in general, but when the conversation comes close to personal finances people become defensive and feel threatened? One can safely express an opinion on the price of gold on the European money market, the rise and fall of the Dow Jones Index, real estate values, recession, inflation, and the fluctuation of the prime interest rate. But it is considered both bad taste and an invasion of privacy to ask directly how much a person makes, the amount of money in one's savings account, or even when someone will repay a five-dollar loan.

The taboo surrounding money was traditionally shared with

subjects such as sex, aggression, and death. Today it stands practically alone. Thanks to such revolutionaries as Freud, Kinsey, Masters and Johnson, and Albert Ellis; and people in the media such as Hugh Hefner and Helen Gurley Brown, American attitudes toward sex have undergone a radical change in the last thirty to fifty years. No longer is sex something talked about in whispers, nor are personal desires and motivations routinely concealed. In fact, sex is now performed in living color on the screens of movie theaters and described in minute detail in bestselling novels. It is discussed freely in many strata of society in mixed company, and sexual intercourse has all but replaced the handshake and the kiss as a physical expression of affection for dating couples. *Yet the same liberated couple that casually goes to bed on the first date might feel extremely uncomfortable talking about dividing expenses for dinner or the movie they attend.*

Taboos against hostility and aggression are also rapidly disappearing. No longer is the "nice guy" seen as an authentic or a healthy model one would want children to emulate, since psychologists now know that behind the nice guy facade there all too often exists considerable repressed anger. People are becoming more open in admitting their angry feelings and are seeking ways of expressing their aggression creatively.

But with money, society has not progressed very far from where it was in 1844 when Ralph Waldo Emerson observed, "Money . . . is hardly spoken of in parlours without an apology." [1] The well-known existential psychologist, the late Sidney Jourard, concluded that, on the basis of research studies which he helped conduct, self-disclosure about money is rare.[2] And James A. Knight, professor of psychiatry at Tulane University School of Medicine, writes, "They [patients] show far less resistance in relating hatred for their parents or in disclosing sexual perversities than in discussing their money status or transactions. It is as if they equated money with their inmost being." [3] When the subject of money *is* discussed, it is usually talked of in the abstract or with great difficulty. In many cases when the subject of money becomes too personal, there is embarrassment and discomfort and the subject is quickly dropped.

LOVE AND MONEY ARE
A DIFFICULT MIX

Secrecy about money matters leads to many kinds of confused and neurotic interactions between people. For example, few couples discuss their inner money motivations openly before they get married. Friends and relatives, in fact, would become suspicious of her love if the prospective bride were to admit that one of the reasons she was marrying her future bridegroom was that he was earning a large salary and had the promise of becoming well-to-do. In fact, she may not even be aware of that feeling since well-socialized people are taught not to think that way. Money motives are considered among the lowest of all motivations. Even worse would be the groom's admission that he *suspected* that money was a factor in *her* marrying him or that he was marrying her because she had a good job and would be able to contribute substantially to the family income. He might acknowledge his appreciation of the fact but not that this was a key factor in his marriage choice.

Somehow people need to believe that love is too important an experience to be contaminated with considerations of money. If money is a consideration, people generally think that their love is not real. There are feelings that money will somehow magically find its natural, rightful place. Those who openly indicate that money is a factor in their marital choice might be labeled gold diggers, parasites, rank materialists, and so forth. Few believe that love could possibly exist in an atmosphere where money played a role in the decision to get married. Though it is said that it is as easy to fall in love with someone who is rich as it is with someone who is poor, if one happens to fall for someone who is rich, it is necessary to feel that this happened by chance rather than by conscious design.

Since money is supposedly ruled by the head and love is ruled by the heart, money views are usually hidden and individuals get married pretending money does not exist. But money feelings are all too real, and if conflicting feelings about money are present, as they often are, they will soon become evident. Too often, the course of the relationship goes from (A) denial of the importance of money during courtship, to (B) arguments over money during marriage, to (C) an attempt to destroy each other financially during divorce.

Denying one's monetary attitudes doesn't make them go away any more than denying one's sexual desires or hiding one's angry feelings causes them to disappear. Attitudes about money are an integral part of people's lives and will affect and be affected by everything else they do, think, and feel; if not directly, then indirectly. Like neurotic problems of sex and aggression, irrational uses and abuses of money can only be resolved by a willingness to take a close look at one's relationship with money and find out what money means psychologically. Perhaps then it can be put into realistic perspective, something which few people are now able to do.

One reason people are loath to discuss money prior to marriage is the prevailing worship of romantic love. In other times and in other cultures, marriage was primarily a business agreement. Either the bridegroom bought the bride or the father of the bride bribed the bridegroom by means of a dowry. In either case, a monetary value was put on the bride in much the same way that a price was established for a cow or a piece of furniture.

That kind of dehumanization has not been tolerated in this country for a good many years. Long before the advent of Women's Liberation, such blatant male chauvinism became totally unacceptable. Over the years, the only acceptable alternative to purchasing a mate has been to fall in love. This creates certain problems since love is a very personal experience that is difficult to define or measure. Most people can agree on the definition of three cows or a dowry of two thousand dollars, but how does one measure love?

While love may well be the most noble of all motives for getting married, it has taken such an exalted position that no other motive is even considered respectable. So, to avoid any possible taint, one's tendency is to hide other motives, including monetary considerations.

Some spokespersons for the Women's Liberation movement advocate that since money is the universal measure of value in our society, wives should be paid for their services. Germaine Greer, for example, maintains that women should bargain for better terms and should enter marriage with some kind of business contract.

For these and other reasons, the idea of a financial agreement signed before marriage is slowly gaining acceptance. Surely, too many people, both male and female, have been financially ruined by divorce.

When the former Jackie Kennedy married the late Aristotle Onassis, many romantics became disillusioned. To them her marriage was more a business arrangement than an affair of the heart. Whatever her motivation, there was more than a little comment when it was learned that a formal marriage contract was a precondition of the marriage. In this agreement, she allegedly would receive nearly ten million dollars for each year of marriage if he should leave her, a flat sum of approximately eighteen million dollars if she should leave him, and about twenty-five thousand dollars a month for expenses and spending money while married.[4]

Whether one agrees with this type of arrangement or not, it is one way that the role of money can be brought out in the open where it can be discussed rationally. And who is to say that it is impossible for a logical consideration of money matters to co-exist with the emotion of love?

FAMILY SECRETS

Janet Rogers announced proudly to a close friend that after three years of psychotherapy she was now able to discuss sex openly with her fifteen-year-old daughter without a sense of embarrassment. That was a real milestone for Janet, considering her repressed, puritanical background, and she justifiably felt elated and liberated.

Less than an hour later, however, Janet was heard to say in a very self-righteous tone of voice, "Tom and I don't think our financial affairs are any of the children's business. There's no reason for them to know how much money their father makes or how we choose to spend it. We give them an adequate allowance, and that's all they need to be concerned about."

The Rogers family is not unique in this respect. In millions of homes throughout the country, children are kept in ignorance of their parents' finances. They have no idea about the family income, the cost of housing and food, the family indebtedness, savings and investments, taxes. And it is usually the case that the more secretive the parents are in general, the more likely they are to withhold monetary information from their own children.

If one should ask these parents why they are reluctant to reveal their finances to their children, they would probably attempt a logical explanation. Among the more common are, "We want to spare them the problems of dealing with money. Why burden them with these problems? It's our responsibility and we'll handle it," or, "These are adult matters. What do kids know about money? When they get older we'll tell them," or, "They would not understand anyway. They might be so discouraged when they find out how much it costs to support a family that they would decide not to have one of their own." Actually, these answers are rationalizations. The parents are trying to give logical reasons for illogical behavior. In most cases they are unaware themselves of the deeper, underlying reasons that are embedded in the framework of their personalities and that are involved in all aspects of their character structure and not limited only to their perception of money.

Children are not the only ones shielded from information about and involvement in the world of money. Even today, there are wives who have absolutely no knowledge of the family's finances and no experience coping in the arena of money or business.

Margaret Bradbury is such a woman. Her situation is not at all uncommon. Margaret's husband, Peter, was a successful attorney. He not only made considerable money in his law practice, but also through timely real estate investments. His relationship with his wife was, at best, overprotective; at worst, demeaning. He never discussed finances with her, claiming that he did not want to bother her with the sordid problems of money. He paid all the bills, made all the major expenditures, kept all the family's financial records. He dabbled in commodity futures and stock options and was involved in a number of limited partnerships. It made him feel powerful and protective to indulge his wife like a favorite child and to maintain her dependence on him by keeping her ignorant of financial matters.

For her part, Margaret's only concern about money was how to spend the generous allowance Peter gave her. She disclaimed any other interest in money, considering it "unfeminine." She saw Peter as the strong, masculine figure and she enjoyed being pampered and indulged by him. She liked the luxury of not having to think about money and often joked about her ineptitude at balancing the checkbook.

If ignorance is bliss, Margaret Bradbury lived in a state of financial euphoria. At least she did until Peter died suddenly of a heart attack. Then she had to pay for her years of isolation from the real world. And she paid dearly. She paid attorneys and accountants and stock brokers to help straighten out her affairs. She also paid a heavy price emotionally. She realized that the pampered and protected status she had had with Peter all but disqualified her from coping without him.

She felt stupid and inadequate when confronted with the hundreds of decisions she had to make and became somewhat paranoid about people taking advantage of her. Most of all, she felt anger toward Peter for keeping her in a helpless, infantile monetary state and she felt angry with herself for letting it happen.

Wives and children who are excluded from free and open discussion about the family's finances, as many are, often get distorted ideas about money. They are likely to either underestimate or overestimate the family's wealth. They may scrimp unnecessarily or spend recklessly. They will most likely use poor judgment in financial matters. When the time comes to face their own financial transactions, they feel insecure and ill-equipped and uncomfortable about asking for help since they have learned by example that money is a taboo subject.

Nowhere is the taboo against honest discussion of money more apparent than in the interaction between middle-aged children and their aging parents. If the children want the parents to make a will so there will be fewer conflicts about how the estate will ultimately be divided, they are afraid to say much about it for fear the parents will think them mercenary.

The parents may procrastinate about making a will because they don't want to face the decision of assigning a monetary value to each child. Or they may use the will as blackmail to extract more attention from the children. Not infrequently, the children will vie with each other to be the nicest or the closest to the parents so they will be favored in the will. Greed and deception to gain parental inheritance is a time-honored reality and was a central theme in Shakespeare's tragic play *King Lear*. Cordelia, the favored daughter, is disinherited because of her modest but honest statement of affection for her father, while her older sisters are rewarded for their dishonest but flowery endearments.

A symptom sometimes present in senility is paranoia. It is not unusual for the elderly to harbor delusions that someone is out to rob them and steal their possessions. Since delusions are often based on a grain of truth, it is perhaps accurate to surmise that in this case the delusion is based on the awareness that whoever stands to gain from the elderly person's demise is more interested in the inheritance than in the person. Not infrequently, if there is a sizable estate, the children start to worry about whether the parents are in full control of their faculties or whether they will squander all their money before they go. Worse yet, will they become financially dependent on the children? Will Dad, now that Mother is gone, marry some manipulative young woman who will take him for his money? Will Mother donate all of her money to cancer research or the church as she sometimes threatens to do? The children may spend hours pondering questions about their parents such as, "To protect them from themselves, should we get a power of attorney, or put them in a sanitarium?" All of this, of course, is discussed without ever mentioning personal financial gain and usually with the attitude that money is the least possible consideration.

Sensing these concerns, however, the elderly parents become defensive and suspicious. They hide money here and there so they won't feel helpless. And they try to figure ways to protect themselves from having their assets taken from them. On rare occasions they may even take a lesson from the movie *Auntie Mame* and try to spend it all, enjoying life as much as possible before they die. Any exaggerated retention or spending of money is likely to be considered peculiar behavior, regardless of the motive.

Some people are so conditioned to depriving themselves in order to save money that they continue to do so long after it is necessary. Even when their children are grown and they have no responsibilities, they don't eat properly, they dress shabbily, they never go out to dinner or to a show. Whatever it is, they can't afford it. Their children worry about them, try to give them presents of money, and dread the time when their parents will be totally dependent. It is not until the parents die that the family realizes that they had thirty or forty thousand dollars in the bank.

"Crazy" money habits and money neuroses rarely disappear with age. The person who unnecessarily hoards money for a rainy day at the age of thirty is usually still waiting for the rain at seventy, only now the hoarding is done more rigidly.

THE HIGH PRICE OF HIDING

The inability to discuss money openly can be a factor in all sorts of psychologically unhealthy states, such as depression, hate, paranoia, and self-destruction.

When Fred lent his neighbor Bill Jordan ten dollars during a poker game, they were still the best of friends. When Bill forgot about the loan and had not repaid it after a week, Fred became a little cool. Bill sensed that something was wrong and asked Fred about it. Fred was too embarrassed to admit he was miffed about the ten dollars and denied anything was wrong. Over a period of time the rift widened and eventually their friendship turned into cold detachment.

Jerry Farmer was a tool and die maker, a skilled craftsman

who was well thought of by his foreman. It was generally assumed that he was next in line for promotion. When a new man was hired, Jerry thought nothing of it—until he heard a rumor that the new man, although less experienced, was being paid more than he was. The "injustice" of the situation began to gnaw at him and he became increasingly more sullen and depressed. Both the quality and quantity of his work suffered. The foreman tried to talk with him, but to no avail. When the next promotion went to someone else, Jerry quit his job in anger.

Soon after Sue and Gregg had their first baby, Sue's aunt Dora offered to baby-sit so Sue could accompany Gregg on a business trip. Of all the relatives, Dora had been the most enthusiastic about Sue's pregnancy and, when the baby came, she was delighted. Whenever she was around, it was hard to tell she was not the doting grandmother. While Sue was reluctant to leave the baby with Aunt Dora, she finally agreed because she felt it would mean so much to her. And while Dora seemed to thoroughly enjoy herself and the baby, she never volunteered to baby-sit again. When Sue approached her on subsequent occasions, she always had an excuse as to why she was unavailable.

Sue and Gregg had the uneasy feeling that they had offended their aunt, but they weren't sure how. At one point they thought that possibly they should have offered to pay her for sitting, but they dismissed the idea since they felt that that would offend her, knowing how much she cared for the baby. Dora, on the other hand, had fully expected to be paid for her time and effort. She was hurt that her favorite niece would "take advantage" of her, but she was too proud to ask for the money.

Sally was an outspoken feminist and found herself particularly comfortable with Ted, who seemed to really appreciate her assertiveness and independence. After four dates Ted stopped calling. He had built up increasing resentment because Sally was not offering to split expenses on their dates as he had fully expected. He had been too uncomfortable, however, to ask her to do so. Meanwhile, Sally had never offered to pay for fear of offending Ted. She never found out why Ted stopped seeing her even though she had called him to ask. He simply evaded the issue. He was afraid he would sound cheap or ridiculous.

Few people deal openly with money. This is a phenomenon that is not unique to the present time or the present culture. In India there is an old proverb which indicates that secretiveness about money matters has been around for a long time: "Never make known one's wealth, one's remedies, one's lover, where one has hidden money, the good works one does, the insults one has received, or the debts one has contracted." [5]

Even in psychotherapy, that most intimate relationship where supposedly no secrets are held sacred, the subject of money is often avoided. It is amazing how many people undergo therapy without dealing with their anxieties about money—largely because the subject never comes up. And the fear of disclosure is not solely the problem of the patient. Therapists, too, including even the existentialists who believe in self-disclosure to their patients, may be reticent to reveal their guilt feelings about charging fees, their financial dependency upon their patients, or their resentment toward patients who fall behind in their payments.

In all of the above cases, the hurt feelings, the disappointment, the anger, suspicion, and frustration might have been alleviated if money had not been a taboo subject, laden with guilt and anxiety. Yet money, which is one of the most powerful motivators of human behavior, has such a negative connotation to most people that they try to deny the importance it has in shaping their lives. And then they suffer the consequences.

Money is surely an unromantic subject. It is a significant factor in everyone's life and, at the same time, a source of great discomfort. The way it is dealt with, or better yet, the way it is *not* dealt with, allows for a potentially destructive element in the lives of most people. It is time to cast more light on the subject and to focus on the way money and the psychology of the individual intermingle, the way hidden money motives serve to impair and distort human relationships.

3

PARADOXES, HYPOCRISIES, INCONSISTENCIES, AND LIES

To some, money is the root of all evil. To others, the lack of money is perceived to be the basis of all their troubles.

People who are rich are often envied and hated. Those who are poor are frequently scorned.

Many who have little or no money are obsessed with obtaining it. Others seem compelled to act in ways that insure they don't acquire it. Many who are rich are obsessed with holding onto money. Some who have money are apparently not content until they dispose of it.

Any attempt to make sense of the confusing and paradoxical attitudes that people have toward money is a monumental undertaking. It seems that for some people money is the most important thing in the world. Yet they pretend it is the least important. The worship of money and the condemnation of money exist side by side, sometimes even within the same individual. And this is not a new phenomenon. Even a cursory glance back through history suggests that ambivalence toward money is the rule. While Horace was proclaiming, "Money is the foremost thing to seek; cash first and virtue afterwards,"

Cicero was warning that, "Of evils current upon the earth, the worst is money." Alexander Hamilton called money, "an essential ingredient to happiness," and Tolstoy regarded it as "a new form of slavery."

When people are bombarded with two opposing philosophies or ideologies, it might seem logical that they would accept one and reject the other. But the human mind is extremely flexible. At different times it can accept completely opposing points of view and somehow juggle them so that the contradictions are not readily apparent.

Most people, for example, believe in and accept maxims such as "You get what you pay for," or "If you want the best, you have to be willing to pay for it." They have been taught those clichés all their lives and they accept them as fact. Yet those same people will spend hours and hours trying to get *more* than they pay for—to get a bargain, or, better yet, "to get something for nothing." The dilemma this attitude poses for every merchant is, "Should I put my prices high so people will think they are getting better quality or put them low so they will think they are getting a bargain?"

To covet money openly is generally considered to be socially unacceptable behavior. To be selfish or greedy is usually thought of as repulsive, "sinful," and in poor taste. Those who openly put the accumulation of money ahead of human values are usually viewed with contempt. At the same time, it is obvious that money commands respect. Money is not infrequently used as a measure of personal worth, so that people who have money are perceived as somehow superior to those who do not. People with money can often intimidate those who want it, and those who do not have money may allow themselves to be manipulated in humiliating ways in order to get it. The humorous novel *The Magic Christian* by Terry Southern [1] is built around this theme. The hero is a billionaire named Guy Grand who spends $10 million a year humiliating people or "making it hot" for them. His crowning glory is constructing a vat in downtown Chicago which he fills with a mixture of manure, urine, blood, and ten thousand one-hundred dollar bills. The movie version of this novel shows a very dramatic shot of people diving fully clothed into this mess to extract the money.

People often give each other double messages in regard to money. They claim it is "good" to strive to obtain money but "bad" to admit that one wants a lot of it. Money is viewed as the most important commodity in the world, but social etiquette demands that it be spoken of as having no value. People give lip service to the democratic ideal that everyone is equal but give differential treatment to those who have money and those who do not. Hypocrisy about money is therefore inevitable. In fact, *hypocrisy becomes the norm*. People who deviate either by openly avowing their desire for money or by not devoting most of their time and energy working to acquire it are looked upon as peculiar.

Most of the great religions of the world preach the virtues of poverty and self-denial. Foregoing personal and material pleasure is believed to enhance holiness, righteousness and spiritual development. One of the most frequently quoted passages in the Bible is Christ's proclamation that, "It is easier for a camel to go through the eye of a needle, than for a rich man to enter into the kingdom of God." Yet it is obvious even to the most confirmed believer that some of these same religious leaders apparently do not practice what they preach. The late Kathryn Kuhlman, the well-known evangelist, reportedly left a very sizable estate. The teenage guru, Maharaj Ji, was denounced by his mother and deposed as head of the Divine Light Mission for living in opulent splendor. In 1975, for example, he received a personal income of $200,000 from the donations of his followers. And the controversial Rev. Sun Myung Moon made headlines with his extensive real estate purchases. While his followers donated thousands of hours of time to raising money for the cause, the Reverend Moon was buying some $20 million worth of property.

While church leaders stress the value of sacrifice and penury to their congregations, many churches, cathedrals, and temples of even the most traditional denominations are impressive architectural masterpieces, richly adorned with gold and silver, and housing some of the most valuable art collections in the world.

Despite their stated beliefs, it would seem that most church leaders and churchgoers prefer to worship in attractive and expensive surroundings. The "success" of the ministry is too often measured less by the "spiritual impact" on the congregation than by the amount of money donated by the congregation to erect an imposing house of worship.

Occasionally, a religious leader comes along who preaches that it is better to receive than to give, rather than the other way around. Such a person was Russell Herman Conwell, a Baptist minister at the turn of the century. He went about the country giving a speech called "Acres of Diamonds," in which he proclaimed that acquiring wealth was an honorable ambition. According to Conwell:

> Money is power. Every good man and woman ought to strive for power, to do good with it when obtained. I say, get rich, get rich![2]

Conwell followed his own advice. By the time he had given his speech to some six thousand audiences, he had accumulated approximately $8 million, which was certainly a lot of money in the 1890's.

The modern counterpart to Reverend Conwell is the Reverend Frederick J. Eikerenkoetter II, better known as Reverend Ike. As head of the United Christian Evangelistic Association, Reverend Ike has sixteen Rolls-Royces at his disposal, as well as six residences in the United States and others throughout the world. His wardrobe costs approximately $50,000 a year and he has enough jewelry to start a small store. He is a self-proclaimed hedonist and admits to being a multimillionaire. Addressing his huge congregation, Reverend Ike says something like this:

> "Now repeat after me! . . . I have a wonderful relationship with money. . . . Money loves me. . . . I see a mountain of money piling into my arms. . . . I see myself on shopping sprees . . . taking fabulous vacations several times a year—with money to spare. . . . Oh bless you, money, you're wonderful stuff!" [3]

Paradoxical attitudes toward money are found in every lifestyle and every profession or business. Ideally, the amount of money one spends in a month or a year should be related to one's income. However, some people live beyond their means whether they have a little money or a lot, and others refuse to spend much money regardless of their financial circumstances. For example, when one of baseball's highest-paid players, Willie Davis, filed for bankruptcy, he listed assets of only $15,000 and debts of nearly $120,000, although he had earned $234,000 during the preceding two years.[4] This is not uncommon among professional athletes, entertainers, and other celebrities. Joe Louis, shortly after he retired from the ring as the champion heavyweight boxer of the world, owed the Internal Revenue Service more money than he could expect to make in the rest of his life.

In contrast is the story of a woman in Delray Beach, Florida, known as "Garbage Mary." Although reportedly worth more than a million dollars, she dressed in rags, lived in an apartment amid mounds of garbage, and spent much of her time rummaging through garbage cans and begging cigarettes from neighbors.[5]

J. Paul Getty during his lifetime was considered the world's richest man. He was also known to be one of the stingiest. Sheila Graham, the columnist, tells of observing him while on vacation at the Imperial Hotel in Vienna. He gave the concierge the equivalent of twenty-five cents to pay for a stamp and then asked for change.[6] Getty also had pay telephones installed in his seventy-two-room mansion, presumably so guests would not run up his phone bill. On the other hand, he would freely spend hundreds of thousands of dollars for a piece of art to add to his extensive collection. Although recognizing that fine art is a fine investment, his interest in collecting was motivated by the enjoyment and beauty of art rather than its monetary worth. H. L. Hunt, the Texan whose wealth was perhaps second only to Getty's, drove his own car to work and parked three blocks away to save fifty cents in parking fees.

Pablo Picasso accumulated more wealth in his lifetime than any other artist. After his death his estate was valued at something over $250 million, including two large estates in France and an extensive art collection. When his paintings began selling for very high prices, he was able to fulfill one of his earlier stated dreams: "I should like to live like a poor man, with a great deal of money." [7] Yet for many years Picasso was an ardent supporter of communism, an economic system which advocates equal distribution of wealth.

During the sixties many rock singers, such as Bob Dylan, became rich writing and singing protest songs which berated the establishment for its concern about money and materialism rather than human rights and social reform. Later Dylan built an ultraposh home overlooking the Pacific Ocean in Malibu at a cost in excess of $2 million. Examples of paradoxical attitudes and ambivalent feelings toward money are endless. People denounce the value of money yet worship it. Too often they envy and hate those who have more money than they do and fear and hate those who have less. Some people would do anything in the world to get money; others treat it like dirt. To wind one's way through the maze of confusion and contradictions regarding money and to discover the origins and meaning of the paradoxical behavior toward it, it is necessary to leave the world of reality and common sense and enter the world of fantasy and unconscious motivation.

UNCOVERING HIDDEN CONNECTIONS

There is very little actual research on the psychological meaning and use of money. What literature is available is almost exclusively the product of Sigmund Freud and the psychoanalytic school of thought. Other theoretical approaches to psychology have almost totally overlooked or ignored the subject. The fact that such a critical area of behavior has received so little close psychological scrutiny probably indicates that it is an area of great discomfort and one that contains powerful truths about people and their motivations; truths that even for psychiatric and psychological professionals may be too close for comfort.

The underlying premise of Freudian psychology is that the individual is endowed with certain basic instincts and that the interaction between these instinctual drives and the environment molds the personality. The analyst is a mental archaeologist. The terrain for exploration is the unconscious mind of the patient, and the buried treasure consists of the bits and pieces of truth deposited there in the past because they were too difficult or too traumatic to cope with at that time.

The psychoanalyst as *therapist* is concerned with probing the patient's unconscious mind to find the particular combination of instinctual drives and environmental experiences that make that person a unique human being. The psychoanalyst as *scientist*, on the other hand, tries to find similarities and patterns of interaction between drives and experiences in many patients in order to develop laws and theories of human behavior.

THE "ALMIGHTY DOLLAR" IS REALLY "FILTHY LUCRE"

The generalization most often cited by psychoanalysts and those familiar with the Freudian literature pertaining to the unconscious psychological meaning of money is that *money equals feces*. This certainly is not its only meaning, although perhaps it is the most frequent unconscious equation.

The psychological derivation of this equation is as follows. One of the basic instinctual drives is for sensual gratification. This drive is called "libido." During the first year of life, the highly developed nerve endings in the mouth provide the greatest opportunity for libidinal gratification. By the second and third years of life, the nerves in the anus have also become sensitive to pleasure, and anal activity is the focus of libidinal energy. This later shifts to the genitals during the fourth and fifth years.

According to psychoanalytic theory, it is during the second and third years that personality patterns are most likely to develop which later influence one's perception of money. Several things are going on during this anal period which play a role in that development.

1. The child finds instinctual libidinal pleasure in eliminating fecal matter.

2. This process meets a variety of reactions from the environment.

3. The most typical response is to subject the child to some type of toilet training procedure.

4. Reaction of the parents to toilet training may range from ecstatic praise when the child defecates in the prescribed receptacle to threats and punishment when it does not.

5. During this period, the child is also striving to achieve autonomy and a sense of self-worth.

6. Toilet training may then become a battleground in which there is a power struggle between child and parents, a conflict as to whether the child feels in control of sphincter muscles or feels compelled to submit to parental demands out of fear of punishment or threat of loss of love.

7. At the same time, children are known to have extensive and often distorted fantasies about their feces; there may be great pride because the feces are a creation out of their own bodies; their expulsion may represent bodily mutilation (like the loss of a penis), or be confused with giving birth, as a mother does.

8. These fantasies are influenced to a degree by feedback from the environment, but the likelihood of perceptual distortion remains high because of the child's limited experience and limited intellectual understanding.

9. Confusion is amplified if parents express great pleasure with the feces the child deposits in the potty chair, treat it like a gift of gold, and then later communicate that it is dirty and smells bad.

Few people remember their toilet training experiences. Most of the process takes place on an unconscious level. Much is repressed. However, if the anal stage of development is traumatic, normal psychological development will be partially arrested at that level. The source of trauma most emphasized by Freud is premature and excessive demands for toilet training by the parents, although any severe threat to the child's security or sense of autonomy during this time period might produce the same results.

Where the child's needs are severely frustrated and psychological development is fixated at the anal stage, other important aspects of life, including money, will be dealt with in the same way as the retention and elimination of feces. For example, the miser's hoarding of money can be thought of as symbolic of the child's refusal to eliminate feces. The defiance with which the child withholds its precious feces in the face of parental demands is generalized over a period of time to the withholding of all precious possessions from a world perceived as hostile and demanding. Since it is readily apparent even to the developing child that most people view money as a prized possession, the transition from feces to money is an easy step.

In contrast to the miser, the spendthrift has learned that submission to parental authority in the elimination of feces leads to approval and affection. Having learned to equate elimination with receiving affection, some individuals develop diarrhea whenever they feel insecure and in particular need of approval and affection. Others, who have substituted money for feces, may spend money freely instead of expelling feces. This is a symbolic form of diarrhea.

The similarity between money and feces lies in the extremes of emotion and value attributed to them. Money is vulgar and repulsive to some, yet to many it is the most prized possession in the world. The same is true of feces. They are the most worthless of waste material with an offensive texture and aroma. Yet to the small child the creation of excrement out of its own bodily functions is a source of pleasure and wonder, and feces themselves are perhaps the most valuable commodity in the child's young life. It was this similarity that led Norman O. Brown, the noted professor of classics, to observe, "In its famous paradox, the equation of money and excrement, psychoanalysis becomes the first science to state what common sense and the poets have long known—that the essence of money is its absolute worthlessness." [8]

In trying to substantiate the validity of unconscious motives, Freud and his followers not only learned from the dreams and free associations of their patients, they also sought confirmation in other representations of the unconscious—myths, fairy tales, folklore, and superstition. Clues may also be garnered from observing linguistic expressions, since idiomatic and vernacular language often provides insight into unconscious meaning. In the language of money, there are a number of commonly used phrases which point to an anal association. Money is referred to as "filthy lucre." The person who is wealthy is called "stinking rich." The poker player puts money in the "pot." The dice player shoots "craps." The gambler or investor who loses everything is "cleaned out."

The equation of money and feces is not necessarily universal. In a culture where there was no money or no incentive to accumulate money, such an equation could not exist. People use what is available to express their emotional conflicts. If there were no money, some other outlet would be used. Also, in cultures where there is no excessive demand for bowel control, relatively less importance is attributed to money. Among the Dakota Indians, for example, toilet training was very permissive. Likewise, little value was attributed to personal possessions, and the accumulation of great wealth was nonexistent. If a warrior admired a neighbor's horse, it was given to him with no expectation of getting anything in return. Among the Dakotas there was a noticeable lack of greed, envy, and struggle for power. If a person had something that someone else needed, that was sufficient cause to give it to the other person.[9]

Attitudes toward both child rearing and the private ownership of money have changed dramatically in China since the takeover by the Communists. Punishment is less severe and discipline is maintained through subtle coercion and pressure to conform to a common standard of behavior rather than by spanking or physical force. Toilet training is completed fairly early but through encouragement and with essentially no emotional overtones.[10] Pressure to conform to the group norm is applied by the family, the school, and the state. Society is placed before the individual. Consequently there is minimal opportunity or incentive to accumulate much wealth or personal property. Individual differences are minimized and money is not used as a measure of superiority.

The one-to-one relationship between attitudes toward money and feces is obviously too simplistic. Variables other than those associated with toilet training influence one's perception of money. However, other things being equal, in families and in cultures where early and demanding toilet training is in vogue and anal fixation results, certain character traits such as orderliness, punctuality, compulsive cleanliness, and obstinacy are most likely to evolve. *It is out of character traits like these that one is psychologically predisposed to react in certain ways to the important things in life, including money.* The miser, for example, not only withholds money, but most likely also withholds knowledge, feelings, time, and everything else of value. Attitudes toward money are never isolated phenomena. They are intricately related to the person's total personality structure, value system, and cultural background. Therefore, knowing a person's secret attitudes toward money makes it easier to understand that person's attitudes and behavior in many aspects of life seemingly unrelated to money.

While internal tensions associated with anal activity give rise to the symbolic equation of money and feces, internal tensions arising during other stages of development will predispose the individual to form other unconscious associations with money. During the first year of life, the oral stage, conflicts center mostly around dependency, trust, and problems of weaning. If trauma occurs during the oral stage of development, oral fixation is likely to occur. This means that the individual will be predisposed to resolve tensions through feeding behavior or something symbolically related to it. Money might then become a substitute for the breast or the bottle and the person may attempt to gain a sense of warmth and security and affection from it. Lack of money, in turn, might be perceived as a threat to one's safety or it might give rise to feelings of emptiness and depression or loss of love.

The genital stage of psychosexual development follows the anal stage. Problems at this stage are primarily related to bladder control and emerging genital sexual impulses. Consequently, excessive frustration and resulting fixation at this level might ultimately lead to an association of money with sexual desire and physical attractiveness.

Because the symbolic linking of money with instinctual drives takes place unconsciously, not even the person who has made such a connection is necessarily sure that for him, or for her, money is a substitute for milk, security, love, sexuality, or feces. But simply because a drive is unconscious does not mean it is any less powerful a motivator of behavior. An unconscious drive is only less obvious and more difficult to discover. Few people really have any understanding of where their attitudes toward money come from, although they may offer rationalizations. And basic attitudes toward money rarely change in a lifetime. Despite increased knowledge and experience, a person's perception of money at sixty is generally similar to what it was when the person was twenty. This lends further support to the idea that attitudes toward money have an unconscious and irrational basis.

When Nick Scanlon graduated from high school, he left the small town in Pennsylvania where he had spent his first eighteen years and headed for Los Angeles. He was an ambitious young man who was determined to do well.

His first job was as a busboy in an expensive West Los Angeles restaurant. He rented a cheap room, ate only what was given him free where he worked, and spent most of his money on clothes. When he had acquired an adequate wardrobe, he began going out one night a week either to a nightclub or a fancy restaurant. When he could afford it he took a date, but whether he went alone or with someone else, he always went first class. He dressed immaculately, ordered the best seats and the most expensive food, and tipped generously.

Over a period of time, Nick moved up from busboy to host to night manager of the restaurant. When he was thirty-two, he opened his own bar and grill with backing from friends. During the next thirty years, Nick owned or managed a number of the better resturants in Hollywood, Westwood, and West Los Angeles. Some were successful, others were not. But from the way Nick spent money, no one would ever know whether he was broke or riding high. He always bought the best.

Now Nick is in his sixties, has no money in the bank and is living on social security. Or, as Nick puts it, "I *live* one day a month. The other twenty-nine I just exist." On that one day of the month Nick goes calling on a woman friend with flowers, candy, champagne, and box seats to the theater. The rest of the month he struggles to survive until the next social security check arrives.

Freudian psychoanalysis provides the most extensive theory of personality development available. It is also the only one that attempts to explain the origin of the irrational, emotionally charged value that people have attributed to money. Understanding the major Freudian tenets helps to make sense out of what otherwise seems nonsensical. However, Freudian theory doesn't provide all of the answers.

OTHER VIEWS OF THE
PARADOXICAL MAZE

Other psychological theories disagree with Freud's emphasis on instinctual drives, but most accept the fact that nearly all behavior is learned. Most would also agree that irrational behavior in adulthood is an outgrowth of previously learned behavior, perhaps dating back to childhood. Many, however, would emphasize more strongly than did Freud the role of cultural and social influences in the learning of basic attitudes and values. It is obvious that attitudes toward money and the acquisition of money will be influenced by whether one lives in a capitalist or socialist country, whether one grows up in a period of affluence or economic depression, whether one is born into an upper-class or lower-class family, and whether one lives in a developed or underdeveloped country.

Cultural influences cannot be ignored. They play an important part in shaping the individual. But still only a part. Some individuals apparently turn their backs on the culture of their heritage and make a satisfactory adjustment to a culture that is radically different from the one they grew up in. Joseph Hirshhorn, an immigrant who grew up in some of Brooklyn's toughest slums, amassed a fortune of over $100 million in stocks and mining and moved ultimately into a social circle where he was on an equal footing with heads of state and heads of other mammoth corporations. The story of Frank Woolworth is much the same. He came from a poverty-stricken small farm in upstate New York, started into business with borrowed capital, and gradually built a chain of five- and ten-cent stores across the United States and Europe. On the other hand, Albert Schweitzer, the brilliant philosopher, musician, clergyman, and physician, gave up a comfortable, intellectually stimulating and potentially lucrative life in Europe to become a medical missionary in the jungles of Africa.

Another part of the puzzle can be pieced together by drawing on the research of social psychologists. Their studies of the nature of group conflict throw light on why both the rich and the poor are hated and/or feared by a large number of people in between. Hatred of the poor is not usually admitted openly. It is often disguised as pity. Sometimes it is intertwined with racial prejudice. At other times contempt may be directed at some aspect or behavior which the majority attributes to the poor, such as "They're lazy," or "They're dumb."

Conflict between groups as well as conflict between individuals can be traced to two main sources—envy and threat to security. Envy involves a feeling of resentment toward another person or group that has something desirable. It is a powerful motive. It fosters hostility and aggression and often leads to the destruction of that which is prized as well as the person or group that possesses it. If money is highly valued, as it generally is in the American culture, those who have more are likely to arouse the envy and hatred of those who have less but covet it.

Threats to group security that lead to intergroup conflict may be real or imagined. They may involve threats of physical violence or financial destruction. Most threats, however, are to the status, reputation, or ego of the group. Those who have money often see those who have less as a potential threat to their "superior status" and they fear being "dragged down" to the level of the poorer group. This leads to feelings of hostility and antagonism toward those who are at a lower socioeconomic level. If, in addition to the psychological threat, the poor are perceived as an economic threat because they are willing to work for lower wages, hostility toward them is likely to increase.

Conflict between groups, with resultant fear, hostility, and distrust, is likely to be increased as group membership is restricted. An organization which anyone can join and from which anyone can withdraw is not likely to arouse much resentment. Where membership is limited, however, group identification becomes intensified and barriers develop between those who are members and those who are not. As barriers increase, communication between groups lessens and suspicion takes the place of understanding. On many college campuses an invitation to join a social fraternity or sorority is in part dependent upon the financial status of one's family. The exclusiveness of these organizations often sets them apart from the rest of the student body and a certain amount of animosity commonly occurs between those who belong and those who do not.

Money, or lack of it, is itself frequently a barrier. It is difficult to live among the wealthy without wealth, although it is occasionally done. There are some who can cross the money line and pretend to be what they are not. A few poor persons can pass for being wealthy by dressing and acting the part, much like Cinderella. Some rich persons are able to dress and act on a par with poorer people and relate to them in such a way that the economic difference is not a factor. Generally, however, the wealthy people in a community use their money to separate themselves from less affluent community members. Differences become barriers and the more different the wealthy group becomes in dress, housing, language, customs, moral standards, and the like, the more it alienates itself from the majority and the more resentment and hostility it is likely to attract.

In the same way, if the poor of the community, by necessity or by choice, live together in the same neighborhood, dress alike, develop a common vernacular, and have similar interests and activities, they may develop an in-group feeling and a sense of security through belonging to the group. However, to the extent these characteristics set them apart from the majority, they are seen as a threat, and the more likely they are to arouse suspicion and hostility in members of the larger society.

FEELING GUILTY ABOUT MONEY

One of the cultural forces that has helped shape the American character is the Puritan ethic, also known as the Protestant ethic. One does not, of course, have to be a Protestant in the religious sense to function in the mode of the Protestant ethic. Its style is often seen as clearly in the Catholic, Jew, or atheist. All that is required is that from infancy one be indoctrinated with a moral philosophy which teaches that hard work, self-sacrifice, and suffering are virtuous and that pleasure and self-indulgence are sinful.

Of all mortal sins, "selfishness" is probably the worst from this Puritan point of view. Lesser sins can be forgiven under certain circumstances, but selfishness is a sure-fire ticket to hell. To indulge oneself in any kind of self-oriented pleasurable activity is an abomination, and to possess or covet anything of monetary value for one's own personal satisfaction constitutes an unpardonable sin. Toys are to share. Ice cream, if any, is equally distributed. Vanity and bragging are abhorred.

Children brought up under the Protestant ethic are constantly reminded about their evil, selfish ways. And they are promised all sorts of dire punishments, both here and in the hereafter, because they do not put the feelings and welfare of their parents, siblings, friends, neighbors, and all of the miserable and suffering people in the world ahead of their own selfish desires. Of all the punishments invoked, however, the most damaging is guilt— that all-pervading sense of guilt that haunts people every time they want something a little bit better than their neighbors have, every time they dare to profess to want to be different or better or faster or smarter or richer than someone else.

This style of child rearing is, of course, visible to all. If it hasn't happened to you personally, it has happened to someone you know. For example, you probably know someone like George Hanson. George grew up in a small Midwestern town, the only son of immigrant Scandinavian parents. As a child George could never please his father no matter how hard he tried. His father was a hard working, God-fearing man who did not believe in frills or praise. He always gave his best effort and expected everyone else to do the same, especially George. No matter how well George did at anything, his father found areas that could stand improvement. The emphasis was always on the negative. George never gave up trying to please his father, although he also built up a lot of resentment toward him. Feeling anger toward his father was too frightening and upsetting, and George repressed the feeling most of the time so that he was generally unaware of it. Occasionally, however, when he was reprimanded by his father, his frustration and rage would get the better of him and he would clench his fists and mutter to himself, "I wish he were dead! I wish he were dead!"

Ellen Murphy lived across the street from George. Her father was a butcher and earned a good salary, yet money was scarce since there were seven children to feed and clothe. Ellen was the youngest of five girls. She was an energetic, happy child with a lively imagination. She would spend hours dreaming and pretending that she would someday become a movie actress, wear beautiful clothes, and have handsome suitors. The clothes she actually wore were hand-me-downs and anything but fancy. Ellen's mother constantly berated her for her frivolity and vowed, in her sternest Irish brogue, that "No good will ever become ye!" She preached of thrift, piety, hell and damnation, and the virtues of self-sacrifice.

Next door to the Murphys lived the Fergusons. The Fergusons had three sons: Thomas, Warren, and Wade. On weekends and summer vacations, Thomas and Warren helped their father in the lumberyard, but Wade, whenever he could get away with it, stayed in his room listening to rock music or singing and playing his guitar. He occasionally made some money playing and singing at local clubs. Even his music teacher, who was classically trained, felt that Wade had talent and could make a career for himself in music. His parents, however, were most upset at that possibility and were determined that he would enter the family business.

Millions of Americans have grown up with backgrounds similar to those of George Hanson, Ellen Murphy, and Wade Ferguson. Backgrounds which help insure a reasonably successful economic future based on hard work and dedication but which, in many cases, limit the accumulation of wealth and prevent the enjoyment of whatever money the person does acquire. The end result of such training is a personality characterized primarily by self-denial, self-deprecation, and an overwhelming guilt complex. Working provides a sense of accomplishment and satisfaction. Nonproductive leisure time, on the other hand, may make one feel anxious and uncomfortable.

Values such as honesty, sobriety, punctuality, thrift, and conscientiousness are also a part of the value system propounded by the Protestant ethic, but they do not play as essential a role in the present discussion. While part of this tradition is fading from the current American scene, remnants of it still remain. Most of our ancestors were steeped in this philosophy and tried as best they could to pass it on. And, being a strong, demanding and persistent lot, many of them succeeded rather well.

It is not uncommon, therefore, for many people with an ingrained value system based on the Protestant ethic to feel guilty about acquiring a lot of money. Not that the system is opposed to money per se, but only to *too much* money or money acquired *too easily* or displayed *ostentatiously*. Money is all right as long as it is the result of hard work, since hard work is believed to build character. Unfortunately, however, the amount of energy expended is rarely the sole criterion of what a job pays. A successful rock singer may make more money for one performance than a successful jackhammer operator makes in a year. In fact, there are probably not enough hours in a lifetime for the jackhammer operator to make a lot of money by the sweat of his brow. Yet the Puritan code equates "easy money" with dishonesty or sinfulness and lauds hard work whether it leads to poverty or riches.

Guilt produced by adherence to the Protestant ethic works in one of two ways. It can either precede or follow the act itself. If, for whatever reason, a person does something which produces a feeling of guilt, the person experiences a sense of discomfort, discontent, unhappiness, self-loathing. If guilt feelings precede the act (this is sometimes referred to as "anticipatory guilt"), the person will likely find some reason or rationalization for not performing the deed. If a person feels it is morally wrong to make too much money too easily, it is possible to avoid situations where that is likely to happen and thus eliminate the probability of feeling guilty later.

When they deliberately do something they consider to be wrong, most people experience a feeling of guilt consciously and directly. Many things people do, however, are not so obviously "wrong," and the resulting guilt is also not so obvious. The discomfort one feels may not even be recognized as guilt. Wade Ferguson, for example, used to suffer frequently from an upset stomach or other vague physical symptoms when his mother complained about him wasting time playing the guitar.

When people are aware of guilt there are positive steps that can be taken to eradicate it. They can try to undo the acts that cause the feelings of guilt. They can seek to make restitution or perhaps seek forgiveness if they have wronged another person.

On the other hand, when guilt is unconscious and not directly experienced, the solution is not as easy. Since the person is unaware of what was done to cause the guilty feelings and since the discomfort is usually not even recognized as guilt, it is extremely difficult to take positive steps to rectify the situation. In this case, guilt may result in psychosomatic complaints or be transferred to feelings of depression or to unconscious attempts at self-punishment. It is not uncommon for people who feel guilty about making money to donate to charity, to lose money through poor investments, or to spend lavishly until the money is all gone. Fortunes are lost and opportunities to make money are missed by people who seek to atone for their guilt feelings by deliberately but unconsciously making the wrong decisions— decisions that lead to failure rather than success.

Poor money decisions are what caused George Hanson to seek professional advice. When he was thirty-five, George consulted a psychologist because he was beginning to see a pattern developing in his business dealings which upset him and which he couldn't understand. He was an intelligent, hardworking, creative person who was still trying to prove something to his father by striving to become a success in the business world. After graduating from college he went to work for his father, who owned a small but profitable printing company. After a couple of years he decided to go into business for himself. He had saved a little money and was able to borrow more from the bank. With that he purchased a small furniture store from a neighbor who was about to retire. He worked hard, added some new lines, redecorated, tried some unique sales promotion ideas, and business began to boom.

When the building next door became vacant, George leased it and expanded his operation. He hired more employees and began advertising on television. Business continued to improve. Next, he decided to open a second store across town. This time, however, he picked a poor location. Although he put a lot of effort and money into the venture, he soon lost not only the second store but also the first. After three years of hard work, self-sacrifice and creative ingenuity, George was out on the street without a dollar and without a job.

George, however, did not give up easily. The second time he was on the verge of becoming a financial giant, he took a partner who absconded with the company's funds. The third time, he parlayed his hard-earned profits on a product line that wouldn't sell. Now, on the brink of his fourth fortune (or his first fortune for the fourth time around), he anxiously sought professional help to find out why he inadvertently took that crucial step which caused him to fail just when he was about to cash in on months of hard work and meticulous preparation.

After a number of sessions with the psychologist, it was discovered that the underlying self-destructive behavior was motivated by *guilt*. To summarize and simplify the process, it seems that:

1. From early childhood, George harbored strong but repressed hostile feelings toward his father because he felt rejected by him.

2. His drive to become successful was an attempt to win his father's approval.

3. Becoming extremely successful financially and in business, however, would make him more successful than his father.

4. Being more successful than his father was unconsciously equated with destroying his father and taking over the father's role.

5. Consequently, to keep from feeling guilty for symbolically destroying his father, George managed a last-second reprieve by blowing everything he had worked for, and thus he could remain in an inferior but safer financial position.

When he was able to understand and accept his angry feelings toward his father, George no longer had to bury them. As he became more able to express his emotions openly and to understand them, he was able to resolve the negative feelings he held toward his father and he no longer felt guilty. He not only developed a healthier, more mature relationship with his father, but he no longer felt driven either to become the greatest financial success in town or to fail.

Unconscious processes are by far the most difficult to deal with because, by definition, they are beyond the scope of conscious awareness. Before he went into therapy, George would have completely denied that he harbored hostile feelings toward his father. Consciously, he respected his father even though they were not very close to each other. And, since he considered himself an enlightened and liberated man of the world, he would have been even more incredulous if someone had suggested he felt guilty about these feelings he did not know he had. Yet, it was *guilt about his angry feelings* that made him repress them in the first place.

Ellen Murphy's problem was a little different. She left home after high school and went to a large city where she found a job in an advertising agency. She gradually developed a flair for writing copy—conservative, but in good taste. When the agency went broke, a business acquaintance persuaded Ellen to go into business for herself. For a while she did free-lance work and eventually had a small agency of her own. She did most of the work herself. She had only a few clients but the ones she had were very loyal and were pleased with her work. Although she was an attractive woman, she never married and devoted her life to work, using it as an outlet for her imagination and fantasy.

Ellen's social life was limited. Although she had a few close friends, she found little time for them. Her personal wants were few and her tastes were simple and Spartan. In a field of business which grows and expands largely on the basis of personal and social contacts, Ellen's remained essentially the same year after year. Despite the invitations of friends and associates, she avoided cocktails parties, social gatherings, conventions, and all of the settings which might logically lead to increased contacts and increased business. In the meantime, competitors with less ability were progressing while her business remained static.

Although she offered a variety of excuses and explanations for her asocial behavior, psychologically she still perceived herself as that little girl in hand-me-down clothes. She felt no compunction about telling clients they had to spend money to make money, but she felt too guilty to spend money on herself for expensive clothes, an attractive apartment, or entertainment, even though she knew it would be good for business.

And Wade Ferguson never made it big in the music world. He and his two brothers each own a one-third interest in the family lumberyard. Wade is married, has two children, and lives in a comfortable three-bedroom house in a newer section of town. He attends the Rotary Club luncheon every Thursday and is the master of ceremonies at their Christmas benefit. He sings in the church choir.

For a while, however, the family was disappointed in Wade. They tolerated his "laziness" as best they could while he was growing up, but when he quit college in his freshman year and went to Hollywood, he had gone too far. At first they tried to console themselves that it was some nonsense he had to get out of his system, and they waited for him to grow out of it. As time went on, Wade took little jobs at various clubs and spent his days sunning on the beach and composing music. When he telephoned excitedly one day to tell them that a publishing company had expressed interest in some of his songs, the family was convinced that Wade's style of life was becoming permanent and that something drastic had to be done.

In letters and on the telephone, Mrs. Ferguson increased her pleading and crying, Mr. Ferguson lectured more emphatically, and Thomas and Warren relentlessly pursued their campaign of "man-to-man" talks with Wade. Finally, in a mood of depression and frustration and partially as a result of this steady barrage, the seeds of guilt implanted during childhood flourished, and Wade "came to his senses." He gave up his dream of music and show business and riches and returned to the safety and stability of the family business. He couldn't cope with the guilt of getting paid for something he enjoyed doing, for something that was creative and pleasurable. Eventually, he began to feel virtuous about working ten hours a day at a job he disliked.

The Puritan ethic, with its emphasis on hard work, thrift, overcoming adversity and, to some extent, the virtue of Yankee shrewdness in business, has helped to make America the prosperous industrial nation it is. It has also contributed to the confusing and paradoxical views of money that most Americans have. The ethic teaches that people should work hard and sacrifice to earn money but should not enjoy it once they have earned it; that a lot of money made too easily is the "work of the devil," but that a lot of money accumulated over a period of time and as the result of hard work proves that one is "favored by God"; that both money and lack of money produce feelings of guilt; and that money can both protect and destroy one's virtue.

UNSCRAMBLING THE MAZE

If, like most people, you feel caught up in the confusing maze of money but aren't sure how you got there or what you can do to get out, you are certainly not alone. You may wonder why you spend money freely on luxuries and resist buying tomatoes because they are three cents a pound higher than they were the day before. You may find that when you win a bet or earn extra money for doing some simple task you feel depressed instead of elated or you feel you want to spend that money on an extravagance. You may complain bitterly about your job and the low salary it pays and then realize that you have never seriously thought of quitting or of trying to find another position.

Whatever inconsistencies you find in your own money behavior, you may be sure that they are the result of previous learning. Money behavior, like all complex behavior, is learned; and it is learned because it satisfies certain psychological and emotional needs. Positive and negative experiences during infancy and childhood, cultural impact, and early training all help to define attitudes and behavior toward money. If those attitudes and behavior now prove troublesome or inappropriate, they can be unlearned. In the following chapters we will explore the psychological meanings of various forms of money madness and the means by which they might be handled so that money may find its rightful place in our lives.

4

PURSUING AN ILLUSION

FAME AND RICHES ARE THE STUFF THAT DREAMS ARE MADE OF. In fairy tales like *Cinderella* and *Sleeping Beauty*, the ending, "And they lived happily ever after," implies not only that the happy couple are deeply in love but also very wealthy. Visions of money and stardom stir the imaginations and longings of millions of American young people, and the promise of wealth is the lure that shapes the lives of many of all ages. What child has not had daydreams of someday becoming a movie star, or entertainer, or professional athlete—both famous and wealthy?

Alice Cooper, the male rock star with the feminine first name, is one whose dream became a reality when he was still in his early twenties. After a dismal beginning, Cooper, whose bizarre act included singing to a live boa constrictor and chopping up a fake baby, became an overnight millionaire. "The idea all along was to make $1 million. Otherwise the struggle wouldn't have been worth it," said Alice. "I'm the most American rock act. I have American ideals. I love money." [1]

For every Alice Cooper whose dream comes true, there are thousands whose dreams don't. But the odds don't seem to stop anyone who is determined to make the dream a reality. The magic of money is such that few people react to it with logic or reason.

MAGIC FROM THE START

The magical quality of money dates back to antiquity. Early coins bore the likeness of the king of whatever country issued them, and the magical powers attributed to the king presumably were then transferred to the coins. These coins served the function of a talisman more than that of an instrument of commerce.

The magical power of money has multiplied over the last twenty-five hundred to three thousand years. As more and more people have come under its spell, the quality and quantity of its magic have increased. The myths and rituals have become more complex, and the money priesthood has expanded to include bankers, legislators, accountants, lawyers, stockbrokers, economists, and financiers.

Through it all, however, the basic magic is unchanged. Like the king, the person with money is endowed with great power. By waving a handful of money in the air, an otherwise insignificant man can command others to wait on him and to satisfy his every need and whim—shine his shoes, clean his clothes, pour his wine. In short, to treat him like a king. A twenty-dollar bill can magically make a nonexistent table suddenly appear in a crowded nightclub. Twice that amount might conjure up two tickets to an otherwise sold-out theater performance.

The power of money has been used to build and to destroy. To create empires, to wage war. To save lives and to kill. To get to the moon and to pollute the earth. To support scientific research that seeks to improve life for millions and to provide the means of mass destruction.

The course of history, for better or worse, is continually changed by the power of money. The international balance of power today is shifting because of the economic value of Arab oil. Wars are fought for economic reasons as much as for ideological differences. The American Revolution, for example, began with a dispute over taxes. The whole concept of labor unions emerged as an organized struggle for higher wages. Organized crime, on the other hand, owes its existence to the fact that some people are willing to accept money for performing illegal services. Jesus Christ was betrayed for thirty pieces of silver, the equivalent of about $24.

Not only does money provide magical power to help people control and manipulate others and the environment, it also serves as a kind of amulet which protects them from presumed evil and harm. In a world filled with many known and unknown dangers, money can sometimes provide a sense of emotional security. The person who is emotionally insecure frequently seeks to offset that unpleasant feeling by stacking up money as a bulwark against anticipated attacks on his or her ego.

For some, money has magical healing powers. With people whose anxiety level rises as their finances dwindle, an infusion of money will bring about a sudden return to normalcy. Where a person's sense of adequacy as a human being is dependent upon the amount of money in the bank, a drain on funds may create a depressed emotional state. For those people, money is a better mood elevator than anything that medical science has yet developed. Short of intensive psychotherapy, a shot of money is probably the treatment of choice for many persons with neurotic monetary problems—although the relief is temporary and the symptoms will soon return.

Karl Schroeder owned a small but thriving neighborhood bakery. Most of the year he maintained a somber, almost sullen mood. If sugar went up two cents a pound, he would go home with a headache, feeling depressed. During holiday seasons, however, especially during Christmas, Karl was a changed person. He greeted customers with a cheery smile and joked and kidded with the salespeople. To those who did not know him well, his behavior might be thought of as a reflection of the holiday spirit. Only his wife and a few close friends knew that Karl's happy mood was the direct result of increased sales and increased profits during the holidays.

It is said that "money talks," "money opens doors," and "money makes the ugly beautiful." There seems to be no limit to the magical feats money can perform. It can even change the human character. To quote from Jean Giraudoux's *The Mad-woman of Chaillot,* "To have money is to be virtuous, honest, beautiful, and witty. And to be without it is to be ugly and boring and stupid and useless."

THE BLACK MAGIC OF MONEY

Not all of the magic of money is positive. At times it is more like a curse. When José Sanchez, a grocer in Miami, Florida, went to a palm reader for help with his personal problems, he was told they were the result of the "evil" in the money he had earned and saved. He was instructed to bring his money to the palmist to have it "exorcised," which he did. Sometime later he went to the authorities complaining that he still had his problems, but that his life savings of $20,000 had disappeared.[2]

While it might be easy to think of Mr. Sanchez as being naïve and gullible to entrust his savings to an unknown palm reader, it is not as easy to dismiss his superstitious belief that he might be the victim of "evil money." Not a few are convinced that money contains "black magic" that corrupts souls and creates misery and unhappiness. Many people firmly believe that "money is the root of all evil." Therefore, to be poor means one is not tainted and is deserving of protection against sin, corruption, and all evil forces.

Money and virtue are often seen as opposite polarities. Phrases like "poor but honest" have become hackneyed, whereas "rich but honest" sounds more like a contradiction than a statement of fact. Crime, vice, and dishonesty generally produce considerably more money than does honest toil. In most cases, the person who desires a large sum of money in a hurry is forced to choose between wealth and virtue. And not infrequently money wins.

Sophocles, in 441 B.C., wrote, "It is money that sacks cities and drives men forth from hearth and home; warps and seduces native innocence, and breeds a habit of dishonesty." Except that the language sounds a little stilted, it might just as well have come from the pen of a contemporary writer. More than two thousand years later in a speech before the United States Senate, for example, the gifted orator and senator from Kansas, John Ingalls, displayed a similar distrust and contempt. "Gold," he proclaimed, "is the instrument of gamblers and speculators, and the idol of the miser and the thief. . . . No people in a great emergency ever found a faithful ally in gold. It is the most cowardly and treacherous of all metals. It makes no treaty it does not break. It has no friend whom it does not sooner or later betray."

Ill-gotten money is referred to as "dirty money." Many people who "sell their souls" for money suffer later. Guilt about their transgressions can take many shapes, but it is obvious that many persons who have achieved fortunes by unscrupulous means feel compelled to cleanse themselves by giving their money away. A number of the world's great charitable and humanitarian foundations owe their origin to the guilt feelings of their founders. Alfred Nobel, for example, who became one of the world's richest men from his invention of dynamite, set aside a part of his fortune to award prizes annually to persons who have made valuable contributions to the "good of humanity." Nobel felt guilty because the explosives that made him wealthy killed his brother, contributed to his father's stroke, and could be used as instruments of war rather than peace.

THE FEAR OF AFFLUENCE

To aspire to riches is as American as apple pie. To *fear affluence* is also a part of American tradition. The Puritan ethic stipulates that affluence is permissible only in the presence of "good character." Character is developed through dealing with and overcoming adversity. The traditional model has been Horatio Alger, who starts at the bottom with broom in hand and, through hard effort and good work, ultimately becomes president of the company. Any shortcut to the top is deplored since that limits the development of character, which is necessary to withstand the temptations to which wealth subjects one.

From the Puritan point of view, the speculator and the gambler are looked down upon because they hope to become wealthy without facing adversity and without contributing to society.

Andrew Carnegie, who was something of a speculator himself, was nevertheless a spokesman for the Puritan ethic. In a speech entitled, "The Road to Business Success; A Talk to Young Men," he commented, "As an end, the acquisition of wealth is ignoble in the extreme; I assume that you save and long for wealth only as a means of enabling you the better to do some good in your day and generation."[3] Speculation, by contrast, is based on the conviction that it is possible to become affluent quickly and without the prescribed amount of suffering and hardship. This is antithetical to the American tradition, which might be summarized as, "You only get ice cream after you eat your spinach."

Professor John P. Sisk of Gonzaga University, in a scholarly treatise on the fear of affluence, claims that the basis of the fear is that "affluence like passion means loss of control."[4] At one level, this means that as one accumulates more and more money, the money controls the person rather than vice versa. The wealthy person may easily become chained by money and possessions and thus lose the freedom to function independently. Money dictates where and how one lives. It restricts a person's circle of friends and associates, and limits one's activities.

When Bill Harvey was promoted to vice-president, with a substantial raise in salary, the family moved to one of the more expensive suburbs. The children attended private schools and Bill's wife, Beverly, had help with the housework twice a week. The Harveys joined the country club and between club activities and entertaining customers and business executives, Bill and Beverly seldom had an evening alone, and rarely time to visit former friends and neighbors. Beverly felt compelled to spend more money on clothes and beauty treatments in order to keep up appearances in her new surroundings, and Bill no longer felt at ease lounging around the house in comfortable but beat-up slacks and sweatshirts.

Before they moved, Bill used to enjoy working in the yard. He looked forward to Saturday afternoons, which he spent mowing the lawn or trimming the hedge and sharing a beer with one of the neighbors while discussing the complexities of eliminating crabgrass. In the new neighborhood, however, everyone employed a gardener. Bill felt self-conscious being the only one to mow his own lawn, so he took up golf instead; but it was never quite the same. Golf wasn't casual fun and exercise. It was much too serious and competitive.

While he was a junior executive, Bill occasionally bought a few shares of stock. At breakfast he would enthusiastically pore over the financial page to see how his stocks were doing and to try to figure out why they went up or down. Now that he was more affluent and his investments were extensive, trying to outguess the market was a deadly serious business. The fun was no longer there. More and more, Bill and Beverly were beginning to feel that they had lost control over important areas of their lives, but they were not really sure how the transition had come about.

At a deeper level, loss of control has a somewhat different significance. Affluence implies a *superabundance* of money, a limitless supply of what is necessary for the most satisfactory life possible. In contrast, the Puritan perception of the world includes *limits to everything*. Therefore it is necessary to conserve things like money, time, resources, energy, sex, and emotions. The development of "character" enables the individual to resist the temptation to waste or squander any of these essentials. If, however, one had an unlimited amount of something—money, for example —there would be no reason to conserve, save, or invest it. In short, there would be no logical reason to exercise any type of control over the expenditure of it.

In *Julian and Maddalo,* the poet Percy Bysshe Shelley captures the essence of the perception of limitlessness when he writes:

> I love all waste
> And solitary places; where we taste
> The pleasure of believing what we see
> Is boundless, as we wish our souls to be.

EASY MONEY

In times past, alchemists tried to convert cheaper metals such as iron into gold. Some alchemists were motivated by greed, but a few, striving for a nobler cause, believed that if gold were readily available and affluence became universal, corruption, greed, and crime would disappear. Alchemy, which is a blend of science, magic, and religion, failed. However, the dream of "streets paved with gold" or an endless supply of money still persists in the minds of many people. It is the dream of the gambler who tries to design a system to beat the horses or the gaming table. It is the dream of the speculator, the inventor, the business tycoon. And the cornerstone of some current economic theories is the conviction that the resources of the earth are plentiful enough to satisfy the needs and desires of all.

While the validity of this theory is debated in economic circles, how does it apply to individuals? Since money generates money, it is theoretically possible for a person to develop a never-ending supply of dollars. A Howard Hughes or a J. Paul Getty, for example, could invest $100 million in eight percent tax-exempt bonds. The interest on this investment would produce $8 million a year spendable income, without ever touching the principal. Conceivably, this income could go on forever.

Although it is generally conceded that there is a limit to the amount of oil beneath the burning sands of the Near East, some Arab oil magnates act as if it will last forever. And they appear to spend money about as fast as the oil pours out of the ground. Adnan Khashoggi, a Saudi Arabian businessman, reportedly has an annual income of $500 million! On a visit to New York he rented an entire floor of the Waldorf Towers. He travels in a 727 jet furnished with gold fixtures, and owns a yacht bigger and better than that of the late Aristotle Onassis. The biggest spender of all, however, is the Emir of Kuwait, Sheikh Sabah al-Salim al-Sabah. The Sheikh hires eighty people who have nothing else to do but help him spend money.[5]

Most individuals who see their personal resources as limitless, however, are experiencing an illusion rather than viewing reality. This is particularly true where a good deal of money is acquired in a short period of time and/or without a lot of effort. In these instances, it often appears to the recipient as if the money has appeared almost by magic, making the person feel as if he or she has a favored position in the eyes of fate or some higher authority. To test this illusion, the individual often seems driven to find out whether the money can be disposed of faster than it comes in, or if, in reality, there is an inexhaustible supply.

One of the people caught up in this obsession was Michael Nesmith, at one time a member of the wildly acclaimed rock group the Monkees. Overnight, he went from a starving self-taught musician to a teenage idol. In two years he made approximately $3 million and spent more. In 1969, when the Monkees disbanded, Nesmith owed the government $330,000 in back taxes and surrendered his expensive cars and his $500,000 home to his creditors. "It all seemed so unreal," he said. "At one time I had nearly $1 million in my checking account." [6] But by buying everything in sight, he was able to get rid of it faster than it came in, thus confirming that there really were limits to his money supply.

If affluence is perceived as limitless and such a superabundance of money eliminates any need for control or conservation, what are the underlying implications? If there were truly an endless supply of money, why not throw it away, burn it, spend it with abandon? Why does the possibility of such uncontrolled behavior arouse fear and anxiety?

The answer is that obviously money has many underlying emotional meanings. Every psychotherapist has heard patients express fear of losing control of their feelings, particularly feelings of hostility and aggression. The loss of control of one's emotions is equated with going insane, with dying, with being a helpless victim of something or someone more powerful than oneself, or with committing murder or rape. Maintaining control, on the other hand, provides the person with a sense of security —*or at least the illusion of security.*

The process of turning an uninhibited infant into a civilized adult involves the teaching of rules and laws and limits. Parents who fail to set limits for their children's behavior most likely produce insecure children. On the other hand, parents who are too strict and demanding are apt to make their children fearful, rigid, and overly inhibited. When they grow up, these persons use repression excessively and become terrified of revealing the emotions they have been taught are bad and unacceptable. The more that feelings and emotions are repressed, the more powerful they appear to be and the more threatening loss of control becomes. And the fear is sometimes warranted, as in the case of the very quiet, very passive, emotion-repressing individual who suddenly turns into a mass murderer when repressed rage erupts and overwhelms defensive controls.

To the extent that the fear of affluence is symbolic of the fear of loss of control of one's unacceptable pent-up emotions, such fear might help explain why so many people who suddenly come into a lot of money are unable to cope with their wealth. They lack the self-discipline to handle it. Their behavior is not unlike that of the overly controlled adolescent who goes away to college and can't cope with the unexpected freedom. After a period of uninhibited acting out of impulses, the student becomes so unnerved that any excuse to submit to external authority will be welcomed. Where controls have not been internalized and realistic self-discipline has not evolved, the individual is dependent upon external controls to provide a sense of security.

Michael Nesmith, previously mentioned, was convinced that subconsciously he was trying to get rid of his money. "I flat wanted out of the whole insane deal," he commented. He claimed the happiest day of his life was when he turned his back on his Rolls-Royce and his Bel Air mansion and drove off into the sunset in a Volkswagen.

It is not money per se which is frightening to many people, but the misperception that there are no limits to the amount of money available and, hence, no control over the spending of it. An unlimited amount of money gives permission to use it with abandon, to wallow in it without concern for the consequences. When this uncontrolled behavior creates anxiety, the person frantically seeks reassurance that there really are limits, that there is a sense of order and control; and there is a return to a feeling of security. If the source of money dries up and the person is broke, an unexpected sense of relief often sets in because the individual is now reassured that limits exist and order is restored to the world. The knowledge that one's income is limited provides a necessary restriction on how much money can be spent. It acts as an external control which compensates for lack of internal controls.

The giving up of affluence restores a feeling of normalcy for some people. Humans seem to adjust to almost anything if given enough time, but rapid change creates chaos for many. People who suddenly acquire a lot of money often make many drastic changes in their life-style. If these changes are too radical, such people may consciously or unconsciously see getting rid of the money as the only way back to normalcy.

In cases where affluence isolates and alienates one from former friends and leads to a high degree of suspicion and distrust of others, the relinquishing of wealth may even represent a healthy desire to return to a time of relationships and a life-style that felt real. It may in this case be a movement toward positive growth.

THE MAGICAL ANSWER

Despite evidence everywhere to the contrary, millions of people seem to think that money is the panacea that will solve most of their problems. And if a little bit of money doesn't do the trick, they are convinced that more money will. Money has an almost universal magnetism that draws people from every level of society. And not a few of these people have an insatiable thirst for it that can never be quenched regardless of how much money they accumulate. To them the quest is an end in itself.

The greed to acquire a superabundance of something that cannot be used defies a rational explanation, even when that something is money. The explanation lies in unconscious emotional drives. Studies of self-made wealthy men, for example, show an extremely high incidence of parental death and parental divorce, which resulted in a high degree of insecurity early in life.[7] Many of these men, as young boys, apparently set out to amass so much money that they would never be left stranded again. They also were faced with assuming adult responsibility while still children, and then tried to prove to themselves and others they didn't really need to depend on parents.

The search for wealth and the search for happiness often go

hand in hand. Not infrequently, however, it is the pursuit rather than the attainment of wealth that produces the most happiness. Time and again men and women who have become rich recall that the happiest times of their lives were the years in which they were struggling to make ends meet. People who aggressively pursue money often find that having acquired it, it does not fulfill their dreams. In the words of one wealthy patient confessing to his therapist, "By the time I found out that money can't buy happiness, I already had $5 million. What do I do now?"

The fallacy of trying to achieve happiness through money has been expressed as well by Benjamin Franklin as by anyone. "Money," he observed, "never made a man happy yet nor will it. There is nothing in its nature to produce happiness. The more a man has, the more he wants. Instead of its filling a vacuum, it makes one."

One of the reasons that people who acquire wealth are disappointed or embittered with their acquisition is that they expect too much from it. They endow it with magic and power it does not possess and then feel betrayed because it did not live up to their fantastic expectations. As with sleight-of-hand entertainment, what appears to be magic is simply an illusion. The nightclub performer does not really pull a live rabbit out of thin air. It only seems so. If one believes in miracles, the chances of being disappointed are great. If one truly expects money miraculously to solve all of one's problems, one will probably feel deceived when the promises of money prove empty. On the other hand, if nothing magical is expected from money, it can be appreciated for what it can do rather than being despised for all the things it can't.

Much of the magic of money is really an illusion. Like Santa Claus and gremlins and ghosts, who also are real to those who believe in them, money magic is an outgrowth of unconscious needs and perceptions. As has already been discussed, money can be symbolically associated with a number of unconscious needs and desires.

Money greed, from the psychoanalytic point of view at least, is related more to oral than anal frustrations. The person with an insatiable appetite for money is not unlike the starving person whose sole preoccupation is devouring food. Such a person attacks food with a vengeance, disregarding normal table etiquette, perhaps even to the point of stuffing food into his or her mouth with both hands. Each bite of food is perceived as if it might be the last portion left in the world, and it is gobbled up before it disappears. The person who is greedy for money reacts to money much the same way as the starving person does to food. And it is probably more than coincidence that slang words for money are frequently terms like "lettuce," "bread," and "dough."

The money-hungry person inevitably felt deprived as a child. During the first weeks and months of life, the deprived infant is not always able to tell whether it is hungry for food, affection, or some other form of dependency gratification. It accepts whatever is available. If its needs are continually frustrated, however, it never learns to trust. As the deprived child grows older, he or she learns to *take* whatever will satisfy the craving rather than waiting for someone to offer it as a gift. And, in taking, the child grabs as much as possible because there is no assurance that there will be more later. As Alfred Adler, the founder of Individual Psychology, pointed out, ". . . [the child] may show an abnormal interest in eating and eatables, and its tendency to collect and hoard things may develop in later life into a concentration upon money-making." [8]

ENVY, GREED AND THE HUNGER FOR MONEY

Melanie Klein, the British child analyst who made an extensive study of the fantasies of young children, particularly fantasies of an oral nature, provides an explanation of the origin of greed and the hunger for money. While the infant is in the womb of the mother, all of its needs are taken care of without effort on its part. And even after it is born there is a short period of time when the infant perceives itself and its mother as one and the same. Before long, however, the infant learns to distinguish between the self and non-self and develops a vague sense of being dependent upon the external world for its survival. Since the world of the infant at this age revolves around feeding and other forms of oral gratification, the non-self is primarily the breast, or its equivalent, the bottle. When the infant is fed and satisfied, it feels relaxed, secure, and loved. When it is hungry it feels threatened, deprived, and angry.

According to Klein, the infant, in order to cope with the stress caused by an inconsistent world, perceptually splits that world into the "good breast" and the "bad breast." The good breast satisfies; the bad breast deprives. If the bad breast predominates, that is, if the world is more frustrating and rejecting than rewarding, the child experiences overwhelming anxiety and a threat to its existence. In order to cope with this trauma, the child may develop a longing for the security and comfort it once knew, a fantasy of "the inexhaustible breast." [9] This desire to seek "a land flowing with milk and honey" is, in reality, an attempt to regress to a state in which one's needs were automatically satisfied, as in the womb or at the mother's breast. The more frustrating and threatening the world seems to the infant, the more desperate will be the desire to regress to dependency on the good breast.

In this way, the infant exaggerates the "goodness" of the good breast, believing it can fantastically satisfy the ego's needs forever. Having thus endowed the breast with magical qualities, the child envies it when it is withheld. Envy leads to hostility and a desire to devour the breast, partly out of anger and partly to get it inside oneself where it will always be within one's control. This might allow the infant to feel safe rather than frustrated except for the guilt that ensues for wanting to destroy that which is perceived as the most valuable thing in its life.

The drama which goes on in the unconscious of the child who seeks the ever-flowing breast predisposes that child to seek limitless wealth as an adult. The child who attributes magical qualities to the breast becomes the adult who seeks magic in money. The hunger, the greed, the envy, and the guilt now apply to money as they once did to the breast. The person feels empty and deprived and perceives money as a means of satisfying the hunger. Only an inexhaustible supply of wealth, like the vision of the overflowing breast, will seem to satisfy the greed, and the person is envious of any source of money outside of his or her control.

Since many of these people have learned to feel guilty about their greed and envy, it becomes impossible for them to enjoy money once it is acquired. It is then necessary to dispose of it to atone for guilt. This process might account for the fact that so many people who start their careers with nothing but an obsession to acquire money seem driven to dispose of it after it has been obtained.

Furthermore, if what has been sought under the guise of making a fortune is really an inexhaustible breast, it is obvious that the basic need can never be satisfied with money. Money in this case is a symbol or a substitute, and a substitute can never satisfy the real need that the infant had but which was not fulfilled. As Sigmund Freud said, "Happiness is the deferred fulfillment of a pre-historic wish. That is why wealth brings so little happiness; money is not an infantile wish." [10]

5

THE MANY SIDES
OF THE COIN

MONEY, PERHAPS MORE THAN LOVE, IS WHAT MAKES THE world go 'round. It is one of the most powerful motivators of human behavior. People rob and kill for money. They also work and toil for it. If you are an average wage earner, you can expect to spend approximately 83,000 hours of your life working in order to earn the money to buy the things you deem necessary for survival and enjoyment.

But what is money? From the economist's point of view, money is anything which has an agreed upon value that can be exchanged for goods and services. In most cases it is a piece of metal or paper. In many primitive societies it has taken the form of animal skins, feathers, or beads. Natives on the island of Yap in the Caroline Islands use large rocks. In our culture, checks and credit cards are gradually replacing coins and paper money as the medium of exchange. While money, or its equivalent, is necessary for survival since we exchange it for food, clothing, and shelter, it also provides the comfort and luxuries we desire. In addition, it can be used to purchase power, security, freedom, and other psychological satisfactions.

Theoretically, the economic value of money is determined by the government that issues it. At one time in the United States the value of a dollar was pegged to a certain amount of gold or silver held in reserve by the federal government. Ultimately, however, its value is determined by the law of supply and demand. Money is worth what someone is willing to give in return for it. Because the United States government has so determined, a dollar is always worth one hundred cents, but, at different times, it may be worth eight, ten, or eighteen eggs—depending on their availability.

When it is said that a dollar is worth a hundred cents or ten dimes or fourteen eggs or a gallon and a half of gasoline, there is general agreement on its economic value. Its psychological value, however, is judged more by a personal yardstick. If one is poor, for example, one is likely to place a higher value on money than if one is rich. This contention has been demonstrated by the much-publicized experiments of psychologists Jerome Bruner and C. C. Goodman with the relative perception of money by rich and poor children.[1] When asked to draw circles representing various coins, poor children exaggerated the size of the coins and drew circles significantly larger than did rich children. And the higher the monetary value of the coin, the greater this disparity in judgment between the two groups. The researchers interpreted the results as meaning that poor children overvalue money more than do rich children. A recent study of rich and poor children in Hong Kong confirms Bruner and Goodman's results and indicates that socioeconomic differences in the perception of money are not limited to Americans.[2]

The psychological value or meaning of money is usually distorted by emotional needs. There is an irrational quality about it that often overshadows its more conventional meaning. There is nothing very logical, for instance, about a man who calmly makes or loses thousands of dollars on the stock market lying awake half the night worrying about the three dollars he lost in a friendly poker game. Or his wife, who bought five heads of lettuce because they were on sale and then let three of them spoil because she could not use them. Or his daughter, who took six months to get up the courage to ask her boss for a raise even though she felt it was long overdue. Or his brother, who becomes undone whenever his checking account falls below ten thousand dollars.

The meaning attributed to money significantly influences how a person will choose to earn, save, and spend it. Since that meaning reflects a dominant need in the person, it will be evident in all major areas of that person's behavior.

In one of the few research studies done on the meaning of money, two psychologists at the 3M Company in Minnesota, Paul Wernimont and Susan Fitzpatrick, found not only that money means different things to different people, but that there are significant differences between occupational groups. Among their conclusions are the following:

> The results here indicate some very consistent and rather sharp differences in the meaning of money between those groups employed full time in industry and those groups not so employed. Employed groups view money much more positively, as a good, desirable, important and useful commodity. Non-employed groups and college students particularly, seem to take a tense, worrisome, unhappy view of money, yet they tend to downgrade or play down the importance of it in terms of economic values and to look down on those who do value money more highly. In short, they appear to be very uptight about money but are reluctant to admit to those feelings. They "pooh pooh" such values.[3]

MONEY IS A STATUS SYMBOL

Many of the meanings associated with money are symbolic and closely intertwined with other needs and values. If having money makes a person feel important or superior, it has more impact on the person's life than if its only value is the goods it will buy. For many persons, money is a status symbol. One of the benefits of having money in our culture is that it raises one's value in the eyes of many people. The more money people have, the more "important" they become. The bank manager is likely to fawn over the large depositor and ignore the person with a small savings account. The stockbroker, the store owner, and the hotel bellhop rush to give personal service to the wealthy patron while customers of moderate means fend for themselves.

Conspicuous consumption—whether it be of clothes, jewelry, automobiles, furnishings for the home, or food and drink—is an attempt to flaunt one's wealth in the face of others as a means of trying to prove one's superiority. Oddly enough, it is sometimes successful.

Ideally, we judge people by their deeds and not by their pocketbooks. But ideals are rare in the marketplace. It matters little whether money is obtained through hard work, inheritance, fraud and corruption, or a lucky ticket on the Irish Sweepstakes. When it comes to status, the question is not how, but how much.

THE ORIGIN OF MONEY

In primitive societies and in the subhuman animal kingdom, survival belongs to the strongest and the swiftest. In modern civilized society, the means of survival—food, clothing, and shelter—are purchased with money. Over a period of several thousand years, money has become a substitute for strength and speed. People no longer compete directly with each other for the game to feed their families, but indirectly for the money to buy food. During this transition, money has had many uses and many meanings.

Strangely enough, from the very beginning money has had more of a psychological or symbolic than an economic meaning. William Desmonde traces the origin of money to ancient religious rituals in which money was used as a symbol in sacrificial food ceremonies.[4] Its use as a medium of exchange in commerce came later. In ancient times, particularly in Greece and Rome, the ritualistic killing and eating of a divine bull played an extremely important role in the religious sacrificial system; and it was from this ceremony that coinage later evolved.

In these early communion ceremonies, the god received part of the flesh of the sacrificial animal and the rest was distributed to the participants in the ritual. The portion that each person received was determined by his social rank. Receiving a part of the roast was a symbol of citizenship. To be excluded from the feast meant one was a social outcast.

This ritual continues in England today with only slight modifications. Monarchal gifts of quarters of venison from the royal herds are bestowed on people of prestigious position, such as the prime minister, the chancellor of the exchequer, the governor of the Bank of England, the lord chief justice, and the archbishops of Canterbury and York.

In general, however, coins of metal gradually replaced portions of meat as symbols of status. These coins, like the portions of flesh of the sacred bull, were given by the king to his subjects as a sign of esteem and honor. They also symbolized the contribution each individual made to the state. The greatest honor was to receive a gold medal, followed in turn by a medal of silver, then bronze—a custom still performed today in athletic events such as the Olympic Games.

Chronologically, then, money as a status symbol preceded money as a medium of exchange. The deep psychological significance of money as a measure of social rank has not changed in the unconscious minds of human beings for over two thousand years. In contrast, the conscious, rational mind has altered the perception of money until it is sometimes claimed that its only real value is what it can be exchanged for in tangible goods and services. The schism between so-called rational and irrational meanings of money has thus widened considerably with time.

THE PSYCHOLOGICAL
MEANINGS OF MONEY

Status is not the only symbolic meaning of money. It can represent any of a number of psychological needs and can be used in many ways to promote and/or satisfy those needs. Among the more common needs with which money becomes involved are security, power, love, and freedom.

Security (The Safety-First Syndrome). Emotional security is often intertwined with financial security. In such cases, security-oriented people develop a sense of safety in proportion to their bank accounts. The more money they have, the more confident they feel in coping with the "dangerous" world around them. Money helps to stave off anxiety. It becomes an emotional life jacket, a bulletproof vest, a security blanket. Security-oriented people hold onto money as if their lives depended on it. Without it they feel frightened and vulnerable, unable to function with self-assurance or decisiveness. With it they feel safe.

Jim Harper, a product of the Great Depression of the 1930's, came from a large family in which there was never enough of anything—money, food, affection—to provide a real sense of security. The family moved often and there was little opportunity to make lasting friends or to put down roots. Jim was rather shy and sensitive and had trouble relating to other children, especially girls.

As an adult, Harper had seemingly outgrown most of the obvious signs of shyness and insecurity. He had a steady job and put part of each paycheck in a savings account and government bonds. He chose a position in a large company with a strong union. This provided him solid job security, an excellent company pension, and ample fringe benefits. On several occasions he turned down opportunities to take jobs offering more pay because they were less secure.

Like most people who view money as security, Harper thought of it as something to *save* rather than to *spend*. When spending was inevitable, it was done cautiously, sometimes grudgingly. Bills were paid promptly because that made him feel safe. A bill was considered an obligation—something that had to be taken care of to avoid anger or attack or ridicule from the outside world. There was a big difference in his mind between the "have to's" in life and the "want to's." You fulfill obligations like paying bills because you have to, but to spend money just because you want to—to eat dinner out or go to a movie or buy clothing that just strikes your fancy—is a painful experience.

Jim Harper kept meticulous financial records and a tight budget. Consequently, he knew to the penny where his income went. When purchases were necessary, he studied *Consumer*

Reports, checked with experts, and always shopped around for the lowest possible bids. By the time he parted with his money, he was sure that he was getting the best bargain that money could buy.

There was little time, place, or money in Harper's life for fun and enjoyment, but he did receive a great deal of satisfaction in watching the figures in his bankbook grow. In fact, by his standards, life was not too bad. Therefore, it came as quite a shock to him when one day his wife announced she wanted a divorce. So much of a shock, in fact, that, despite the cost, it drove him to seek professional counseling.

Harper knew that his wife had been unhappy and that she complained a lot, but he was used to that. He had heard it all his life, from his mother. He supposed women were like that, and he accepted it. What really troubled him was that his wife was leaving him for another man, a free-lance writer. Why she would give up all that security for something as financially unpredictable as life with a professional writer was the question that plagued him the most.

In therapy Jim Harper learned that at the root of his insecurity was a deep-seated fear of being abandoned. This was an exaggerated reaction to the helpless and dependent status he had had as a small child in relation to very rigid, cold, and insecure parents. He picked up their anxiety and overconcern about money, and the theme of his life became, "If I have enough money, I can survive even if everyone deserts me." Money became the symbol of security, a more reliable substitute for the tenuous security he experienced with his parents. He also learned that his preoccupation with money, which was originally designed to forestall abandonment, was actually a major factor in his wife's leaving him.

Turning toward money for security inevitably leads to a sense of alienation from people. The individual transfers the need for significant people to a need for money as a means of allaying feelings of insecurity and anxiety. In time, however, it is the fear of losing money that becomes the main source of anxiety. Unable to become emotionally involved with people because the anticipated pain of future rejection is too great, these individuals build an emotional wall around themselves to keep other people at a distance. *In the extreme, they turn their fear of being hurt and rejected by others to the fear that others will deprive them of their money.* A prime example of this type of paranoia was the comedian W. C. Fields, who was so afraid that he would be swindled out of his money that he deposited it in some two hundred different bank accounts throughout the world—each under a fictitious name. He was so successful at foiling his "persecutors" that after his death in 1946, only forty-five of those accounts were ever located. It is estimated that approximately $600,000 of his estate has never turned up.

Power (The Green Giant Syndrome). To some people, money means power. It is not used to purchase cars, houses, or food so much as it is used to buy importance, domination, control. The need for power is a compelling drive. It is usually associated with aggressiveness and a determination to win at all costs. It is often the key ingredient in "greatness." Politicians, generals, labor leaders, and business executives are usually driven by a need for power.

Where money is concerned, its primary value is its usefulness in clearing away obstacles that stand in the path of the person seeking power. In face-to-face combat, the victor physically overpowers his opponent. In more complex, sophisticated power games, money may substitute for physical strength in overcoming one's adversary. One can buy out the competition, hire attorneys and tax experts, buy advertising and public relations, or do whatever is necessary to gain an advantage in the struggle for superiority.

While money may be the stated goal the power-oriented person strives for, the chances are that acquiring all the money in the world would not slow the person down. The story of John D. Rockefeller is a case in point. Considered one of the most successful and ruthless of the so-called "robber barons" of the turn of the century, Rockefeller amassed a vast fortune by the time he was still a comparatively young man. Despite his wealth, he lived frugally and spent little on himself. He preferred bread and milk to fancy French cuisine. His family had to goad him to buy new suits when the old ones wore out. Finding no practical use for the money he so tenaciously acquired, he began giving it away. In the year 1919 alone, he reportedly gave away over $138,000,000.[5]

J. Paul Getty retired at the age of twenty-four, having made his first million. After two years of idleness, he reentered the business world and went on to become the richest man in the world.[6] Although he had fulfilled the dream of most Americans of being able to retire on a substantial income, he was not satisfied. Money, as such, was not the goal.

The use of money to obtain political power is as old as politics itself. With few exceptions, the candidate who spends the most money is elected to office. Votes and favors are exchanged for donations. Corruption in all levels of government is commonplace, but governments topple when it becomes too blatant. The American public was outraged when its vice-president was accused of accepting bribes that were delivered to him at the White House, and the Nixon regime fell partly as a result of the disclosure that millions of dollars were donated illegally to the president's reelection campaign fund.

The story of former Prime Minister Kakuei Tanaka of Japan also illustrates the relationship between money and political power. Born in a small town in Niigata Prefecture, Tanaka made his way to Tokyo at the age of fifteen with only a grade school education and less than three dollars in his pocket. Being ambitious and hardworking, he parlayed his small stake into ownership of a contracting business by the time he was nineteen. Within a few years, he was doing a multimillion dollar business. In 1947 he became a member of the Diet and from there worked his way up the political ladder. At the age of fifty-four he became the youngest prime minister in the history of postwar Japan.

Tanaka's political success was built on what the Japanese call *kinken*, or "money power." It was reported that in 1972, for example, he spent at least thirty-four million dollars on loans and cash gifts to fellow members of the Liberal-Democratic Party to insure his selection as chairman of the party, which meant automatic selection as prime minister.[7] During his rise to political power, charges of corruption were repeatedly hurled at Tanaka, but he managed to avoid legal action until mid-1976, when he was arrested and charged with accepting bribes of five hundred million yen from Lockheed Aircraft Corporation. In 1974, however, he had been forced from office when a Japanese magazine printed an exposé of his *kinken* record, describing secret bank accounts, dummy corporations, and false tax statements.

Tanaka believed that since he did not have prestigious educational or family ties like most successful big-time politicians, he had to rely solely on himself and his power. Unfortunately for him, however, power also meant money; and at a time when Japan was searching for morality in its leaders, Tanaka's extravagant exploitation of money power became unacceptable.

The equation of money with power can be traced back to ancient times. The participants in the sacrificial feast of the bull supposedly took on the characteristics of strength and heroism which previously had belonged to the bull. Presumably, too, ancient coins carried the *mana* ("magical power") of the king. Like the bull, the king was filled with a magic power that overflowed into every object with which he came in contact. Therefore, coins originally served as charms, possessing great power for their owner.

The consuming hunger for power is rooted partially in the infantile experience of omnipotence. It is generally agreed that for a short time after birth, the infant is unable to distinguish between itself and the external world. It is assumed that the infant perceives itself as the center of the universe and everything else as an extension of itself. This condition is called "infantile omnipotence," an unconscious perception of being able to control the world. When this illusion is shattered by the emerging awareness that the self and non-self are not one and the same, a certain amount of anxiety is evident in the infant. Rather than perceiving itself as all-powerful, the infant is now faced with the reality that it is helpless and almost completely dependent on others for its survival. The amount of anxiety and frustration this awareness arouses depends upon the needs of the infant, the degree of satisfaction from the environment, and the infant's perception of how safe or dangerous it is to be dependent.

One of the ways of coping with a world perceived as dangerous is to regress to the stage of infantile omnipotence. Since this is an impossible task in reality, the goal is never reached except through fantasy or delusion. The seeker of omnipotence becomes obsessed with the *search*, even though there may be some subconscious awareness that the prize at the end of the rainbow is unattainable. Money and power often become the symbolic expressions of that search.

The noted psychoanalyst Otto Fenichel has suggested that irrational uses of money in the search for power are often unconscious attempts to recapture infantile feelings of omnipotence.[8] The irrational need for power and the irrational need for security both stem from unconscious feelings of helplessness and fear of abandonment. However, in contrast to security-minded persons who try to protect themselves from anticipated desertion and death, power-oriented individuals endeavor to become strong enough to force others to stay with them and to do their bidding.

To the infant, the source of strength, as well as of security and tension reduction, is nourishment. Deprivation of the breast or bottle when the baby is hungry provokes both fear and rage. If deprived for long, panic sets in since the infant instinctively senses a very real threat to its existence. It is an attempt to avoid further exposure to this kind of trauma that motivates the development of ego defenses such as striving for omnipotence. For many who have been so deprived as infants, an insatiable hunger exists and money becomes the symbol of nourishment. But since it is a substitute for the ever-flowing breast of fantasy, it never fully satisfies the insatiable thirst. *Power-oriented people never get enough power and they never get enough money. Like many who have never had enough to eat, they become greedy.* Their motto is not unlike the dictum of Horace, who some two thousand years ago said, "Make money; if you can, make money honestly; if not, by whatever means you can, make money." [9]

When the power structures of the Kakuei Tanakas and the Spiro Agnews of the world come tumbling down, people are generally aghast at the high-handed way in which these power-motivated individuals have set themselves above the law of the land and the morals of society. It has been speculated that unconscious guilt is at the bottom of their downfall. The openness with which they flaunt their power is interpreted as a bid to get caught and punished in order to atone for their underlying guilt.

Perhaps that interpretation is true, or partly true. From our clinical experience in working with power-oriented persons of this type, however, an alternative hypothesis appears more accurate. The arrogance with which they command the world to do their bidding and by which they assume that the rules of ordinary people do not apply to themselves suggests they truly believe they have regained their lost feelings of omnipotence. Their behavior indicates that, at least for a time, the delusion of omnipotence is accepted as reality, and they assume that their actions are not to be questioned by mere mortals. This delusion is reinforced by the fact that they have been able "to move mountains" and to achieve goals most people have been unable to reach. It is only when their political or financial empires crash around them that they are faced with the harsh reality that they are, after all, human rather than omnipotent.

It has been theorized that the more intensely one is driven by the desire for power, the more that person strives to overcompensate for the underlying feelings of helplessness and humiliation. Business executives, politicians, and others motivated by power are sometimes thought to be channeling their energies into work to bolster their egos because they feel insecure sexually.

An interesting study of the relation between money and sexual dysfunction was conducted by Dr. Paul Frisch, a former psychology professor at Adelphi University, and his wife, Ann, also a psychologist. Based on an investigation of thirty males who were involved in the stock market, either as investors or Wall

Street employees, and who were in counseling for nonsexual problems, they found a definite correlation between the sexual behavior of the subjects and the Dow Jones industrial average.[10] When the market went up, sexual drive went up; when the market went down, there was a high incidence of sexual problems.

While the results of this study raise intriguing possibilities, to conclude that this is an obvious cause and effect relationship is probably much too simple a deduction. The problem of sexual dysfunction is rarely a unilateral problem. Sexual relations are a basic means of communication. Therefore, what is important is not only what the male tells himself about his adequacy when the market goes down, but also what his sexual partner tells him, either directly or indirectly, about his attractiveness as a powerful male when he is winning and when he is losing.

Love (The Santa Claus Syndrome). For some, money is symbolic of love. Emotionally inhibited parents who are unable to freely express love and affection to their children may offer cookies, presents, or money instead. As these children grow up, the equation sticks. Money equals love. Money, or its equivalent in the form of gifts, is given or withheld as a token of affection or rejection. Not only does this hold in interpersonal relations, but such an individual may indulge or "love" himself or herself when feeling depressed by purchasing some unnecessary luxury. One may, on the other hand, do without necessities when feeling guilty.

When money means love, it is extremely difficult to be objective about how one gives or receives it. Do you pay a restaurant check even when it is in error because you are afraid the waitress might be angry with you? Do you buy a particular stock recommended by your broker because you want him to like you rather than because you feel it is a good investment? Do you overpay your secretary or overtip your hairdresser because you want them to be fond of you? Do you give your children too large an allowance because you want them to love you?

When Frances Morgan began therapy, she was inclined to do most of these things. She was the only child of fairly successful, professional parents. They found time to go to meetings and lectures and cocktail parties, but rarely time to read to Frances or listen to her problems. They hired the best baby-sitters and sent her to the best schools. They bribed her to be good and to get good grades. Frances was a good student and learned her lessons well. For every dollar she received for getting an A on her report card, she found that she could buy four ice cream cones for her classmates and a few minutes of their friendship.

Frances went through life buying and selling affection—or anything closely resembling it. However, her need for love was so great that frequently she got shortchanged. Sometimes "friends" took advantage of her generosity or her gullibility. They often used her hunger for affection to manipulate her. She was a sucker for almost any request, whether legitimate or not, because she had never learned to say no.

Few would deny that love is an important psychological need. To some it is the most important. To Frances, who had never really known the experience of *being* loved, the need for love was all-pervasive. It was what the eminent psychologist Abraham Maslow called "deficiency love," or love-hunger, a pathological deficiency of a necessary ingredient for growth, much like a vitamin deficiency.[11] And the gnawing hunger for love drove her to seek love in neurotic ways, including trying to buy it.

Whereas the power-oriented person uses money to overcome feelings of vulnerability, the love-starved person uses it to overcome feelings of being unlovable. Love-starved people are inclined to be alienated from other people and unable to give love to others because they have so little to give. Some, like Frances, use money as a gauge of emotional worth and caring. After she married, she saw her husband's inability to earn a lot of money as a sign of his not loving the family enough. She felt devalued as a person if she did not have at least fifty dollars in her purse. Her children were never given a regular allowance, but a variable amount depending on how much they pleased her. Her equation in interpersonal relations was essentially an economic one, a sort of 365-days-a-year Christmas. The more she cared about people, the more she spent on them; the more they spent on her, the more, she assumed, they cared about her.

In working through her neurotic problems in psychotherapy, Frances found that there were two major reasons why she linked money and love. The first was a simple imitative learning of a behavior pattern set forth by her parents. Because they were unable to show affection openly and directly, they gave, instead, that which they valued most—money.

The second reason was less conscious and, in some ways, was an extension of the first. It substantiated essentially the psychoanalytic equation "money equals feces," which was discussed in Chapter Three. During therapy, Frances was able to recall with great clarity the pains she took as a little girl to please her mother and father and to win their love. She learned that the main ingredients were being "good," being clean, and being compliant. When it came to toilet training, Frances was very compliant. She wanted to do what was "right" in order to win the approval and love of her parents. When she learned that they were pleased with her gifts of feces, she tried to outdo herself to give them these tokens of love.

One of the tragedies of people who use money symbolically is they don't know that the symbol is just a symbol and not the real thing. The person who tries to satisfy a love deficiency with money is not unlike the person who eats a lot of sugar to correct a salt-deficient diet. No matter how much sugar one eats, salt will still be lacking in the diet. A man who feels unattractive and unlovable may feel that beautiful women would find him desirable if he were rich. But if he becomes rich and women do flock to him, he is likely to feel they are really attracted to his money and not to him. He will still feel deprived of love.

In his autobiography, *As I See It,* published posthumously in London, J. Paul Getty claimed that his money couldn't buy love —although he tried. Getty, divorced by five wives, stated, "Each was jealous and resentful of my preoccupation with business. Yet none showed any visible aversion to sharing in the proceeds." While hundreds of women proposed to him, he was not under the illusion that it was because of his blue eyes. Rather, he wrote, "The magnetism I exert is of another color—green." [12]

Freedom (The Declaration of Independence Syndrome). Another intangible that people sometimes try to buy with money is freedom. Freedom, of course, is relative and the pursuit of freedom may take many turns. The role of money in relationship to freedom also varies. Some people are enslaved by their desire to accumulate money, while others find freedom by turning their backs on money and materialism.

Freedom and security are in some ways incompatible. Where the need for security is predominant, the individual may prefer a steady job with regular hours, routine activities, limited responsibility, and a predictable future. Where freedom is the stronger drive, the person generally rebels against the nine-to-five routine, regimentation, restrictions on movement or initiative, and anything that implies unnecessary dependency. These individuals are likely to work longer hours for less pay if it means more independence. They want the chance to chart their own lives, to make their own decisions and to have the opportunity to succeed on their own merits. They are usually adventurous and willing to take chances.

People who are motivated by a desire for freedom and independence often see money as the means to buy the time to do what they want to do. If they have the money to provide the necessities of life, they can devote their time to pursuing their varied interests and whims rather than to pursuing money itself. If creative, they can write, paint, or sculpt. If not, they are free to travel or study. Doing their own thing is what is most important to them and money may well be the vehicle which allows them to do it. Money per se is not important. They may spend it wisely or foolishly by other people's standards, but always in ways that are personally satisfying. They may gamble recklessly or invest cautiously depending on their mood and finances, but usually they are looking for something new and different that presents a challenge to them.

Art and Henry Stevens were brought up in a rather permissive atmosphere. They were exposed to a wide variety of activities and both developed numerous interests and hobbies. In school they leaned toward debate and drama. They did well in subjects that interested them and poorly in those that did not. From an early age they were included in family discussions and their opinions were sought regarding major family decisions. Few onerous demands were made of them, and frequently they could talk themselves out of the ones that were. They resented anything that tied them down or interfered with their freedom.

At college, Art majored in English and obtained his teaching credential. He decided on teaching as a career because it would allow him time off in the summer to travel and write. After two years of teaching, the regimentation and red tape got to him and he quit. He began making instructional aids, which he was able to sell to the school district where he had previously taught. His ideas were unique and his materials were effective in facilitating learning. Before long he had his own printing shop and a full-scale production line. A few years later, Art sold his business, invested his money in tax-exempt bonds and now spends his time writing books which he can't sell. But he says he has never been happier.

Art's younger brother, Henry, dropped out of college. He tried a number of different jobs but couldn't find one that suited him. So he dropped out of the job market. He spent the next year "trying to find himself." At the last report, Henry had joined a commune and was "living off the land." According to Art, who still keeps in touch with him, Henry claims to be very contented. It would appear that Art and Henry each found freedom and independence in his own way—Art through the acquisition of money, Henry by giving up the chase.

The dynamics underlying a strong need for freedom vary from a generalized rebellion against authority to a high degree of self-fulfillment. Some people drop out because they feel they can't compete; some are so self-confident they welcome any challenge. A number of studies based on the social learning theory of psychologist Julian Rotter involve a personality dimension known as "locus of control." [13] Persons with an *internal* locus of control view rewards as a consequence of their own behavior, while those with an *external* locus of control attribute them to forces outside themselves, such as fate, chance, or other persons. People who have an internal locus of control believe that they are largely masters of their fate rather than pawns of external forces. They are governed more by their own needs, values, ideas, and desires, and less by the persuasion of other people. From this frame of reference, it would seem that most, if not all, of those with a decided need for independence would have an internal locus of control.

At one time or another, most people have had the dream of obtaining enough money to free themselves from the necessity of working and to allow themselves to spend their time doing whatever they wish. If the dream should become reality, however, many are disappointed. For example, there are thousands of people who eagerly look forward to retirement. They anticipate with relish the free time to do all of the enjoyable things they have never had time to do. Shortly after they retire, however, they find their lives empty and boring and they rapidly go downhill both physically and mentally.

On the other hand, there are some like Art Stevens who, given the freedom to pursue their interests, use their time to develop to their highest potential. After Somerset Maugham made enough money to pursue a full-time writing career, he claimed that this money provided him the freedom and privilege to master his craft. As he put it, "I found that money was like a sixth sense without which you could not make the most of the other five." [14]

The goal that Art Stevens was striving for, and which Maugham ultimately achieved, is an example of what Maslow calls "self-actualization." [15] He contends that all human needs develop in a hierarchical pattern. As lower-level needs are met satisfactorily, higher-level needs emerge. The most basic needs are physiological. When the needs for food, air, and water, and other physiological needs, are satisfied, the person can then pursue the next higher level of need gratification, which is safety. Safety needs are followed in turn by the needs for love, esteem, and finally self-actualization. If one is forced to devote all or most of one's energy to the pursuit of lower-level satisfactions, progress toward becoming a mature, self-actualizing adult is either halted or impeded.

To a large degree, physiological and safety needs can be purchased with money. Higher-level needs, obviously, cannot. However, as in the case of Art Stevens, money can sometimes be used to buy the time to pursue self-actualization.

If the loss of infantile omnipotence is a critical period in the development of personality, how the infant perceives and reacts to the experience of helpless dependence upon the significant others in its life will help set the direction for future behavior patterns. The security-oriented person will strive to feel safe, the power-oriented person will try to avoid humiliation and regain omnipotence, and the love-starved individual will become compliant to seek love. Freedom-minded people try to deny dependence on others and seek to become epitomes of self-sufficiency. Generally these people become fearful of entrapment of any kind, including close emotional involvement with others. They are more likely to be leaders than followers, but frequently are loners. They use money to buy their way out of the slavery of conformity and control by others. Independence of thought and movement are essential to their happiness, and they resist becoming indebted to others either financially or emotionally.

Security, power, love, and freedom are not the only psychological motives for acquiring and using money. While they are among the most common, many others might be mentioned, such as comfort, revenge, knowledge, and even sexuality. It should also be noted that psychological needs do not always show up the same way in all people and that several needs may occur simultaneously within the same person. Each human being is different, with different combinations of needs, which in turn are based on different backgrounds and experiences. Consequently, everyone sees and uses money somewhat differently.

To the extent that you understand how money is used and what it means to you psychologically, you can better assess whether your handling of it is rational or not. Recognition of a problem is the first step in solving it. But, like any emotionally tinged problem, using money irrationally is usually denied. "Others may use money neurotically, but not I!" is the feeling most people have. However, the following is a small sampling of the hundreds of clues which suggest an irrational use or view of money:

1. You put money ahead of everything else in life, including health, love, family, recreation, friendship, and contentment.

2. You buy things you don't need or don't want because they are on sale.

3. You buy things you don't need or want because they are the "right" things to have, or because they might impress others.

4. Even when you have sufficient funds you feel guilty about spending money for necessities such as a new pair of shoes.

5. Every time you make a major purchase, you "know" you are being taken advantage of.

6. You spend money freely, even foolishly, on others but grudgingly on yourself.

7. You automatically say, "I can't afford it," whether you can or not.

8. You know to the penny how much money you have in your purse or pocket at all times.

9. You have difficulty making decisions about spending money regardless of the amount.

10. You feel compelled to argue or complain about the cost of almost everything you buy.

11. You insist on paying more than your share of restaurant checks or bar bills just to be appreciated or to make sure that you do not feel indebted to anyone.

12. If you have money left over at the end of the month, you feel uncomfortable until you spend it.

13. You use money as a weapon to control or intimidate those who frustrate you.

14. You feel inferior to others who have more money than

you, even when you know they have done nothing of worth to get it.

15. You feel superior to those who have less money than you, regardless of their abilities and achievements.

16. You firmly believe that money can solve all your problems.

17. You feel anxious and defensive when asked about your personal finances.

18. In making any purchase, for any purpose, your first consideration is the cost.

19. You feel "dumb" if you pay a little more for something than your neighbor did.

20. You feel a disdain for money and look down on those who have it.

21. You prefer saving money to investing it because you're never sure when things will collapse on you and you'll need the cash.

22. The amount you have saved is never quite enough.

23. You feel that money is the only thing you can really count on.

6

THE SECURITY COLLECTORS

DEMOSTHENES, THE FAMOUS GREEK ORATOR, IS REMEMBERED more for the unusual method he employed en route to becoming a public speaker than for anything he said after he became one. In order to overcome a speech impediment, Demosthenes went to the ocean, filled his mouth with pebbles, and learned to articulate over the sound of the crashing waves on the beach. While few of his hard-won words have withstood the test of time, an excerpt from one of his speeches, given some twenty-three hundred years ago, bears repeating as it pretty well describes the basic attitude of those who adhere to the safety-first syndrome of money use, discussed in the previous chapter. "There is one safeguard known generally to the wise. . . . What is it? Distrust."

Distrust is the cornerstone of the security collector—distrust of people, of the world, of the future. The possible exception is money. Money is considered the most trustworthy of all commodities; not because one can depend on its purchasing power, but because the possession of it makes the anxious owner feel safer. The frightened, insecure person needs most of all to feel safe. If dependency upon parents or others in authority does not provide a feeling of protection and security, the child learns to distrust people and to seek something else to rely on. Frequently, that something else is money. If having money reduces anxiety by making the person feel less dependent on others, money may replace people as a potential source of security.

People who develop a sense of distrust are constantly on guard to protect themselves from getting hurt—physically, psychologically, or financially. Originally, the fear is most likely physical—the fear of physical pain and suffering, possibly even the fear of death. If the infant's needs for food, oxygen, and so forth are not satisfied, suffering and death are possible. Next, the fear may be psychological—the fear of rejection, loss of love, humiliation, and the like. Eventually, however, as the person depends more and more on money for ego satisfaction and security, the fear of *financial* loss becomes paramount.

Distrust and the constant fear that someone or something will cause the person to lose money may be the best protection against such a loss taking place since the owner will be constantly on guard. However, such distrust also makes it impossible for the person to enjoy the luxury and leisure that money might otherwise allow. Preoccupation with the threat of losing one's means of security certainly does not create an atmosphere conducive to pleasure.

There are a variety of ways in which people who are emotionally insecure latch onto money to bolster their feelings of safety and self-esteem. A few of these ways will be discussed, along with an explanation of the underlying personality characteristics, the payoff in psychological satisfaction, and the cost to the self in terms of unhappiness and emotional damage. However, since all security collectors have some characteristics in common, two underlying themes run through the various types, (1) turning a distrust of people into trust in money, and (2) finding a feeling of safety in money to offset a feeling of emotional insecurity. It should also be noted that many persons who manifest the safety-first syndrome show characteristics of more than one type.

THE COMPULSIVE SAVER

The compulsive saver carries the idea of thrift to an illogical extreme. Saving for emergencies is prudent. Saving to accumulate capital is necessary if one wants to invest or go into business. Saving money in order to make major purchases later is sound financial planning. For the compulsive saver, however, saving becomes an end in itself. Saving is not done for some future reward; *saving is its own reward.*

People who suffer from a compulsion have an irresistible impulse to perform some act. If they resist performing the act, they feel anxious. When they perform the act, they feel relieved. They may or may not view the act as rational, but whether they do or not, the act *must* be carried out in order for them to feel safe and secure enough to function in other areas of their lives.

The compulsive saver *must* put a certain percentage of every paycheck in the bank before paying bills or taking care of other financial obligations. Money designated for savings is not considered as income. It is taken off the top like a withholding tax. What is left is budgeted for the necessary expenses until the next payday. If any money is left over at the end of the month, it also is most likely deposited in the savings account rather than spent frivolously, or even for necessities that can be put off until later.

Paying full price for anything is a painful experience for the compulsive saver. Satisfaction in spending money does not derive from pleasure in the item purchased but from the fact that it was purchased at a substantial savings. The obsessive preoccupation with money overshadows everything else so that the only aspect of any object or event that registers in the mind of the compulsive saver is the cost. A show or a ball game is not seen as an evening's recreation but as the expenditure of a ten dollar bill. A vacation cannot be enjoyed as an opportunity for a change of pace and a chance to unwind and relax. Instead, it is an experience of mixed emotions, with the pleasure ultimately measured by the amount of money painfully extracted from purse or wallet. To the compulsive saver, the "sin" of wasting money on a vacation is compounded by the "sin" of also wasting time in nonproductive activity. Compulsive savers agree with Benjamin Franklin that "Time is money." And time not spent in making money is time wasted.

Edmund Bergler, the late, well-known psychiatrist and author, relates a story told to him by a patient, which illustrates the extreme to which an obsessive preoccupation with money can lead. During World War I, the man was stationed in a village where meat was very scarce and, therefore, very expensive. One evening he was invited to dinner by a well-to-do family and miraculously a roast appeared on the table. Everyone expressed delight at their good fortune, except for the hostess, whose eyes were fixed on the carving knife. She seemed to be counting each slice as it fell. When the portions had been passed, she shifted her gaze from one diner to another. As each person put a piece of meat in his or her mouth, she would mumble, "You are now consuming ten francs' worth of meat! You are now consuming twelve francs' worth of meat!" Each bite was being weighed in her mind and given a price. The poor lady was not only miserable at the consumption of so much money, but was so busy watching and counting that she forgot to eat.[1]

The Underlying Personality. Case histories of compulsive savers show that as children they were anxious and insecure and felt incapable of coping with a world seen as overpowering and threatening. Because their parents did not provide them with a sense of security and protection from the real and imagined dangers of infancy, they never developed what Erik Erikson, the distinguished professor of human development at Harvard, calls "basic trust." [2] Basic trust or distrust is dependent upon the quality of mothering the infant receives in early life. Erikson sees trust as the first stage of development en route to social maturity. Without trust, responsible adulthood is impossible.

Such was the experience of Harry Burns, whose mother died when he was born. He was "mothered" by a series of aunts, older siblings, and baby-sitters. Harry's father was a construction worker who made a lot of money when he worked but who often went for months at a time between jobs. Frequently, it was necessary for him to move around the country to find work. When he was working, Harry's father put in long hours and saw the family only rarely. When he was not working, he was depressed and irritable and worried about not having enough money to pay the bills.

Like so many people who become compulsive savers, Harry, early in life, associated security with money. When his father was working and earning money, there was a sharp reduction in the tension and the sense of impending doom that permeated the family. Not only were there more toys and new shoes, but sometimes when Harry's father was home, he would smile at the children and tell them stories or take them to a movie.

Over a period of years, Harry evolved a dream of someday having a lot of money. He made the assumption that if he only had enough money he would be free of all insecurity and would be protected from all possible danger. In attempting to cope with the anxieties of life and never having had the inner security that comes from feelings of trust and dependency-gratification from people, Harry narrowed his view of the world. Since he felt unable to deal with the world, he focused his entire attention and energy on one aspect of it—money. By ignoring practically everything else in life, he was now able to function with a minimum of anxiety. Because of his early experiences, Harry was unable to cope realistically with stress as it arose. Instead, he retreated in the anticipation of impending disaster and relied on the protective power of money to make him feel safe. When his fiancée broke off their engagement because he was so tight with money, Harry took a second job and put the entire salary in the bank.

For the compulsive saver, no amount of money is sufficient to provide enough security to stop saving money. The craving is insatiable. It matters little whether the figures in the passbook are in the hundreds, thousands, or millions; there is always that recurrent fear that some tragedy could come along and wipe it all out. In case the bank might fail, the compulsive saver is likely to hide sums of cash around the house. But this gives rise to the fear that someone will break in and steal it, which only adds to the person's anxiety and distrust.

The Payoff. Not only does money in the bank reduce the feeling of emotional insecurity, but the compulsive saver is often looked up to as an example of the virtue of thrift. Many people staunchly believe in the adage, "a penny saved is a penny earned." They believe that people get rich by saving their pennies. The leaders in this crusade are, of course, the bankers and the compulsive savers. Some compulsive savers, convinced that their approach to money is sanctioned by society, turn thrift into something akin to religious zeal. Saving thus makes them feel noble and somewhat superior to those who are less thrifty.

Some of these people become wealthy if their income level is substantial, and they may gain respect and admiration from others because of their social and financial status. Those who have sufficient savings and investments have the added advantage of being able to withstand real economic crises as well as the imaginary doom that never comes.

The Cost. Perhaps the biggest cost paid by compulsive savers is in wasted opportunities to enjoy interpersonal relationships. Focusing their attention almost exclusively on finances makes these people rather dull and boring. They don't enjoy life and are not much fun to be around. They are rarely at ease with other people, partly because they are suspicious that others are trying to do them out of their money. The more money they acquire, the more they worry about losing it. And the more they worry about it, the less they are able to enjoy it. They become defensive rather than relaxed, and many who acquire wealth become more secretive, withdrawn, and suspicious as their savings grow.

In addition to deprivation of social pleasure, compulsive savers are sometimes vulnerable to physical illness. Some skimp on nourishment and neglect their personal health because of the cost. With most, physical needs are subordinate to financial desires, and even if there is enough money for both, the preoccupation with money is often so overriding that physical discomfort or minor illnesses may go unattended. When money is the goal, many compulsive savers will work long hours and endure severe fatigue in order to acquire additional money. Also, because of the constant tension and anxiety these people subject themselves to, a variety of psychosomatic complaints are likely. For the compulsive saver, even good health is less important than money.

THE SELF-DENIER

Even more than the compulsive saver, the self-denier neglects physical well-being and goes out of the way to avoid pleasure or enjoyment in life. For the compulsive saver, these self-destructive tendencies are an outgrowth of a preoccupation with saving money. Being overly attuned to the saving and protecting of money, the compulsive saver finds other considerations, such as health and happiness, relatively unimportant. To the self-denier, however, there is reward value in "self-sacrifice" itself. Such a person is saying to the world, "See how deprived I am. It is a mean, cruel world, and no one cares whether I live or die, but I will not let it get me down." These persons put on a show of maintaining a "brave front" in the face of doom and gloom. However, much of their adversity is self-imposed.

Self-deniers feel guilty about spending money on themselves. Their food is purchased more for its price than its taste or nutritive value. They are likely to buy day-old bread and store-brand canned goods. It hurts them to buy expensive clothes, and their wardrobes are purchased primarily from outlet stores and at month-end sales. They frequently live in poorer neighborhoods than others with the same income because rents are cheaper. Self-deniers generally let it be known that they would like a better way of life, but that they simply "can't afford it."

Regardless of the actual amount, their incomes never seem to stretch far enough to allow self-deniers any of the little extras that most people work for. *If they do have any extra income, they find some excuse to spend it on others rather than themselves since they firmly believe it is better to give than to receive.* Although they are obviously reluctant to indulge themselves, they are not necessarily adverse to spending money on their children, spouses, or friends. They may even give generously to charities or other worthwhile causes in which they have no special interest, because in these instances they need not deal with the guilt they would feel over being "self-indulgent."

Self-deniers have a "poverty complex." They are pessimistic about the future and feel fortunate to survive in the present. They tend to treat each day as if they expect to enter the poorhouse tomorrow. Consequently, they resist indulging themselves in any way and seemingly try to put off inevitable financial disaster as long as possible.

In some cases, self-deniers rationalize their self-imposed austerity by proclaiming they are saving for retirement or saving for a rainy day. For these people, however, every day is a rainy day; yet it never rains as hard as it might rain sometime in the future, so they continue to put off spending. And by the time they are ready to retire, it becomes obvious that they are going to continue to deny themselves and be unable, after years of deprivation, to accept the rewards they have promised themselves.

The Underlying Personality. Like all security collectors, self-deniers are primarily concerned with safety. They have learned to cope with life by playing up their financial and emotional deprivations with the expectation that others will feel sorry for them, and perhaps even offer assistance. They perceive self-sacrifice and self-denial as virtuous and expect others to reward them and compliment them on their unselfish, martyr-like behavior. Thus, they feel safe.

At twenty-two, Peggy Gordon was working forty hours a week as a salesclerk in a cut-rate drugstore and going to college three nights a week. She was not a particularly gifted student, but by studying most of the time she was not working, she was able to keep up. Her parents offered to help her with her expenses so she would not have to work full-time, but Peggy felt guilty about taking money from them and refused. "Besides," she said, "you have worked hard for your money for a long time. Now, you should enjoy it. And I don't want to be a burden to you."

While she was growing up, Peggy's parents provided for her

adequately. She dressed as well as her peers, and had as much spending money. However, the money was always given reluctantly and she was made to feel guilty, as she was told that if it were not for her, her parents would be affluent. It was evident that they resented the money they spent on her. Consequently, in order to minimize guilt and to maintain her parents' approval, Peggy learned to deny her desires and to feel proud of her decision to restrict any kind of self-indulgence. And, in many small ways, her parents communicated that the less she cost them financially, the more they approved of her.

Self-deniers try to conceal their envy of, and hostility toward, those who are substantially better off than they are. While they frequently harbor resentment toward those who are more affluent, they are also in awe and fear of them because, in their own minds, wealth is associated with power and authority. Therefore, by denying their anger and implying they are satisfied with less, self-deniers seek to protect themselves from retaliation by powerful authority figures whose rejection they fear.

The Payoff. Safety and security are the goals of self-deniers. By their self-sacrificing behavior and by denying they need or want anything from others, they hope to elicit admiration and sympathy from people rather than contempt or rejection. If they can thus assure other people that they are satisfied with their Spartan existence and that they pose no threat because of envy or resentment, other people will be more likely to relax and treat them kindly. In this way, fear and distrust of others is minimized and a dangerous world is made to seem a little safer. In some cases, self-deniers can manipulate others into turning feelings of sympathy into overt acts of help and support in the form of gifts, subsidies, or loans.

The Cost. Since self-deniers must maintain their state of self-imposed deprivation in order to feel safe, it follows that any activity that might ordinarily be associated with pleasure will, instead, bring about a state of anxiety and insecurity. Fear and distrust are not conducive to enjoyment and satisfaction in living or in promoting meaningful interpersonal relations. Self-deniers maintain a standard of living below their potential and find satisfaction only through proving they can do without. This limits the areas in which they experience a sense of accomplishment. Consequently, self-esteem is often eroded and self-actualization is virtually impossible to achieve.

Living with a self-denier is likely to be depressing. It is difficult to enjoy life when one's companion is unable or unwilling to join in the fun. Even if the self-denier indulges others, the recipients are made to feel guilty since they are aware that the cost is not only monetary, but also involves a good deal of self-sacrifice and self-denial. In most cases self-deniers' guilt rubs off on their children, who also learn to avoid pleasure and to feel guilty for self-indulgence.

THE COMPULSIVE BARGAIN HUNTER

The compulsive bargain hunter is a fanatic when it comes to spending money. Unless the situation is exactly right, money is fiercely retained, but once the bargain hunter spots a chance to buy something cheap, there is no holding that person back. The object purchased may be shoddy or the person may have no real use for it, but that is no deterrent if the price is right. The thrill is not in acquiring something, but in buying it at a cheap price.

One such bargain hunter was twenty-six-year-old Mark Mercer, who worked as an account executive for a television station and lived with another bachelor in an expensive apartment complex for young singles. He made $55,000 a year, yet he looked forward all week to Saturday, the day he devoted to saving money by "shopping wisely." The first thing he did on Saturday morning was to spread out the week's newspapers on the floor and systematically read all of the advertisements. Then he cut out all of the food coupons and put them in an envelope for safekeeping. Next, he made a list of the sale items featured at all of the supermarket chains. The rest of the morning, Mark spent going from store to store purchasing whatever items happened to be on sale. This usually took most of the morning. Afternoons were spent shopping for clothes, furniture, appliances, automobile accessories, and whatever else happened to be on sale. If he ran out of sales, Mark might spend an hour or two window-shopping or browsing through department stores, antique shops, or second-hand stores searching for bargains.

A succesful shopping trip for Mark was not measured by what he bought or how much he spent, but by how much money he *saved*. He considered it a personal defeat if he had to pay full price for anything. He would drive ten miles across town to save two cents on a can of tomatoes. If he was out of butter and butter was not on sale anywhere in town, he would either buy margarine on sale or do without the butter. Mark took great pride in his ability to always get a bargain, and he kept a running account of his savings in his head as he went from store to store. But he never figured in the value of his time or looked at the possibility that he spent a dollar's worth of gasoline to save sixty-five cents on groceries.

The Underlying Personality. Buying, for the compulsive bargain hunter, is not a rational process. It is an attempt to bolster one's ego by seemingly outsmarting others—both the sellers and those who pay full price. Most people, in purchasing something they want, weigh the usefulness of the object against the price. The bargain hunter considers only the price. Given a choice between a valuable object at a reasonable price and a practically worthless item at a "giveaway" price, the bargain hunter will most likely take the less-expensive item. Such a person may buy six shirts at five dollars apiece and hardly ever wear them because of their poor quality rather than buy two fifteen-dollar shirts that are well-made and would look attractive for a long time. The feeling of triumph accompanying such a purchase validates the irrationality of the act.

Beneath the exterior of compulsive bargain hunters is a nagging feeling of emptiness, a feeling of having been deprived of something essential to a sense of security and contentment. They may have come from homes where death or divorce or conflict limited the amount of affection available from parents. Or they may have felt that brothers or sisters were favored and received more than their share of love and attention. In most cases, money as well as affection was in short supply when they were young. They learned at an early age to get as much as possible for whatever money they did have since there was never enough to satisfy all of their needs and desires. Now, as adults, they continue the pattern. Regardless of their income or net worth, they try to get more than their money's worth from every purchase.

Symbolically, compulsive bargain hunters are trying to even the score. Having felt shortchanged as children they are now trying to manipulate the world into giving them more than their share. The elation of getting a "bargain" is at least partly the result of unconsciously equating the act with having outsmarted one's parents into giving more affection than they had originally offered.

The dividing line between bargain seeking and greed is sometimes hard to find. The difference between the two is primarily one of degree. Some bargain hunters become so caught up in the pursuit of getting something for nothing that greed takes over and they lose all sense of control. Not only do they buy peaches which they don't like because they are cheaper than pears, which they do like, but they buy peaches by the case to save an additional five cents a can.

The Payoff. Bargain hunters receive a payoff in several forms. First, they derive a sense of security in perceiving that they can survive longer than most because their money goes farther. Second, because they believe they are more clever than others and can outsmart them, they can feel superior. Up to a point, friends may look up to them or envy them because of their bargaining ability and others may seek their advice in making purchases. This reinforces their feelings of superiority. Third, they feel secure believing they can manipulate the environment into giving them more than they pay for, which temporarily alleviates some of their underlying feelings of insecurity and vulnerability.

The Cost. Despite their self-perception of being clever buyers, compulsive bargain hunters frequently get shortchanged. They focus on the price rather than the quality and are often sold inferior merchandise. Or they buy clothes that don't fit because they have expensive labels and are on sale. The compulsiveness of their spending often leads them to purchase things they don't need, with money they don't have. They may haunt discount stores and buy many dollars' worth of trinkets they throw in a drawer and never use. Not infrequently, they squander excessive amounts of time to save a minimal amount of money—time that might more profitably be spent otherwise.

Although it might appear on the surface that they have found a satisfactory solution to the problem of insecurity and distrust, that is not usually the case. An underlying self-destructive tendency is frequently operating in the compulsive bargain hunter, and it may be found in the bargain-hunting behavior itself. What looks like a legitimate bargain, may, in fact, be a fraudulent get-rich-quick scheme. More than one compulsive bargain hunter has become a sucker for easy money schemes and wound up losing everything by investing in false promises. Overly confident of their shrewd bargaining ability and blinded by their avarice, they are likely to disregard sound judgment and helpful advice and become sitting ducks for shrewd promoters.

Compulsive bargain hunters who brag about their cleverness or the number of items they bought at discount prices may irritate their friends and acquaintances. Recipients of gifts that are obviously shopworn and bought at sale prices are likely to feel resentful and uncomfortable. Being entertained inexpensively when it is unnecessary may cause guests to feel rejected or unappreciated. Consequently, the very people who might provide the warmth and friendship that compulsive bargain hunters need to feel secure are apt to withdraw from them. These people see the bargain seeker as "cheap" and resist becoming too involved emotionally because of the bargain hunter's annoying and endless obsession with price.

THE FANATIC COLLECTOR

While some people collect money, others collect stamps, bottles, campaign buttons, paperweights, old clocks, or any of a thousand other things. And, like saving money, collecting can be an enriching pastime or it can become an obsession. The difference between normal and obsessive collecting is the intensity of the desire to obtain a collectible item, the lengths one will go to in order to add to a collection, and the extent to which collecting dominates the collector's life. Some things that people collect, like gold coins or Goya etchings, have an intrinsic value. Others, like matchbook covers, do not. Sometimes the value of a collectible item is sentimental; sometimes it is symbolic; sometimes it is artistic or aesthetic. People may find pleasure in the object they possess or in the power associated with possessing it; perhaps both. Regardless of what other values collected items may have, for the fanatic collector there is almost always a monetary value.

The Underlying Personality. Like the squirrel that hoards nuts to stave off starvation during the cold winter, the obsessed collector acquires a collection of snuff bottles, Mickey Mouse watches, baseball trading cards, Boy Scout knives, or almost anything in order to feel capable of surviving in a cold and rejecting world.

Fanatic collectors turn away from people as a potential source of affection and security and seek gratification instead through possessing things. And, being afraid to love other humans, they bestow love and devotion on these same inanimate objects. From earliest childhood, fanatic collectors found they could not depend on their parents for the love and security they needed. They were given toys instead of love, or they were children who had no siblings to play with and had to spend many hours alone amusing themselves. Their only source of identity was through their possessions.

Serious collectors not only seek to acquire more and more or better and better specimens for their collections, they are also usually reluctant to let go of any of the objects they have accumulated. That is, they have a retentive as well as an acquisitive nature.

They also are inclined to be very competitive—at least in their struggle to have the best collection of whatever it is they collect. Their egos are likely to become invested in the superiority of their collections and any threat to the status of their collections is perceived as a threat to their self-worth.

Mary Lou and Georgia had been next-door neighbors and best friends for eight years. Their children played together and their husbands were on the same bowling team. They visited back and forth constantly and they were affectionately known in the neighborhood as the Bobbsey Twins. When Mary Lou's grandmother moved into a retirement home, she gave away most of her possessions, including a number of silver spoons, which she gave to Mary Lou.

From time to time, Mary Lou would see an interesting spoon and add it to her collection. Frequently, she and Georgia went shopping together and Georgia would accompany her if she stopped at an antique store or a garage sale to look for souvenir spoons. Both women became knowledgeable on the subject, and Mary Lou encouraged Georgia to collect spoons also so they could share their interest and information.

In time, however, they became mildly envious of each other's collections. They stopped shopping together because they frequently spotted the same treasure at the same time and each would say, "Here, you take it! You saw it first," and then would feel resentful if the other bought it. Fortunately, before resentment and competition became intense enough to destroy their relationship, Georgia gave her souvenir spoons to Mary Lou as a birthday present and began collecting ornate napkin rings.

The Payoff. By devoting hours on end to collecting, displaying, and admiring one's treasures, the fanatic collector can attain a sense of purpose and avoid feelings of loneliness and isolation. Many collectors who are inhibited and uncomfortable in social interaction surround themselves with favored objects upon which they project humanlike qualities. They practically talk to these objects; they find comfort in being with them and regard them as friends. And objects are certainly safer to relate to than are people. They don't make demands, compete, arouse anger, or abandon one.

By building the world's largest collection of, say, beer cans, the competitive collector can also achieve a feeling of superiority and power. This is more difficult if one collects only money, since no matter how much money the average person acquires, there are still hundreds or thousands of people who have more. Even J. Paul Getty, although considered the world's richest man, admitted in an interview that he never felt *really* rich because others in the oil business had accumulated more money than he. He was comparing himself not to other men, but to Standard Oil, Gulf, Shell, and Texaco. If, however, one is collecting shaving mugs or first-edition comic books instead of money, it is possible that with perseverance and a few thousand dollars one could eventually have the world's largest and best collection and be the envy of all other collectors of that item.

Also, by collecting something other than money, even though it is a substitute for money, one avoids the stigma of being thought of as a miser or penny pincher. One might even develop a reputation as an authority on the object collected, and being an authority usually carries with it a certain amount of respect and admiration from others.

The Cost. People who collect as a hobby find a sense of satisfaction in their search and in their acquisitions. Obsessed collectors, however, are driven. The acquiring of a certain oil painting or a rare jade carving becomes a matter of life and death. Their obsession overrules every other aspect of their lives and they devote almost every waking minute to thinking and planning how to obtain the next object for their collection or how to display it. Objects ultimately become more important than people, and fanatic collectors progressively alienate themselves from friends and family, occasionally even becoming suspicious that others will take away their prized possessions. They tend to withdraw from interpersonal relationships and often do not concern themselves with everyday problems like paying bills or getting the car serviced.

Carlos Ortega was considered a reliable and capable policeman. He had been on the force for six years, after having served a hitch in the navy. His wife, Rita, taught kindergarten and told friends, "I want to learn as much as I can about children before I have some of my own." At parties and social events they were an attractive couple. Carlos was quiet and reserved, but always poised and in control. Rita, on the other hand, was vibrant, outgoing, and a comfortable conversationalist. Carlos was secretly in awe of her, and more than a little jealous. He frequently accused her of flirting with other men. Gradually he spent more and more of his off-duty time engrossed in his gun collection. At first it was simply a diversion, a way of relaxing after a tense day on the job and a way of avoiding a confrontation with Rita. Eventually, it became almost a total preoccupation.

Ultimately he became so involved with his hobby that it began to interfere with his work. He found it difficult to pay attention to the radio calls in his squad car. He found himself daydreaming about a particular gun he wanted to buy and he became less alert to what was happening around him. One day he turned the wrong way on a one-way street and drove half a block before he realized what he was doing.

His affection and concern for his prized guns drove an ever-widening wedge between him and his wife. She became resentful of the time and attention and money he devoted to his collection and of the hours he spent at gun stores and on the firing range. And she felt helpless to compete with his collection. She knew that Carlos was diverting his attention and affection from her to his guns but was at a loss to explain why she couldn't compete with these pieces of metal. Neither could Carlos understand why Rita went into a rage one day and threw his guns all over the living room floor. Nor could their friends understand why two such charming and intelligent people as Carlos and Rita soon afterward filed for divorce.

UNDERSTANDING THE SAFETY-FIRST SYNDROME

While there are many different varieties of the basic pattern, security collectors—those who adhere to the safety-first syndrome —have certain characteristics in common. Their primary goal in life is not to be happy or successful or productive, but to remain *safe*. In fact, they spend so much time and effort in not losing, that they rarely think in terms of winning.

Security collectors concentrate their attention on money and various symbolic extensions of money. Their answer to all of their problems is accumulating more and more money, which will then make them impervious to any potential catastrophe. When they feel anxious or threatened in any area, they seek security by increasing their money supply.

The basic problem, however, is clearly not one of money, so it can hardly be solved by money. The real issue is one of distrust; not so much a fear that others will take advantage of them in financial matters, but rather a fear of trusting others with their emotions. Since safety is their prime concern, however, security collectors withdraw from people and put their trust in money and things. They resist becoming dependent upon others, while hiding their cravings for dependency. They view people as being undependable and unpredictable, while money can always be relied on. People can reject or abandon one, but one can hang onto money.

The compulsive saver, the self-denier, the compulsive bargain hunter, and the fanatic collector are but a few of the many variations of the safety-first syndrome. Many others could be mentioned. For example, the mourner, who bemoans the opportunities that got away and dwells on the fantasy of what life would be like if only other choices had been made. The mourner can feel safer believing that next time fate will be kinder. Or the self-punisher, who courts disaster by consistently losing money, and tries to prove that by *surviving* defeat after defeat, one really has nothing to fear from a threatening world. Regardless of the variation, however, the underlying process is the same. The person who as a child did not develop a sense of basic trust has learned some method of coping with a world perceived as dangerous by relying on money instead of people.

HOW TO RECOGNIZE
THE SAFETY-FIRST TRAP

People who are caught up in the safety-first syndrome tend to lock themselves into it so that it becomes increasingly difficult to get out. They are often unaware they are in this trap, and almost always unaware of what they do to stay there. While every human being is unique in many ways, all are alike in some other ways. And all security collectors have some of the following characteristics in common.

Despite any pretense to the contrary, money is more important to the security collector than people.

Money is a primary consideration in making or dropping friends.

Spontaneity is lacking in interpersonal relations since a preoccupation with money interferes with free-flowing communication. In the course of half an hour at a cocktail party, for example, the thoughts of a security collector might go something like this:

"I wonder if I'm obligated to return the invitation to the host and hostess."

"I'll bet this party cost them plenty."

"The guy with the pipe looks interesting, but I think he sells insurance. I'd better stay clear of him."

"I better move on. If I get too friendly with this group, they may want to get together later on and I can't afford it."

"I wonder why this guy is so inquisitive about my job. He's probably trying to find out how much money I make."

"I wonder what he paid for that suit. It looks just like the one I saw on sale this afternoon."

"That couple in the corner looks familiar. Oh, yes! They are the ones who drove up in the Bentley. I think I'll go meet them."

"I'd like to cut out of here, but if I do I'll probably have to buy my date something to eat. I guess I'll stay an extra hour, then I'll tell her I don't like to eat late. If we do go out, I wonder if she would consider going dutch."

With friends or acquaintances, the main topic of conversation of the security collector is money. Although the discussion may involve taxes, inflation, recession, government spending, wages, or investments, the underlying theme is always, "How can I accumulate enough money to feel safe against any possible catastrophe?"

Nearly every happy event produces ambivalent feelings for the security collector. The pleasure is offset by the cost. An invitation to a birthday party means spending money for a gift. Going to a show or a concert means purchasing a ticket. Buying a new sweater is accompanied by feelings of guilt. Receiving a gift means having to return one at some future date. Nothing that costs money is totally pleasurable.

In exchanging gifts with friends or relatives, the security collector's first reaction is, "Did the present I gave cost more than the one I got?"

The security collector is inclined to be secretive about savings, income, assets, and all other personal financial matters. Others rarely know the real worth of the security collector, but are led to believe it is less than it actually is.

The patterns of saving, self-denying, bargain hunting, and dependency on money to solve all problems continue, and even intensify, as the security collector's money increases.

More and more, money becomes an aspect of almost every decision made by the security collector. "If I wear this dress one more time before I get it cleaned, I can save a little money." "If I wait until the end of the month, maybe I can buy that shirt I need on sale." "If I move my savings from one bank to another in the first ten days of the month perhaps I can get double interest." "I guess I'll reupholster that old chair instead of buying a new one." "If I wear the same old suit to work every day, maybe the boss will notice and give me a raise." "I might make more if I invest my money, but it is safer in the bank." "I would really like to take a trip this summer, but I can't afford it." Not only is money a consideration in such decisions, it ultimately becomes the *major* consideration.

Friendships rarely last for very long since the security collector's concern about money becomes a barrier to the development of close, intimate relations. If the security collector becomes wealthy, then it is likely that suspicion and distrust will increase and the person will withdraw more and more from human interaction, believing other people are interested in him only for monetary reasons.

Price rather than quality or personal preference dictates what the security collector buys. If a security collector is crazy about Chanel No. 5 but can buy My Sin on sale for a lot less, she will buy and wear My Sin.

These are some of the more common characteristics that distinguish people who manifest the safety-first syndrome. The more of these traits that apply to a person, the more likely it is that the person is a true security collector.

BREAKING OUT OF
THE SAFETY-FIRST TRAP

Assuming a person is identified as a security collector, what is involved in breaking out of the safety-first trap? Because distrust is learned very early in life, it is an extremely difficult attitude to change. The roots of this attitude are deep. Over a period of time, the individual has learned to reduce anxiety and a feeling of vulnerability by relying on money instead of people. Money is dependable and predictable whereas people are not. Since relying on money seems to work and is in its way reassuring, the pattern, though self-defeating, is also self-reinforcing.

Furthermore, the security collector has learned to relate to people in ways that insure they will prove as untrustworthy as he or she believes them to be. This happens in many ways, but regardless of the form it takes, the unconscious motive is to justify and perpetuate one's distrust.

For example, Ben Foreman, a forty-two-year-old salesman, found most people boring. He particularly thought them stupid when it came to handling money. He was attracted to people who were "doing things" and who had ideas about "making it big" financially. He was flattered that some of these people recognized his "astute business sense" and his "keen judgment about investments." Because they told him what he wanted to hear, he invested in a number of their schemes and lost a good deal of money. Because of his greed and his alienation from more authentic people who related to him honestly but perhaps not always in a "fascinating" way, he became a sucker for the ploys of these con artists and thus repeatedly proved to himself that people can't be trusted.

After Joan Weismann finally divorced her husband, who was a chronic gambler, she vowed she would never trust another man and certainly would never marry again. She had always worked hard, and being able to save her money again made her feel more secure. In time, she accumulated enough money to consider a few small investments. It was then that she met Melvin Diamond. He handled her account at the brokerage office and helped her select some safe investments which paid a reasonable dividend. His sophistication and business acumen impressed Joan, and she eventually forgot her resolve to distrust men.

When she finally agreed to see Melvin socially, Joan was flattered that he took her to expensive restaurants, ordered exotic wines, and introduced her to perfumes with strange foreign names. After they were married, however, she resented the high standard of living Melvin insisted on, and their bitter quarreling over money led to another divorce.

After forty years of instilling in his children the idea that money is the only thing in the world that can be trusted, and, therefore, should be accumulated at all costs, Ralph Dickenson was dying of a terminal illness. He bitterly bemoaned the fact that his children's only interest in him was in how much of his money they would inherit when he died. He took no pride in the fact that they had learned well the lessons he taught them.

Some security collectors feel they have a winning system. They are convinced that people are untrustworthy and that they would be foolish to risk becoming vulnerable by depending on them. Their money gives them a feeling of security that no one or nothing else can provide. As long as they feel that way, they are not likely to want to change. It is only when their dependency on money is more painful than rewarding that they are motivated to give it up. If they feel they are missing too much by alienating and being alienated by others, if they dislike being alone and isolated by their money, if they feel that the possibility of finding happiness is worth risking safety for, they might then be willing to change.

To overcome the safety-first syndrome, one must learn to take a chance on people, to trust others with one's feelings, not indiscriminately, but selectively. It takes time, however, to unlearn the long-established pattern of distrust and to learn how and whom to trust. Some people can be trusted with money. Some cannot. Some people can be trusted with feelings, others can't. It is not intelligent to trust one's money to a known embezzler, or to trust one's feelings to a person who abuses them. Trust must be earned, and it is usually earned slowly over a period of time. By expressing some of one's feelings and then sitting back and observing the consequences, one can learn whether the other person can be trusted further.

To begin the process of learning to trust calls for a conscious effort. Keeping the process going depends on how rewarding trusting becomes. One of the spin-offs of developing trust in others is an increased trust in oneself and one's abilities to cope effectively with the problems of everyday living.

Trusting, becoming involved, loving, being dependent, needing, all involve risk. The person who dedicates every waking moment to being safe essentially avoids living. As Helen Keller once said, "Life is either a great adventure, or nothing."

More than anything else, the price of being a security collector is, in all cases, too high. That is, the safety-first defense inevitably backfires. The security collector is swept into a corner. The basic insecurity that produced the preoccupation with money increases rather than decreases with the accumulation of money; life increasingly becomes a process of erecting stronger defenses against real and imagined exploiters, to the ultimate end that after he passes away, the security collector's money is greedily divided up among the family members whose lives have been impaired by the experience of living under the constant threat of doom.

Reclaiming intimacy with people after one has been hiding

for years behind the illusory protection of money is not an easy or comfortable process. The alternative, however, is the eventual annihilation of one's humanness and its replacement by the emptiness, dehumanization, and despair that comes from trying to find nourishment and satisfaction in things.

7

THE POWER GRABBERS

WHEREAS THE GREEK ORATOR DEMOSTHENES WAS THE SPOKES-
man for security collectors, power grabbers take their cue from
the biologist Charles Darwin. Their motto is "Survival of the
fittest." Their theme song might well be taken from the poetry
of Robert Service, who wrote:

> This is the Law of the Yukon, that only
>   the Strong shall thrive;
> That surely the Weak shall perish, and
>   only the Fit survive.

Money is seen as the key to survival. It turns helpless, infantile
rage into usable strength and power. It transforms an otherwise
ineffectual and pitiful weakling into a Green Giant. Money protects the power grabber from experiencing the dreaded "humiliation" of being weak. Loss of money, on the other hand, means
the loss of power and a return to the terror, experienced originally in childhood, of being helpless, weak, and scorned. This is
avoided at all costs.

Power grabbers have been taught early in life that any show of
emotion is a sign of weakness. Consequently, most have learned

to repress their feelings. Because they are often not in touch with what they are really experiencing emotionally, they are inclined to react mechanically or superficially in their dealings with others. However, if their power supply is threatened, their repressed rage may take over and explode openly and directly. And the force of their adult rage may not be impotent, as was their remembered rage from early childhood.

Power grabbers come in all shapes and sizes—from pool hall hustlers to giants of industry. Sometimes they operate outside the law, sometimes within it. And sometimes they make the laws. Whatever their calling, they seek to dominate and control everyone within their sphere of influence. While exploiting the weaknesses of others, they deny any sign of weakness in themselves. Since they view life as a "dog-eat-dog" existence, they can justify their power-grabbing behavior. "That's the way the world works," they will say. "It's survival that counts. And anything it takes in order to survive is okay."

While there are many types of power grabbers, only a few will be discussed here in detail. Since humans do not always fit precisely into types and categories, many people have characteristics of more than one type. It should also be remembered that the traits and behaviors associated with any given power-grabbing syndrome may occur in varying degrees, from mild to extreme.

THE MANIPULATOR

Like all power grabbers, the manipulator uses money to get power and power to get more money. To the manipulator, life is a contest. But it is a contest played with little fun or enjoyment. The manipulator is likely to appear competitive, yet only participates in contests where the possibility of losing has been all but eliminated. Importance is placed not on the process but on the victory.

Manipulators play on the pride and greed and vanity of their victims in order to exploit them. Frequently, they are fast thinkers and fast talkers who use flattery, promises of easy wealth, and a variety of manipulative promotional and sales techniques to induce people to part with their money.

A reporter investigating unethical, high-pressure telephone stock-brokerage firms, known as "boiler room" operations, gave the following account of a salesman's conversation with a prospective client. The client's name was obtained from a "sucker list" purchased by the brokerage firm, and the stock being pushed was Texas Western Oil, a stock that was essentially worthless.

"He started off by calling her Rosie—her first name being Rose. He asked if she was Jewish, and when apparently she replied yes, he said he was too. He told her he would make her enough to take a trip to Israel.

"It developed her husband was paralyzed and that they had very little money, but did have some Columbia Gas stock. So the salesman told her he would sell that for her and put the proceeds into Texas Western Oil. She finally agreed." [1]

Fast-talking hucksters appeal to their victims' emotions rather than their intelligence or logic. The manipulative door-to-door salesman tries to make parents feel guilty if they "deprive" their children by not buying a set of encyclopedias. "What good is it to put food in your children's stomachs if you starve their minds?" he will ask.

After selling his customer a piece of inexpensive furniture, the manipulative salesman commonly uses the gimmick of saying rather casually, "I know this piece over here is way beyond your means and I'm sure you will be happy with the chair you bought —for an inexpensive piece of furniture it's quite satisfactory— but I would like you to just look at this exquisite fabric, this handsome styling. I know it's more than you can afford, but . . ." Many emotionally insecure customers are thus induced to buy the more expensive chair to "prove" to the salesman that they are not impoverished and that they can indeed afford the more expensive item.

The Underlying Personality. One of the most obvious characteristics of the manipulator is a seeming lack of guilt. Although the manipulator may have broken promises, taken advantage of others, even swindled them out of money, little or no remorse is evident. The conscience of the manipulator seems not to be working much of the time. Therefore, it is all right to misrepresent oneself or one's product, to play off one person against another, or to take advantage of loopholes in the law or in contracts in order to gain more money or more power. In the minds of manipulators, life is made up of only winners and losers, the "hip" and the naïve. All of their energy, therefore, is directed toward ending up on top, since the only alternative is the bottom.

Reuben Walters is an administrative assistant to a high-ranking public official. He grew up in a black neighborhood of southwest Los Angeles. His father, a policeman, was killed in a gun battle during a liquor store holdup when Reuben was less than two years old. His mother went back to work teaching school after her husband was killed, and Reuben was left primarily in the care of a neighbor woman and his three older sisters, the youngest being nearly ten years older than Reuben.

Reuben's baby-sitter was very permissive with him. She let him eat when and whatever he wanted. He napped only when he felt like it. His sisters treated him more like a doll than a person. "Here, Reuben, let me comb your hair!" "Let's have a tea party for Reuben!" "Reuben, sit in the chair till we get back!" There was no consistent discipline or training. Very early in life, he learned to capitalize on what his mother called his "angelic look." If he wanted money for candy or ice cream, he would turn on his angelic look and say, "Mama, I need money to make me sweet." And she would always answer, "Reuben, baby, you're already the sweetest one in the world, but here's some money anyway!"

When his mother was not around, Reuben frequently took money from his sisters' purses, and occasionally from the baby-sitter's billfold. Whenever the theft was discovered, Reuben looked so wide-eyed and angelic that no one ever suspected that he was the guilty one.

Reuben got through school more by charm and wit than by academic effort. His teachers would "fall in love" with him and would go out of their way to help him, even giving him grades he didn't deserve. Only his fellow students knew him for what he was—a manipulator.

After graduation, he held a variety of jobs for short periods of time, but mostly he just drifted, waiting for the right opportunity to come along—"something that will make use of my talents," he would say. Eventually, the right opportunity did arrive. Through the influence of a friend, he was hired as an investigator for a government agency.

Reuben was a fast learner. By being extremely observant, he soon found that power makes one very much in demand and that one's services have a monetary value. He learned who was getting payoffs and who was willing to pay for services rendered. He also discovered that the head of the agency he worked for was a very honest man.

"What could be better?" thought Reuben. "All I have to do is discreetly let the boss know who the 'dirty crooks' are and he'll fire them. Then I'll get promoted into higher and higher jobs and I'll be in an even better position to cash in." Before long, Reuben was in a position where he could help a company land a government contract—for a price. For a price, he could also get someone a job, either with the agency or with a company doing business with the agency. He even managed to conceal vacations and other personal expenses under the guise of government business. Eventually, kickbacks and "fringe benefits" exceeded his salary.

While his manipulating paid off financially, it was the wheeling and dealing that really made his efforts worthwhile for Reuben. "Man, this is the life!" he said to himself. "With a little luck, I'll be running this whole damn city in a few years!" If one of his many girl friends expressed concern about the money he was spending or the questionable honesty of some of his dealings, he would become annoyed and yell, "Look, forget it! That's the way the game is played. These clowns are happy to pay me for what I can do for them!"

Reuben, like most manipulators, had an exaggerated need to feel important in order to offset an underlying feeling of inadequacy. While his background was not as deprived as that of some manipulators, a number of specific events and circumstances, not uncommon to manipulators, were present in Reuben's childhood. These helped shape his life.

1. His father died when he was young and his mother never remarried. This left him with no strong male with whom to identify, and, having been left exclusively in the care of females, he adopted some of their characteristics. This made him the target of ridicule from other boys.

2. He never felt able to compete with other boys physically. He felt humiliated by them, but learned early in life that he could outsmart them and compete successfully on an intellectual, manipulative level.

3. Part of his sense of inadequacy stemmed from the feeling that he could never compete with the image of his dead father, who became something of a folk hero in the Walters family.

4. While he got a lot of attention from his family, he also felt ignored much of the time. He never had the feeling that any of them was really involved with him or cared enough about him to know whether he ate or went to school or was unhappy. They never listened to him or considered his needs or feelings. They told him how cute and clever he was and his mother gave him money whenever he asked for it or whenever she felt guilty about leaving him. But he never felt loved for himself. He was usually treated like a cute toy to be played with and shown off. Because of the type of attention he received from his family, he never really felt "connected" to them.

5. He never learned self-discipline because no one bothered to teach him and because he had no immediate examples to follow.

6. He never learned to delay impulse gratification because money and other rewards were either given immediately or not at all. The many promises made to him about future rewards were usually forgotten.

Being able to control other people like puppets makes manipulators feel powerful by comparison and assuages the fear of being helpless and frustrated themselves. In many cases, it is also a way of symbolically striking back at those who manipulated and controlled them in the past. It is a means of making the score even. This is particularly true when the original threatening and humiliating persons were authority figures, such as parents or schoolteachers, and the target of the manipulator is also an authority figure, such as an official of the government or some other symbol of the establishment.

Since manipulators view sentiment and tenderness as signs of weakness, they resist showing warmth and compassion for others —unless, of course, they use the show of sentiment and tenderness for manipulative reasons—and, hence, feel no qualms about taking advantage of them. Their feeling is that people who are weak or dumb or gullible deserve to be exploited and manipulated.

The Payoff. The most obvious rewards for the manipulator are money and power. The more "successful" the manipulator, the more of each is acquired. Fortunes have been made by shrewd individuals who have been able to manipulate stock prices through maneuvers ranging from company take-overs to the precipitation of mass hysteria by buyers and sellers. Manipulative attorneys and financial advisors have become wealthy and powerful through misadvising their clients, directing customers' funds into their own accounts, or having themselves made beneficiaries in the wills of aged persons they represent. Even the most honest car dealer may try to persuade customers to finance their cars through a certain lending agency, which gives a kickback to the dealer for signing the buyer to a contract with an unnecessarily high rate of interest.

Manipulators are everywhere. Some physicians have been known to perform unnecessary medical procedures on patients, including expensive surgery, to obtain more money. Real estate developers sometimes use misleading advertising and confusing contracts to induce people to buy. Testifying before a group of state legislatures, Florida congressman Alan Becker stated, "Buyers have purchased units in 'tennis club condos' that had no tennis courts or found that the 'Olympic-sized pool' described in the sales brochure was little larger than a bathtub. One project bills itself as a waterfront community, but residents said the only time they ever saw water was when their roofs leaked." [2]

In Detroit, two mothers sued a major toy manufacturer for false and fraudulent advertising in its television commercials. The mothers charged the toymaker with using deceptive advertising methods to manipulate children into asking their parents to buy them the toys.[3]

There is probably no area of endeavor that some manipulator has left untouched if it offers the opportunity to glean fast money and power. In addition, there are secondary gains for many manipulators. Successful ones often lead "exciting" lives. Top-echelon manipulators mingle with important, successful people and become involved in high-level financial or political encounters. Even less successful ones may gain some measure of respect and approval from others since that comes almost automatically with money and power.

Although manipulators are nearly devoid of any deep feelings for others, some are so clever and charming that many people are attracted to them. While they are apt to be strong initially, relationships with manipulators usually fade out quickly. In extreme cases, however, even people who have been swindled or cleverly manipulated continue to admire their deceivers. Spouses and lovers have been known to suffer repeated indignities at the hands of their manipulators, yet continue to express loyalty and devotion to them.

An actress who is married to a wealthy businessman openly exploits and humiliates him by squandering his money and having affairs with other men. However, when she tires of playing around or fears that her husband is angry enough to cut off her money supply, she apologizes so contritely that he forgives her "misbehavior" and seems to be convinced that this time she has found out how much she really loves and needs him.

In some cases, a payoff for the really clever and intelligent manipulator is the challenge of matching wits with others or the satisfaction of mapping a brilliant strategy and seeing it executed successfully. The manipulator, in this sense, is much like a general in the army who maneuvers his forces adeptly, following a well-conceived plan of attack, in order to defeat the enemy.

The head of a nationally known "religious" organization has been very successful in getting his followers to do his bidding, run his errands, and recruit other members—all without remuneration. They are all trying to please him and to get his "love"—which they will never succeed in doing because they are simply discardable pawns in his manipulations. In the meantime, millions of dollars pour in.

The Cost. Loss of integrity is one of the costs paid by the manipulator. While this may not bother the out-and-out con artist, who considers integrity nothing but a hang-up anyway, it may be a heavy price for some who gradually slip into the manipulator role. The purchasing agent who accepts a bottle of Scotch for Christmas from a grateful salesman does not necessarily feel his integrity has been violated. However, if the same man accepts a weekend vacation at a fancy resort, it is generally assumed that he is obligated to purchase a sizable amount of merchandise from the firm that pays the bill. The next step is to actively solicit bribes. The difference between a gift and a bribe may seem inconsequential, but the latter implies a definite loss of integrity. The price for which one will sell his or her integrity or morality varies, but once sold it is difficult if not impossible to buy back.

Frequently, as manipulators become successful, they also begin to live increasingly in their own private worlds, making their own rules. The laws are for fools; the clever learn to use the law for their own benefit. The consequence of this disregard for law is that manipulators tend to hang themselves. By crossing legal boundaries they become increasingly more blatant until they finally get caught. Then, to their dismay and amazement, they cannot talk their way out of their predicament. Such has been the fate of many of the master manipulators throughout history. When they lost their sense of limits, they were finally apprehended.

Some psychologists have suggested that there is a strong self-destructive strain in manipulators. As they become increasingly more successful, their desperation increases. The rewards are empty and even boring. Consequently, these people become more and more extreme in their attempts to enjoy life and make it exciting—until they so blatantly violate the social rules that they are done in.

Even the sharpest manipulators are at times manipulated by someone else. Not infrequently, their greed for power and money blinds them to reality and allows them to be hustled by someone a little more clever than they are.

For example, the owner of a chain of fast-food restaurants decided to eliminate competition in a number of areas where his outlets were located. By buying food and supplies in larger quantities than most of his competitors, he could buy for less. In addition, by selling food at cost for a period of time, he could greatly underprice them. This forced a number of independent restaurant owners out of business, and he had a virtual monopoly in those locations. Then he could raise prices substantially.

On the advice of his treasurer, he next decided to set up a dummy corporation to buy out his competitors for a fraction of their real worth. In this way, he could prevent another chain from buying up the rival food businesses and he could guarantee his monopoly by operating two, three, or even four establishments in the same geographical area.

Things moved rapidly and the owner felt very smug and self-satisfied. Then one day it became evident that he had over-extended himself and that he was greatly undercapitalized. He could not borrow enough money to cover his commitments and was forced to sell not only his new acquisitions but controlling interest in his original chain of restaurants. He did not find out until later that his treasurer was involved with the syndicate that bought him out and was largely responsible for greasing the skids for his financial demise.

The manipulator becomes increasingly isolated while struggling to make it to the top. For example, a manipulative man who has little or no capacity or patience for a real give-and-take relationship is prone to "falling in love" with a manipulative woman, who will then exploit him for his money.

The wife of one such forty-seven-year-old insurance broker manipulator died of a terminal disease. During her illness, although protesting his love and concern for her, her husband was also preoccupied with possible malpractice suits against the hospital and the doctor.

Within six months after she died, he had a twenty-nine-year-old girl friend who fancied herself to be a nightclub singer, although she had little talent. He gave her his wife's jewelry, invested money in her career, and tried to introduce her to "important" people. Yet, when his son asked him for financial help with college expenses, he exploded. He cried poverty, accusing his son of using him and caring about him only for his money. To those who knew him, it was obvious that he was being blatantly used by his girl friend. He, however, was euphoric with "love." After a lifetime of manipulating and exploiting others, he was now being used himself but could not see it.

Because of their inability to form close interpersonal relations, many manipulators become increasingly more lonely and unhappy as they grow older. Since they have spent a lifetime denying their own feelings for fear of being exploited, they distrust overtures of love and affection from others. In addition, they have often alienated the very persons who might otherwise be close and supportive. Increasingly with age, they are surrounded by manipulators who are now using them as they have used others.

THE EMPIRE BUILDER

Like the kings of old, empire builders set out to expand their domain and increase their sphere of influence and power. While manipulators are usually looking for shortcuts to riches and power (and the avoidance of intimacy), empire builders are more likely to be aggressive, driving, ambitious persons who are willing to work hard for what they get.

One of the prime characteristics of the empire builder is an overriding sense of independence and self-reliance. A typical event of early childhood among these individuals is rejection by one or both parents. The cause might vary from death to divorce to emotional deprivation, but to the child the result is the same.

The child learns not to rely on other people, but only on himself.

In an extensive study of the self-made rich, Dr. Alfred A. Messer, professor of psychology at Emory University and chief of the Georgia Mental Health Institute's Family Study Laboratory, found that many of these people had a childhood background similar to that of the empire builder (although not all empire builders are rich). According to Messer, "The child grows up with the understandable feeling that he can't rely on other people, he must prove himself worthy *by himself*. He seeks to prove it with money." [4]

For the most part, empire builders are adherents of the Protestant work ethic. They believe in dedication to hard work and self-sacrifice. The Henry Fords, the Frank Woolworths, the Cornelius Vanderbilts, the George Eastmans, the John D. Rockefellers, the Andrew Carnegies, and thousands of lesser empire builders are stamped from that mold. They started out in life with little, but all had a burning desire to succeed at all costs and a strong conviction that they could do so regardless of the odds.

Empire builders tend to be leaders rather than followers since they equate following with being weak. They also consider indecision a sign of weakness and, hence, strive to become decisive and to assume responsibility. They usually function with an air of authority, and are often autocratic and dogmatic. They dislike having their decisions questioned and may even become violent and aggressive if others make fun of them or challenge their authority. The empire builder seeks to increase personal strength by the acquisition of money, property, resources, and people, which then can be used like an army to go forth and bring back more plunder, which, in turn, means more power.

The Underlying Personality. The primary motivation of the empire builder is to deny underlying feelings of weakness and helplessness that are carried over from childhood. The alternative to being vulnerable is to be strong. And that is the goal of the empire builder, as it is with all power-grabbing Green Giants. They cannot tolerate being dominated by others, although they have a strong underlying need for dependency. They repress this need because they fear being exploited if they express a need for anything from anybody.

While they repress and deny their own dependency needs, they try to make others dependent upon them. The empire-building husband tends to marry a passive-dependent, "faceless" wife and is so overpowering that his children become deeply dependent upon him. He can then feel totally masterful. To break the hold, the children often need to rebel and reject the life-style of their empire-building fathers. Status among empire-building department heads in the bureaucratic hierarchy depends not on how much work the department turns out, the service it provides, or the money it saves the taxpayers, but on the number of employees under the department head's control.

Bob St. John is a somewhat typical empire builder. From where he started, he has come a long way. But, according to Bob, he has just begun. There is still a long way to go.

Born in Canada, Bob and his family moved to the United States when he was four. His father, a mechanic, had a drinking problem and drifted from job to job and place to place until his mother could no longer tolerate it and filed for divorce. She took Bob and his two sisters and moved to Denver.

Although Bob was a good student, he disliked school because he couldn't afford to dress as well as the other students and didn't have much money to spend since his family was on welfare. He was also self-conscious and did not make friends easily. He would have been ashamed to take anyone home if they had been willing to go since, although she denied it, his mother often had more to drink than she could handle. At times, Bob would get angry. "Look, Mom. You divorced Dad because of his drinking, and now you're doing the same thing! What's wrong? Why do you do it?"

"Now, Bobby," she would reply tearfully. "Your father was an *alcoholic*! I just take an occasional glass of wine. It relaxes me so I can face the terrible life I have to live. It's not fair of you to accuse me of such an awful thing! Haven't I always been a good mother to you? I don't know what I ever did to deserve . . . ," and she would run sobbing to her room, leaving Bob frustrated and angry, but with no place to vent his feelings.

Bob was determined from an early age to become rich enough someday so that no one would ever look down on him again or make him "feel like dirt." He felt that both his parents were weak and that's why people pushed them around. He promised himself that would never happen to him.

Since he had little social life and was not athletically inclined, Bob spent most of his spare time working at whatever odd jobs he could find—delivering papers, cutting lawns, shoveling snow. And he saved his money. When he finished high school, he took a job as an apprentice carpenter and learned as much as he could about the building business. He read books on various phases of construction and took some courses at night school. When he accumulated enough money, Bob bought a lot and built a house, doing most of the work himself on weekends and in the evenings when he was not going to school.

The profit from that first house was the beginning of what later became a thriving contracting business. Bob also has a major interest in a lumberyard and a mortgage finance company. His son, Bob Jr., although he always wanted to be a musician, is enrolled in architectural school, and his daughter is studying urban planning.

When Bob built his own home, he chose a big lot with trees, overlooking a private lake. It was a large, rambling house with lots of brick and wood paneling to create a feeling of strength and permanence. "This is *me!*" he mused, smiling with a deep sense of satisfaction. "The St. Johns now have roots. Never again will we be pushed around by other people or be forced to take charity from them. My children and my grandchildren will have a heritage they can be proud of."

The Payoff. Empires may be large or small, but anyone who builds an empire of any size is, to some extent, successful. And success always carries with it some reward. Success is the story of America. It is here that Abraham Lincoln, born in a humble log cabin, rose to become president. This is the carrot held in front of every schoolchild. And those who achieve success are admired and respected by the majority of their fellow Americans. Those who "make it" also have an internal satisfaction, a feeling of accomplishment or achievement.

Successful empire builders are able to provide some of the "better things in life" for themselves and their families. They are able to live in the "better" neighborhoods, drive new cars, and take expensive vacations. Many empire builders feel a sense of pride and accomplishment in the knowledge that they have enough money and power to provide their families with the security, protection, and comfort they never knew themselves as children.

As long as they hold onto their bank accounts and their estates and their business enterprises, empire builders avoid the dreaded feelings of helplessness and impotence. Their money and power tend to soften their underlying feelings of rage and generally keep them under control. Sometimes a sufficient amount of money may even make empire builders seem benevolent and protective.

The Cost. The drive that makes empire builders successful in business is often the very thing that makes them poor marriage partners and poor parents. They often try to run their families as they do their businesses. "Turn off that damn T.V. and do your homework!" "You've been making gravy for thirty-five years and it still has lumps in it! Can't you *ever* learn to do it right?" "Who stole the financial page?"

They make demands and give orders with authority and frequently tyrannize the whole family. They expect their spouses and their children to share their dreams of power and to be productive and contribute to the building of the empire. Although they take pride in the fact that they are building an empire to be enjoyed by their heirs, they are apt to dominate their children and grandchildren to the point where they are hated rather than worshiped or admired by them. The children may then end up rejecting everything the empire builder stands for.

Too often, empire builders can relate to others only in terms of a power struggle. They come alive when they are working, struggling, and building, but they know little about warmth and tenderness. This makes them poor partners in an intimate relationship.

At forty-two, Dan Evans was promoted to Chairman of the Board of a fast-growing company that manufactured tennis and racquetball equipment. On the way to the top, he worked long hours to the exclusion of other interests and activities. At one point he told his wife, "I want to become rich. And if I have to choose between you and my career, you lose."

Now that he runs his own empire, he works even harder. He rarely sleeps over four hours a night and never takes a vacation. His income is over two hundred thousand dollars a year and his assets are over two million. He owns a townhouse, a country estate, and a mountain retreat. He drives a Rolls-Royce and a Pantera and he has over a hundred custom-made suits. But he is not satisfied. "No matter how much I have, it is never enough," he stated. "I want the best of everything, and you can't do that on just a few million dollars."

Their obsession with work deprives empire builders like Dan Evans of the enjoyment of their labors. In their younger years they dream of the many luxuries they want to obtain. However, as they become more successful they are too busy to spend time enjoying the possessions they strive so hard to acquire. They feel guilty when they are not working and producing, and they often dread holidays and social events. Friends and acquaintances are frequently made to feel unimportant. Most often they are selected from business associates and are exchanged as the empire builder's business interests vary. Since their friendships are superficial and rarely lasting, empire builders often find themselves alone and friendless as they grow older.

The rise to power and the acquisition of money enable empire builders to fulfill an unconscious desire to isolate themselves from a world perceived as hostile and competitive. They see the world as a battleground and divide people into allies and enemies. The fantasy of the empire builder is to move from the crowded urban apartment to a single-family house to a home in the suburbs to a country estate. This ultimate symbol of "having arrived" is envisioned as a baronial castle surrounded by acres of lawn and high fences, with guards at the gates. Each step in the progression indicates not only that empire builders have achieved more wealth and power, but are also able literally to put more distance between themselves and the "enemy." Even the "old warrior" who still enjoys the competition in the business arena may feel the need to have a peaceful retreat in which to retire and prepare for the next battle. In many cases, also, as empire builders grow older, they develop a preference for conducting "push-button wars" from their penthouses or country estates rather than engaging in "hand-to-hand combat."

The ultimate in isolation and alienation during the declining years is depicted in the life of the classic empire builder, Howard Hughes. In the last years before his death, Hughes was completely shut off from friends and from the world—a billionaire hermit.

THE GODFATHER

"My mother," complained Manny, "will be the death of me yet! She's really a nice lady and I love her, but sometimes I feel like I'm on a leash." He stuffed the letter he had been reading back in the envelope and tossed it on his bed.

"I know," replied his roommate. "Mothers are like that."

"Not like mine," Manny answered. "Even though I'm away from home and going to college, I have the feeling she knows everything I'm doing and everything I'm thinking. If I don't write home every couple of days, she sends me stamps. If I write home for money, she says I'm not studying hard enough and am fooling around too much. If I don't write home for money, she thinks I'm starving. I have no privacy. I have no freedom. But if I complain, she gets hurt feelings and tells me it's for my own good and makes me feel guilty. For a ninety-four-pound weakling, she sure has a lot of clout. I sometimes think of her as my mother, the godfather!"

The primary characteristic of the godfather syndrome is summed up in the adage attributed to Theodore Roosevelt, "Speak softly and carry a big stick." Godfathers take a benevolent role toward those under their control as long as they conform and do what is expected of them. Control is maintained largely through a system of financial rewards and punishments. When subjects conform to the demands of the godfather, they are monetarily rewarded; when they rebel, money is withheld. To modify the oft-quoted biblical observation, "The godfather giveth and the godfather taketh away!"

The godfather parent bribes children to be good, to get A's in school, and to do chores. Money is the only medium of communication for such parents and they are determined to teach their children the power of money. If the children misbehave, their allowance is immediately cut off. The godfather employer demands loyalty and obedience through giving or withholding pay raises, bonus checks, opportunities for advancement or overtime work, and threats of being fired. Payoffs for political favors insure the power of the godfather politician.

One godfather, a mild-mannered banker, had eaten lunch at the same restaurant every working day for eleven years. He was a generous tipper and was always given a preferred table and the best possible service. He knew each of the waiters by name and inquired solicitously about their wives and children. He joked pleasantly with the hostess and sent her roses on her birthday.

Yet he had become something of a legend among the staff. Not once in all that time had he eaten a meal without some complaint and at least one request for special service. "The coffee is too cold. Could you please bring me a fresh pot?" "The steak is too rare. Please have the chef grill it a little longer! This is rare and I asked for *medium* rare!" "This wine is the wrong year. I wanted a 1970 and this is 1973. And the bouquet is all wrong. 1973 was not a good year." "The soup has a little too much pepper in it. Would you exchange it for the salad?" "The salad fork is dirty!" "The napkin is stained!" "It's too dark in this corner!" "The sun is shining in my eyes!"

It was not that the banker was displeased with the restaurant. He recommended it highly to his friends and he entertained customers there frequently. One day, however, he felt that his waiter had ignored him for an unreasonable length of time and that the busboy had taken longer than necessary to refill his water glass. Although the restaurant was unusually busy, the banker took his complaint to the headwaiter, who apologized, but with a slight hint of impatience in his voice. The banker felt that he had been humiliated and the headwaiter had been ungrateful considering all that the godfather had done. Since that day, the banker has never been back and tells his friends to stay away.

No matter where he ate, his behavior would be the same. It simply makes him feel important and powerful to order people around. He makes the same kind of unreasonable demands on his wife, children, friends, employees, and anyone else he happens to deal with. It is important for him to feel dominant. Yet his benevolent and paternalistic manner takes much of the sting out of the resentment of those he controls and usually makes his otherwise unreasonable demands somewhat tolerable.

The Underlying Personality. Behind the quiet and often kindly exterior of the godfather is a very angry individual with an oversensitivity to being humiliated. "Respect" is a key word in the vocabulary of the godfather, and it indicates a powerful obsession with not being made to "feel small." The godfather was overly controlled as a child—to the point of humiliation and embarrassment. Consequently, the dread of humiliation leads to a supersensitivity to any form of reaction that might be perceived as a put-down.

Anger and hostility are often repressed or at least kept under tight control. When they are expressed, it is likely to be in a violent eruption. As long as the godfather's authority is not threatened, however, anger may be expressed indirectly and impersonally.

When Kathy Garrett was a child, she was very quiet and submissive. On the rare occasions when she got into trouble, a stern look from either parent would send her to her room crying. Whatever punishment she received she felt she deserved, and she accepted it without protest, promising to be better in the future.

With her brother, Craig, it was not so simple. Craig was by nature more rebellious. But when he questioned his father's orders or protested his own innocence of wrongdoing, his father went into a rage. No matter how harsh the ensuing punishment, if Craig cried or showed fear, his father would yell even louder and call him derogatory names. After his father left, Craig's mother would come into his room and comfort him. She would put her arms around him and hold him tight until his sobbing stopped.

One day Craig got in a fight after school with a tough Irish kid named Terry, who was a head taller and ten pounds heavier. Craig came out on the short end of the fight and went home nursing his injured pride and a swollen lip. When his father found out what had happened, he called Craig a sissy with such scorn that Craig could hardly stand it. He took the two dollars he had been saving toward the purchase of a record album and hired an older kid to beat up Terry.

When he was ten, Craig's sexual curiosity prompted him to suggest to a girl who lived on the next block the usual, "I'll show you mine if you'll show me yours." His request was met with "I'm going to tell your mother!" But he found he was able to "buy a look" when he offered her a dollar.

In these, as well as in many other situations, Craig learned what all potential godfathers learn: (1) that people and power can be bought with money, and (2) that the rage caused by humiliation can be channeled into getting the money and power to dominate and control others instead of being at their mercy.

The Payoff. Godfathers, because they wield power, are usually respected. The respect may be more an outgrowth of fear than of love, but if the godfather is able to project the image of a kindly patriarch, admiration or even affection might also be forthcoming.

Loyalty and devotion are also purchased by the godfather. If one is willing to spend the money, it is possible to buy a whole army of yes-men who will bow and scrape and devote their lives to doing the will of their "master." For the godfather, the power to control the lives of other people helps erase the memory of the feelings of frustration, humiliation, and helplessness that came from being dominated by someone else.

An obscure football player on a mediocre college team, with more ego than talent, ultimately made a fortune in business and bought his own professional football team. He was thus able to hobnob with some of the finest athletes in the business and have them call him, "Sir." He acted as father confessor to the team and frequently helped players with their financial problems. From time to time he would coerce the coach into giving preferential treatment to one or another of his favorite players but would bellow in rage if anyone accused him of tampering with the team. As owner of the team, he got more newspaper publicity than he could ever imagine as a college player. Even when the publicity was bad, he received a good deal of satisfaction from seeing his name in print. He was even accused, on occasion, of firing a coach or hiring a quarterback for the publicity involved and to prove that he had the power to buy and sell the people he had always envied.

The Cost. The godfather, like all power grabbers, seeks to dominate in interpersonal relations. Either the godfather is on top or the relationship ends. It is a vertical rather than a horizontal relationship. And the person on the bottom must agree to stay there or get out. The male godfather, for example, will never let his wife develop her own potential. He may buy her expensive presents, cater to her whims, even put her on a pedestal; yet he controls her because, in his mind, he owns her much as he owns his car and his house. At some level, he is likely to be very dependent on her. At the same time, he does everything possible to maintain her feeling of dependency on him and to convince her that, except for his benevolence, she would be nothing. This kind of deception is typical of the godfather, and does little to build meaningful relationships.

Those who are involved with godfathers usually have to walk on eggshells because of the tendency of the godfather to shift suddenly from a quiet, controlled demeanor to a violent rage when challenged. Many insecure people are attracted to godfathers because of their apparent strength and protective qualities. "I really got sucked in," claimed one young divorcée. "After my first marriage ended, I wasn't feeling too good about myself and Aaron seemed so protective and understanding. I needed that. But before I knew it, I felt like a zombie. I was thinking his thoughts, doing his thing. I had no mind of my own. I had to get out."

Too often godfathers destroy the initiative and independence of all those who come under their control. By systematically giving and withholding money, the godfather tends to view people more as coin-operated machines than as human beings with needs and feelings. Put money in the slot and the machine works. Withhold the money and it stops. This view of people does not lend itself to the establishing of warm, intimate relationships. Instead, it tends to demean and dehumanize all those who come under the domination and influence of the godfather.

For this reason godfathers tend to attract the weak and the insecure. Followers with any ambition and self-respect leave. In the end, the godfather is left with only the most passive and ineffectual dependents, sycophants who contribute nothing except their presence. Eventually, the godfather is apt to realize the trade-off is no longer satisfying. "All of my life I have given! I have given my life's blood! And what do I get in return? *Nothing*! People are like vultures! My friends. My children. They pick my bones, but where are they when I need *them*? *Nowhere*!"

It is not unusual for an elderly godfather to regress to an infantile, dependent state—the very condition that power-grabbing behavior was designed to prevent. The male godfather, for example, may turn more and more to his wife for nurturance and support. She, in turn, frequently does a role-reversal. Instead of being the docile, dependent wife she has been, or the kindly nurturing fairy godmother he envisions, *she becomes the godfather*. Whereas she used to complain about his stinginess, she now puts him on a tight allowance and doles out money to the children in smaller amounts and with more strings attached than he did.

WHAT MAKES A
GREEN GIANT TICK?

Security collectors felt threatened by their environment at a very early age and learned to distrust it. They reacted with fear and gradually found that they could use money to build barriers between themselves and the threatening world and thus feel safe. Power grabbers also felt threatened as children. Instead of reacting with fear, however, they became enraged. They consider fear a sign of weakness and look down on security collectors for succumbing to such emotions.

Faced with threat or danger, people, like lesser animals, are faced with two basic choices—attack or withdrawal. Attacking behavior is associated with the emotion of anger, while withdrawal is linked with fear. Evidence indicates that both fear and anger are usually present in each behavior, but to different degrees. If one is more fearful than angry, the probability of withdrawal is more likely, but attack is probable if anger is predominant. Security collectors and power grabbers might then be distinguished by the imbalance between fear and anger in their reactions to early threats from the environment, particularly threats from parents and family. The degree to which this difference is the result either of inheritance or learning is not always evident.

Anger is not always expressed overtly, nor is it always experienced consciously. It is, however, *always found in abundance among power grabbers.* And the anger stems originally from excessive frustration of early childhood needs and the feelings of helplessness and humiliation resulting from an inability to overcome the source of frustrations—be it parents, society, or "fate." The behavior of power grabbers conforms to what is sometimes called the "frustration-aggression hypothesis." This concept, developed by a group of research psychologists at Yale University, maintains that some form of aggression is evident whenever a person is frustrated in trying to complete some goal-directed activity.[5] Aggression is linked with attack and anger but is not always conscious or overt.

In contrast with many others who feel thwarted and desire to strike back, those who become Green Giants do not usually resort to physical assault or unite with others in a group attack. Instead, they find their source of strength in money. Their anger and rage and desire for revenge are motivators to gain the money which provides them with the power to attack and intimidate others and overcome their underlying feelings of impotence and humiliation.

The majority of power grabbers are men. And a majority of the power-grabbing men have had poor relations with their fathers. Some fathers have been weak and ineffectual, possibly alcoholic. Some have died or abandoned their families. In these cases, the boy did not have a positive identification with the father. Some of these boys have become overly attached to their mothers, becoming "mama's boys."

Another common pattern is the macho father, or the "marine drill sergeant" father, who will tolerate no emotion, and especially no sign of weakness, in his son. These fathers are determined to make "men" of their boys if it kills them. Their sons are punished unnecessarily and then are told, "Take your punishment like a man!"

Faced with this kind of abusive treatment, potential Green Giants do what many, including some who develop into murderers and a few prisoners in German concentration camps, have done; *they identify with the aggressor.* They accept and internalize the value system of their tormentors. This process, first expounded upon by Freud, enables the son to cope with his feelings of helplessness. By identifying with his aggressor, the boy *no longer feels like a helpless victim of an external threat.* The threatening quality is now perceived as *inside* himself, something which is now under his control.

Power grabbers have a cynical view of the world. They tend to believe the worst about people and expect to be mistreated by others if they let their guard down. While there is enough evidence of a dog-eat-dog attitude in the world to deny that power grabbers are completely paranoid, much of the hostility they see in others is a projection of their own underlying rage.

Although most Green Giants are men, there are exceptions—Helena Rubinstein, the late cosmetics tycoon, for example. The richest self-made woman is thought to be Lucille Ball, the actress-entrepreneur. Her current net worth is reportedly in the neighborhood of $50 million.[6] Reasons given for the limited number of women power grabbers range from (1) lack of cultural and economic opportunity available to women, to (2) a lack of the "killer instinct" in women, to (3) the traditional repression of aggression in female conditioning and the assumption of an overtly passive-submissive role by women.

In the past, the woman who sought money and power did not necessarily go out and build an empire on her own. In some cases (for example, Scarlett O'Hara in *Gone With the Wind*) she would seduce, manipulate, and control men who had money in order to further her own ambitions. In other cases, she would be the power behind the throne who pushes and manipulates the man in her life into becoming a financial giant. Another common role has been the woman who sits quietly in the shadow of her husband but keeps her finger on the pulse of the business while her powerful husband makes it grow. When he burns out or dies, she steps in and takes over where he left off, and becomes a Green Giant in her own right.

Not infrequently, an aggressive power grabber marries a passive power grabber. B. J. Burnside Enterprises was a small, wholly owned conglomerate consisting of a blueprint company, an advertising agency, a cardboard box manufacturing company, two printing companies, and a distributorship for janitorial supplies. B.J., as he insisted everyone call him, was a combination empire builder and godfather. His employees feared and respected him. They never questioned his decisions, and those who stayed in his organization for any length of time seemed to think he could do no wrong. They, in turn, were rewarded with handsome salaries and bonuses.

Betty Burnside was the daughter of a wealthy manufacturer. It was partly her money that started B.J. in his first business venture shortly after they were married. She had gone to private schools and had developed expensive tastes and proper manners.

Although reserved, she talked easily with people and was a gracious hostess. As B.J. began to make money, he took great pride in entertaining and showing off his lovely home and his attractive wife.

While B.J. bragged to friends that he had "the filthiest vocabulary in the United States," he never swore or told a dirty joke in front of Betty. When one of his business associates commented on the difference in his behavior at home as compared with his usual style, B.J. replied haughtily, "I respect my wife too much to degrade her with that kind of talk!" It was generally known that B.J. had countless brief affairs and, over the years, a number of mistresses. However, if Betty suspected, she never let on. The relationship between Betty and B.J. could best be described as "friendly but formal." So formal, in fact, that one of Betty's closest friends once remarked, "I know they've had sex at least twice because they have two kids."

While he generally dominated and intimidated everyone he came in contact with, including his own children, B.J. never felt altogether sure of himself with Betty. He was usually flattering in his comments about her but occasionally, when he had had a little too much to drink, he would try to humiliate her by introducing her as "Saint Elizabeth, her holiness, the patron saint of virgins and virtue!" Or he would make some remark like, "She's so saintly they named a hospital in Washington after her. You know, Saint Elizabeth's Hospital for the Insane!" Most of the time he was a little in awe of her, however, and if he began to get out of line, she could get to him by reminding him that he came from the wrong side of the tracks and that his father was a drunk. On rare occasions this would send him into a rage, but usually he would sink into a state of insecurity and humiliation.

Although he never admitted it to anyone, one of the driving forces behind B.J.'s power-grabbing behavior was to become wealthy and powerful enough so that Betty would respect him rather than reject him. For her part, Betty saw through B.J.'s facade. She knew how dependent he was on her and that he couldn't openly admit it. Most of the time he put her on a pedestal and indulged her. It was similar to the way she had been adored by her father, and she reveled in it. It didn't bother her that her husband discouraged her from becoming independent, or assertive, or sexual. As long as she could manipulate him into buying her expensive clothes, a prestigious home, a sports car, and numerous other trinkets, she was content.

HOW TO SPOT
A GREEN GIANT

Sometimes Green Giants go undetected by the untrained eye of the casual observer. On close inspection, however, they can usually be spotted, particularly if one is aware of their telltale characteristics.

A common characteristic of Green Giants is a cynical attitude toward life. They are inclined to sneer if someone suggests people can really be persuaded to act out of compassion or humanitarian motives. They are firmly convinced, on the other hand, that everyone and everything can be bought if the price is right.

Contrary to other power-oriented persons, the power of Green Giants is located solely in money. Power grabbers feel impotent if their supply of money is cut off.

Power grabbers are rarely able to give or receive love. They may demand loyalty and respect from their underlings but are secretly convinced that without money they would be worthless and would be abandoned and scorned by the very persons who are devoted to them when they have money and power. They may fantasize that more money will bring more affection; but as they accumulate more and more money, they become even more isolated from people, more suspicious, and more easily enraged.

What relationships power grabbers do have with people tend to be volatile. When pleased with another person or not feeling threatened, the power grabber may be magnanimous in rewarding that person with praise and presents. The next day, feeling less secure or displeased with the person, the power grabber is likely to explode with rage and vilification.

Power grabbers live in an unreal world of fantasy. They so

terrorize their friends, family, and employees that people are afraid to challenge or confront them. Power grabbers are seldom given authentic opinions because others are conditioned to parrot what power grabbers tell them or what they want to hear. Since they hear their own ideas stated over and over, they are more convinced than ever that they are right—even when their ideas are totally irrational. For example, they may have paranoid delusions about an employee, or be on the verge of becoming alcoholics, but no one will level with them.

Because they detest weakness and infirmity, power-grabbing Green Giants are inclined to burn out early in life. They ignore physical complaints and do not take care of themselves when ill. After a serious illness hospitalized a well-known power grabber, his wife arrived at the hospital to take him home to recuperate further. On the way home, however, he demanded to be dropped off at his office because he had work to do.

After extensive research on the subject, two well-known cardiologists, Dr. Meyer Friedman and Dr. Ray H. Rosenman, concluded that individuals with certain personality characteristics are most prone to heart attacks and other cardiac problems. People with these characteristics are labeled Type A by Friedman and Rosenman.[7] Type A behavior is typical of the power grabber. Type A persons are characterized, in part, by a compelling sense of time urgency—"hurry sickness"—aggressiveness and competitiveness, usually combined with a marked amount of free-floating hostility. They engage in a chronic, continuous struggle against circumstances, against others, and against themselves. They don't know how to relax and enjoy life. They are so busy *getting the things worth having* that they don't have the time to *become the things worth being.*

STAYING OUT OF THE CLUTCHES
OF THE POWER GRABBER

Power grabbers are disinclined to see anything pathological in their behavior and are not often motivated to seek counseling or psychotherapy. The world is a jungle and anyone who suggests otherwise is naïve or trying to be misleading. Admitting they need help of any kind is a sign of weakness, and this they avoid at any cost. If led into therapy at the instigation of a spouse, power grabbers are resistant and defensive. They are fearful of revealing any flaws in their personality and equally fearful of the intimacy that is implied in most approaches to therapy. Those who become deeply involved with power grabbers, on the other hand, are likely to feel squeezed and manipulated to the point where they sense they are losing their own identity.

You may be involved with a power grabber if:

1. You are overly fearful of antagonizing the person.

2. You try overly hard to please the person.

3. You orient all your behavior around the person's moods.

4. You have an obsessive devotion to the person. You feel the person is a truly superior human being, but greatly misunderstood by others.

5. You find that you accept the person's ideas even though they would ordinarily conflict with your own.

6. When the person owes you money, you are afraid to ask for it.

7. Even though you have earned the money, when the person pays you it is done in such a way as to imply it is a gift.

8. When you work for the person, you always feel underpaid but you also feel unneeded and are fearful of being fired if you protest.

9. Even when you badly want or need money, you try to hide this fact because you don't want the person to feel you're working *only* for money.

10. Even though the person procrastinates in paying you or pays you less than you bargained for, you still feel humble and grateful when you are finally paid.

If you find yourself identifying with a number of these or similar experiences, perhaps you are in the clutches of a power grabber. If it makes you uncomfortable and you want to get out, you can do so but it is not easy. The thing that locks most people into an untenable relationship with a Green Giant is the conscious or unconscious fear of unleashing the rage which lies beneath all power-grabbing behavior. Courage to risk being the target of this rage is necessary if one is to confront a power grabber or to break away from one.

In order to extricate oneself from the clutches of a power grabber, it is important to determine what payoff one receives from being a victim of such a person. It is easy to say, "I was taken in," or, "He changed after we got married." But such is rarely the case. Children may be the victims of power-grabbing parents, but adults tend to gravitate to people who satisfy their psychological needs. If they become victims, it is because they receive some sort of payoff.

People who are attracted to power grabbers usually feel weak, invisible, ineffectual, and insecure, and seek to attach themselves to someone they see as strong and capable. They particularly negate their own ability to survive and make money. They are likely to have a strong money hunger, but tend to deny it because of their lack of confidence in getting money. By tagging along after a "winner" they hope to gain a certain amount of power vicariously and receive some share of the winnings as payment for their loyalty and support. In effect, they form a parasitic attachment to the Green Giant.

In trying to become free, it may be helpful to note that what looks like strength in power grabbers is mainly an illusion. They are manipulative, controlling, and angry, but not necessarily strong. Like a good actor, the power grabber is often able to play the role of a strong character without really being one. The individual who really needs strength in another person would do well to look beyond the power grabber. The typical male godfather, for example, is likely to become more and more dependent upon his wife as he grows older and turn to her for the nurturance and affection he was deprived of early in life. If she married him for strength, she will be very disappointed.

Gaining a feeling of personal strength and independence is necessary to break the neurotic tie to a power grabber. The business associate must deal with the fear of making independent decisions and the feeling that, "Everything I have I owe to the boss. If I had to go it alone, I'd be out on the street and broke!" The spouse will need to get in touch with his or her own aggression and desire for power and dominance, and take responsibility for them. Breaking the feeling of financial dependence is extremely important. Power grabbers rule because they have the money others are willing to grovel for. If they had no money, people would not feel intimidated by them. If people were unwilling to "sell their souls for money," the power grabber would have little clout. *The essence of resolving an unrewarding attachment to a Green Giant is to develop a realistic perception of money and a change in self-image.*

THE GREEN GIANT VERSUS
JACK AND THE BEANSTALK

While a few Green Giants are successful in manipulating people and property and wielding power until they die peacefully in their sleep at an advanced age, a surprising number come crashing down while still in their prime or wind up lonely and bitter in their old age. Much like a young revolutionary who builds a bomb to destroy the enemy and has it go off in his or her own face, many power grabbers seem to be victims of the power they create.

Two of the most successful manipulators of modern times, Bernard Cornfeld of Investors Overseas Services and Stanley Goldblum of Equity Funding, came to the end of their careers before they were fifty. Through innovative sales approaches, perfect timing, and considerable daring, each created an immensely lucrative and monstrous sales organization, which ultimately became as unmanageable as the monster created by Dr. Frankenstein. In order to keep their pyramids growing, they resorted to a variety of unethical and illegal manipulations, which ultimately became their undoing.

Empire builders frequently end up buying their own tombs with their fortunes. As they accumulate more and more money, they become more and more suspicious of people. They believe, and often correctly, that people are primarily interested in them for their money. As their suspicions grow, they tend to become bitter and disillusioned and isolate themselves from other people. Such was the fate of some of the world's most famous empire builders—Howard Hughes and J. Paul Getty, for example.

One of the world's richest men is so anonymous and secretive that few people even know his name. He owns a private shipping fleet which is larger than that of either the late Aristotle Onassis or Stavros Niarchos. He also owns savings and loan companies, hotels, office buildings and other real estate, coal and iron deposits, and petroleum refineries. For years he has refused to talk to reporters and few people have even as much as a speaking acquaintance with him. His vast empire is reportedly a one-man operation in that even his most trusted executives know only a section of the empire. Only he knows the total operation, and there is no heir apparent to the throne. When he goes, the entire enterprise may collapse because he never trusted people enough to groom them to run the vast and complicated empire which he built.[8]

One of the most determined power-grabbing cadres in history was the so-called palace guard—the men who built a wall around President Richard Nixon.[9] Their prime mission was to protect him, but their arrogance and zeal in the pursuit of more and more power, and their illegal fund raising to insure continued power, led to one of the worst political scandals the country has known.

The desire for power is itself a powerful motive. It drives people to do things they otherwise would not do. Those who are most vocal in denouncing the power of others often are motivated by power themselves. Rebel leaders seek to overthrow governments and free the people from oppression, but often, on assuming power themselves, abuse it as much or more than did their predecessors.

The achievement of power too often leads to the desire for more power until one loses all perspective and all humility. Money begets power and power begets money, which begets more power. This progression, if carried to its ultimate, leads to a delusion of omnipotence—the belief that one is *all-power-*

ful. The irrationality of this belief blinds one to the consequences of one's behavior and ultimately leads to errors in judgment, which set in motion the mechanism of self-destruction. The Jack who chops down the beanstalk and destroys the Green Giant is the delusion of omnipotence.

8

THE LOVE DEALERS

LOVE IS A COMMON THEME FOR POETS, A FIELD OF STUDY FOR psychologists, a preoccupation of teenagers, and the gift of doting grandparents. There have been more books, songs, and poems written about love than perhaps any other single subject. It is necessary for physical and emotional growth, and essential for mental health.

Yet despite its importance and the volumes written about it, there seems to be little agreement as to exactly what love is. Sir Walter Scott claimed, "love is heaven," while Shakespeare said, "love is blind," and Conrad Aiken stated, "love is bitter." In recent years, love has been defined as everything from "a warm puppy" to "not having to say you're sorry." Perhaps the late English poet laureate John Masefield summed it up best when he wrote, "we make Love what we choose." It might be likened to a Rorschach ink blot that looks like something different to everyone who views it.

Less romantic but equally significant, a large number of people see love as money, or money as symbolic of love, while others act as though love is a commodity that can be bought and sold.

Most people consider both love and money to be very important, and it is not uncommon to use similar descriptive terms for both. This is apparent in the metaphors that have been used by poets and songwriters to describe the attributes of their beloved. After reading any anthology of poetry, one might form a vision of the composite love goddess as follows:

> Her eyes sparkle like *diamonds.*
> Her teeth are like *pearls.*
> Her skin is the purest *ivory.*
> Her hair is burnished *gold.*
> From her *ruby* lips pour
> *Gems* of wisdom, reflecting
> A heart of *gold* and a
> *Million-dollar smile.*

LOVE IS A THIN DIME

To the small child observing a parent reaching into a pocket or purse time after time and continually extracting a handful of money which will purchase some desired object, the supply of money is likely to appear inexhaustible. The money seems to magically replenish itself. It is always there when the parent wishes to buy something.

At the same time, the child is learning that money can be exchanged for pleasure in the form of candy, ice cream, and toys. William Kaufman, a physician who became interested in the emotional uses of money by his patients, observed, "Because money becomes associated with pleasures in the child's mind, parents can now use it as a reward to reinforce habit development of various desirable forms of behavior. It is at this time that a child first makes the connection between love and money." [1]

Since the child believes the parents' supply of money is unlimited, the refusal of money is often interpreted by the child as punishment or withdrawal of love. Not infrequently, the child who is denied a dime for a piece of candy screams out in frustration, "You don't love me anymore!" When told by his mother that she didn't have the money to buy him an expensive toy, one disbelieving little boy retorted, "If you don't have any money, write a check!"

How children learn to cope with the realization that there *is* a limited supply of money available to them and how they learn the relative value of spending versus saving help set the tone for future emotional reactions to money. Ideally, children learn that, depending upon the situation, either the giving or withholding of money can be a loving act, but that love itself can be neither bought nor sold. This, however, is a lesson not learned by love dealers—those individuals who are caught up in the Santa Claus syndrome.

THE LOVE BUYER

The man who pays a prostitute to "make love" knows that he is really buying sex and not love, but for a few moments he may fantasize to the contrary. The same is true with most people who are so starved for love that they try to buy it. Except for a few brief moments here and there, it is unlikely that they truly delude themselves into believing that they can buy the love they feel they so desperately need. Most people who are hungry for love basically feel unlovable under any circumstance. They are usually willing to settle for "being liked" if not loved. They can buy attention, even admiration. They can try to become "nice guys" and avoid being rejected. While these conditions are related to love and act as substitutes for it, they never quite satisfy. Still, there are many "love buyers" who keep trying.

Love buyers may make generous contributions to civic benefits or charity in order to win the admiration of friends and recipients. They are likely to give large tips to waitresses and bellboys in return for a smile and a friendly word. Love-buying employers pay high salaries not only for work received but for the "devotion" of their employees. Love buyers love to play Santa Claus. Money and gifts are to them the means of making others happy and thus winning their friendship and affection.

Love buyers tend to spoil their children. In an attempt to buy their love, they give in to the wishes and desires of their children and buy them candy and presents they don't need and may not really want. As they become older, they are apt to become jealous of their children's friends and spouses and will then try to compete by offering money and expensive gifts. Elderly love buyers often attempt to keep control of their families and insure periodic visits from them through gifts of money and promises of a sizable inheritance. The wife of a successful businessman was so enmeshed in a love-money relationship with her aging parents that when they became ill, she divorced her husband, left her two teenage daughters, and rushed halfway across the country to minister to her parents and to wait to collect the lion's share of their wealth.

Some people are not content to purchase human friendships, they also try to buy the love of God. By paying heavy tithes and making large contributions to the church, they hope to ingratiate themselves with God and to be favored in His eyes.

The Underlying Personality. Whatever their social role, love buyers basically feel not only unloved, but unlovable. They avoid feelings of worthlessness and rejection by trying to please other people and by being generous. They buy companionship to keep from feeling lonely and to purchase the admiration and attention they believe will never be freely given to them.

Because they have never experienced love sufficiently to know what it is, love buyers are incapable of truly loving others. Emotionally, they are still like children who want things given to them, but are relatively incapable of reciprocating. As adults they might feel guilty about taking love without giving love in return, but by giving money instead, they feel they have evened the score.

Some love buyers are not only unable to love, they are filled with anger and hostility toward parents and the world because their needs have not been met. These hostile feelings are unacceptable to them, however, because they might further alienate those they want to love them. Therefore, they may try to deny and "undo" their negative feelings by bestowing monetary or material gifts of "love" on those they unconsciously hate. Their overt "loving" behavior masks their true feelings of hostility toward those they depend upon. The pattern is similar to that of a criminal adopting the behavior of a model citizen to avoid detection.

Children who are abandoned and grow up in orphanages and foster homes are frequently starved for love and affection. Sooner or later they find out that people are being paid to take care of them and that there is a price tag on the attention they receive. They learn that love is not given freely, but that it can be bought for a price.

Parents of children who become love buyers are frequently love buyers themselves. They are emotionally inhibited persons who try to glean from their children the love and affection they never received from their own parents or from each other. In many cases they are too insecure to risk emotional involvement with other people but feel safer with their own children and deal with them by offering presents and gifts in return for affection.

Gary Richmond was a high school biology teacher. Because his salary never quite paid all the bills, he also moonlighted part-time clerking in a liquor store. His wife, who was studying art, offered many times to go to work to help with the expenses, but Gary always convinced her that, in the long run, it would be more profitable for her to keep on with her art. Inwardly, however, he preferred her to stay financially dependent upon him. He was afraid he would lose his hold on her if she could support herself, because then she might leave him.

Gary was popular with his students, largely because he gave parties for his classes every semester and he offered prizes as incentives to induce students to work harder.

Two other teachers rode to work with Gary. Although he went several miles out of his way to pick them up, he refused to accept any money for gasoline from them. He assured them he was "glad to do it" and that it was "really no inconvenience at all." He was mildly annoyed, however, that they did not include him in their Thursday night bowling league.

As an adult, Gary was continuing a pattern he had learned as a child. He had been awkward and shy and had had difficulty in making friends. His mother would induce other children to play with him by offering cookies and ice cream. His father would take a group of boys to a movie or a ball game and pay the bill. If Gary was particularly unhappy, they would try to cheer him up by buying him a new toy.

The Payoff. For the love buyer, an adequate supply of money staves off feelings of anxiety and depression associated with an underlying fear of abandonment and loss of love. The essence of the love buyer's "Santa Claus syndrome" is that by bestowing gifts on all the deserving people in the world, one expects to receive their undying love and devotion. To a degree, this may happen.

The world is filled with people whose time and talents can be purchased to perform acts of simulated adoration. The person who spreads money around freely is seldom lonesome. From freeloaders to faithful and devoted employees, people can be found who, for a price, will fulfill almost any whim or desire known to mankind—with the exception of love. In the entertainment business, it is well-known that the creation of a star that millions of fans can "fall in love with" is "good box office." It is not so well-known by the adoring public that before the mass hysteria gets started, it is often contrived. When Frank Sinatra was virtually unknown in the early forties, it was rumored that an enterprising public relations man urged a number of girls to "swoon" at his performances. Soon the craze caught on and women all over America yelled, fainted, and tore at his clothes whenever they saw him. And they showed their "love" by buying millions of Sinatra records and standing in long lines to buy tickets to his concerts.[2]

A wealthy man may feel pleased and flattered by having attractive women at his beck and call or by winning a young and beautiful wife, something he might not be able to accomplish without money. And a relatively unattractive woman with money might acquire a handsome lover, a devoted husband, or a baronial title.

The Cost. In the final analysis, love buyers get what they pay for—a substitute. The noted psychiatrist Frieda Fromm-Reichmann defines mature love as "the state of interpersonal relatedness in which one is as concerned with the growth, maturation, welfare, and happiness of the beloved person as one is with one's own." [3] Her view in this regard is similar to those of many other eminent theorists and writers in the field of psychology, particularly Erich Fromm and Harry Stack Sullivan. And it is obvious that this kind of emotional relationship is not for sale on the open market. It is sometimes earned, but never bought.

The love buyer not only is unable to buy real love, but is also unable to give it, since the capacity for mature love is dependent upon having developed a solid sense of self-respect. Persons who become love buyers do so partly because they are lacking in that regard. In most adult relationships, it is unrealistic to expect to get from another person a more mature and healthy emotional response than one is able to give in return. Yet, that is what love buyers do, and that is why they usually come up short.

The desperation some love buyers feel makes them likely targets for manipulators and unscrupulous salesmen. They buy things they don't need because they can't say no and risk being "rejected" by the salesman who shows them "consideration and caring." Because of their hunger, many love buyers cannot tell the difference between real love and a sales pitch. Their need for *instant* love makes them vulnerable to buying anything that remotely resembles the real thing without inspecting it too closely.

Because they fear loss and rejection, love buyers often panic when they think they are losing someone's "love." They may spend lavishly when they are pursuing the person, but if they sense rejection, they will spend even more, and faster. The love-buying husband whose wife threatens divorce or the older man whose young mistress is about to leave him may throw money around recklessly in a last desperate attempt to avoid abandonment.

In extreme cases, the love buyer who feels hopelessly alienated may join a lonely hearts club, sign up for a course of dance instruction, or pay a fee for a computer-selected date. Some of these organizations are legitimate, some are not. Even the most respectable, however, may be hangouts for marriage bunco artists. In return for promises of "love" (and frequently marriage), the victim is swindled out of whatever money he or she can come up with.

In Los Angeles, which abounds in such things, perhaps the champion human marrying machine was a man named Emil "Brigadier" Drake. Drake was a short, gray-haired, dignified-looking man who made a career of marrying and fleecing women. Shortly after his thirtieth marriage ("maybe more, I'm not certain"), he was arrested for parole violation. He had been out of jail for less than a month after having been convicted on another bigamy charge, and remarrying was a violation of his parole. Although he bilked these love-starved women out of hundreds of thousands of dollars, he took pride in the fact that not one of them ever divorced him.[4] Not only was he such a convincing actor that his victims believed him, but they were so fearful of rejection they couldn't even express their anger when they found they had been duped.

Regardless of their protestations to the contrary, it is apparent that many love buyers, unconsciously if not consciously, prefer a simulated rather than a real relationship. A real love relationship involves an emotional commitment, which is a terrifying thought to love buyers because of their early experiences. Thus, they are resigned to a life that is made up of superficial relationships.

Love buyers sometimes alienate their family and friends by being too quick with the checkbook and always too quick to pick up the tab at the restaurant. There are many people who resent "being bought" or constantly feeling that they are "indebted." The love buyer, by trying to play Santa Claus in these cases, actually accomplishes the opposite of what is intended. The people whose friendship and affection are most worth having are the very ones who are most likely to be offended by the love buyer's insensitivity and the ones who are most likely to pursue friendships elsewhere. Only the leeches and parasites hang on.

THE LOVE SELLER

Whether the commodity is gasoline or love, buyers cannot purchase unless there is someone willing to sell. And history shows that the buying and selling of "love" has been going on for thousands of years. Wives and slaves and harem girls have been sold throughout many parts of the world, and, presumably, the buyer was sometimes interested in more from his purchase than work, since a premium price was usually paid for beauty. It is also generally accepted that the world's oldest profession is prostitution, the selling of "love."

About the only real difference between the prostitute and the "gold digger" or the "gigolo" or the many other types of love sellers is that the prostitute is somewhat more open and honest about the transaction being strictly a business proposition. There is little need to rationalize or pretend that the "love" being offered for sale is real or deep or meaningful. The financial arrangement is made openly and the buyer knows what to expect for the price. However, the prostitute who can effectively simulate "real love" or caring stands out among her competitors, and customers often "fall in love" with her and wish to marry her.

In contrast to the prostitute, there are many love sellers who promise affection, entertainment, sex, endearment, devotion, and other attributes of love, but never set a specific price on their services. In fact, many lead the buyer to believe they are free. It is only later that the buyer discovers the price of love was dear.

When the buyer can afford the luxury of such a purchase, perhaps no harm is done. Certainly, the much-married Woolworth heiress, Barbara Hutton, and Anna Gould, the daughter of the notorious robber baron, Jay Gould, could afford it—at least financially. At nineteen Anna Gould had practically everything that money could buy except a husband and a European title. Fortuitously, she met Boniface, Count de Castellane, who had not only a title but also manners, charm, and a burning desire for money. Arriving in New York penniless, the Count talked a fellow Frenchman into grubstaking him, for a percentage of the future spoils, while he set out to marry a rich American woman. When Anna Gould accepted de Castellane's proposal, she had no idea that the brief but spectacular marriage would cost her $12 million.

When asked how he had managed to spend such an enormous amount of money, the flamboyant count replied, "My general existence, my chateaux, my palaces, my *bibelots*, my race horses, my yachts, my traveling expenses, my political career, my charities, my fetes, my wife's jewels, and loans to my friends." He also added, "I claim to represent the best investment the Goulds ever made." [5]

On a far smaller scale are the high school girls who date only boys who drive expensive sports cars, college athletes from the ghetto who use their charisma to attract wealthy sorority girls, and secretaries who flatter and act seductively around their bosses in order to get a raise.

Many incompetent workers save their jobs and endear themselves to their employers by capitalizing on the boss's need for approval and attention. These love sellers are paid as much for inflating the employer's ego as they are for productive labor that adds to the company's financial assets.

Like merchants who deal in other commodities, love dealers are sometimes involved in both buying and selling. Like the prostitute who sells herself to the "trick" to get money to buy affection from her pimp, love dealers may try to buy love with the money earned from selling it. The yes-man who earns his salary by pampering and flattering his boss may shower his wife with gifts to win her love. The boss, on the other hand, may go home and indulge and cater to his own wife, who happens to be the owner's daughter. In most cases, however, love dealers tend to specialize—either buying or selling love.

The Underlying Personality. The role of the love seller is usually established early in life. It stems generally from a symbiotic relationship with one or both parents, who happen to be *love buyers*. The parent has more money than love to offer the child and uses it to bribe the child into being sweet, considerate, and "loving" to the parent.

The perceptive child learns to pick up cues from the parent and knows when to respond with flattery, an affectionate hug, or an approving smile. Like a well-trained actor, the truly effective love seller is able to play a convincing love scene on cue—without any underlying emotion. Approval and security from the parents, as well as money, are earned by such acts.

In the backgrounds of many love sellers is a heavy burden of guilt. Not only do their parents reward them with money when they show love and attention, but indoctrinate them with guilt feelings when they do not. "How can you be so cruel as to forget my birthday?" "You obviously don't love me or you wouldn't wipe your grubby hands on my new skirt!" "If you gave a damn about me, you wouldn't embarrass me by bringing home such a terrible report card!"

For individuals so conditioned, playing the love game not only reaps rewards in the form of money, but also avoids the punishment of guilt. Guilt does not play a role in all love selling, however. Much like power-grabbing manipulators, some love sellers seem to be lacking in anything resembling a guilty conscience. They view the love buyer as a "sucker" or a "pigeon" and show no remorse about taking such a person's money. There are wives who are loyal and loving to their husbands while the money flows and who seek a good divorce attorney when the husband declares bankruptcy. "Good friends" also tend to disappear about that time. Those who treat love like a commodity that is sold in the marketplace are inclined to subscribe to the motto of the marketplace: *caveat emptor*, let the buyer beware. As one such individual, who bilked a number of women out of their savings with promises of marriage, told the sentencing judge, "If women are stupid enough to believe my stories, they deserve to lose their money." [6]

The Payoff. The basic premise of all business transactions is the law of supply and demand. And as long as love is in short supply, love sellers will be in great demand. The plethora of activities and organizations designed to merchandise love indicates there is indeed a big demand for their product.

Apartment complexes, complete with recreation directors, that cater to single people have sprung up in many areas. Travel agents advertise "singles cruises." Extension courses and night school classes offered by colleges and universities are designed to attract single people and to teach them to relate to each other more effectively. Self-awareness and consciousness-raising centers and many other groups with psychological and pseudopsychological overtones offer a promise of understanding and "love" for a fee. A scholarly book on psychotherapy was published a few years ago with the title *Psychotherapy: The Purchase of Friendship*,[7] and thousands of hypochondriacal patients pay their physicians regularly for a little "love" and attention.

Psychologists have learned from studies what sales managers have learned from experience, that sellers who come across as warm, sincere, decent human beings generally have a receptive audience even when their product is worthless. Most people want to see the "good guy" win and many will buy something they don't want just to help the seller get ahead. "So what if I paid two dollars for a lousy pen that doesn't write? It's for a worthy cause!" When the seller offers to sell something the buyer really wants, the task is obviously much easier. Not only will the buyer probably not question the price but will most likely not inspect the merchandise too closely and will overlook many obvious flaws. With this bit of sales psychology in mind, it is easy to see why love sellers generally have an easy time of it. They come across as warm, affectionate, decent human beings and apparently have what their customers so desperately want—love.

When she was twenty, Debbie Morrison told her sorority sisters she had decided to lead the "good life." She was a pretty, dark-complexioned girl with an easy, friendly smile. In her junior year at college she was both a pom-pom girl and a homecoming princess. As a major in business, she also had learned what it means to be in a seller's market. Since she had a choice among several possible dates for each free evening, Debbie made it a point to take the best possible offer, which usually meant the biggest spender.

She enjoyed going to expensive restaurants and lavish parties and opening-night performances. In return, she had the knack of making every man she went out with feel as if he were the most important person in her life. She talked easily and laughed appreciatively when he said something clever. But most important was the way she looked at a man—a look that was a mixture of innocence and boldness that usually blew his composure, but also made him feel very special.

At twenty-eight Debbie is still living the "good life." She still believes it is as easy to love a rich man as a poor one, but the "right" one hasn't come along. Besides, she feels she is having too much fun to settle into a serious relationship, although she has had a number of offers. In fact, her present boss would divorce his wife in a minute if Debbie would promise to marry him. In the publishing company she works for, she has advanced rapidly, not so much because of her ability but because "everybody loves Debbie." Even the other women are fond of her and one of the female executives once remarked, "I only wish my own daughter was as sweet and lovable as Debbie!"

Love sellers like Debbie Morrison find out it not only pays financially to spread a little sunshine, but it also reaps a good deal of positive attention and recognition from others. While the love and affection being sold is usually pretty superficial, it does provide at least a temporary interaction between the buyer and seller and may help alleviate the loneliness of one or both.

Some love sellers gravitate to the so-called helping professions like teaching, social work, nursing, and counseling, where their affection and concern can be channeled into helping people in trouble. They are, in a sense, professional love sellers, who are paid a salary or a fee to minister to the emotional needs of people who are crippled by a lack of love. Not only are these professional helpers paid in money, but they are also frequently reimbursed with gratitude from those they have helped.

The Cost. Ideally, a love relationship is a trade rather than a purchase. Two people exchange love and affection in approximately equal amounts rather than one selling and one buying. The love is given freely by both persons with no price tag on it. They give because they want to and because they enjoy doing things for each other. Love sellers also have needs and desires for love, but love buyers don't have the love to give. Therefore, regardless of their desires or expectations, as long as love sellers are involved only with love buyers, all they are likely to get in return for their "love" is money.

Cindy Franklin turned down marriage offers from several younger men and married a man twice her age because he was wealthy and could give her "all the things a woman could ever want." Like many love sellers, however, Cindy soon found to her chagrin that there were things she wanted from a relationship that had nothing to do with money. Her husband gave her a new car and expensive clothing and plenty of spending money. He did not give her consideration, respect, or any type of emotional satisfaction. She was angry and frustrated because she somehow expected these things *in addition* to money, although she managed to ignore them in her pursuit of an "ideal" marriage partner. Her husband, on the other hand, had little sympathy for her. It was clear to him what he was buying and the price he was committed to pay. The only thing he had promised her was money, and he had lived up to his end of the bargain.

Not all love buyers are as aware as Cindy Franklin's husband. Because they want to or need to, some believe that they are truly loved for themselves and not for their money and are then deceived by love sellers, who are mainly interested in money. Doting parents, for example, may even give money to their children out of a feeling of love, and then find they are ignored, rejected, or sent off to a retirement home by their love-selling children when their money is gone.

Much of the commercial entertainment business involves the packaging and selling of love. Millions of fans are willing to pay money to indulge their love fantasies, but often the "love object," although adored by fans and paid tremendous amounts of money, feels exploited, empty, and insecure. Some, like Marilyn Monroe and Freddie Prinze, commit suicide. Both were love-starved and unsure of themselves when they were younger, and continued to feel that way even though millions of people professed love for them and showered them with gifts and money. At seventeen, Freddie Prinze was lucky to get a date with anyone. At twenty-one, "He was one of the biggest stars in the country, loved by millions, earning hundreds of thousands of dollars, dating Raquel Welch, and pursued by every starlet in Hollywood." [8] At twenty-two, he was dead.

THE LOVE STEALER

While some love dealers buy love and others sell it, some are not in the position to do either, and feel compelled to steal it. People steal for different reasons. Some because they have no money to buy, some for the thrill or excitement, some for revenge, and some for other psychological reasons. Sometimes things are taken because the temptation is too great to resist.

Stealing love involves a special kind of theft. What is taken is frequently not love itself, but a symbol of love. Some kleptomaniacs are love stealers. A true kleptomaniac is a *compulsive* stealer, a person with an uncontrollable impulse to steal. These people do not ordinarily set out with the idea of stealing, but when faced with temptation are unable to control themselves. The overwhelming impulse to steal is initiated by the object or thing stolen, whether it be money or something else of value, because it has a strong unconscious significance for the kleptomaniac. The kleptomaniac does not steal indiscriminately, but only takes things which symbolize satisfaction of a strong unfulfilled need. Not infrequently, that need is love.

All kleptomaniacs do not steal love symbols, nor are all love stealers kleptomaniacs. Some are more subtle, perhaps more resembling embezzlers than shoplifters.

Love-stealing schoolteachers can take the love from their students without getting hurt because they do not let themselves really feel affection for their students. Love-stealing bosses can pretend to care for their employees and can trade on the affection they get in return to induce their workers to put in more effort for less pay. Entertainers who are love stealers may have contempt for audiences privately but may be willing to bask in the admiration and affection, as well as the money, they receive from them. The classic example is the host of the children's radio program who, thinking he was off the air, remarked at the conclusion of his program when thousands of listeners could hear, "There, that should hold the little bastards!" Many entertainers who thrive on the admiration of an audience wouldn't voluntarily spend two minutes with any member of the audience on a personal basis.

Love stealers deal in stolen merchandise. In contrast to love buyers, who purchase love by their own efforts and their own money, love stealers obtain it through work or money contributed by others. In short, they take what they don't own and haven't earned and exchange it for love and affection they pretend they don't need.

The Underlying Personality. While buyers and sellers of love contract to do business with each other, love stealers pretend they have all the love they can use and then steal it wherever they can get it. They are basically very hungry for love and affection but, like all love dealers, don't feel they deserve it. They have also learned from early experience that to let their need for love be known makes them vulnerable to rejection and hurt from those upon whom they depend for affection. Their parents invariably have been unable to provide the love they needed, but promised the love they couldn't deliver.

Danny Covelli is probably the best-liked supervisor in his company. He always gets top ratings from his superiors and has the reputation of being a warm, generous person who would do anything for anyone. More than once, the people working for him have been known to comment, "Danny doesn't have a selfish bone in his body," or "Danny is just too good to be true!" In informal discussions, Danny talks freely about his big lovable family and the fun he had as a kid and the scrapes he got into with his many brothers and sisters.

He never speaks of the bitter fights between his mother and father, or the times he cried himself to sleep because he felt lonely and frightened, or the many times he stole pennies from his mother's purse and hid them in an oatmeal box in the closet. When he felt particularly unhappy and rejected, he would take the box of pennies and pretend it was a fortune given to him by his mother as a sign that she loved him more than she did his brothers and sisters. And in his fantasies, he would build hospitals for the needy and houses for the homeless and feed the poor people of the world to show his love for mankind.

At first Danny, like all children, had no conception of where money came from or how much was available. He knew only that sometimes his parents bought him things he wanted and sometimes they didn't. Since they constantly stressed the difference between right and wrong, he assumed there was probably a connection. And later, when it became "obvious" that he was loved for being good and punished for being bad, he reasoned that money was given for his being good and withheld for his being bad. Therefore, when he felt deprived of love and affection, he would steal the love from his mother symbolically by taking money from her purse.

Over the years, Danny learned to conceal his need for approval while developing a knack for getting the need satisfied. On the one hand, he appeared to be totally self-sufficient, needing nothing from anyone, whether it be love, money, or self-confidence. Yet, on the other hand, he was able to sense what would please other people and win their approval and affection. And he secretly thrived on the praise and admiration he received from others, while maintaining the facade of a "good guy" who was merely sharing his surplus. Friends, lodge brothers, even casual acquaintances could always count on Danny for little favors such as having papers typed or duplicated, phone calls made, reservations handled, or information gathered. "It's no trouble at all," he would assure them. "I'm always happy to help a friend." He would then turn the task over to his efficient but overworked secretary, who often spent her lunch hour doing the jobs for which Danny was receiving kudos.

A week before the department manager's birthday, Danny suggested to one of his office staff that it would be a nice idea to take up a collection and buy the manager a present. He mentioned the advantages to everyone in the department from having the manager's good will and appreciation. The staff person agreed and enthusiastically solicited contributions from all of the employees in the department. When Danny presented the gift to his boss, however, he did not mention that it was from the whole staff. The manager was under the impression the gift was from Danny himself, and Danny did nothing to correct that misperception. But when he reported back to the employees, Danny exclaimed, "Gee, gang, the boss really appreciated that handsome desk set you gave him, and I just wanted you to know how thrilled he was with it. I also want you all to know how fortunate I feel to be working with such a great bunch of people as you."

While love stealers take love wherever they can find it, they go out of their way to let others believe they can "take it or leave it." Admitting they *need* anything threatens their whole defensive structure. The admission of need would establish a *motive*. And as long as there is no motive, the theft of love is more likely to go undetected.

The Payoff. Love stealers try to take the risk out of loving. By taking without giving anything in return, all the love and affection they get is a bonus. They may utilize the time, energy, and money of others, but never their own. Theirs is locked safely away where it will never be touched. Because they appear to be generous, people admire and respect them and rarely suspect that what they are giving away is either a sham or belongs to someone else.

In addition, by pretending to have a surplus of love themselves, love stealers avoid situations in which they might otherwise subject themselves to the possibility of being rejected. By denying they need or want love from anyone, they cannot have love withheld from them.

Love stealers often go through life being the "good guys." Good guys avoid all sorts of unpleasantness and generally avoid open confrontation with others. They are liked and accepted by many because they don't rock the boat.

The Cost. Love stealers usually pay a heavy price for their "safety," however. By not risking their own love in a relationship, they stand to win very little and possibly lose a great deal. Love cannot grow by withholding it. And the love stealer is a love withholder. Consequently, whatever relationships such a person has with others are bound to be superficial.

Chronic love stealers are likely to get caught eventually. This can not only prove very embarrassing, but may also result in the loss of the very things the love stealer needs most—love and affection from others. For example, Lois and Michele decided to give a bridal shower for their mutual friend Karen. Since Michele had the larger apartment, they agreed to have the shower there. Consequently, Lois volunteered to pay for the refreshments and prizes. When the party was over Karen and all the guests thanked Michele profusely for a wonderful evening. She beamed happily while Lois became more and more angry. The next day Lois called Karen on the phone. "Look," she said, "it's no big deal, but did you know that Michele *and I* put on the shower last night?"

"I had no idea! I'm . . ."

"That's all right," interrupted Lois. "I didn't want to say anything, but it just made me angry. It doesn't matter as far as the rest are concerned and I don't care about the money, but since I consider you such a close friend, I wanted to do something for you. And I wanted you to know! That's not the first time Michele has tried to take credit for something I've done."

From that day on, Lois and Michele have become cool to each other and the relationship between Michele and Karen has been strained. Interpersonal relationships with love stealers are usually tenuous. People are rarely allowed to get too close because they might discover the fraudulent nature of the relationship. They might see through the disguise and find out how hungry for affection the love stealer really is. To avoid that disclosure whenever possible, the love stealer settles for shallow and superficial relationships.

Employees who feel "unloved" and unappreciated by their employers sometimes steal money from the company or waste time as a means of retaliation. It is a pattern of behavior reminiscent of stealing money from parents when they felt unloved as children. As adults, however, if they are apprehended, they are likely to be arrested, or at least fired.

People who interact closely with love stealers often get shortchanged. Whatever they offer in the way of love and friendship is demeaned rather than treasured by love stealers, who pretend they neither need nor want such emotions and, hence, that they have no value.

WHAT MAKES SANTA RUN?

Those who are caught up in the Santa Claus syndrome suffer from a deficiency of love. Early in life a confusion between money and love evolved, and in the minds of those who eventually become love dealers, the two somehow seem interchangeable. They learned from their interaction with parents and other significant people in their lives that money was more plentiful than love, although not necessarily more valuable. Whereas most parents provide money for their children *because* they love them, parents of potential love dealers give money *instead* of love.

In the process of growing up, love dealers never get the feeling of being loved unconditionally. Whatever tokens of affection they do receive are payments for good behavior. Money is also given for good behavior. And "good behavior" is "loving" behavior. "Good little children love their mommies and daddies and try to please them." And good little children don't yell, don't get dirty, don't get in the way, and don't hit or fight. Before too long the child learns that "love" can be exchanged for money and money can be exchanged for "love."

The most common parental pattern encountered by future love dealers is rigid, intellectualizing, emotionally inhibited parents who are not in touch with their own needs and feelings. They are often striving, upwardly mobile people who measure success and personal worth by a monetary standard. They don't dislike their children and don't intend to be cruel to them, but sometimes feel the children are in the way. And they don't understand their children any better than they understand themselves. Not uncommon is the mother who, when her child falls down and scratches a knee and comes home crying and seeking comfort and reassurance, feels only discomfort. Instead of hugging the child and expressing affection, she pats him awkwardly on the head and says, "Stop your crying now, and I'll give you a cookie!"

The experience of being loved is necessary in order to develop a healthy self-concept and self-respect. People who have never known love find it virtually impossible to love others. Satisfaction of the need for love is as important for psychological development as satisfaction of the hunger need is for physical survival. Children who have never felt loved grow to feel worthless, unwanted, inferior. They not only feel unloved, but unlovable. In most cases, they begin to believe that they are unworthy and do not deserve to be loved. Consequently, the only way to get love is either to buy it or steal it.

Motivated by their gnawing hunger for affection, many love-starved individuals set out to make the money they feel they need to buy the desired love. If the amount of money they can earn honestly does not produce the love they seek, they may become desperate and seek drastic ways to get more money. Such was the plight of a thirty-six-year-old Michigan divorcée. As the assistant vice-president of a bank, she admitted to embezzling $760,000, most of which was spent on a lover she ultimately lost. Among the gifts the female Santa Claus bestowed on her lover were a $200,000 home, a $65,000 boat, a Rolls-Royce, a Mercedes, and a vacation retreat worth $137,000.[9]

Without money, love dealers, especially love buyers, are merely spectators rather than participants in the game of life. They feel lonely and alienated and sit on the sidelines watching life go by. Like a gambler, the love dealer needs money to get into the game. And like the compulsive gambler, life is empty and meaningless for them unless they are playing. In fact, some compulsive gamblers are also love dealers. While the dynamics vary, many compulsive gamblers report that they feel "dead" inside most of the time, and only "come alive" from the time they put the bet down until they find out whether they have won or lost. Some admit that winning or losing is the symbolic equivalent of being told one is loved or rejected by Dame Fortune, who is really a substitute for mother. As one compulsive gambler described it, "When I win, I feel a warm glow all over, like a baby at its mother's breast. But when I lose, I get a cold, clammy feeling that grabs me by the throat, and I feel depressed and empty."

HOW TO TELL THE REAL SANTA CLAUS

The problem in identifying the real Santa Claus stems from the fact that there are so many impostors. Some godfathers, for example, give away gifts and money and at first glance may be mistaken for Santa. On closer inspection, however, it becomes clear that the godfather is more concerned with dominating and controlling people than with buying their love. And some loving parents bestow gifts and money on their children. But they are gifts rather than bribes. They are given *out of* love, not to *buy* love. Such parents can easily be distinguished from the mother described in the following letter to Dear Abby:

Dear Abby:

What do you think of a 55-year-old mama's boy who gave his girlfriend an engagement ring in 1970 but does not allow her to show it to anybody because he doesn't want his mother to find out?

Well, I am the girlfriend. I have gone with Arthur for 10 years and I am pretty sick of this setup. I met his mother just once, when Arthur took her to the eye doctor. He let me go along for the ride. He never told her I was his girlfriend, though. The problem is, Arthur's mother has money, and she says if he marries, she will leave it all to the church.

He was so confused two years ago he wrote to you, and you told him to talk to his pastor. He said he did, and the pastor told him he was lucky to have such a wonderful mother.

What am I supposed to do now? I am 48 and not getting any younger.

ARTHUR'S GIRL [10]

Although in the song "Santa Claus Is Coming to Town," the

lyrics state that "He's making a list, and checking it twice. He's gonna find out who's naughty and nice," the real Santa Claus can't say no to anyone. No matter how ridiculous the request or how undeserving the asker, love dealers are compelled to accommodate. They buy raffle tickets they don't want, donate time and money to causes they don't believe in, spend more for presents than they can afford, and give them to people they don't like. They are conditioned to say yes to any request from anyone, and the word "no" seems to be missing from their vocabulary. They are so afraid of being unloved if they refuse anyone that people frequently take advantage of them.

The real Santa Claus is rarely found alone. Not only does the compelling need for love make isolation unbearable, but the trade-off between them demands that a love seller team up with a love buyer and vice versa. Unfortunately, since neither buyer nor seller has any capacity for mature love, the commodity that they exchange is pretty superficial and not very satisfying. They are both dealing in a commodity that they don't understand, and, in the end, neither profits from the transaction. Love stealers are also surrounded by people. They often resemble the department store Santa Claus, who has lines of people waiting to receive goodies and promises which, if forthcoming, are paid for by someone else. To maintain their disguise as givers, love stealers need a receptive audience. Also, as with successful pickpockets, the bigger the audience, the more chance of stealing and the less chance of getting caught.

Some of the most successful Santa Clauses double as politicians. They have learned that to win the endearment of their constituents as well as to win elections, they must make elaborate promises to the voters. However, most campaign promises cost money, which ultimately comes from the people themselves. The clever politician, therefore, combines the best of Santa Claus with the best of Robin Hood by promising to take from the rich and give to the poor. Since the poor outnumber the rich, the politician wins the undying love and admiration of a majority of the voters.

TAKING OFF THE SANTA CLAUS SUIT

Love dealers, because they have never learned to give or accept love freely, feel compelled to buy, sell, or steal it. And, in the process of growing up in a money-oriented society, they find it difficult to accept the fact that something that is *given away* is really more valuable than something which people are willing to *pay* for. Yet, if they are dissatisfied with the quality of love they are dealing in, as all love dealers must ultimately be, they will have to come to that conclusion. They will have to learn to say, "Why should I pay for it when I can get it for free?" or "Why bother to steal it when they're giving it away?"

Karl Abraham cites the case of a young man he saw while serving as an army psychiatrist in Germany during World War I. N., as Abraham refers to him, was the youngest child in a large but rather poor family. The other children were at least half grown when N. was born—unplanned and unwanted. As a small child he was regarded simply as a burden on the family budget. He felt that his parents and his brothers and sisters not only did not love him, but were hostile to him. By the time he was five, he scorned his parents as they scorned him. He wanted to have rich parents who would not regard him as a financial liability. In kindergarten, he would play only with the children of well-to-do families. Beginning at that early age, N. stole money to buy toys on a par with those of his wealthy playmates. He also made an effort to show his most attractive side to every person who could substitute for his mother or his father or his brothers and sisters. Every teacher and every student would have to be fond of him, would have to provide a perpetual source of gratification.

As he grew older, he claimed his greatest pleasure was to feel that "everything is revolving around me," which was the opposite of what he ordinarily felt as a child. Although he was able to make a large number of surrogate parents and siblings "love" him, he also felt compelled to disappoint them as a matter of revenge. He did this primarily through stealing money, embezzling, and running up bills he never paid. Dr. Abraham's evaluation of N. was that he was essentially incurable; that his pathological state was permanent and unalterable.

Shortly after his discharge from the army, however, N. met an older woman who took a maternal interest in him. She was a widow who owned a business and offered him a position where he could develop his artistic talents. Later their relationship became more romantic and they were married. The marriage provided him an increased social status as well as financial stability and a feeling of being truly loved by his "little mother." After N. had been married four years, Dr. Abraham saw him again and felt that a tremendous transformation had taken place, possibly even a "cure through love." [11]

While the case of N. is somewhat extreme and the "cure" is somewhat unusual, it does point out the underlying basis of the love dealer's psychological makeup. First, there is a void created by the lack of a loving relationship with parents or parent substitutes during childhood. Then the individual confuses money with love and begins to get involved in unhealthy interpersonal relationships because of the confusion. And, finally, the only way to resolve the Santa Claus syndrome is to learn how to give and accept love.

Most people claim that love is an important, if not *the most* important part of life. And few would deny that they want a deep and meaningful love relationship. Yet millions of these same people, including love dealers, avoid emotional intimacy at all cost. They give it lip service, but secretly they are terrified of it. By not allowing themselves to "fall in love," they avoid the possibility of being rejected by others. Saying "I love you" with meaning makes one vulnerable to potential ridicule or emotional hurt by the other person. For love dealers this is a frightening thought since they have been there before.

On the other hand, treating love as a business proposition makes life much safer. Only one's money is at stake, not one's ego. If love is offered for a price and is turned down, no one feels particularly devastated or humiliated. It is a relatively impersonal transaction. There may be some haggling over price or terms, or some excuse about why the deal cannot be consummated, but not the empty, depressed, and desolate feelings of the stereotypical rejected lover. Some people mourn the loss of a business deal, but not with the pathos and anguish that have been captured in Shakespeare's *Romeo and Juliet* or W. C. Handy's "St. Louis Blues."

For those who are tired of the sham of bartering for love, it is necessary to stop hiding behind the safety of money. Money is the Santa Claus suit that conceals the real feelings of the love dealer and protects the person from a real emotional encounter. Like the "Ho, ho, ho!" of the department store Santa, the emotional response of the love dealer is shallow and indiscriminate. It is applied equally to anyone and everyone.

Once the money manipulation defense is dropped from intimate interpersonal relations, one is confronted with the possible anxiety that comes from being in a position of loving and being loved. Loving another person involves some kind of commitment to please and satisfy that person. Accepting love requires a responsibility not to take advantage of the other person's vulnerability.

It is no doubt difficult for the very wealthy person to become involved emotionally with others without feeling that money is partly responsible for the involvement. The late J. Paul Getty, for example, received thousands of proposals of marriage from women he had never met but who knew of his financial status. Many even stated that they would be willing to waive the formality of marriage and overwhelm him with love and companionship provided appropriate financial arrangements were made beforehand.[12]

For most people, however, the buying, selling, trading, and stealing of love is a defense against emotional commitment. If they really want to experience the fulfillment of a rewarding love relationship, they must be willing to become involved, to make a commitment. They must be willing to give love without expecting anything in return except the pleasure of giving. And they must learn to accept love without feeling unworthy or guilty.

9

THE AUTONOMY WORSHIPERS

ADDRESSING AN INDIANA REGIMENT TOWARD THE END OF THE Civil War, Abraham Lincoln remarked, "I have always thought that all men should be free; but if any should be slaves, it should be first those who desire it for themselves, and secondly those who desire it for others. Whenever I hear any one arguing for slavery, I feel a strong impulse to see it tried on him personally."

This remark by Lincoln aptly states the enduring theme of autonomy worshipers. Their burning desire is to escape the shackles of domination and control by others and to live their lives exactly as they see fit. Theirs is a "live and let live" attitude toward others, with a tendency to become enraged if anyone seeks to interfere with their freedom. In this regard, power grabbers are seen as potential enemies, security collectors are viewed as "slaves," because they are willing to give up their freedom and independence for money, while love dealers are viewed as pathetic.

Autonomy worshipers fall into two groups. The first perceives money as the means of buying freedom, while the other perceives it as the enemy of freedom because of its power over people.

Specifically, the former group accepts money as a necessary evil and sees its accumulation as a passport to autonomy. The more one can accumulate, the less dependent one is on the structure of a job or the dictates of other people. Also, the more money one has, the less time must be devoted to earning it, and the more time is available to do what one pleases. The second group, however, views money as an unnecessary evil. From this perspective, the greed for money and power is the cause of people seeking to dominate and manipulate others and, thus, to deny them their freedom. Consequently, some in this group turn their backs on money and thumb their noses at the economic system, while others actively rebel against it and seek to destroy the system they see as oppressive.

In most cases, neither group is strongly attracted to work. While many are gainfully employed, they work out of necessity rather than by choice, or in some instances are fortunate in being able to earn money doing the things they most enjoy doing, such as painting, dancing, sailing, or professional sports, and, thus, do not consider it work. Rebellion against regimentation and resistance to rigid hours of employment or any type of confinement are the basic attitudes. Many drift into selling jobs, not only because of the independence of action these positions provide, but also because being on a commission basis may mean there are no limits to the amount of money they can make. Some go into business for themselves so they won't have to take orders from anyone.

The life-style of autonomy worshipers varies with their income, but the pattern is likely to be the same—only on a lesser or a grander scale. One young, little-known artist, for example, made more money painting house numbers on curbs in residential areas of Southern California than he did painting landscapes. When he earned enough money to buy a tank of gas, he would head for the beach and spend the rest of the day surfing. A few years later, when his paintings became much in demand and he had more money than he ever imagined possible, he gave up painting house numbers but not surfing. Now when he hears the surf is up in Australia, he will hop on a plane and fly to Australia for an afternoon of surfing and return a few hours later.

THE FREEDOM BUYER

Money, to freedom buyers, is the means of escaping an intolerable life of servitude. To this group servitude means something a little different than it does to most people. For them, it means any order, command, or suggestion that restricts autonomy or limits independence. While most people take a certain amount of these demands in stride, freedom buyers inwardly bristle, become incensed, and vow to create a life that makes it possible to resist ever submitting to such "indignities."

Money is seen as providing the clout to protect one from being pushed around. Unlike power grabbers, however, theirs is not a hunger to control or dominate others, but rather the desire to be left alone. Only enough power is sought to make it possible to tell anyone who tries to intimidate or tell them what to do to "go to hell!"

Money also means not having to be dependent upon anyone for a job or a favor. In this sense, freedom buyers will often *insist* on paying their own way to avoid the feeling of being indebted to anyone. When they argue unreasonably about picking up the tab at a restaurant or bar, their motive, unlike that of love buyers, is not to win friends or to play the "nice guy." They want independence, not love.

The more money, the more freedom. Preferably, they would inherit it so they wouldn't have to waste time in onerous activities earning it. Because they have developed a strong time-urgency, stemming from a feeling that doing anything other than what one wants to do constitutes wasted time, they feel a pressure to get the money in a hurry.

The Underlying Personality. The primary driving force behind most of the behavior of freedom buyers is the avoidance of dependency. They do, in fact, have strong dependency hunger, but they devote an exorbitant amount of energy to denying and repressing it and pretending it doesn't exist. This fear of dependency often makes them appear aloof and distant and, in extreme cases, almost paranoid in their suspicions and distrust of those whom they perceive might want to entrap them.

Ken Mason, an autonomy worshiper, was a thirty-three-year-old bachelor. Tall, ruggedly handsome, and perpetually suntanned, he found women attractive and enjoyed their company, but never let himself become too involved. While enjoying the chase, whenever the relationship seemed to get too serious, he managed to break it off.

Ken became a physician because science came easily to him and the practice of medicine could provide him with freedom and income sufficient to allow him to do the things he really wanted to do. Unlike his father, who was a country doctor in a rural community in Iowa, Ken moved to the city and specialized in anesthesiology. "In something over thirty years, Dad has never taken a vacation," he would tell himself with some feeling of disgust. "He's been on call twenty-four hours a day, seven days a week. Ever since mother died when I was born, his patients have been his whole life, and surely there is more to life than that. I plan to find it!"

As an anesthesiologist, he was hospital based and therefore he was not tied down to a private practice. When surgery was finished, so was his responsibility. His reputation was good so he could get as much work as he wanted and make as much money as he needed for comfortable living. The great flexibility of his life-style was what appealed to him most.

He would take three- and four-day weekends to go skiing or backpacking. He often attended medical conferences, not because he was particularly interested in the program, but because it gave him a chance to break up his routine, see another part of the world, and meet new people; and it was tax deductible. In general, whenever he had enough money to take off, he went. Occasionally, he decided not to work simply because he got involved in reading a book and didn't want to put it aside or because he really would rather spend the day in bed. Since he refused to keep a rigid schedule, or make any kind of advance commitment, his social and professional calendar was rarely planned more than a day or two in advance.

Some of the colleagues he was friendly with would chide him about his "immaturity," his "irresponsibility," or his lack of "financial stability." When they tried to advise him about investments or ways to develop financial security, Ken would laugh and reply, "Security is for the scared, the miserly, and the old. Talk to me about it when I'm sixty-five."

A colleague who had gone to medical school with Ken and who later went into psychiatry approached him one day in the hospital dining room. During the conversation over lunch, he suggested to Ken that his obsession with freedom might, on a deeper level, be an attempt to run away from something he feared. Ken tried to hide his annoyance, and replied half-kiddingly, "The trouble with you, Charlie, is that you read so many of those damn psychiatry books that you begin to believe them. You think there is something sinister in the unconscious of everyone." But Charlie's observation stayed with Ken and it bothered him. Ken kept his distance from Charlie from then on.

What Charlie was responding to was Ken's inordinate resistance to any kind of dependency. His mother died in childbirth, and his father employed an aging housekeeper to care for Ken. His father partially blamed himself for his wife's death and, in a sense, devoted the rest of his life to atoning for it by taking care of the sick and dying. And he partially blamed Ken because if she hadn't been pregnant with him, his wife would not have died. Although he knew it was irrational to hold the baby responsible, it affected him enough so that he could not be very affectionate with his son. Besides, in the little time he was at home, he was too tired or too preoccupied to take much interest in Ken or really even to get to know him.

In the kind of atmosphere in which Ken found himself while growing up, it was necessary to become self-sufficient. Ken got recognition for dressing himself, feeding himself, brushing his teeth, learning to read, and especially for not bothering anyone or asking for anything. When he did seek attention, he was either ignored or called a "baby."

While still very young, Ken would sometimes watch the housekeeper bake bread and iron clothes, but his presence seemed to irritate her and she would shoo him outdoors. "Don't be bothering me now," she would tell him. "Get on outside and play!" Occasionally, when his father sat in his favorite chair reading the paper, Ken would sit nearby or try to crawl up in his lap, but the response would usually be negative. "Not now, Son! I'm tired. Can't you find something to do?" When older, Ken would be given money to go bowling or to the movies when he "got in the way."

Like all freedom buyers, Ken learned that to feel dependent —to want to be close, to need comfort and reassurance, to lean on others for support and guidance—was to open himself up to pain and ridicule. Therefore, these needs became something to overcome and repress. He spent many hours in solitary activity, reading in the library, fishing in the lake outside of town, and inventing things in his garage; anything to avoid having people tell him what to do or push him aside.

Freedom buyers know that with money they have more options available to them and more control over what they do with their lives than they have without it. With sufficient money, one can choose whether or not to work, whether to stay home or to travel, and, most of all, whom to be with and for how long.

The underlying frustration and craving for dependency is there, however. Occasionally these needs prevail and the freedom buyer falls in love with someone who also appears to be a free spirit. Ironically, this usually ends in disaster as the underlying, all-consuming dependency comes pouring through and suffocates and drives the loved one away. This rejection further convinces the freedom buyer that it is dangerous to love or depend on anyone else.

In fantasy it is possible to have a relationship with another "free spirit" in which both can experience freedom and togetherness simultaneously. However, the reality of this actually happening eludes them because their independence is a facade, and, when in love, they quickly become possessive and dependent, although they deny it.

The Payoff. Freedom buyers are often interesting people to know socially. Since they tend to lead unconventional lives and may even flout contemporary mores, they present a kind of original and rebellious view of life and values that seems attractive to others. Also, since they tend not to have strong attachments, they are mobile and free to do and experience many things that others are not.

Because they have the "courage" to do what many other people would like to do, freedom buyers are likely to win the admiration as well as the envy of friends and acquaintances. While love dealers live for approval and never get enough, freedom buyers don't really care about it one way or another and often wind up getting more than they want. Since they "march to a different drummer" and seem unconcerned about what the rest of the world is doing or thinking, they are often a source of fascination to the conventionally "tied-down" conformist.

The Cost. Because they are impatient to get at whatever it is that turns them on, freedom buyers sometimes turn into freedom gamblers. They take big risks to try to get money in a hurry and often pay the consequences in significant losses.

The two adjectives most often used to describe freedom buyers by their friends, family, and employers are "undependable" and "irresponsible." While freedom buyers may protest and claim they are not irresponsible but merely insuring they are not being tied down, they are inclined to be a source of pain to those they get involved with. Hosts and hostesses never know whether or not to expect them until they arrive. If they go golfing or water skiing over a weekend, they may not show up for work until Wednesday. About the time an employer feels they have learned their job and can do it without supervision, they are apt to quit.

The people who are likely to get hurt most by freedom buyers are those who become romantically involved with them. Freedom buyers, while they may be attractive, charming, and interesting, have an aversion to emotional closeness because of their fear of dependence. At one level, they desire closeness but are inclined to run, leaving the other person frustrated, hurt, and angry. Parental responsibility is often felt as restrictive and confining, and it is not uncommon for freedom buyers to walk out on their children as well as their spouses. The children are all too often left with a burden of guilt for "driving the parent away" because of their needs and demands.

Because they are unable or unwilling to relinquish a portion of their independence and freedom for intimacy, freedom buyers not only hurt those who love them but ultimately find themselves painfully isolated, particularly as they grow older. The price they pay for independence is a constant frustration of dependency hunger. The end result of extreme independence is aloneness and isolation from the world.

THE FREEDOM FIGHTER

Whereas freedom buyers seek money to purchase their independence from the regimentation and drudgery of social conformity and to buy the time to pursue their dreams and desires, freedom fighters reject money and all it stands for. Money and the materialistic society that worships it are seen as the cause of enslavement of the majority of the people.

The anti-money contingent may cover a broad spectrum of the population. Among them are the politically oriented ones, who ally themselves with Communist and Socialist groups and advocate equal distribution of wealth and limitations on the accumulation of money and material possessions. Also included are the technocrats, who believe in the elimination of money altogether and think of it as an obsolete holdover from a primitive age, not at all suitable to a time of high technology and social enlightenment.[1] Money would be replaced with a certificate based on a measure of energy, rather than gold or silver. Each adult would receive a certificate equal to the amount the person contributed to the production of the nation's energy. The certificate would be for immediate use and could not be hoarded, therefore eliminating the possibility of accumulating wealth.

The freedom fighters also include some of the militant minority groups, a large part of the "drug culture," the commune movement, revolutionary activists, and others. Some simply turn their backs on the scramble for money and refuse to compete. Others are more militant. Like the Hungarian Freedom Fighters of 1956, these militant freedom fighters view their struggle as a holy war.

"One radical youth leader whose father was a top U.S. utilities magnate and who regularly received a handsome allowance from his indulgent sire remarked about this incongruity: 'If [the old man] wants to finance the revolution, that's okay with me.' The lad summed up his social program graphically: 'Kill all rich people. Break up their cars and apartments.' When reminded that his parents were prime candidates, he replied, 'Yeah. Bring the revolution home. Kill your parents, that's where it's really at.' And still the allowance checks kept coming." [2]

Like Patrick Henry, freedom fighters have as their motto, "Give me liberty or give me death!" They want complete freedom in the way they conduct their lives. Not all are militant in their opposition to the monetary and social philosophy of the establishment. Some express their aggression passively by defying conventions and assuming a life-style that scorns money and all it represents.

As an example, a former mathematician and systems analyst quit his top-secret job in 1966, after trying psychedelic drugs, and became a wandering poet. He travels barefoot around the country, riding the rails and living with hoboes. According to a friend, "He lives on very little and virtually never works for money, knowing that if he doesn't get a meal within the next two or three hours he can go a day or two or three without food. This attitude gives him enormous flexibility. . . . If he felt he had to eat at 6:00 P.M. sharp he might not get food very often. He would probably get so wrapped up in the meal-getting process, would get so hassled by it, that people wouldn't love him as a poet or be as likely to give him a meal in the first place just for the fun of having him around." [3]

The Underlying Personality. Freedom fighters, even more than freedom buyers, feel alienated from the mainstream of American life. Frequently they are products of the youth movement. There are few late bloomers among their ranks. The in-group of the adult establishment, as seen by the freedom fighters, is a competitive, enslaving, money-worshiping society.

Outsiders have three choices open to them: (1) They can try to become eligible for membership in the in-group by adhering to the rules and by identifying with the values of its members. This essentially is the pattern of the empire builder, who not only joins the establishment, but becomes a leader of it. (2) They can decide it is not worth the effort to become accepted. This may either be an honest appraisal of comparative values, or it may be a rationalization because they don't really feel they can qualify or compete. This second alternative has been taken by the drop-outs, hippies, flower people, commune members, and followers of certain religious sects, such as the Hare Krishnas—persons who might be termed passive-aggressive freedom fighters. (3) They can denounce the values of the in-group and seek to destroy it. This is the position taken by the more revolutionary and militant freedom fighters, such as the student activists, the New Left, and the so-called urban guerrillas.

The majority of both the passive-aggressive and the militant freedom fighters are struggling to resolve internal conflicts and clarify confused values. Their perception of money and the capitalistic system as the evil and oppressive ogre is basically the outgrowth of highly personalized feelings and experiences, and is covered over with idealism, humanism, and concern for the underdog. For example, the rebellious adolescent son feels inadequate and overwhelmed by a powerful, perhaps empire-building father, and also feels he can never compete successfully with his father and can never become the kind of person his father would be proud of. Intensifying these feelings, his father may continually cut him down and make him feel inadequate. The only way for him to escape being swallowed up in the money-power struggle is not to compete. If he is strong enough or angry enough, he may actively seek to destroy the system. If not, he may simply turn his back and walk away. The following excerpt from the notes of a college revolutionary of the sixties illustrates the conflict between father and son:

Long hair on men, however, has been known to make some people sick.

My father, for instance. On July 8, 1968, he alleged that long hair on his sons made him sick. "You look like a woman," he said. "I'll get a haircut," I said. That threw him off, but only for a moment. "If I were a girl," he continued, "I wouldn't like the way you look." "You are not a girl," I said, "and anyway, I said I'd get a haircut." "I don't see how your hair could possibly get any longer," he added. "Would you agree," I asked, "that if I let it grow for another two months, it would get longer?" "Maybe," he conceded, "but it just couldn't possibly be any longer."

My father talks about the bad associations people make when they see someone with hair. I come back with the bad associations people make when they see someone replete with a shiny new Cadillac that looks like it should have a silk-raimented coachman standing at each fender. But as for bad vibrations emanating from my follicles, I say great. I want the cops to sneer and the old ladies swear and the businessmen worry. I want everyone to see me and say "There goes an enemy of the state," because that's where I'm at, as we say in the Revolution biz.[4]

Some people drop out of the money rat race because of religious conviction or because they find sufficient satisfaction in what they are doing in life so that material possessions and money are not important to them. It would seem easy to understand why people who are born into poverty and see no legitimate way of getting out, while others around them have an overabundance of wealth, might rise up in rebellion and turn on the privileged few. It is much harder to fathom why the sons and daughters of the very rich would do the same thing. Yet that has been a common trend in the United States during the past decade or so. As one writer on the subject put it:

> The Weathermen, that iconoclastic wing of the student movement that espoused Jacobean terrorism, displayed a pattern of behavior that will fascinate psychologists and sociologists for years to come. They numbered during the peak of their influence only several hundred members, the vast majority of whom were sons and daughters of America's richest families. Indeed, the Weathermen joked that the number-one qualification for membership was that one's father must be earning at least $50,000 a year.[5]

Freedom fighters from well-to-do homes, however, have a number of explanatory factors in their backgrounds. Many see their families as slaves to fortune making and resent the time and energy their parents spent on business rather than on them. At the same time, they never knew the feeling of being in want or need of money, and most people tend to discount anything that comes too easily.

Some felt guilty about their own affluence when others in the world had little. By rejecting money and living in squalor or off the land, they could dispose of guilt feelings, as they also could by idealistically supporting a revolution. Many sons and daughters of wealthy and important persons feel that whatever success or recognition they achieve in life is due to the money and power of their parents and not their own merit. To them there is no way of winning, and, consequently, they resent the money and influence and seek to dissociate themselves from it.

While the vast majority of passive-aggressive, noncompetitive freedom fighters and the rank-and-file militants seemed to be rebelling against the political and economic values of their parents, the tiny majority of hard-core "activists" actually came from a different background. According to a study by Yale psychologist Kenneth Kenniston, "The fathers tended to be college faculty, lawyers, doctors, rather than businessmen, white- or blue-collar employees. Family incomes above $15,000 were ordinary. Moreover, the activists were *not* rebelling against parental politics; instead, they were pushing an already liberal or leftist attitude to an extreme. They were frustrated by the differences they thought they saw between the high ideals and values their parents espoused and the lives their parents actually lead. They tended to be students of humanities and social sciences, with extraordinary interest in abstract thought and religious liberalism. And they suffered from greater anxieties, a trait with a well-documented tendency to convert to frustration and hate." [6]

Public opinion pollster Samuel Lubell, who interviewed more than 1,100 students at thirty-six college campuses over a four-year period, also found that the ringleaders of the student violence movement were the sons and daughters of radical parents.

Lubell concluded, "These students comprised the organizing core for the Students for a Democratic Society; they also supplied the 'revolutionary' ideology and tactics. . . . Far from being in family revolt, these students were projecting the radicalism of their parents." [7]

Freedom fighters can thus be considered to comprise a heterogeneous group—revolutionary activists, frustrated idealists, passive noncompetitors, members of oppressed minority groups, spoiled brats, concerned liberals, misfits, political and economic dissidents, nihilists, and a smattering of other types. What they all have in common is a belief that money is the root of all evil and that by abolishing money or distributing it more evenly, the quality of life could be improved. Behind this belief, they feel that the struggle to acquire money is a trap and that if they get caught up in it, it will rob them of their freedom and independence to live their lives as they choose.

The Payoff. Dedication to a cause gives meaning to a person's life, and many who become freedom fighters had previously felt alienated and without an identity to define themselves by. Many had dropped out of the rat race to "find" themselves. By identifying with the counterculture they acquire a purpose. Whether the opposition to the money culture is passive or active, there is now a goal in life and, by identifying with that goal and striving to accomplish their mission, they gain a sense of self-worth and importance that had previously seemed unattainable.

Camaraderie and companionship are also often rewards for joining the anti-money forces. Sharing a common enemy leads to mutual support and reassurance, and many freedom fighters have had a past history of "not belonging." They never felt accepted by their peers until they took a stand against their parental upbringing and joined forces with similar dissidents.

Andrea Compton was shy and awkward; she felt ill at ease in social relationships with peers of both sexes. She attended Catholic girls' schools until her junior year in high school, at which time she persuaded her parents to let her attend public high school in the hope that her social life would improve. It didn't. Classmates regarded her shyness as an air of superiority and snobbishness since they knew that her father was an officer of a major corporation and that she lived in the most expensive house in an expensive neighborhood.

Shortly after she graduated from high school, she happened to run into a girl she had known slightly a few years earlier. The other girl had left the Catholic Church and had become a follower of the Reverend Sun Myung Moon. She recognized Andrea and approached her, asking for a donation. Andrea was flattered that the girl recognized her and gave her twenty dollars. Because it was the first time Andrea had been asked to join anything, she was also receptive to the other girl's proselytizing on behalf of the Unification Church. It didn't take much convincing before Andrea decided to join. Since she had long ago determined that it was money that isolated her from other people and kept her from the friendships she so desperately wanted, it was not difficult for her to give up a life of affluence for the Spartan life of the religious commune. The acceptance and the feeling of belonging she got were well worth the sacrifice.

The Cost. It has been said, "Idealism and revolution are luxuries that only the young can afford." Certainly, most people become more cynical and more conservative as they grow older. Freedom fighting is rarely a lifetime occupation. Most of the people caught up in the movement eventually make some sort of compromise with society. A few of the former leaders capitalize on their switch to more conventional social, political, and economic philosophies. Former Harvard psychologist-turned-drug advocate Timothy Leary returned from exile and became a highly paid public speaker. And former revolutionary student activist Tom Hayden ran for the United States Senate from California. Some freedom fighters, such as Richard Neville, one-time editor of the underground paper *Oz*, became disillusioned. Before he dropped out of the freedom-fighting business, Neville was complaining about hippies who gave him bad checks and stole his possesions after using his house as a crash pad.[8]

Freedom fighters confuse idealism with feelings, whereas, in reality, their idealism is a *defense against* feeling. Consequently, many have wasted their early creative years as well as their energy and talents fighting the wrong battles.

Families of freedom fighters also pay a price. Parents whose children have joined religious groups like the Hare Krishna movement, Scientology, or the Unification Church frequently claim that their children have been brainwashed by these groups. Some have been involved in lengthy and expensive legal battles to try to extricate their offspring from the "control" of these organizations. Rather than finding freedom, the parents claim their children have become slaves. One ex-Moonie, in explaining her indoctrination, stated, "It's easy to get pulled into it. Sometimes there are 40 days of lectures where they talk about God, love, support and changing the world. Everything seems so logical." Once one becomes a follower, she claimed, "Your *whole life* is dedicated to Rev. Moon." Although it has the trappings of freedom, this is really an illusion. Followers have virtually no freedom. "The day was always organized for you and decisions were always made for you." [9]

A more far-reaching cost, however, is the shock and disillusionment that faces so many freedom fighters sooner or later. For many and varied reasons they become frustrated, unhappy, and angry people. Either for logical or emotional reasons they view money as the root of their problems. They see it as some sort of cancer that destroys people and society and the environment. And they see themselves as engaged in a holy war to rid the world of this scourge. However, money is but the scapegoat upon which to vent their frustrations and bitterness. Even if they manage to establish a relatively money-free life-style, their problems do not disappear. It is just as psychologically naïve to believe that doing away with money will solve all of mankind's problems as it is to think they can be resolved by putting a million dollars in everyone's pocket.

UNDERSTANDING THE AUTONOMY WORSHIPER

While autonomy worshipers fear dependency and seek to avoid it by adhering to a life-style based on independence and freedom, some also deny an underlying desire to control and manipulate others. Their stand for freedom and independence is an attempt to repress and deny their underlying desire to dominate. However, leaders of many nomadic religious cults and revolutionary groups exert rigid controls over their members, and a number of entertainers who have made fortunes appealing to the counterculture have built their own empires and hired their own lackeys.

To what extent, if any, primitive psychological or even perhaps genetic factors play a role in the development of freedom-worshiping traits is not known, although these traits are sometimes obvious very early in life. The parents of one freedom-worshiping boy observed that at the age of only a few weeks, before the infant could even crawl, he was content to be placed on a blanket on the floor. Any attempt to place him in a playpen, however, was met with cries of rage until he was removed.

The one consistent theme that runs through the backgrounds of autonomy worshipers, however, is that for one reason or another, dependency on other people and on the world early in life was perceived as a threatening rather than a rewarding experience.

While the conflict between the idealism of the young and the pragmatism and cynicism of their parents is nothing new, the protests of the youthful counterculture of the sixties reached epidemic proportions. A number of factors contributed to that phenomenon. First was the sheer number of young people. The babies of the post-World War II boom had grown up and overflowed the college campuses. In a little over a decade, the college population swelled from 2.6 million to 7 million. Second, the parents of these college-aged youths had survived the Great Depression of the thirties and a major world war in the forties. They were determined their families would have the financial advantages that they themselves had been denied. The prosperity of the times made that possible in many cases, although often parents had to work long hours or hold down more than one job to provide the standard of living they desired. Many young people, observing their parents' drive to get ahead financially and to accumulate bigger houses and cars and bank accounts and more expensive furniture, decided the struggle for money wasn't worth the effort and dropped out.

A third, and somewhat related, factor in the protests of the sixties was the great advance in technical and scientific progress during this period. Many believed the pendulum was swinging too far in the direction of scientific objectivity and away from human and spiritual values. The original hippie movement was at least partly a protest against that trend. Fourth, although many children growing up after World War II felt their parents were too busy making money and becoming slaves to possessions to offer them the love and attention they desired, in many ways postwar America was a child-centered society. Children were generally treated with a good deal of permissiveness, and many were pampered and spoiled to a much greater degree than had been true in previous generations. Parents had been made to feel so guilty about the potential psychological trauma that might befall their children if they were frustrated, that they were conditioned to give in to most of their children's demands, financial and otherwise. This even carried over into campus protests. Perhaps for the first time in history, their elders listened to the complaints of student dissidents and gave in to many of their demands. Some observers were not only amazed at this capitulation, but felt that "rewarding" young people for their rebellious activity actually escalated campus violence. On the other hand, Dr. S. I. Hayakawa, the acting president of San Francisco State College when riots broke out on campus, took a strong fatherly stand and was uniquely successful in restoring order.

Rebellion against parental demands and parental values is certainly nothing new. For a long time it has been considered a normal part of growing up—an aspect of the rites of passage. It was generally accepted that children were, for the most part, molded by their parents, became adolescents and rebelled against their parents, then quit rebelling and became part of the adult establishment. Over the years, however, a strange transformation has been taking place. Parents and other adults have not only been *listening* to the younger generation, they have been looking to it for guidance. The young lead and the elders follow.

Young people are setting the styles in hairdos, clothes, music, automobiles, housing, and moral values.

The anthropologist Margaret Mead views this phenomenon of older people madly trying to keep up with their children and grandchildren as an outgrowth of the very rapid social change that has been taking place in America. Since young people are much more adept at coping with change than are older people, the older generations turn automatically to the younger for guidance. For example, young people generally know more about calculators and stereo components and the effect of nonbiodegradable pollutants on the environment than their parents will probably ever know. And their parents will turn to them for answers. This is essentially what happened during the campus riots of the sixties. There were some violent confrontations such as at Kent State, but to a larger extent than at any time in history, the students' complaints were heard and they had an impact on the adult society. They brought about definite changes in the "in-group" establishment. Not only were students given much more of a say in running the colleges and universities in the country, but their antiwar sentiment was fairly well accepted by a majority of the population; and some of the emphasis on federal spending was even shifted away from missiles and space programs to human rights and environmental programs.

WHEN DOES FREEDOM
BECOME ANARCHY?

Freedom, like love, security, and power, is a virtue in proper perspective. The telltale signs that freedom loving is becoming a manifestation of emotional and social anarchy can be identified, however.

Freedom lovers resent any injustice to themselves or others; anarchists rebel for the sake of rebellion.

Freedom lovers are generally positive in attitude; anarchists are angry and have a chip on their shoulders.

Freedom lovers accept a limited amount of obligation good-naturedly if they can't avoid it; anarchists rebel against *any* interference with their complete autonomy.

If you suspect your own freedom worshiping is a defensive flight from dependency, observe George Norris, whose friends, family, and acquaintances had been trying for years to tell him he was an irresponsible autonomy worshiper. After a heated argument with his wife about his "bullheadedness" and her "unreasonable demands" on his time and patience, George decided to listen to what other people were saying to him. The following is a partial list he collected within a few weeks' time.

His sister, Joan: "We'd love to have you and Virginia over for Thanksgiving, but I'm sure you won't decide what you're going to do that day until after the rest of us have eaten. I wish you'd learn to plan ahead."

His banker: "I'm sorry, Mr. Norris, but we can't approve your loan without a cosigner. If you could only establish a better credit rating . . ."

His employer: "I'm sorry, George. You've only been working here three days, I can't possibly let you have the rest of the week off."

His barber, Sam: "I know you've been a loyal customer for three months, but I can't let you have any more credit. Why don't you let your hair grow long like everybody else?"

His wife, Virginia: "Where on earth did you buy that ghastly tie? Last week you ran around in an undershirt and today you wear a purple shirt and a pornographic necktie!"

His ex-wife, Lois: "George Norris, I don't give a damn how inconvenient it is for you, if I don't have the child support money by Monday, I'm going to take you to court!"

His wife: "George, did you take the money out of my purse to play golf? I was saving that for the phone bill."

A fellow worker: "I can't believe it, George. You're forty-two years old and never had a savings account?"

His wife: "Sure, it would be nice to go to Acapulco, but we can't afford it."

The travel agent: "I know I said you could put the trip on a credit card, but this one has expired, and when I checked with the company, they said that you have already exceeded . . ."

A personnel clerk: "How's the application coming? Another piece of paper? Sure! Wow, how many jobs have you had?"

While freedom perhaps more than any other concept symbolizes the American ideal, autonomy worshipers, by being out of touch with the roots of their obsession, corrupt the concept by confusing freedom with license and by too often ignoring the rights and freedom of others in the name of autonomy and independence.

THE VARIABILITY OF MONEY MEANINGS

Although only four of the many psychological meanings of money—security, power, love, and autonomy—have been discussed, others could easily be added. It should also be noted that to some people money has more than one meaning. A person could have characteristics of both a love buyer and a security collector, for example. As one's finances and emotional development change, it is also possible to change one's perception of money. A person could conceivably change from a security collector to a power grabber to an autonomy worshiper. The types described in the preceding chapters should be viewed merely as examples of the many possible ways that human beings relate to money.

10

TREATING MONEY MADNESS

PSYCHOTHERAPISTS SPECIALIZE IN MARRIAGE COUNSELING, AL-coholism, sexual dysfunctions, childhood disorders, depression, or acute psychosis, but never money madness since money problems are usually considered to be secondary. And people rarely go into therapy because of money hang-ups since they are unlikely to see the connection between their money orientation and other problems. They talk about their unhappiness, their problems in interpersonal relations, their nightmares, and their ulcers, but not money. Consequently, they may even go through an entire experience of psychotherapy without mentioning this aspect of their existence.

Paradoxically, the type of money personality one has will largely determine the type of therapist one will seek out. For example, the freedom fighter will more likely be drawn to a less conventional therapist while the security collector will look for a bargain, picking the least expensive therapist available. The power grabber, of course, wants only "the best," meaning the most expensive.

PAYING FOR HELP—
AND WHAT IT MEANS

Psychotherapy is a service and therefore one of the first considerations is cost. Most psychoanalysts believe that successful analysis cannot take place without a financial sacrifice by the patient any more than it can without free association, dream interpretation, or the examination of transference. Therapists from other schools sometimes disagree. Just as they feel it is possible to do effective therapy without free association or the use of a couch, they believe that successful therapy can, under certain circumstances, take place when the patient pays a reduced fee or even no fee at all. Most psychotherapists expect to get paid for their services, however, and there are both rational and irrational factors that go into the determination of how much. It is not true, as many people think, that the quality of treatment is necessarily related to the cost.

Many underlying variables help determine fees for professional services. Therapists, like other people, have emotional investments in money and their own monetary styles and hangups. Some find security, prestige, or power in making large sums of money, driving expensive cars, and practicing in plush offices. Some have a need to work with the underprivileged, or with minorities; others have a need to serve the wealthy clientele of Beverly Hills or Park Avenue. Some therapists underestimate their worth and charge too little; some, in their grandiosity, overestimate their ability and charge too much. And some therapists feel guilty about charging for their services and are embarrassed about focusing on the issue of payment for therapy because therapy is supposed to involve caring. Caring and charging money are a difficult mix.

Entering psychotherapy generally means a decision to invest a substantial amount of money in oneself, with the hope of leading a more meaningful, more productive, and happier existence. No one can realistically predict how much it will cost, how long it will take, or what the results will be. Yet many people plunge into such a commitment with the same irrational money attitudes that prevail in other situations. For example, they may agree to higher fees than they can realistically afford because they want to impress the therapist. Or because admitting they can't afford the fee makes them feel worthless and inadequate. On the other hand, there are prospective patients who do a lot of comparison shopping—not for quality, but to find where they can get therapy the cheapest.

It is commonly accepted in the American culture that what is cheap has little value and what is expensive is valuable. Psychotherapists know that as well as anyone. One therapist expressed it as follows, "I know I'm a good therapist and I value my time. Therefore, I put a high price on it. In turn, patients value therapy more because they pay dearly for it. And they work harder and put more into it to get their money's worth."

This point of view is not uncommon among therapists, and in many cases it might be an accurate appraisal. In other instances it might simply be a rationalization. Certainly motivation is necessary for a patient to make progress in therapy, and money is a great motivator for many individuals. However, if there is sufficient motivation of other kinds, progress is also possible. Obviously, money is not the only motivator of human behavior. Both clinical and research evidence indicate that some people make great strides in therapy without making a significant financial sacrifice. Nor is it always true that the person who pays less has lower expectations or puts less effort into therapy. If therapy is less effective with the low-fee patient, it may be because the *therapist* expects less progress or doesn't work as hard because of the reduced fee. Conversely, some therapists have been known to *raise* their usual fee when they anticipate working with a particularly difficult patient. One well-known psychologist confessed, "Sure, I have a sliding scale of fees. I charge less for interesting, challenging patients and more for the tough ones and the boring ones. If I have to work harder or suffer more, I might as well get paid more for it!"

While psychotherapy is usually expensive by some standards, its cost in terms of money and emotional trauma must ultimately be weighed against the results. Some therapists reassure clients that if they are able to function more effectively because of therapy, they could conceivably earn many times the money they have invested in therapy. On the other hand, these same therapists may say to an ambitious empire builder, "I might be able to help you relax and enjoy life more, but you may lose your burning desire to make millions." Whatever fee is decided on by therapist and patient, and for whatever reasons that particular amount is chosen, the real value of psychotherapy can be determined only by the patient who has gone through it. The eminent psychiatrist Frieda Fromm-Reichmann speaks for all psychotherapy and not only psychiatry when she says, "Psychiatric services—that is, the attempt to help a person overcome his emotional difficulties in living—are priceless if successful or worthless if they fail." [1]

MONEY AS A MEANS
OF COMMUNICATION

Discussing fees with a therapist is frequently an unnerving experience—for both patient and therapist. Therapists who work in clinics can usually avoid this unpleasantness by delegating it to the intake worker or the receptionist. Therapists in private practice who can afford a receptionist can do the same thing. Some of the anxiety about dealing with fees can be minimized when the patient has insurance that pays at least part of the bill.

In the multitude of books and articles devoted to the subject of psychotherapy, very few mention the role of money as a therapeutic agent or the use and abuse of fees. The few that do deal with the problems of money lament the limited literature on the subject and stress the importance of being open and honest in discussing money and fees with patients. The authors then end their discourse by observing that apparently few therapists are able to live up to Freud's classic admonition to discuss money as frankly as one would discuss sexual matters: "By voluntarily introducing the subject of fees . . . he [the therapist] shows the patient that he himself has cast aside his false shame in these matters." [2] A few back up their contention that false shame still abounds in the minds of therapists by quoting from one of the rare research studies on the subject, such as the one conducted by the humanistic psychologist James Bugental. In polling a group of highly experienced therapists throughout the country, Bugental found that ninety percent could conceivably, under certain conditions, openly express anger toward a patient; seventy percent could conceivably socialize with a patient; but less than twenty-five percent felt that there might be *any* circumstance in which they would lend a patient money or ask for advance payments as a way of borrowing from a patient.[3]

Most of the writers who mention money in relation to psychotherapy limit their discussion to the setting of fees in the first interview. The impression one gets is that money is such a nasty subject that it is best to get it over with in a hurry so that it won't contaminate the relationship between patient and therapist later on. A few go beyond fee setting and talk about the pros and cons of charging for missed appointments. Rarely, however, does an author come to grips with the rich source of material available to the therapist who looks at the exchange of money between patient and therapist (or the withholding of it, as the case may be) as a means of nonverbal communication.

Rather than dispensing with the subject of money in the first interview, *the therapist needs to focus on the meaning of payment and nonpayment for services throughout the course of therapy.* Changes in the pattern of payment frequently reveal underlying changes in the client's perception of his relationship with the therapist. Understanding what is communicated through money transactions between patient and therapist then becomes the basis for understanding the use of money in other interpersonal relationships. The following examples illustrate some of the conscious and unconscious meanings of money in patient-therapist transactions.

1. Steve, a twenty-nine-year-old engineer, had been going to therapy on a weekly basis for several months. He habitually paid for each session at the end of the hour, since, "I don't like a lot of loose ends. I like to keep my bills current. That way I always know just where I stand." When two weeks went by

without the usual payment, the therapist decided to discuss the meaning of this withholding behavior. It turned out that Steve was angry with the therapist for making him look at the cowardly way he related to his father. He was trying to "punish" the therapist by withholding money, just as he tried to get back at his father by withholding his emotions.

2. Wanda, a very anxious thirty-four-year-old housewife, had been seeing a therapist twice a week for almost a year when her husband lost his job because of a drinking problem. Her therapist felt it would be unfortunate for her to interrupt therapy since she was just beginning to accept and deal with some important aspects of her personality, especially her repressed anger toward her father and her husband. Wanda agreed but stated that she simply could not afford to continue. It was finally agreed that the therapist would see her once a week instead of twice, and at no charge, until her husband went back to work. This arrangement seemed to work out for several weeks. Then one day Wanda came to therapy, angrily placed an envelope full of money on the therapist's desk, and exclaimed, "Now I can tell you what I really feel about you!" And for the rest of the hour she proceeded to let out the hostile feelings she had been harboring toward the therapist, who in her mind was partly confused with her father and her husband. While she was being seen for free, she had felt too guilty about her angry feelings to express them, but when she was able to pay what she owed the therapist, she no longer felt indebted to him and felt free to express herself and work through her hostile feelings.

3. Ramona was an attractive twenty-year-old college student. She consulted a therapist because she was having trouble concentrating on her studies since breaking up with her boy friend. In a short period of time, she developed an intense dependency upon the therapist. At the same time she stopped paying his bill. When the therapist was able to get Ramona to look at her feelings, it became clear that she had developed a strong attachment to him. In her fantasies, the therapist reciprocated her romantic feelings and their relationship was no longer one of patient and

doctor. As she phrased it, "It seemed profane to lower such a profound relationship to the level of prostitution, the kind of thing you can buy on any street corner."

4. Ed was referred for therapy by his family doctor because of a series of psychosomatic complaints. He began each session by handing the therapist a check and then saying, "Now Doc! This is what I want you to do . . ." As he did in his various business enterprises, Ed felt that when he paid the bill, he could give the orders.

5. Toni, a twenty-eight-year-old fashion designer, was offered an attractive position in another city after she had been in therapy for about eight months. After discussing the opportunity at length with her therapist, Toni decided to take the job. She had been delinquent in her payments to the therapist for reasons beyond her control, but with her new position, she was able to pay off her debts. Every month she sent the therapist a check until the bill was down to fifty dollars. The bill then went unheeded for a number of months, and the curiosity of the therapist was aroused. He wrote to the patient, inquiring about the unpaid debt. A short time later, the therapist received the following letter:

Dear Doctor _____:

I am a little embarrassed to say this, but I have been unable to bring myself to pay off the last of your bill. This may sound strange to you, but I see that fifty-dollar debt as an umbilical cord that ties me to you. I don't yet feel strong enough to cut it, but someday soon I know I will. Then I will send you a check. I hope you will understand.

Love,
TONI

6. Gordon was a graduate student in psychology. His father was a well-known psychiatrist and his mother had been a psychiatric social worker. Gordon grew up on Freud and Adler, and he often remarked that, with both his mother and father,

he felt more like a patient than a son. He was a bright but moody student and at times he would sink into deep depression. He had been in psychotherapy on several occasions, but not for long. He would usually begin feeling better and use that as a reason to quit therapy. On the last occasion, when the therapist was beginning to make him feel uncomfortable by exploring his insecurities, Gordon stopped paying his bill. He made excuses and promises, but no money was forthcoming. When the bill amounted to a few hundred dollars, Gordon announced that owing the therapist so much money made him feel too guilty, and he would have to terminate therapy until his finances got better: thus avoiding having to face his problems.

In all of these instances, money style and expression of feeling were interwoven. Since money is such an integral part of everyday living, it is unlikely that one could have a neurotic life-style of any kind without it affecting one's perception and use of money.

Psychotherapists differ in their approaches to treating patients, but in the following pages we will present a few examples of approaches and encounters that have been used in dealing with irrational attitudes toward money.

Dennis Patterson was a thirty-four-year-old accountant and an intense security collector. He went into therapy begrudgingly because his wife threatened to leave him if he did not. After comparing the cost of a divorce, including property settlement, he decided that therapy might be cheaper.

During the first interview, Dennis pleaded poverty and claimed he could not possibly afford the therapist's "outrageous" fee. He tried to haggle but the therapist stood firm. "I'm afraid you wouldn't respect me if I let you take advantage of me," he said quietly. Eventually, Dennis gave in and reluctantly agreed to pay the full fee. The therapist, sensing Dennis' bargain-hunting behavior, ran the risk of losing the patient over the question of fees rather than cater to his neurotic need to get something for nothing. He suggested that if Dennis was really unable to afford private therapy, he would be happy to recommend a clinic where help would be less expensive. It became obvious that the problem was not a lack of money but the reluctance to part with it.

Resistance in security collectors like Dennis may be handled in many ways. Dennis' therapist used the security-collecting hang-up to make Dennis so uncomfortable that he would give it up and try to resolve his problems. "Dennis," he would say, "do you realize that you have avoided talking about anything meaningful for the past twenty minutes? You pay me the same amount of money if we sit here and stare into space or if you open up and tell me where you're at. It doesn't matter to me either way, but if I were you, I'd resent wasting all that time and money." This invariably got a reaction from Dennis. He felt anxious and angry because he realized he couldn't withhold both his feelings and his money.

The objective in Dennis' therapy was to encourage him to become more involved with people so he could explore the experience of trusting. As in most such cases, Dennis first had to learn to trust the therapist. He actually set up tests for the therapist, who managed to pass them and ultimately prove that he was trustworthy. In the area of money, he deliberately overpaid the therapist, who caught the mistake and returned the money. Then Dennis revealed an experience which he had never told anyone before, and checked to see if the therapist, who was also seeing Dennis' wife in therapy, had passed it on to her. He found the therapist had not. He gradually discovered he could express his feelings, including anger and affection, toward the therapist without destroying the relationship. Eventually, he was able, with pressure and encouragement from the therapist, to trust his wife and a few close friends with his feelings and emotions.

At times, Dennis' therapist discouraged him from discussing money or anything directly related to it. He recognized that this was the one area in which Dennis felt safe, and that when he felt threatened talking about his problems in relating to people or his difficulty in being spontaneous or in enjoying life, he would resort to discussions of financial matters: how much money he saved on his new stereo set; how he could get an extra half-percent interest by putting his money in the credit union rather than the bank; how his wife was being extravagant. Not only did the therapist convey that the subject of money was therapeutically unproductive under these circumstances, but he also made it clear that in comparison to other subjects it was relatively unimportant. At times the therapist pointed out why Dennis resorted to this safety device. Following the therapist's lead, Dennis gradually began to put money in perspective and see it for what it really is.

As Dennis found more satisfaction in relating to people, he put relatively less importance on financial security. His own self-confidence and self-respect also rose. He began to take an interest in trying new things and developing new interests and friendships. And eventually he understood what his therapist meant when he said, "There are other ways to enjoy money besides stacking it up in the bank."

Power grabbers, even more than security collectors, are loath to seek out psychotherapy. The security collector resists because of the cost, the power grabber because it is unacceptable to admit that one has any weakness or fault, or needs help from anyone else.

Mike Gregory never intended to go into therapy. He is still not too sure how it happened. His wife, Helen, began seeing a psychologist because she felt "depressed and lonely and terribly, totally worthless." Mike was annoyed with her for not being able to "get up and get going." He took time out from his "busy schedule" to see the psychologist in order to help him understand his wife and tell him how to treat her to get her over this "nonsense."

Before he knew it, Mike was talking about his own background—his struggle for survival in the Bronx as a child, dropping out of high school to join the merchant marine, a short stint as a professional boxer, and finally his rise as a successful businessman with a chain of appliance stores. Mike and Helen had married young. When Mike opened his first store, Helen kept the books and worked closely with him. As he became more successful, she quit working for Mike and devoted her energies to running their new home, entertaining, and looking after their two lively sons. As they grew more affluent, they became more distant and alienated from each other.

The psychologist tried to point out that, despite Mike's protest, Helen did have some real problems and that some of her problems had to do with their relationship. It seemed probable, too, that Mike had some problems and that his relationship with Helen compounded his problems. The psychologist observed that if Mike really wanted to change things with Helen, as he said he did, he might try to understand how his behavior affected her, and vice versa.

Mike was irritated by the bluntness of the psychologist. He was not used to having people confront him that directly. But he saw no way of refusing to see the psychologist again since he had presented himself as a concerned and loving husband.

Since there was enough evidence to indicate that Mike was not above cutting corners to further his own interests, the psychologist took pains to spell out precisely the terms of the "therapeutic contract" so there could be no possible misunderstanding. The fees, the length of appointments, conditions for cancellation of appointments, and telephone calls between appointments were stated in businesslike form. When, in the course of therapy, Mike tried to renege on the contract, the psychologist reminded him of the agreed-upon conditions and would not relent. "You know our agreement, Mike. If you fail to show up for an appointment without notifying me forty-eight hours in advance and for a legitimate reason, you will have to pay for the missed hour." "No, I can't give you an extra half hour now even if you do pay double! I have another patient waiting. If it's urgent, I can see you at two o'clock tomorrow or it will have to wait until next time."

It was frustrating to Mike to find someone he couldn't manipulate and couldn't buy, but ultimately it caused him to become a little less cynical about people and to become somewhat more honest in his dealings with customers.

Throughout therapy Mike competed with the psychologist for a position of dominance in the relationship. The psychologist, feeling no need to compete, but understanding Mike's need to do so, simply pointed out the irrationality of Mike's behavior. When Mike felt frustrated or not in control, he became sullen or demanding, and occasionally even cursed the psychologist; but the therapist refused to play his game.

Gradually, Mike began to see that his domineering attitude was not only ineffective in his relationship with the therapist, but also unnecessary. Here was an authority figure who was not impressed with either his "toughness" or his money. When this fact dawned on him, Mike found himself looking forward to his meetings with the psychologist. They were about the only place where he could let down his defenses and be himself. Occasionally, he even talked about some of his anxieties and other "shameful" feelings. He found to his amazement that the therapist didn't laugh or ridicule him the way his stepfather did when he was a small boy. Most of the time, however, Mike confined his activities in therapy to intellectual discussions and decision-making sessions.

Of all the money types, the one most likely to seek psychotherapy voluntarily is the love buyer. On first exposure to therapy, love buyers see it as similar to other relationships they have had. They pay the therapist so much an hour to be nice to them. While their conscious intent is to overcome their loneliness and desolation, unconsciously love buyers are frequently content to stay in therapy forever and maintain a permanent love-for-hire relationship with the therapist.

Linda Boothe was a slightly obese twenty-six-year-old elementary school teacher. She had no close friends and only occasionally did she find anyone to spend an evening with. When she did, it was most likely someone as socially awkward and love starved as she was. Linda had never felt close to her parents or her older sister. She found some comfort in eating and she spent a lot of time reading—usually romantic novels and love stories, but also enough academic material to get through college and obtain a teaching credential. She got some affection from her students, but she never had a boy friend.

Linda had seen a counselor briefly while in college, and she was determined to seek more intensive professional help now that she had graduated and was working. In the beginning Linda felt quite anxious in the presence of the therapist and didn't know what to talk about. However, she was thrilled to have the therapist, whom she saw as an attractive older man, all to herself for a whole hour. Between visits she would indulge in fantasies in which the therapist would find her exciting and would ask her out socially.

After she had been in therapy for a while, she "overlooked" paying her bill one month. By the middle of the following month, when the bill still had not been paid, the therapist asked her about it. After much probing, she finally admitted that she really wanted the therapist to be her friend rather than her doctor. That would make her someone very "special" and not "just another patient." She would like to think that the therapist was helping her because he liked her and not because she was paying him money.

On a number of occasions, Linda would become upset with herself or with her relationship with the therapist, and would say something like, "I'm such a mess, I don't see how you can stand seeing me every week," hoping to get the therapist to reassure her that he cared about her. Or, "You *have* to like me because that's your job; that's what I pay you for. If I weren't a patient, you wouldn't even look at me!" To which the therapist would reply, "You pay me to *help* you, not to love you. If I like you that makes it easier, but that's not what I get paid for." In time, Linda was able to separate the financial transaction from the emotional transaction in therapy and not confuse the two.

Linda's constant complaints were, "I'm ugly!" "I'm lonely!" "Nobody loves me!" "I'm worthless!" "I'm unhappy!" When the therapist felt that he understood Linda's personality, he confronted her directly, "Linda, I want you to understand something. All behavior is learned, and it is learned because in some way it is rewarding. If you have learned to be miserable and lonely and unhappy, there has to be a payoff. Let's see what it is."

At first, Linda denied that she could possibly be getting any reward from her loneliness and depression. During the course of therapy, however, she became more and more aware that her behavior, as unpleasant as it was, felt preferable to the anxiety of becoming emotionally involved with someone and running the risk of being "destroyed" emotionally. It felt safer for her to exchange money, rather than her own feelings, for love. If her money couldn't provide the love she needed, it was no big loss. But to put herself on the line was terrifying.

In time, however, Linda became more willing to take risks and began to take significant steps toward becoming involved with other people. She lost weight, developed outside interests, got over much of her self-pity, became less self-centered, and began to take an interest in other people. She found more reasons to like herself, and found that others responded more positively also. Eventually she saw that the love and friendship that she could not buy with money she could obtain when she was willing to invest herself instead.

Whereas love buyers are inclined to become overly dependent on the therapist, autonomy worshipers who undergo therapy make a conscious effort to resist such dependency. Their motive for going into therapy is to seek help in extricating themselves from domination and control, not to burrow into a confining relationship.

Barbara Davis was a thirty-two-year-old divorcée and would-be artist. She went into therapy because she was having problems in her relationship with Tom, the man she had been living with for the past two years. They met when both were wallowing in the effects of a difficult divorce. After dating for a few months, they decided to live together, with a clear understanding that there was no commitment on either side and that each was free to see other people and do as he or she pleased. Barbara still felt that way but Tom was becoming jealous if she saw other men, and she felt that in many ways he was becoming too involved and making too many demands on her.

Because of her disorganized, chaotic life-style, Barbara was frequently so engrossed in her painting or some other activity that she forgot her appointments with the therapist. When she became aware of what she had done, she was most apologetic and promised to try harder to remember; but the pattern continued. After she had missed several appointments, the therapist reminded her of their discussion during the first interview in which it was pointed out that except for emergencies she was responsible for paying for missed appointments, and that, under the circumstances, he was going to have to enforce that condition. Barbara agreed that this was only fair and that maybe having to pay for the missed visits might force her to remember. Quite the contrary. Not only did she continue to miss appointments, but she began to overlook paying her bill. Despite a good deal of resistance on Barbara's part, the therapist pushed her to explore the meaning of her behavior. Gradually it came out that her "forgetting" was partly a passive form of rebellion. When she felt she was becoming too dependent upon the therapist, she stayed away. She was also beginning to see the therapist as something of a father figure, which aroused the ambivalent feelings she had had toward her own father. Her nonpayment was an expression of her negative feelings.

Since early childhood, Barbara felt that her father neglected her and gave too much of himself to his law practice, which she hated. When he died from a heart attack at the age of forty-eight, he left Barbara with a comfortable inheritance, which provided her the freedom to pursue an art career. While the freedom appealed to her, she had some underlying guilt feelings about accepting the money, which she regarded as tainted. Consequently, her handling of money was erratic and frequently she seemed compelled to spend it with abandon just to get rid of it. As a result, she often had to borrow money from Tom or rely on his generosity to get through the month.

Although Barbara went into therapy complaining about Tom's emotional dependence upon her, she was ultimately confronted with her financial dependence upon him. The therapist, by continually pointing out to her how she used time and money with him, made her see the pattern she used with Tom and others, and what it represented to her psychologically. She did not want to make a commitment to keep regular appointments, but would have preferred to see the therapist whenever it suited her convenience. Her mishandling of money and haphazard bookkeeping made it financially impossible for her to function autonomously. Rather than terminate her therapy because of her missed appointments and overdue bills, the therapist forced Barbara to see that she was trying to manipulate him and others into continuing the protective role of her father. Her first major step toward "growing up" was taking responsibility for keeping her appointments and paying her bill to the therapist.

Since attitudes toward money and the handling of money reflect underlying personality dynamics, they provide a rich source of information for therapists and patients alike. One of the few psychologists addressing himself to the need for dealing with money styles in therapy concludes, "The many deep emotions and conflicts often associated with money cannot be suppressed and brushed under the carpet, and are bound to interfere with the therapeutic process if not brought out into the open and dealt with frankly. It is likely that the widespread uneasiness and difficulty experienced by many therapists in confronting the money part of their work, and the money aspects of the lives of their patients, contributes appreciably to the number of failures and partial successes in psychotherapy." [4]

11

WHY THE RICH GET RICHER, THE POOR STAY POOR, AND MOST DON'T DO EITHER

THERE IS AN OLD SAYING TO THE EFFECT THAT IF A PERSON HAS a hundred dollars and makes a million, that is incredible; but if a person has a hundred million dollars and makes a million, that is inevitable. The dream of rising from rags to riches is as much a part of the American heritage as is baseball and apple pie. The fact that a number of people, for example Ray Kroc, the owner of the McDonald's hamburger empire, and Conrad Hilton, the hotel magnate, have achieved the incredible keeps the dream alive. And, despite increasing taxes, controls, and other barriers imposed by government agencies, the number of millionaires continues to grow to the point where one wit recently remarked, "Soon millionaires will be a dime a dozen." Still, the odds against someone who is poor or middle class becoming rich are much greater than those against the rich getting richer.

THE RICH HAVE MORE MONEY

When the novelist F. Scott Fitzgerald made his oft-quoted observation, "The rich are different from us," Ernest Hemingway replied, "Yes, they have more money."

This simple dialogue is actually more profound than it might appear. While many personality and character traits have been attributed to the rich, individuals do not always conform to a class stereotype. A number of studies have even stressed the similarity of the very rich, especially those who inherit wealth, and the very poor. Both groups tend to live off of unearned income, have a disdain for hard work, and espouse greater sexual freedom than do the middle classes.

Another similarity between the very rich and the very poor is their immunity to the necessity of making choices and assuming the responsibility that goes with such choices. Roger Starr, housing administrator for the city of New York, makes the following comparison.

> This characteristic distinguishes the very rich from all the rest of us; immune from having to give up one apparent good in order to attain another, they do not understand the more or less painful weighing of alternatives which constitutes daily business for the rest of us, and permeates our view of the seriousness of life itself, since we know that choices are not usually refundable.
>
> The very poor are also immune from the need to make choices. They lack the monetary means with which to choose. It is in this respect that the pangs of poverty are painful in relation to the wealth of the surrounding society. The poor man in American society is dehumanized, not because his actual standard of living is below the level at which human life is possible (clearly hundreds of millions of people survive on standards far lower). He is dehumanized because his relative poverty deprives him of the human responsibility of choice.[1]

Dr. Roy R. Grinker, Jr., described before a meeting of the American Psychiatric Association his experiences in treating fifteen patients who were multimillionaires by inheritance. "The similarity to children of the poor is startling," Grinker claimed. Both groups are deprived of adequate parenting and lack adults they can admire. They feel unloved, unvalued, and never gain a positive self-image.[2]

Certainly, not all who inherit great wealth are "emotional zombies," as Grinker called the sample he saw. Not all are "defensive, self-centered, mildly depressed, bored, shallow, disinterested in work, short on values, goals or ideals, and operating on the notion that they could spend their way out of all frustrations." On the other hand, the term "emotional zombie" probably fits more of the super-rich who inherit money than it does the super-rich who make it. The latter are more inclined to be ambitious, hard driving, work oriented, decisive individuals.

Psychological studies of personality factors common to the rich have generally come up empty. Typical of the conclusions of researchers in the field is that of Dr. Frederick Herzberg, professor of psychology at Case Western Reserve University, who states, "There is no commonality among highly successful men. Their personality types are as varied as all other people's." [3] Similarly, studies attempting to define a personality type characteristic of the poor have been equally unsuccessful. The most that can be said is that there are certain factors which may hinder or promote the likelihood of accumulating or increasing wealth. As Hemingway noted, the only thing that sets rich people apart from all others is that they have more money. This was also the opinion of Joseph P. Kennedy, father of the noted political clan. When a Princeton University psychology student sent him a long, involved questionnaire in an attempt to probe the personality characteristics of the rich, Mr. Kennedy returned the questionnaire unanswered with a note stating, "I am rich because I have a lot of money." [4]

It Takes Money to Make Money. There are many ways to make money. Nearly all the ways to make a *lot* of money legally, however, involve some type of investment. One can invest in real estate, the stock market, a lottery ticket, or a business. However, by whatever means one chooses to invest in an attempt to make a fortune, it is necessary to have money to invest. And, as the philosopher Rousseau observed over two hundred years ago, "Money is the seed of money, and the first guinea is sometimes more difficult to acquire than the second million."

Except for a few corporate executives, entertainers, and professional athletes, it is impossible to become rich on a salary. Most wealth comes from unearned rather than earned income.

Rather than, or in addition to, putting themselves to work, the rich put their money to work for them. Naturally, the more money they have working for them, the more they are likely to get back in return. If one has enough capital to start with, it is possible to make a lot of money with no effort, no intelligence, no business know-how, and virtually no risk. If one invests $100 million in the safest tax-exempt bonds, for example, it will yield approximately $6 million spendable income a year. Or placed in a long-term bank account, it will double in less than ten years. If one is knowledgeable and willing to take greater risks, it is possible to make considerably more money.

Future Orientation. Successful investment depends on the ability to forecast developmental trends, to predict future growth. It involves the principle of planning for the future, of putting off immediate gratification in favor of long-term rewards. The wise farmer doesn't use all of his corn. He saves part of it for seed for next year's planting. The successful merchant puts some profit into advertising with the hope of selling more merchandise. The wage earner may try to save a few dollars from each paycheck to invest in a home or to eventually go into business. But it is a hardship. For the average person, some sacrifice is necessary in order to save even a little for investment.

For the poor it is even harder. People who are hungry have difficulty in transcending their present discomfort. It is unrealistic for them to think in terms of doing with even less than they have and investing the difference in the hope of making a profit several years hence. In the ghetto, survival is a day-to-day reality. Tomorrow may never come. Five years from now is forever. Not only is it practically impossible for the poor to accumulate the capital to invest, it is difficult for them to think realistically beyond the present and make any meaningful projections about the future.

By contrast, the rich, whose real needs can be met with little effort, have the time and the inclination to plan ahead. They can afford to put money into ventures which will not pay off for years. If the ultimate return is sufficiently high, they can invest and wait for the profit. Since their present is secure, they can dream about and plan for the future. The very successful empire builders not only have keen vision and foresight regarding the future, they often have the money and power to make their dreams come true.

Individuals who have become rich after starting with nothing but a dream are unusual. Unlike the majority of the poor, they have been future oriented rather than living just for the moment. To accumulate the grubstake to pursue their dreams required considerable sacrifice. Those who are already rich, however, have capital at their disposal, and it does not lower their standard of living or restrict their self-indulgence to invest part of it in some money-making venture.

Modeling. A great deal of learning takes place by imitation. Children learn to talk by imitating sounds they hear others make. They learn to walk by watching adults and by attempting to imitate their movements. Most attitudes and values are learned by unconsciously internalizing those qualities that are held by parents and other significant individuals in a person's life. Sons and daughters of the rich have rich models to emulate. They learn what it is like to be rich, to think in terms of large sums of money, and to become knowledgeable about business and finance. While some children reject these models and rebel against the values of their families, most do not. They not only inherit the family money, they identify with the family's attitudes toward money and imitate its money-making behavior. Howard Hughes inherited approximately $450,000 from his father when he was eighteen and built an empire worth something over a billion dollars. J. Paul Getty's father made millions, which spurred his son to outdo him by making billions. One of the motives for making so much money, Getty claimed, was to prove to his father that he could do it.[5] The Du Ponts, the Fords, the Rockefellers have perpetuated the family name and fortune, with the members of each generation learning from the examples presented to them in the process of growing up.

The models available to the poor, on the other hand, are not wealthy, successful individuals. More likely, they are examples of failure, at least financially. In order to move out of the poverty level, people need hope and opportunity. If a few can pave the way, others will follow in their footsteps. But most people in the ghetto or barrio feel hopeless and trapped. Not only do they not have models of rich people to identify with, but very few even make it into the ranks of the middle class. Until fairly recently about the only visible successful model available to the poor black child was an occasional Willie Mays. Black lawyers, bankers, and college professors were not available to imitate.

Compulsive Drive. While those who inherit wealth are often characterized as indolent and uninterested in work, sometimes even looking down on work as beneath them, this is certainly not true of all who inherit wealth. Ambition, drive, and a penchant for work are not lacking among the Kennedy or the Rockefeller clans, for example. And, among the self-made rich, a compulsive drive to work is commonplace. Many enjoy work as other people enjoy their friends, families, sports, hobbies, and other recreation. One such person remarked, "Why play bridge or golf? Business is more exciting." Most of these people are so hooked on hard work that they cannot give it up even after they have made millions. Work, more than money, seems to drive many of them. As one student of the very rich explained, "Work is part of their being. They can no more easily change their work habits than they can change the color of their eyes." [6]

Hard work alone will not make anyone rich. The compulsion to work is considered primarily a trait of the middle rather than the upper classes. It is, however, a helpful ingredient for rising from the lower to the middle or from the middle to the upper classes. Without it, one must rely on luck or crime to progress upwardly on the financial ladder.

Some compulsive workers will be found among the poor, particularly in rural areas. People may spend long hours working industriously and only squeeze a meager existence out of poor land. In the cities, however, jobs are scarce in the areas of greatest poverty and the work ethic is not as prevalent among the poor as it is among the middle classes. The model of hard work is not seen as frequently by impressionable young people; and where it is seen, there appears to be little payoff or reward for the effort involved. Therefore, hard work is likely to be regarded with a good deal of skepticism.

Propinquity. By attending the right schools, meeting the right people, making the right friends, joining the right clubs, and moving in the right social circle, one increases the opportunity for making money. Associating with people who have money and who are involved in making more money may not only stimulate one's own money-making desires, but may also present opportunities for investments and business transactions that would otherwise be impossible.

Just as one chooses friends from the people in one's own neighborhood or school or work setting, marriages, too, are largely a matter of propinquity. If one associates with the wealthy, the probability is pretty great that one will pick a spouse who has money. In many cases, wealth increases because members of two moneyed families marry and pool their resources. For example, the wealthy Greek shipowner Stavros Livanos had two daughters. One married the wealthy Greek shipowner Aristotle Onassis, and the other married the wealthy Greek shipowner Stavros Niarchos. And when Tina Onassis divorced Aristotle and Eugenie Niarchos died, Stavros Niarchos married his sister-in-law, Tina. That way, the money stayed in the family.[7]

Propinquity applies to the poor as well as to the rich. Poor people associate primarily with other poor people and they learn how to cope with being poor. Most learn to adapt to their environment. Like people everywhere who are locked into a situation from which they feel they can't escape, the majority learn to tolerate their misfortune and to carve out an existence that is as painless as possible. A part of that adjustment involves not rocking the boat or expecting too much since that would lead to more frustration and anguish. Although such an adjustment helps perpetuate the status quo, it may also make poverty bearable.

Luck. In addition to total dedication, good models, an orientation toward the future, propinquity, and capital, there is one other essential ingredient involved in becoming rich. That is luck. No matter how intelligent, hardworking, unscrupulous, or ingenious a person is, an element of luck is almost always involved in making a fortune. The person is at the right place with the right product or the right technology at the right time to capitalize on the right opportunity. J. Paul Getty, Hugh Roy Cullen, Everette Lee De Golyer, and others who have made fortunes in oil, attribute much of their success to luck in picking the right oil leases. W. Clement Stone, who accumulated $400 million selling insurance, was frequently favored by good fortune, including two lucky sales his first day as a frightened young salesman, which gave him the courage and determination to pursue a selling career.[8] Obviously, those who are poor and stay poor have no luck at all, or if they do, it is bad luck.

WHY MOST PEOPLE DON'T GET RICH OR POOR

Millions of people apparently worship money. Even more dream about having millions of dollars and fantasize about the things they would do with it. It is probably safe to say that money is as much a preoccupation with most people as is sex. Yet, the primary reason that more people do not have more money is that, despite their longing, money is really not worth what it would take to get it.

Case histories show that people who start out with little or nothing in life and claw their way to the top of the money heap are obsessed with the acquisition of money and what it stands for. People for whom money is the most important thing in life have a very good chance of accumulating lots of it. Usually, they make lots of money, or land in jail, or both.

People who are willing to work eighteen hours a day while most work eight, or who are willing to work harder than the average person, are likely to make more money than most. If they are preoccupied with money, they are likely to see opportunities to make money that others overlook. If they are really dedicated to making money, they will forego luxuries and pleasures in order to save money to invest. If necessary, they will make the effort to learn all they can about the business ventures they get into, regardless of the cost in terms of time, money, and energy. They will pass up hobbies, social events, and activities with family and friends to concentrate on business. They will sacrifice job satisfaction, social status, and pleasant working conditions for monetary rewards.

From time to time everyone is confronted with decisions regarding the value of money and what each is willing to pay for it. How much is a friendship worth? A marriage relationship? One's self-respect? One's reputation? One's health? One's life? Freedom? Loyalty? Integrity? A possible jail sentence? Most people are unwilling to make money by means in opposition to their beliefs and values. On the other hand, the newspapers, as well as TV and movie scripts, are filled with stories of people who steal, embezzle, murder, and sell hard drugs for money.

With few exceptions, those who rise from poverty or the middle classes to positions of wealth do so because money is the most important thing in their lives. The American wealth builder is described as follows, "A man of action, he is compulsive and repetitive in his single-minded acquisitiveness. He simply does not know what else to do—he substitutes money-making for living and often believes that he is engaged in a great crusade." [9]

It is obvious that most people stop short of giving money top priority in their lives. There are some limitations and restrictions on what they will do for money. In the final analysis, most people put good health, peace of mind, happiness, friendship, self-respect, and similar values ahead of money. The more these values conflict with or inhibit one's drive for riches, the less likely one is to achieve riches. However, even those who rise to the millionaire class generally have some scruples and some limits as to what they will do for money. Other variables are also involved in determining why only a few make it to the top financially.

Dollars and Sense. Making money is an intellectual pursuit. Luck often plays a role, but emotions are usually a deterrent. Many individuals who are otherwise intelligent let their emotions take over when it comes to finances and investments. When they do, they usually lose money. Physicians, for example, who employ logic in their everyday practice, are notorious for making poor investments.

One does not have to be superintelligent to make money, but unless one is very lucky, it is necessary to be knowledgeable. Ignorance is not bliss when it comes to making money. Yet it is amazing how many people put money, even large sums of money, into investments and business ventures about which they know virtually nothing. A physician, who would understandably be aghast at the idea of taking the advice of a first-year medical student on how to suture a wound, blithely invested five thousand dollars in the stock market on the advice of an elevator operator. A biochemist, who studied eight years in a university earning his Ph.D. and another ten years in the lab learning every phase of his profession, casually invested a year's salary in a land speculation without even reading the prospectus. A building contractor who didn't know a Rembrandt from a Dali read an article in the newspaper about the profits to be made in collecting art and began buying oil paintings indiscriminately.

These same people would be horrified if a stock analyst suddenly began practicing medicine, or a real estate developer set himself up as a chemist, or an art curator went into the contracting business. Yet they see nothing incongruous in jumping into some field of investment with no knowledge and no experience, only a naïve expectation of making a lot of money. Just as the weekend golfer cannot hope to compete with Jack Nicklaus, the amateur investor is no match for the professional who has had years of experience and who works full-time managing investments.

For every Colonel Sanders who parlays a small business into an international chain of Kentucky Fried Chicken franchises, there are hundreds of owners of small businesses who struggle along inauspiciously or go broke. Gilbert Lyndon, like millions of Americans, had a dream of going into business for himself. Like many, also, his desire to make his dream a reality was so intense it interfered with his judgment.

Gilbert was considered intelligent by those who knew him

best. He graduated *cum laude* in art history from a leading university. He had worked for several years as an assistant curator in a prestigious municipal art gallery. He was very knowledgeable in the field of art. He also knew quite a bit about appraising, and he had sources from whom he could buy quality work at reasonable prices.

When a great-aunt left Gilbert an inheritance, he decided to open a gallery in a new shopping center. Gilbert's Gallery was one of a number of expensive specialty stores, all with coordinated decor. His friends were enthusiastic about his new venture and assured him he would do well. The shopping center was located in an expanding area of the city and was surrounded by luxury homes. On the surface, one might have expected that Gilbert would have a good chance of making it. Not so.

The yardage shop did well, the drapery shop did well, the hardware store and the paint store did well. Even the gourmet sandwich shop did well. Gilbert's Gallery did not. Visitors came to browse and admire, but few came to buy. Sometimes he took in enough money to pay the overhead; more often he did not. Gilbert found out the hard way that while he knew the art business, he did not know his clientele.

Gilbert had a good product—quality art—but it was expensive. Most of the people in the area were young families—professionals or junior executives on their way up socially and economically. For the most part, they had overextended themselves to buy a home and then went further into debt to furnish it. Art, especially expensive art, was a luxury they could get along without. Those who bought at all were interested in something inexpensive that would match the color of their new sofa. Art for the sake of enjoyment or for financial investment was something they could postpone for a few years.

By the time Gilbert realized he was not making money, his pride would not let him admit he had made a mistake in opening his gallery in that location. He compounded his unwise decision to open with an equally unwise decision not to quit. Instead, he borrowed money, added new items, and had a sale. Eventually, his pride and his money came out even. He lost both.

Since success in business, or any other type of investment, is dependent upon sound decision making, anything that interferes with intellectual efficiency is going to limit one's money-making ability and inhibit one's rise to riches. Pride or "ego," the inability to admit one's mistakes or one's stupidity, as in Gilbert's case, is a common reason for investment failure. Many an investor has watched in frustration as a potential coup, which would make the investor appear brilliant if it had succeeded, backfires. The stock tumbles or the investment erodes and the money disappears. Instead of minimizing the loss by selling or pulling out, the person vainly prays that fate will intervene and vindicate his or her judgment. Meanwhile, more and more money is being lost. Other emotions and personality characteristics may also interfere with good judgment and prevent people from becoming rich.

Greed. While some people become rich because of their greed, more are destined to remain poor or in the middle classes because of it. The lure of instant riches is an opiate that dulls reasoning and common sense. Nowhere is this more apparent than at a race track. Not only will some people risk their rent money and their car payment in the hope of striking it rich, but it is not uncommon for a bettor to "reason" as follows: "If I bet two dollars on the number six horse at two to one, I'll only win four dollars. But if I bet on the number three horse, I'll win over a hundred. I could really use that hundred, so I'll bet number three." This would be all right if the odds were assigned randomly, but obviously they are not. In a horse race the horse with the longest odds is the one considered by experts to have the least chance of winning. The same is true in other types of investments as well. The bigger the gamble, the less chance there is of winning.

Greed is the ally of manipulators and con artists. Although greedy themselves, they are usually able to put their own greed aside while developing a scam to ply on the greed of others. Some of these experts in the psychology of greed come up with brilliantly designed and well-executed schemes for bilking people out of their savings; others rely on swindles that have been used successfully for over a hundred years. One of the old standbys is the story of "a fortune in gold bricks located in a trunk in El Paso, Texas, the property of a once-rich Mexican family forced to smuggle it out because of government restrictions. In exchange for several thousand dollars, the sucker is given the keys to a nonexistent trunk." [10] This scheme and variations of it have been exposed in newspapers for years and it seems highly unlikely that any reasonable person would fall for such an obviously phony pitch. Yet, otherwise intelligent people do. Perhaps the answer lies in the observation made by the British physician Sir Thomas Browne, in 1642, "avarice seems not so much a vice, as a deplorable piece of madness." About the only consolation for the victim of such a "disease" is that many con artists fall victim to their own greed and are taken in by other con artists.

Fear. While greed causes people to gamble recklessly and overrule sound judgment, fear causes people not to gamble at all. Fear and suspicion lead to indecision and the inability to take advantage of possible opportunities to make money. Fearful people may intellectually see the advantage of investing in certain ventures, but no matter how safe the ventures appear to be, these individuals are emotionally unable to part with their money. While they never lose the money they already have, they often lose the money they could have had if they had been more self-confident and decisive.

Don and Tina have been married for five years. They both have good jobs, they have no debts, and they put money in the bank each month. Most of their friends have bought homes or condominiums, but Don and Tina still live in the same apartment they rented when they got married. They have looked at houses to buy, but if they could afford a particular house they were afraid something was wrong with it; if they finally decided to buy it, it was already sold, except for the time they did put a deposit on one and then became so afraid they had made a mistake they forfeited their deposit rather than go through with the purchase. Three years ago, two engineers who worked with Don decided to quit and start their own company. They offered Don a chance to go in with them, but he was reluctant to risk his savings or borrow money from the bank to invest, so he declined. Today, they have several large contracts and seem headed for a prosperous future. Tina works for a firm of stockbrokers. When someone suggests she should take advantage of her position to get inside information on investing, she replies, "If I had any money in the stock market, I couldn't sleep nights worrying about losing it. I'd rather keep my money in the bank where it's safe."

Professional investors, like professional gamblers, know that to be successful one has to make decisions calmly and calculatingly rather than emotionally. They also know that most people invest emotionally and that *the masses are usually wrong*. In the stock market, for example, there is a certain amount of manipulation by heavy investors and insiders who control millions of dollars in mutual funds and pension funds, but the ebb and flow of the market is also influenced by the millions of small investors who follow blindly after the leaders in a kind of mass hysteria. The stock market runs in cycles. Ideally, one buys at the bottom of the cycle and sells at the top. In order to do that, however, one has to be at the head of the pack, which takes courage, conviction, and an intelligent analysis of economic, social, political, and psychological conditions. The timid investor will wait until it is clearly evident that a bull market has been under way for a substantial length of time before risking any money. But by the time all of the sheep are convinced that the market is the place to make money, it is often too late. The peak has already been reached and the market is on a downhill slide. The masses of unsophisticated small investors then panic and sell for whatever they can get, and drive the market still lower. By the time the market has reached bottom and there are bargains galore, these same people cannot be persuaded to invest. They may righteously proclaim that it is impossible to make money in the stock market—and hold onto that belief until the market is near the top of the next cycle.

Envy. The more value people put on money, the more likely they are to envy those who have more than they do. In a volume entitled *The General,* written nearly two thousand years ago, the author, Onasander, drolly commented, "Envy is a pain of mind that successful men cause their neighbors." Many envious persons would be content to get along with less than they now have if it would insure that none of their neighbors had more. One of the problems with envy is that it causes people to spend time and energy attempting to keep others down, which could better be spent in trying to improve their own financial situation.

The richer one becomes, the more one must contend with the envy and hatred of other people. Many, including love buyers, are unable or unwilling to pay the price. Envious people may also limit their own opportunities. The "cut off your nose to spite your face" philosophy stems from envy. As one real estate broker who has been in the business for many years commented, "I never cease to be amazed at how many people will turn down a good buy because they find out somebody else is making a profit. The other day a man was in my office. He was on the verge of buying a piece of property that was ten to twenty thousand dollars underpriced. I could see the dollar signs going around in his head as he was figuring out how much money he was going to make on the deal when he resold it in a year or so. Then he asked how long the present owner had owned the property and what he had paid for it. When I told him, he muttered, 'I'll be damned if I'll help him get rich!' and tore up his check. It happens all the time."

Anger. Of all emotions, perhaps love and anger are the most powerful destroyers of intelligent action. And the more intense the emotion, the more the intellect is shunted aside and behavior is motivated by the force of the emotion. Phrases like "blind rage" or "consumed by anger" describe conditions in which the ego and the intellect are temporarily nonfunctional.

Although a certain amount of controlled anger can be directed toward overcoming a handicap or deprivation, or motivate one to achieve wealth, blind rage inhibits constructive thought and blots out any concern for the future. The entertainer or the athlete who strikes out in anger and cancels an engagement or walks out in the middle of a performance because of a conflict with the management or the audience or the press or within himself, may jeopardize an otherwise lucrative career.

Business negotiations involving large sums of money are often tense and may well produce frustration and considerable stress. Many such confrontations end in anger and hard feelings on the part of one or more persons, with the result that contracts are lost because of impulsive, hostile responses. The owner of a growing manufacturing company lost an important order he had been counting on. In frustration, he queried the buyer as to why his competitor had been given the contract. He was told it was because of a minor flaw in his product and that his price was too high. Rather than taking it as a constructive criticism, he became incensed. "Nobody can tell me how to run my business!" he shouted. "You don't know the difference between a flange and a corkscrew!" When he calmed down, he realized he had been on edge and that the buyer was trying to be helpful. Although he apologized sincerely, the damage was done. The buyer was offended by his outburst and rejected subsequent bids by his company whenever he could.

Self-Concept. Some people never become rich because they can't possibly envision themselves as rich. Even in their wildest fantasies they are unable to imagine themselves having all the money they could possibly want or living in a style so much above what they are used to. The difference between where they are and where they would be with wealth is sometimes more than they can grasp. Although most people have difficulty in adapting to drastic changes in their lives, some cannot even make the transition in their minds.

To reach any goal, whether it be to jog for three miles, learn to play the guitar, or become rich, one must choose a goal consistent with one's self-image and one that is realistically attainable. The person who says, "I could take lessons for a thousand years and never learn to play the guitar," and means it, will never learn to play the guitar. The chances are such a person will not even try. The same holds true for becoming rich. The person who finds the image of being rich too uncomfortable to cope with and the goal too far out of reach, will, at most, make only a sporadic attempt to reach that goal. It matters little whether the self-concept is restricted by guilt feelings in regard to money—a feeling of not deserving more than one has—or by anxiety associated with leaving the familiar; the result will be the same. It is unlikely that people try very hard to reach a goal they feel to be unattainable. Without trying, the chances of reaching it are minimal, and if reached, the probability of maintaining it is even less.

Contentment. Not all personal characteristics inhibiting the acquisition of money are negative. One reason that people make little effort to acquire more wealth is satisfaction with the status quo. People are so constituted that they do nothing unless they are uncomfortable or dissatisfied. Although the rich can get richer while doing nothing, it takes not only capital or extraordinary talent, but also effort for the middle-class person to rise to a position of wealth. Those who are content with their present financial condition are simply not motivated to exert the effort necessary to make a lot more money.

Honesty. While it is possible for an honest person to become rich, the odds are lowered significantly the more dishonest one becomes. Many of the world's greatest fortunes have resulted from business practices which were questionable, to say the least. John D. Rockefeller, Cornelius Vanderbilt, J. P. Morgan, Jay Gould, and Jim Fisk have been included in history books because of their wealth, not because of their ethics. It was not because of their honest business dealings that some of these nineteenth-century multimillionaires acquired the dubious title, the "robber barons." As Ferdinand Lundberg, lifelong student and critic of the rich, states, referring to financial manipulations by the heads of large corporations, "Crime, carefully planned and executed, is demonstrably the royal highroad to pecuniary success in the United States." [11]

Honesty, of course, is relevant. Some people are scrupulously honest in all relationships. Others are honest most of the time. Some cheat anyone they feel they can, while others may cheat only on their income tax. The honest person, generally speaking, is willing to give up possible wealth for peace of mind, to sacrifice financial gain for personal principles and the avoidance of guilt and anxiety.

Compassion. Of all positive emotions that interfere with money making, compassion and its counterparts—love, kindness, sympathy, concern, generosity—are probably the most important. Emotional softness and tender feelings are contrary to hardheaded business decisions, which are concerned only with dollars and cents and not people. Softhearted property owners do not indiscriminately raise the rents of elderly tenants or rush to foreclose on those who are in temporary financial difficulties not of their own making. Compassionate employers try to understand the individual needs and problems of their employees. They don't exploit workers, fire people just short of retirement, or require employees to work under unsafe conditions in order to save money.

In contrast to the typical ambitious, power-grabbing empire builder, the compassionate person does not sacrifice intimate human relationships for money. If a husband and father, he will be concerned about the needs and feelings of his family and will spend time enjoying their company. He will be generous in providing for the education of his children and perhaps give them a helping hand in developing a business or profession. While some compassionate individuals may be love buyers at heart, the truly concerned individual will use money to help others because of genuine caring for people. The more money that is devoted to humanitarian causes and concern for other people, however, the less is available for investment and speculation, and, consequently, the less chance the compassionate person has of becoming rich.

Despite the odds, however, a few do make it. William H. Danforth, founder of the Ralston Purina Company, made millions despite being both honest and compassionate. According to Lundberg, "Danforth [unlike many of his prominent business contemporaries] never engaged in any shady practices, was never involved in any swindles, was never the defendant on criminal charges and was never accused of exploiting his workers. Nor was he, it seems, ever seriously criticized, knocked, called to account or rebuffed in good times or bad. For a portrait of the American capitalist as an extremely good, wholesome, . . . outgoing do-gooder one must turn to William H. Danforth." [12]

Sentiment. Many a movie or TV scenario has been written around the theme of the prodigal son returning home in the nick of time to protect the family estate from being gobbled up by a greedy real estate developer, who is going to turn it into a shopping center. The hero, of course, is motivated by sentiment and a loyal devotion to his heritage and to the land that has been owned and tilled by his family. There are many modifications of the theme, but the underlying thread involves the conflict between sentiment and money, in which the hero or the heroine sides with virtue and resists selling the family racehorse or the Van Gogh painting or the old homestead, regardless of whether the money is needed for a very real purpose or to satisfy someone's greed.

While one person sees the Stradivarius violin which no one plays as a potential grubstake with which to make a fortune, the sentimentalist views it as a nostalgic tie to the past and considers it profane to exchange it for mere money. The person with a strong sentimental attachment to family traditions and possessions will obviously resist exchanging them for so-called progress and money.

These are some of the many reasons why most people never become very rich or very poor. They are locked into a middle-class system that offers them enough rewards to keep them from slipping back and not enough dissatisfaction or incentive to cause them to move up. One middle-aged, middle-class man reflected on his dilemma as follows:

> I think about things now that hardly crossed my mind ten years ago: vague retirement plans; the fact of my mortality; how my wife and I will relate to each other when the kids are grown and gone. I am not a joiner, so she may have a rough time. On the other hand I am easy to please. A good book, a game of bridge or pinochle, a healthy argument disguised as conversation (I'll take either side), a lake with a few fish, TV and a bottle of beer, a tree

to trim, or some solitude in which to think can keep me well-occupied. Contentment! Is that what stops some of us? Perhaps it isn't really stagnation. I continue to study and try to become better at my work, but on the same plateau. I do not have an overwhelming desire to have a larger, newer house, a boat, a club membership, a new car every year, or no debts. A glimmer of desire is there, but not enough to make me act.[13]

Despite what they might say, the vast majority of people do not value being rich sufficiently to achieve it. While most would take wealth if it were offered, and chrematophobia (a morbid fear of money) is practically unheard of, most people limit their rise to riches by both their emotional immaturities and their sensibility and humanness.

12

MONEY SANITY

WITH ALL OF THE ABUSES AND PROBLEMS THAT MONEY SEEMS
to generate, and with all of the self-destructive and crazy
things it motivates people to do, some people question whether
money has any legitimate place in a sane society. Are there any
healthy attitudes toward money? Or is it a seducer that is so
overpowering it drives people mad and causes them to lose their
reason? Is it possible to deal with money rationally, to maintain
control over it rather than to become obsessed with and dominated by it? Is the desire to accumulate money, especially more
money than is necessary to satisfy one's needs, itself a form of
neurosis?

These are not easy questions to answer, and there are many
differing opinions about them. Even among the few experts in
the field of mental health who have focused their attention on
the subject of money and its role in society, there is considerable
disagreement. According to the psychiatrist and author Ernest
Borneman:

> Everything this study has taught us about the pathogenous char-
> acteristics of money and the interest in it must be reminted into a

psychotechnique for overcoming money, for overcoming the tyranny of capital, for teaching participation in a society free of the dictatorship of money . . .

The psychoanalysis of capital must become a psychotechnique for the prevention of capitalism. The analysis of money must develop into a therapy that will cure us of the interest in it.[1]

In contrast is the position of the equally distinguished psychiatrist Otto Fenichel:

Is there an instinctual drive to amass wealth? There appears to be no possible doubt about this. We meet this drive every day in widely-varying degrees in different people. It can assume pathological forms, for example, in the miser, who in order to become rich foregoes the satisfaction of other more rational needs, or in the person who strives to become wealthy in order to ward off a fear of impoverishment and the like. The drive has normal forms; indeed, a person in whom it is completely lacking will in our society be considered abnormal.[2]

MONEY AND SOCIETY

Any consideration of what is normal or abnormal behavior is meaningful only in the context of when and where the behavior occurs. A stranger visiting the island of Dobu in northwest Melanesia, for example, would conclude that the whole society is suffering from paranoia. Distrust and suspicion are considered normal. The fear of being poisoned is constant, and no woman ever leaves her cooking pot untended. No one shares another's food because it is believed to be deadly poisonous to anyone but the owner.

Society helps to shape behavior and it also helps to set the standards of what is acceptable or normal behavior and what is not. A capitalistic system such as is found in the United States creates an atmosphere conducive to certain money values. Likewise, standards of normal behavior or attitudes toward money in such a culture would not be applicable in Communist Russia.

America has traditionally been a culture that values the rights and privileges of the individual, as opposed to the group. It has also emphasized competition between individuals since it has always held out the promise of and opportunity for upward mobility. Any economic system that allows people to improve their lot in life by their own merits also allows them to sink to lower levels. A government that encourages freedom of competition in ideas and in business also provides a climate in which some people will take unfair advantage of others and resort to crime and other shortcuts in order to "win." Lewis Lapham, the editor of *Harper's*, reflects on the paradox of the capitalistic system as follows:

> Hardly anybody likes to admit that the highest achievements of the Western mind spring from the same soils that nourish the lush flowerings of corruption and greed. On the one hand the capitalist system implies the exploitation of any available weakness, but on the other hand it encourages the freedom of thought and experiment. The two genies emerge from the same bottle, simultaneously and without benefit of ideology. In November of last year, in the same week that the usual number of public officials were rounded up on the usual suspicion of fraud, seven Americans received the Nobel Prize.[3]

Largely because of its historical background of opportunity, its industry, its rich natural resources, and its rapid rise to a position of world power, America values success. It is a win-oriented culture. Vince Lombardi, the late coach of the Green Bay Packers, epitomized the win-at-any-cost philosophy which is so prevalent in Western culture. His summation of that philosophy, "Winning isn't everything; it's the *only* thing!" has become so well-known that it is almost a cliché.

Competition begins in the home. Rivalry between siblings is originally for the favor and affection of parents, to become first in the parents' eyes. Competition continues in school for grades, for popularity among one's peers, for athletic superiority. The achievement of success raises one's value in the minds of other people and, in turn, increases one's own self-regard. As one goes from childhood into adulthood, parental approval is gradually replaced by money as the reward for success. The amount of money one commands in the marketplace is a measure of success and of the esteem in which one is held by others.

Success, money, and esteem are often interchangeable as values in our society. The athlete who wins a number of Olympic gold medals or the Heisman trophy not only wins the esteem and respect of millions of people but is assured of significant financial rewards as well. In a study by Joseph Luft, a psychologist at San Francisco State College, college and university students were asked to ascribe personality characteristics to a hypothetical man. Half of the subjects were told the man was poor, the other half that he was rich. In every other respect the man was described identically to the two groups. "The average ratings attributed to the rich man were vastly superior to those projected on the poor man. In other words the hypothetical rich man was seen as relatively healthy, happy, and well-adjusted, while the hypothetical poor man was seen as maladjusted and unhappy." [4]

The original drive may be for a sense of power and respect, whether from others or from within oneself. However, in a society in which power and respect are based upon the possession of money, the need for power and respect then becomes a need for money.[5]

In previous chapters considerable attention was given to the symbolic meaning of money. It was demonstrated how people with exaggerated needs for power, love, security, and autonomy can use money pathologically in an attempt to satisfy these excessive needs. The need for power and respect can be either healthy or unhealthy depending upon the degree to which it dominates one's life. The same can be said of the need for love, or security, or freedom, or even money.

On the other hand, there are those like Dr. Borneman who imply in their denouncement of money that there is something inherently sinister and evil about it. This involves the same fallacious logic that is used by those who misquote the biblical statement as, "Money is the root of all evil." In actuality, money is not the villain. It is people and what they do with and for money who are at fault. The literal quote comes closer to the truth, "The *love* of money is the root of all evil." The statement by the eminent English economist John Maynard Keynes is even more explicit.

The love of money as a possession—as distinguished from the love of money as a means to the enjoyments and realities of life— will be recognised for what it is, a somewhat disgusting morbidity, one of those semi-criminal, semi-pathological propensities which one hands over with a shudder to the specialists in mental disease.[6]

People who hold money in disrepute may be likened to those who claim that if people stopped wearing clothes all social class distinctions would disappear and all social manipulations and game playing would cease. Evidence indicates, however, that even in nudist colonies "pecking orders" emerge. Even without the protection or intimidation of clothing, some people manage to get one-up on others.

Anything that has value can be used as a focus for neurotic or irrational behavior. If string had as much value to people as does money, there would be a lot more unusual behavior associated with string than there is. Occasionally some eccentric or psychotic person invests string with uncommon symbolic meaning or attributes to it some unusual power or worth. If the person saves rooms full of it, people will begin to look askance and question the person's sanity. However, if the whole society puts great value on string, as the people of Yap do on rocks, saving rooms full of string might be considered a good thing to do. On the other hand, it might create a lot of envy in people who had less, and some people might try to steal it and others might worship it or "sell their souls" for it. Societies that put great value on money find that many people do unusual things with it. *People who have emotional problems may incorporate money into their faulty behavior patterns.* This does not mean, however, that everyone in the culture does so or will even lean in that direction. And in societies that put less value on money, other things take money's place as a focus for irrational behavior.

THE REWARD VALUE OF MONEY

The lure of money is the motivation for a large part of human behavior. Money is also the reward or, as experimental psychologists say, "positive reinforcement" for a lot of human behavior.

Just as rats learn to run mazes successfully for the positive reinforcement of food pellets, people learn to perform certain tasks for the reinforcement of money.

Reinforcement for human behavior is basically of two types, external and internal. The behavior of children is molded more by external than internal rewards. They are given approval by their parents for acceptable behavior, and A's by their teachers for outstanding work in school. They receive trophies and medals for winning athletic events and money for doing odd jobs. As people grow from childhood into adulthood, ideally more of their reinforcement becomes internal. It is hoped they become governed more by pride in their work or a feeling of satisfaction for having achieved some goal rather than by being constantly dependent on reinforcement from others.

All internal and most types of external reinforcement are subjective and difficult to measure. How big or how much is a feeling of accomplishment, and how does it compare with two hugs and a handshake from a friend? Of all payoffs, money is probably the most tangible and quantifiable. A hundred dollars is always worth more than ten; a thousand dollars is ten times as much as a hundred, and most people consider it more valuable. To the degree that money is a reward for work or accomplishment, it becomes a yardstick by which the achievements of one person can be compared with those of another.

There are many problems and pitfalls with such a yardstick, but that is true with any measuring device used to compare the worth or value of two human beings or of their accomplishments. The need for recognition and the feeling of self-worth, in proper perspective, are not abnormal. Within limits, the use of money as a measure of those traits, imperfect as it is, cannot arbitrarily be considered abnormal. Unless or until other rewards have sufficient value to compensate people for their time and effort and provide them with a sense of worth and esteem, money will most likely prevail.

Some individuals, of course, have transcended the use of money as a measure of their worth. There are a number of creative people who receive enough internal satisfaction from their artistic endeavors that money is of secondary importance. The internal satisfaction in creating a poem or a picture or a book offers them more reinforcement than any amount of money could. Some professional people put job satisfaction ahead of money, and there are undoubtedly a few in almost any line of work who feel the same. They find great satisfaction in helping others, and the amount of financial reward, as long as it provides a living, becomes secondary. When Albert Einstein was offered a position at the Institute of Advanced Study at Princeton just prior to World War II, he was asked to name his own salary.

> In a state of "flame and fire" to get started, Einstein asked for $3,000 a year. Even for those days, that was a meager salary. The Institute said nothing, and paid him $16,000.
>
> Such people are rare, but they exist. They have no need of monetary riches because their lives are so rich in other respects.[7]

On the other hand, Governor Jerry Brown of California gave as his reason for offering only a token pay raise to the faculties of the University of California and the State University and College System that, as professors, they were partly paid in "psychic" dollars. The professors were not impressed. They claimed they could not pay their rent or buy groceries with "psychic" dollars and would rather have real ones instead.

CAN MONEY BUY HAPPINESS?

The relationship between money and happiness has been debated for centuries. Phrases like, "The best things in life are free," "Money can't buy happiness," and "They were poor but happy," have been bantered about for so long and so often that they have been all but accepted as true. Recent evidence, however, indicates they may contain more myth than reality. For example, George Gallup, who headed the Gallup/Kettering Global Survey on Human Needs and Satisfactions, and his staff interviewed ten thousand individuals in seventy nations and from every economic level. Among Gallup's findings was the following: "In the planning stages of this global survey it was hoped that somewhere in the world a nation would be found whose people are poor but happy. We didn't find such a place." [8]

In line with Gallup's survey are the studies of psychologist Paul Cameron of St. Mary's College of Maryland. In his research on happiness among physically handicapped, mentally retarded, and normal subjects, Cameron found that the affluent, both handicapped and normal, more often said they were satisfied with life than did those who were not as well off financially. Persons with similar incomes, whether handicapped or normal, reported about the same levels of life satisfaction, had similar moods, and were equally optimistic about the future.[9]

The studies of Gallup, Cameron, and others do not show that money actually *buys* happiness, although they suggest that the lack of money may in many cases contribute to unhappiness. People whose needs are unfulfilled, whether due to lack of money or anything else, are going to be dissatisfied. Within certain limits, it is also likely that most people are happier with money than without it. There is no evidence, however, which indicates that, beyond a given level, happiness increases proportionately to an increase in wealth. Moreover, to the degree that money and happiness are correlated, one can only infer that as one increases the other increases, although not to the same degree. Without further information, it would be in error to say that money *causes* happiness or that happiness *causes* one to have more money. A basic personality structure, which includes a healthy self-respect and self-confidence, is most likely the causative factor which produces both happiness and an adequate but realistic supply of money.

The Declaration of Independence provides every American the inalienable right to the pursuit of happiness. And most Americans have been pursuing it madly ever since. The assumption underlying the chase is that happiness is a viable goal. In reality, the more desperately one chases after it, the more elusive it becomes. As Nathaniel Hawthorne phrased it, "Happiness is a butterfly, which when pursued is always just beyond your grasp." True happiness is more likely to come as a by-product of some other experience or the achievement of some other goal rather than as an end in itself. If one is happy as the result of falling in love or having performed a hard day's work, happiness is a bonus or reward. It is an emotion, and emotions are highly personal experiences. Happiness is an internal reward or reinforcement for some particular behavior. As such, it cannot be bought with money; but money might well increase one's range of experiences or one's opportunities to achieve goals, which in turn, will bring about the feeling of happiness.

As with happiness, many people see money as a goal rather than as a reward for the achievement of other goals. To the extent that a person is obsessed with the possession and accumulation of money to the exclusion of how money is acquired—when the satisfaction in *having* money submerges the satisfaction derived from the *process of making* money—then it can be said that the person has an unhealthy attachment to money. Like happiness, money becomes a reward for certain types of behavior, although it is external rather than internal. Most people express a desire for both money and happiness, and the degree of importance attached to either can be healthy or unhealthy. Of the two, money is probably easier to come by than happiness since there are no truly happy neurotics, but there are rich ones!

THE RELATIONSHIP
OF WORK TO MONEY

For most people, the means of acquiring money is payment for work. The concept of work has a variety of meanings. To some it means drudgery and misery and to others, like the workaholic empire builder, it is the most important thing in life. Some very wealthy people consider work, especially hard physical labor, beneath them, and some poor people who are on the public dole feel that work is for suckers. The great middle classes are, for the most part, indoctrinated with the work ethic and accept it as a necessary part of living.

Those who lack money but desire a great deal of it, yet who are unwilling to work long and hard to get it, have few options open to them. Unless they have unusual talent, they are generally limited to luck or crime in order to make their desire come true. They might possibly become manipulators operating just inside the law or, with a little capital, they could become speculators. However, most of these people never find either wealth or happiness, and among those who manage to obtain large sums of money quickly or with little effort, there is likely to be little pleasure—at least, the pleasure is unlikely to last for long. They seem to have difficulty holding onto money or using it intelligently.

For example, a man accused of murdering and robbing a wealthy Indianapolis woman was apprehended shortly after the crime. He had purchased a new Lincoln Continental for $13,500 with new $100 bills in numerical sequence and then returned to trade it in for another new car a few days later because it had a few scratches on it.[10]

The number of highly paid entertainers who have declared bankruptcy is staggering. The community relations director of American International Pictures assessed the situation as follows: "The majority of entertainers can't handle success. They are not equipped for success. You have a situation where the entertainer who is used to living hand-to-mouth suddenly gets more money than he can spend." [11]

The ups and downs of compulsive gamblers and speculators are well-known. Even among those who hang onto their big winnings, however, the prospects of happiness are apparently not great. In 1975, two sociologists from the State University of New York at Buffalo conducted a study of the changing life patterns of persons who had won big on the state-run lottery. They concluded that although the winners had a deep commitment to work, approximately eighty percent of those winning a million or more dollars quit their jobs. "Some of our lengthy interviews," they reported, "resulted from their loneliness and lack of more important things to do. . . . In fact, there were indications that boredom had set in. A series of questions designed to ascertain leisure and recreational activities of winners revealed that most spend a lot of time watching television." [12] Rather than using money to live life more fully, they apparently "dropped out" once the need to work for money was gone.

These observations coincide with the Puritan ethic, which stipulates it is wrong to acquire too much money too easily, although the conclusions of the investigators do not presume to substantiate the moral basis for the Puritan philosophy. Neither do they necessarily imply an underlying feeling of guilt as the reason for getting rid of the money or not enjoying it. This apparent lack of enjoyment is more likely due to the fact that people tend to minimize the value of anything which comes too easily, and find it difficult to adjust to any change that comes too rapidly. The problem of handling the sudden switch from rags to riches, which the community relations director mentioned in connection with entertainers, applies to most people. The social psychologist Leon Festinger calls this type of internal conflict "dissonance." [13] According to his theory of "cognitive dissonance," the tension created by the inconsistency of having money but still feeling poor motivates the person to do something to reduce the tension. This can be either to change one's percept of being poor, or to get rid of the money.

Working long and hard for money does not guarantee that one will either deal with it rationally or enjoy life more fully because of having it. Many industrious individuals obviously do neither. However, for those who are otherwise reasonably intelligent and fairly integrated psychologically, it may help. Increasing one's standard of living over a period of time allows one to adjust to the change gradually, which minimizes the dissonance and makes the adaptation easier. It also facilitates self-discipline in the use of money in that one must learn to put off immediate gratification for future satisfaction if there is not enough money to buy everything one might want. In addition, people generally appreciate the worth of something more if they save and sacrifice and work hard to achieve it. They feel more deserving of it and are less likely to dispose of it indiscriminately.

MONEY IN A CHANGING WORLD

The industrial revolution created a mass migration from farms and rural areas to crowded cities with the lure of more jobs and higher wages. Whether knowingly or not, the majority of people caught up in this migration exchanged a good deal of economic independence for almost total dependence. The person who works for a wage is less free than the one who wrests a living from even a small plot of ground, even though the wage earner may make more money.

The current social revolution, spearheaded by the protests of racial minorities and by the feminist movement, is also heavily involved in economic change. In contrast to the industrial revolution, however, one of the primary forces behind the present upheaval is a desire to exchange dependence for more independence.

Among the feminists, for example, many of the demands for equality have to do with money—equal pay for women, equal job opportunities, and pay for women who stay home and keep house. Books advising women on how to handle money are almost as common as cookbooks. Concern about how to handle money on dates, the pros and cons of separate bank accounts for married couples, and the advisability of marriage contracts are subjects which more and more couples are dealing with today.

The traditional female role of passivity fostered a relationship dependent upon an aggressive and protective male, both emotionally and economically. As more women eschew this role, the pattern of deliberately seeking out a mate who can easily fulfill such a dominant and fiscally sound role becomes less tenable, and there is less pressure for the male to live up to such expectations. Old stereotypes of male and female behavior no longer hold true in relation to money any more than they do in other areas.

The risk-takers' newsmagazine, *Gambling Times,* has reported that women have proved successful gamblers because they are cool, orderly thinkers and have shown that they can handle power. The way to be a good gambler is to walk resolutely away from the table or track when you are ahead of the game—and this is where female prudence outshines male daring, according to psychologists. A man, overcome with emotion and greed, concerned with his external image, tends to stay on and to wind up losing his winnings. The woman—with different, internalized values—is on her way to the bank.[14]

A SANE VIEW OF MONEY

Any discussion of normality is fraught with difficulty since normality covers a wide expanse of behavior. The question of whether a particular act is appropriate depends in part on who does it and when. What is acceptable behavior for a child may not be for an adult; what is reasonable behavior under conditions of stress may not be so under everyday circumstances; what is rational for a pauper may not be for a millionaire; behavior considered emotionally healthy by an Eskimo may not be considered so by an Arab; functional behavior in the twentieth century differs from behavior that was considered functional in the fourteenth century.

In spite of the difficulty in defining normality, certain criteria can be used to exclude some behavior from consideration and to prune the concept to workable size. Money sanity involves behavior which meets all or most of the following conditions:

1. Given the present socioeconomic system, one neither worships nor denounces money.

2. One has the ability to control money rather than being controlled by it; to be able to use and own money rather than being used and owned by it.

3. Since most irrational money behavior involves unconscious motivation, it is necessary to have an optimal amount of awareness and understanding of what meanings money has for one and how one uses it.

4. There is an ability to use money constructively to enhance the quality of one's own life and the lives of those around one.

5. Money is viewed as a just reward for the accomplishment of some worthwhile task rather than as an end in itself.

6. There is a capacity to use money spontaneously at times rather than always rigidly and according to an unwavering formula.

7. Money is used to provide pleasure for oneself and one's friends and family as well as to provide for their necessities.

8. There are realistic expectations of what money can and

cannot do to solve one's problems or to alter one's life.

9. Money is held in proper perspective so that one will not sacrifice one's moral and ethical standards or commit anti-social or criminal acts to obtain it.

While examples of money madness are to be found in great abundance wherever one looks, there is also a plethora of sane money behavior—although being less dramatic and less news-worthy, it may not always be as obvious. The banker who preached thrift and savings to his customers but who died nearly broke because his compassion for people caused him to dig quietly into his own pocket to help them when they needed money may or may not make the newspapers. The carpenter or the schoolteacher or the farmer who go about their business, use good sense about money, and never do anything dishonest or spectacular with it, obviously never will. One is, in fact, amazed at the number of people who manage to cope with the stresses of life and overcome the hazards and pitfalls which constantly confront them and yet never allow their lives to be distorted by destructive money attitudes. Lewis Lapham made a somewhat similar observation in regard to money sanity.

> Nobody can escape the seductions or the intimidations of money. That so many people refuse the offers and resist the threats testifies to their larger understanding of the character of human life. They make their choices not so much on moral grounds as on the basis of empirical observations, because the obsession with money, as witness the long and unhappy life of Howard Hughes, reduces a man to the gibbering sycophancy of a frightened ape.[15]

Those who seek madness in the world can find it. It exists, and it exists abundantly. By the same token, those who seek sanity can also find it, although they may have to search a little harder because it is less spectacular. Healthy and unhealthy be-havior are not always very different or very far apart. They differ more in degree or quantity than in quality. They may be present side by side in the same person, simultaneously or at different times. In many respects, madness and sanity, whether relating to money or not, can be considered as two sides of the same coin.

NOTES

Introduction

1. George Bernard Shaw, *The Irrational Knot* (London: Constable, 1905), p. iv.
2. L. M. Boyd, *Orange County* (Calif.) *Daily Pilot,* December 29, 1976, p. A11.
3. *Los Angeles Times,* November 25, 1973, part 1B, p. 8.
4. *Los Angeles Times,* June 11, 1974, part 1, p. 7.

Chapter 2

1. Ralph Waldo Emerson, "Nominalist and Realist," in *The Complete Works of Ralph Waldo Emerson* (Boston and New York: Houghton Mifflin, 1904), p. 231.
2. Sidney M. Jourard, *The Transparent Self* (Princeton: Van Nostrand, 1971), p. 229.
3. James A. Knight, *For the Love of Money* (Philadelphia: Lippincott, 1968), p. 83.
4. Thomas Wiseman, *The Money Motive* (New York: Random House, 1974), p. 258.
5. James A. Knight, *op. cit.,* p. 83.

Chapter 3

1. Terry Southern, *The Magic Christian* (New York: Random House, 1959).

2. James A. Knight, *For the Love of Money* (Philadelphia: Lippincott, 1968), p. 15.
3. Russell Chandler, "Rev. Ike Preaches That It's Much More Blessed to Receive," *Moneysworth,* June 7, 1976, p. 6.
4. "Morning Briefing," *Los Angeles Times,* May 28, 1976, part III, p. 2.
5. "Garbage Mary: 'From Riches to Rags,'" *Los Angeles Times,* February 25, 1977, part III, p. 20.
6. Sheilah Graham, "The Most Interesting Men I've Ever Known," *Family Weekly,* March 7, 1976, p. 4.
7. *The New Yorker,* April 21, 1973, p. 28.
8. Norman O. Brown, *Life Against Death—The Psychoanalytical Meaning of History* (Middletown, Conn.: Wesleyan University Press, 1959), p. 254.
9. Erik H. Erikson, *Childhood and Society,* 2nd. ed. (New York: W. W. Norton, 1963).
10. W. Kessen, ed., *Childhood in China* (New Haven: Yale University Press, 1975).

Chapter 4

1. "The Rockers Are Rolling in It," *Forbes,* April 15, 1973, p. 29.
2. *Orange County* (Calif.) *Daily Pilot,* September 7, 1976, p. A3.
3. John P. Sisk, "The Fear of Affluence," *Commentary,* June 1974, p. 62.
4. Ibid.
5. Doris Lilly, "My Nominations for the 10 Biggest Spenders in the World," *Family Weekly,* September 19, 1976, pp. 6–8.
6. "The Rockers Are Rolling in It," p. 39.
7. Max Gunther, *The Very, Very Rich and How They Got That Way* (Chicago: Playboy Press, 1972), p. 225.
8. Alfred Adler, *Problems of Neurosis* (New York: Harper Torchbooks, 1964), p. 56.
9. Melanie Klein, *Envy and Gratitude* (London: Tavistock, 1957).
10. Sigmund Freud, *The Origins of Psychoanalysis: Letters to Wilhelm Fliess, Drafts and Notes: 1877–1902* (New York: Basic Books, 1954), p. 244.

Chapter 5

1. J. S. Bruner and C. C. Goodman, "Value and Need as Organizing Factors in Perception," *Journal of Abnormal and Social Psychology,* 13 (1947), pp. 33–44.
2. John Dawson, "Socio-Economic Differences in Size-Judgments of

Discs and Coins by Chinese Primary VI Children in Hong Kong," *Perceptual and Motor Skills,* 41 (1975), pp. 107–110.

3. Paul F. Wernimont and Susan Fitzpatrick, "The Meaning of Money," *Journal of Applied Psychology,* 56:13 (1972), p. 225.
4. W. H. Desmonde, *Magic, Myth and Money* (Glencoe, Ill.: Free Press of Glencoe, 1962).
5. Allan Nevins, *Rockefeller, Study in Power,* Vol. 2 (New York: Scribner's, 1953), p. 479.
6. J. Paul Getty, *How to Be Rich* (Chicago: Playboy Press, 1973), p. 9.
7. "Tanaka: Prisoner of 'Money Power,' " *Time,* August 9, 1976, p. 24.
8. Otto Fenichel, "The Drive to Amass Wealth," in Hanna Fenichel and David Rapaport, eds., *The Collected Papers of Otto Fenichel,* second series (New York: W. W. Norton, 1954), pp. 95–96.
9. E. C. Wickham, *Horace for English Readers* (London: Oxford University Press, 1953), p. 264.
10. "Male Potency and the Dow Jones Industrial Average," *New York,* October 20, 1975, pp. 10–12.
11. Abraham H. Maslow, *Motivation and Personality* (New York: Harper & Row, 1954), pp. 257–60.
12. *Newsweek,* July 26, 1976, p. 56.
13. Julian B. Rotter, "Generalized Expectancies for Internal versus External Control of Reinforcement," *Psychological Monographs,* 80:1 (1966).
14. Somerset Maugham, *Of Human Bondage* (New York: Garden City Publishing, 1939), p. 274.
15. Abraham H. Maslow, *op. cit.,* pp. 340–41.

Chapter 6

1. Edmund Bergler, *Money and Emotional Conflicts* (Garden City, N.Y.: Doubleday, 1951), pp. 135–36.
2. Erik H. Erikson, *Childhood and Society,* 2nd ed. (New York: W. W. Norton, 1963).

Chapter 7

1. Leslie Gould, *The Manipulators* (New York: McKay, 1966), p. 116.
2. "Condo Woes Pace Sales," *Orange County* (Calif.) *Daily Pilot,* January 30, 1977, p. A9.

3. "Toy Scam?" *Orange County* (Calif.) *Daily Pilot*, January 30, 1977, p. B8.
4. Max Gunther, *The Very, Very Rich and How They Got That Way* (Chicago: Playboy Press, 1972), pp. 226–27.
5. John Dollard et al., *Frustration and Aggression* (New Haven: Yale University Press, 1963), pp. 1–3.
6. Max Gunther, *op. cit.*, p. 224.
7. Meyer Friedman and Ray H. Rosenman, *Type A Behavior and Your Heart* (New York: Alfred A. Knopf, 1974).
8. Max Gunther, *op. cit.*, pp. 181–89.
9. Dan Rather and Gary P. Gates, *The Palace Guard* (New York: Harper & Row, 1974).

Chapter 8

1. William Kaufman, "Some Emotional Uses of Money," in Ernest Borneman and Wieland Schulz-Keil, eds., *The Psychoanalysis of Money* (New York: Urizen Books, 1976), p. 229.
2. E. J. Kahn, *The Voice* (New York: Harper & Bros., 1947).
3. Frieda Fromm-Reichmann, *Principles of Intensive Psychotherapy* (Chicago: University of Chicago Press, 1950), p. 34.
4. Walter Wagner, *The Golden Fleecers* (Garden City, N.Y.: Doubleday, 1966), p. 178.
5. Lucius Beebe, *The Big Spenders* (Garden City, N.Y.: Doubleday, 1966), p. viii.
6. Wagner, *op. cit.*, p. 178.
7. William Schofield, *Psychotherapy: The Purchase of Friendship* (Englewood Cliffs, N.J.: Prentice-Hall, 1964).
8. Geraldo Rivera, "Nobody Ever Said 'No' to Freddie Prinze," *New York*, February 28, 1977, p. 33.
9. *Orange County* (Calif.)*Daily Pilot*, January 22, 1977, pp. A1–2.
10. "Dear Abby," *Los Angeles Times*, February 18, 1977, part IV, p. 6.
11. Karl Abraham, "The History of an Imposter in the Light of Psycho-Analytic Knowledge," in Robert Fliess, ed., *The Psycho-Analytic Reader* (New York: International Universities Press, 1962), pp. 316–31.
12. J. Paul Getty, *How to Be Rich* (Chicago: Playboy Press, 1973), p. 194.

Chapter 9

1. Dana L. Thomas, *The Money Crowd* (New York: G. P. Putnam's Sons, 1972), pp. 335–36.

2. Ibid., p. 339.
3. Michael Phillips, *The Seven Laws of Money* (New York: Random House, 1974), pp. 13–14.
4. James Simon Kunen, *The Strawberry Statement: Notes of a College Revolutionary* (New York: Random House, 1969), p. 72.
5. Dana L. Thomas, *op. cit.*, p. 339.
6. Eugene H. Methvin, *The Rise of Radicalism* (New Rochelle, N.Y.: Arlington House, 1973), p. 498.
7. Samuel Lubell, *The Hidden Crisis in American Politics* (New York: W. W. Norton, 1970), p. 188.
8. Thomas Wiseman, *The Money Motives* (New York: Random House, 1974), p. 205.
9. *Orange County* (Calif.) *Daily Pilot,* May 8, 1977, section 1, pp. 1–3.

Chapter 10

1. Frieda Fromm-Reichmann, *Principles of Intensive Psychotherapy* (Chicago: University of Chicago Press, 1950), p. 67.
2. Sigmund Freud, "Further Recommendations in the Treatment of Psychoanalysis: On Beginning the Treatment (1913)," in James Strachey, ed., *Collected Papers of Sigmund Freud,* Vol. 2 (New York: Basic Books, 1959), p. 351.
3. James Bugental, "Psychotherapy as a Source of the Therapist's Own Authenticity and Inauthenticity," in *Voices: The Art and Science of Psychotherapy,* 4:2 (1968), pp. 13–21.
4. Chester W. Feurerstein, "Money as a Value in Psychotherapy," in *Journal of Contemporary Psychotherapy,* 3:2 (Spring 1971), pp. 103–104.

Chapter 11

1. Roger Starr, "A Kind Word About Money," *Harper's,* March 1976, p. 82.
2. Lois Timnick, "Children of Wealthy in Study Called 'Emotional Zombies,'" *Los Angeles Times,* May 4, 1977, part 1, p. 25.
3. Max Gunther, *The Very, Very Rich and How They Got That Way* (Chicago: Playboy Press, 1972), p. 222.
4. Ibid., p. 222.
5. Thomas Wiseman, *The Money Motive* (New York: Random House, 1974), p. 255.
6. Max Gunther, *op. cit.*, p. 228.
7. Thomas Wiseman, *op. cit.*, p. 248.
8. Max Gunther, *op. cit.*, p. 129.

9. Ferdinand Lundberg, *The Rich and the Super-Rich* (New York: Lyle Stuart, 1968), p. 98.
10. Walter Wagner, *The Golden Fleecers* (Garden City, N.Y.: Doubleday, 1966), p. 19.
11. Ferdinand Lundberg, *op. cit.,* p. 114.
12. Ibid., p. 78.
13. Richard H. Weerts, "Middle-aged, Middle-class," *Newsweek,* October 4, 1976, p. 13.

Chapter 12

1. Ernest Borneman and Wieland Schulz-Keil, eds., *The Psychoanalysis of Money* (New York: Urizen Books, 1976), p. 357.
2. Otto Fenichel, "The Drive to Amass Wealth" in Hanna Fenichel and David Rapaport, eds., *The Collected Papers of Otto Fenichel,* second series (New York: W. W. Norton, 1954), p. 89.
3. Lewis H. Lapham, "The Capitalist Paradox," *Harper's,* March 1977, p. 32.
4. Joseph Luft, "Monetary Value and the Perception of Persons," *The Journal of Social Psychology,* 46 (1957), pp. 245–51.
5. Fenichel, *op. cit.,* p. 96.
6. John Maynard Keynes, *Essays in Persuasion,* part V (New York: Macmillan, 1931).
7. Thomas Wiseman, *The Money Motive* (New York: Random House, 1974), p. 208.
8. "Rich-Poor Gap Dominates World Poll," *Los Angeles Times,* September 21, 1976, part I, p. 4.
9. Paul Carpenter, "Three Faces of Happiness," *Psychology Today,* August 1974, pp. 63–64.
10. "Three Held in Murder of Widow," *San Francisco Chronicle,* May 11, 1977, p. 6.
11. Ron Kisner, "The Money Problems of the Stars," *Ebony,* May 1977, p. 142.
12. Charles T. Powers, "Millionaires," *Los Angeles Times,* June 12, 1977, part I, p. 10.
13. Leon Festinger, *A Theory of Cognitive Dissonance* (Stanford, Cal.: Stanford University Press, 1957).
14. Lorraine Davis, "Women Make Good Winners," *Vogue,* March 1977, p. 110.
15. Lewis H. Lapham, *op. cit.,* p. 34.

INDEX